# Africa Overland
## 4x4 • Motorbike • Bicycle • Truck

## THE BRADT STORY

The first Bradt travel guide was written in 1974 by George and Hilary Bradt on a river barge floating down a tributary of the Amazon. In the 1980s and '90s the focus shifted away from hiking to broader-based guides covering new destinations – usually the first to be published about these places. In the 21st century Bradt continues to publish such ground-breaking guides, as well as others to established holiday destinations, incorporating in-depth information on culture and natural history with the nuts and bolts of where to stay and what to see.

Bradt authors support responsible travel, and provide advice not only on minimum impact but also on how to give something back through local charities. In this way a true synergy is achieved between the traveller and local communities.

\* \* \*

When I was a child a colleague of my father visited us once a year, having driven his Landrover from Ghana across the Sahara. I was amazed that it was possible to drive from Africa to England, and enthralled by his stories. This remains the ultimate adventure, yet Bob Gibbons and Siân Pritchard-Jones have done it more than once and have used their experiences to update *Africa by Road* by Charlie Shackell and Illya Bracht. The combined expertise of these four Africa travellers, along with contributions from cyclists and bikers, has produced the book that may literally save the life of a trans-Africa traveller and will certainly enhance the enjoyment of this once-in-a-lifetime trip.

When George and I travelled from Cape Town to Cairo in 1976 there were no guidebooks, so each border was approached with trepidation. We had no idea what to expect, nor even what there was to see in each country. We were using public transport, but occasionally hitched a lift with adventurous souls driving their own vehicles, and envied their freedom to go where they chose and stop when they wanted. But freedom is wasted without knowledge. And knowledge is what this book is about.

*Hilary Bradt*

23 High Street, Chalfont St Peter, Bucks SL9 9QE, England
Tel: 01753 893444   Fax: 01753 892333
Email: info@bradtguides.com   www.bradtguides.com

# Africa Overland

## 4x4 • Motorbike • Bicycle • Truck

Fourth Edition

## Bob Gibbons
## Siân Pritchard-Jones

Bradt Travel Guides Ltd, UK
The Globe Pequot Press Inc, USA

**Fourth edition July 2005**
First published 1991

Bradt Travel Guides Ltd
23 High Street, Chalfont St Peter, Bucks SL9 9QE, England
www.bradtguides.com
Published in the USA by The Globe Pequot Press Inc, 246 Goose Lane,
PO Box 480, Guilford, Connecticut 06437-0480

**British Library Cataloguing in Publication Data**
A catalogue record for this book is available from the British Library

ISBN-10: 1 84162 135 8
ISBN-13: 978 1 84162 135 7

**Photographs**
*Front cover*: Gara Ecker, Algeria (Bob Gibbons)
*Text*: Ariadne Van Zandbergen (AZ), Tricia Hayne (TH),
Chris McIntyre (CM), Geoffrey Roy (GR)

**Illustrations** Illya Bracht, Bob Gibbons, Annabel Milne, Carole Vincer
**Maps** Steve Munns, Alan Whitaker

Typeset from the authors' disc by Wakewing, High Wycombe
Printed and bound in Italy by Legoprint SpA, Trento

# Authors

Siân Pritchard-Jones and Bob Gibbons were both born in the UK, but did not meet until 1983, in Kashmir. By then Bob had already travelled extensively all over Asia, Africa and South America, driving overland trucks and decrepit old buses in India and Nepal.

Before they met, Siân worked in computer programming and systems analysis. Bob, with some fellow students, drove an ancient (1949) Land Rover from England to Kathmandu in 1974. After continuing to Australia by public transport to earn some money for the return trip, their Land Rover expired on the Afghan border.

In Africa, as a client on a bright pink truck, Bob was stuck in Central Africa for weeks as both the drivers and most of the passengers caught hepatitis and left. The truck also became very sick. Bob instigated some drastic repairs and drove it on to Nairobi. He subsequently worked as an overland driver and also lived in Kathmandu as trekking manager for the same company.

As for Siân, her heart was captivated by the Himalayas after a trip there on her way back from working in New Zealand. Working and commuting in London from Kew Gardens station she would watch the flights taking off from Heathrow. To what far-flung corners of the planet were those lucky people going?

Since they met they have been leading and organising treks in the Alps, Nepal, Algeria and Niger, they have hitched across Tibet, driven their overland bus with ageing clients to Nepal, explored the Sahara and driven across Africa to Gabon. They also work each autumn for Pilgrims Book House in Kathmandu and have recently produced a comprehensive cultural and trekking guide to the Kathmandu Valley. Some of this was real work, but luckily that 'proper job' has not materialised. Their most recent journey was by a less ancient (only 21 years old) Land Rover from England to Cape Town, the basis of this new edition.

Is there any cure for this restless bug?

# Contents

# Acknowledgements

Thanks to all at Bradt Travel Guides for giving us this opportunity to share some of our experiences with other would-be travellers across the great Dark Continent. Special thanks to David Mozer, Ariadne Van Zandbergen, Alex Marr and David Lambeth.

To the previous authors of *Africa by Road*, first and second editions, Bob Swain and Paula Snyder, and third edition, Charlie Shackell and Illya Bracht, thank you for allowing us to use your existing material. We are very grateful to Arnout and Saskia, whom we met along the way. Thanks for your time and valuable contributions to this book, with information about buying and preparing a vehicle in South Africa. To Martha, Charles, Angella and Titus in Nairobi, for rescuing us from the roadside! To Dr Liz Molyneux in Blantyre, Malawi, for tea and reminiscences in Doogles. To Professors Kathryn and Larry, and Annette in Durban, for their exceptional hospitality at the end of a long journey. To the others whose stories are in here without their knowing it, thanks, and if you are in here, let us know if you'd like a copy.

A special thanks to our parents, Beryl and Tony, Marianne and John, who have, with a knowing resignation, mostly encouraged and supported us to seek out new horizons. Thanks to Amanda of Travcour, for her help with ever-changing visa prices. We could not have written this book without the help of Rama and Pushpa Tiwari, of Pilgrims Book House in Kathmandu, Nepal, where much of the new writing work was done.

And, lastly, thanks to the land and peoples of Africa for making our trips memorable, fascinating, and so addictive that we can't wait to go back there again.

# Introduction

If you are reading this book, you either have decided to set out on a fascinating, perhaps slightly crazy journey across a vast continent, or at the very least would like to read about it. For those who may be armchair travellers, and there's no harm in that, we have included some anecdotes taken from our various trips. These may or may not encourage you to get out of that armchair and do it for yourself!

So why should you do it? There's really no answer to that question, which has puzzled explorers for all time. Is it just 'because it's there'? Each person will have his or her own reasons for wanting to defy normality and set out on this adventurous undertaking. Perhaps if more people had a true spirit of adventure, and tolerance for other ways of life, the world might be a safer place. As it is, you must be aware that you will be up against it at times, and understand that you are taking risks; but then nothing in life is completely risk-free and there is so much to be gained by third-world travel. Whatever you have read from other early or more recent explorers will only awaken your imagination to the endless possibilities. We didn't have enough time, because we had to get back to work in the Alps. You will never have enough time to do everything; life is not long enough for that. So decide your main objectives and be prepared to change your plans as you go.

Don't necessarily think it will be a once-in-a-lifetime trip; when you return life will never ever be quite the same again. Africa may grab you wholeheartedly; you may find it hard not to return time after time. It is likely that no-one else will understand or be interested in your travels beyond a quick 'Where did you go? What did you see? What was the weather like?'. But your memories will live on forever and you will find inspiration and understanding that no book alone can ever hope to impart.

This book – the first three editions were entitled *Africa by Road* – describes the various ways to travel overland through Africa. The overall cost will vary widely according to your abilities and facilities, and your luck in finding the right type of vehicle, as well as the length of time you have available. Different routes are described in some detail; though the possibilities are endless, some routes may be impossible for a time due to political considerations. Planning and preparation, both before and during your trip, are important; you don't want to miss some vital spare part for example, or forget that favourite bar of chocolate for emergencies! For example, we almost forgot our mashed potato and had to dash to Sainsbury's on the way to the ferry. Although there are more vital things, instant mash is just that, and doesn't use much fuel for cooking, so don't mock it!

Because of politics and other world issues, your route may have to change once you're on the road, so you should always build as much flexibility into your planning as possible. You'll meet other travellers, who may tell you of something they have just discovered and which you really shouldn't miss. But you should certainly have a good outline plan before you start out. Don't rush off without thinking it all over carefully. Try to avoid disasters before they happen.

If you don't think driving your own vehicle is for you, then you may want to join an organised trip. The tour companies will do most of the planning for you, leaving you just

## MARSABIT, MARCH 20 2004

At dawn a grey fog envelops the town, a place of verdant forest in a sea of desert. The heavy dew cloaks everything with a damp veneer. A monkey scurries away, disturbed outside the lodge by the early morning preparations of the guests for the day's journey. Breakfast is a tasty affair; greasy fried eggs cooked in days-old ghee, dubious butter with blackened sweet bread toast and Lipton's tea. It could have been any railway station breakfast in India, but this was northern Kenya, a land of wild-eyed colourfully clad tribesmen, spectacular but harsh desert scrub and stunning isolated boulders the size of mountains.

As the first cracks appeared in the heavy fog clouds, we began the long descent from the island of hills that make Marsabit a rich oasis. We had 'our man' Mohammed from the Kenya security forces, a gregarious family man, our armed guard, with us. We had been advised to travel with an armed guard in view of the fact that bandits frequent the route between Moyale on the Ethiopian border and Isiolo just north of Mount Kenya. Whether Mohammed would deter any determined rogues or make an armed robbery more dangerous was not something to ponder on. At the very least we were providing Mohammed with a comfortable trip to his family home near Isiolo, and ourselves with a chance to gain an insight into life in these torrid zones of northern Kenya.

Once we were down out of the cool hills, the sun broke through and a crystal-clear sky accompanied us across the dry plains. Dramatic rocks reared skyward; acacia scrub and low bushes provided suitable cover for wild animals, and bandits. Just beyond a small village we passed groups of Rendille heading to the market. These amazingly dressed semi-nomadic tribal clansmen and women carried spears. They all wore brilliant red sashes decorated with silvery-coloured braids, ornaments and bangles. Tall and slender, they presented a picture-perfect image of a proud, self-assured independent people. Our guard suggested we should not stop here to say hello, which seemed a great pity.

The road deteriorated from a sandy strip into an unbelievably dreadful rough and rocky gash through the boulder-strewn countryside. Even at 15mph the Land Rover lurched in disgust; the suspension was banging and wearing itself away, the doors rattled constantly. Slowly we progressed into the low hills that marked the approach to the northern slopes of Mount Kenya. Its jagged peak, with icy snowfields, peered out above a wispy band of clouds in the hazy distance.

From Isiolo, where we parted with Mohammed, the desert gave way to the rolling farmlands of the white highlands, where quaint colonial farmhouses illustrated the remarkable change in atmosphere. Gone were the tense testing hours in hostile country, replaced with scenes almost reminiscent of the rolling farmlands of Wiltshire.

to find the money and set off to enjoy yourself – although you should still be prepared to do your share of hard work while on the road.

This book is tailored towards planning, preparation and other details specific to

We passed a smoking belching old Bedford truck, not a local model but a British Army training vehicle; it was none too healthy.

We sailed on by, all the cares of the world blown away by the cool air, the homely farms and a super tarmac highway with fuel stations, shops and animated markets. We galloped along the miles; the Kenyan capital with all its modern towers, coffee houses and vivid happy memories beckoned. We could make it before sunset at this rate. Nairobi at last.

But perhaps one should never be quite so confident of anything happening to plan in Africa. Just 12 miles from the city, in the bright lights of the northern suburbs, a cruel twist to the day unfolded. At the crest of a rise, just before some obviously poor shanty areas, the clutch gave out with a shocking suddenness. With little prior warning, we were engulfed with impatient traffic, horns blasting, drivers fuming. Desperately we pushed the stricken vehicle to the side of the road. What a crowning frustration to a day of incredibly mixed emotions.

'Nairobi is a city with substantial areas best avoided at night, with rampant crime,' quotes a line in a guidebook. Our thoughts were racing, a sudden sense of dread, what if this had happened earlier in the day; then a nanosecond of comic concern, a barely controlled fit of humour and as ever that thought, why are we doing this? And then in a few short minutes, a reality check, a detached sense of resignation, of being in the hands of a higher force and then the need for practical solutions, a wiping of the slate of fear.

Within five minutes we were approached by Charles and Martha, a local couple on their way home from work. They provided an amazing breath of humanity within the sea of hurried, detached masses of evening commuters. Within an hour the Land Rover had been pushed and cajoled into the armed guard security of the local supermarket, and the night staff had been happily rewarded for their kindness and help. Charles and Martha had invited us to stay with them, their enquiring young son and Martha's younger sister. The flat was in a secure compound on a third floor. They offered us a basic but sumptuous dinner, a bed and a hot shower. (The shower was heated by a giant electric ring set in a bucket.) Charles works for the Thika Water Board and Martha commutes into downtown Nairobi to work for a bank.

The unbelievable kindness we were shown was embarrassing. Could we ever image such unashamed humanity in our own country?

On this day we had enjoyed a homely breakfast, endured a harsh, hot and dusty desert crossing, passed sombre nomadic tribal clans, avoided bandits, experienced a stress-relieving exhilaration in the highlands, broken down 12 miles from Nairobi and been welcomed as honoured guests into a private house of strangers.

And all this is just one day in a long journey across Africa.

overland travel in Africa, rather than towards information about particular countries. It does not aim to replace country guides and we strongly recommend that you take along other relevant books.

XII

# Part One

## Before You Leave

# The Basics

You are dreaming of wild animals on the plains, of starry desert nights, of tropical beaches and of camping in the bush hearing the distant beat of drums, but where do you begin? If you have opened this book, the chances are that you will get to Africa one way or another. Africa will be worth every moment and every pound, euro or dollar, but there are important considerations too. The main criteria that will influence the type of trip you plan across Africa are time and money. The salient facts of modern life are that if we have the time we don't have the money, and if we have the finances we can't get enough time off.

Your budget will pretty much determine where you plan to go, for how long and in how much comfort you wish to travel. Once these factors have been thought through, you can begin to look at the other issues. Top of these will be which countries are currently accessible, which routes avoid current hotspots and how the changing local weather patterns will influence the timing of the trip. You will need to take a long look at some maps in order to work out an outline itinerary. Calculating the time to get from place to place will depend on the state of the roads, the nature of the terrain, the mountainous sections, and the type of transport you have as well as the inevitable bureaucratic delays en route. Some countries are expensive, imposing high visa fees or border charges; others are much less costly.

Already you can see the difficulties in estimating a budget. You really do need to keep in mind any number of unexpected costs that will inevitably arise on the way. Of course sometimes it works in your favour, but don't plan on it.

Taking your own vehicle affords you an unrivalled freedom, but you will undoubtedly find that the cost is surprisingly high. Most of it will probably be before you even set off. All the peripheral things add up; the spare parts, the visa fees, insurance, the carnet etc. Basic day-to-day expenses can be very low; fuel is often dirt cheap, and food, where available, is also often very cheap. But if you decide to visit a game park, or the vehicle breaks down, the costs can go sky high.

Taking a motorcycle or bicycle is much cheaper, but you will need to sacrifice comfort, choice of some destinations and some personal space to do it. It is of course possible to cross most of Africa on very public local transport. It will not always be easy and is often extremely uncomfortable. The other option is to join an overland truck group. This is a good option for a first-time trip if you are happy to mix in with other like-minded travellers and can forgo the independence you have when travelling on your own.

You know how much time you have, and it's possible to find out many of the fixed costs in advance, such as visas, ferries, an estimate of fuel costs, and approximate border fees, if any. You can decide which vehicle to take. Remember that the vehicle carnet bond cost will relate to the vehicle chosen, and this can be the most significant consideration when choosing which vehicle to buy. You can estimate the cost of spare parts, equipment and tools. The level of comfort you plan can affect costs. You can map out a route and check costs for each country from relevant guidebooks (Bradt of course!). Invariably the route planning will change according to 'African factors' and even the possibility of unexpected shipping could add considerably to the cost.

What you can't budget for are route changes and delays, whether due to bureaucracy, road damage, breakdowns, border closures or just bad luck. Try to make a realistic assessment of all known costs and then add a couple of thousand dollars or more in case. And then make sure you can get extra funds on a debit or credit card if necessary.

## THE BUDGET
### Expenditure

Trying to predict expenses and work out a budget is very difficult for an overland expedition. Each person has different needs and expectations. Some can survive on only US$10 per day, while others cannot survive on less than US$60 or more per day. You probably need to find a balance between the two. We have indicated below some of the costs involved before you go. Some are more or less fixed; others are very variable, such as the vehicle chosen. We have also estimated the en-route costs, but these too are highly variable according to personal needs.

We spent an average of **US$40** per day, of which $20 was fuel and other costs for the 4x4 vehicle, and the remaining $20 was for personal expenses such as accommodation and living expenses for two people. This was for a three-and-a-half month trip from London to Durban via Cape Town from January 2004 to May 2004, driving over 27,000km with a total on-road expenditure of US$5,500. The previous year's trip worked out at the same daily average. This was a three-month trip from London to Gabon and back. But it would be more reasonable to assume a daily expenditure of nearer **US$50** for two people, and make sure you always have a way of getting more money if you need it. If you have a major breakdown you may need more than you could possibly foresee or carry; be prepared just in case.

As you travel, you will find that in some countries, like Sudan, your expenses will be minimal, as fuel is almost free and there isn't much else to spend money on. But countries like Kenya, Tanzania and Botswana can be much more expensive because of the activities on offer, like climbing Mount Kenya or visiting the various national parks. We found that at times we would spend as much as US$70 one day, and the next only US$12 (sometimes nothing at all in the desert), while game parks can be $100 per person. It will usually balance itself out.

Realistically, if you are buying a vehicle specifically for this trip, you will need to budget for around US$15,000–20,000 in total before you leave, plus US$150 per person per week in your own 4x4 vehicle. Even with a bicycle, the total initial investment will be over US$2,000. Planning a trip by motorbike will fall somewhere between the two.

Your preparation costs will quickly add up: the purchase of a vehicle; equipping it appropriately; getting a carnet, full medical insurance cover and a medical kit; and many more hidden costs that you might not have considered. It is possible to do it more cheaply, but the less you invest, the harder your trip is likely to be. At the other extreme you could buy a fully converted six-wheel drive and spend something like US$100,000 before you even start. We would not recommend this, as the more complicated the vehicle, the harder it will be to fix if it does go wrong. Even an expensive vehicle is not immune to breakdowns. Also remember the cost of the carnet is directly related to the cost of the vehicle.

But don't be put off! If you have the abilities and facilities to do most of the preparation yourself, you can reduce your expenses considerably. The following are some of the major costs you will have to meet, but the figures quoted are only a rough guide. Ideally, you should look at your own requirements under each of the headings listed in *Chapter 2* and check out what these are likely to cost.

## ESTIMATED BUDGET COSTS

The costs listed below are based on taking your own vehicle. Information on taking your own motorbike or bicycle is discussed further in this chapter and *Chapter 2*. The figures below will vary enormously according to the amount of work you can do yourself, and where you get the vehicle, parts and tools. A toolbox bought in a car boot sale will cost much less than one from a good stockist, but be careful. You don't want your cheap spanner to crack up in a dodgy place.

### Before you leave

**Vehicle**
Based on a secondhand Toyota Land Cruiser or Land Rover 110/Defender
Fully equipped, ie: overland ready                US$8,000–12,000
Vehicle only                                        US$3,000–8,000

**Vehicle preparation**
If you were lucky enough to find a fully equipped vehicle, you may only need to check everything works and fine-tune the vehicle for your trip. If you are starting from scratch you may be up for this full amount.                US$3,000–6,000

**Equipment**                                        US$1,500–3,000

**Spares and tools**                                 US$2,000–5,000

**Medical insurance**
Based on each person for one year full cover          US$300–800

**Medical kit**
The lower amount if buying in Africa                  US$100–400

### On the road
Per person, per day, based on two people in one vehicle    US$20–50

## Sponsorship

You might think that sponsorship will fall into your lap as soon as you announce to the world that you are off to explore Africa. Be under no illusions; obtaining sponsorship is a tough nut to crack. Most obvious companies have been approached in the past. They will want you to demonstrate exactly how they are going to get a return on their investment. Local firms are more likely to be sympathetic than nationally known names – but they are also unlikely to have as much to offer. You must ask yourself whether the massive investment of time you will need to find any sort of sponsorship is worth it.

### In aid of charity

With a great deal of forward planning, some travellers have managed to raise cash for charities by approaching sponsors and private donors. Some benefits can be derived from this approach, but a lot of effort will be required. Some of the larger charities such as CARE have given help to overland travellers who have raised money for them. This could be one way of raising awareness and giving something back to Africa. (See *Giving Something Back to Africa* on page 177.)

## ROUTE PLANNING

It has been lamented by some famous travellers that the planning and the expectations of the journey are sometimes greater fun than the execution of the subsequent travel itself.

Maybe, but planning the trip is certainly a lot of fun. Hasty preparation should be avoided; the more information you have, the greater the chances of avoiding problems later. This applies to all aspects of the trip.

## Maps

Africa is big and distances are on a massive scale. Make a mental note that travel times in Africa can be several times longer for a given distance than they are in areas with more developed transport infrastructures.

Although the Michelin maps we highly recommend are excellent for planning, they have been found to have a few surprisingly significant errors. We mention some of these later in the route sections. You will need at the very least the following map numbers: 741 (Africa North and West), 745 (Africa North East and Arabia) and 746 (Africa Central and South). Previously these were numbered 953, 954 and 955. These maps have a wealth of mostly accurate information on them, showing all the salient points, distance, type of road surface, wells and quality of water, dunes, possible fuel and rest stops, altitudes, scenic routes etc. Other Michelin maps that may be of some use are 742 (Morocco), 743 (Algeria and Tunisia) and 747 (Ivory Coast).

Be aware that, although some roads shown as a tarmac highway may be exactly that, quite often they will be pot-holed, have broken sections, have rough uneven surfaces and, at worst, are just plain diabolical with little tarmac left. Other roads shown as gravel might be new superhighways. Some gravel roads are excellent, such as those in Namibia; others, like those in Ethiopia, are exceedingly rough, stony, rocky and tyre-eating.

In the central African rainforest zone, roads can be extremely muddy, with large puddles often the size of ponds. Bridges here may be broken, have planks missing or be constructed of logs. During the wet seasons, some roads are impassable and others might be closed off to vehicles by 'rain barriers (*barrières de pluie*)' across the road until the muddy surfaces have dried sufficiently.

Michelin probably make the best, most easily obtainable maps of Africa. Most travel bookstores stock them. Try to get all the maps you need before you set off, as they are difficult and often impossible to obtain in Africa (except perhaps in places in southern Africa).

## Climate

On the Michelin maps you will see charts indicating the approximate average temperatures, high and low, as well as the rainfall for various cities and towns in Africa. When you are planning a time for your trip, these give a very good basic insight into the climatic conditions of each area.

Attempting to cross the Sahara in summer between late April and early October is pretty crazy. If you plan to invest a lot of money in driving across the Sahara, why go when the dangers are high and the journey exceedingly uncomfortable? The Sahara has a wonderful winter climate, but be aware that in the midwinter months it gets very close to freezing overnight, so good bedding is essential. Remember too that altitude can play a significant part in the effects of temperature and climate. In Ethiopia or on the slopes of Mount Kenya, for example, the highlands bring a welcome relief from the sometimes oppressive heat of the plains.

Further south, planning a trip through any areas subject to seasonal rains really can wreak havoc to daily schedules, particularly where roads are not paved. It is surprising what a short sharp rainstorm can do to some roads. In the Sahel on the southern fringes of the Sahara this can mean seriously sticky conditions, where sand and soil are mixed. In the humid rainforests it can manifest in hours of digging away thick heavy mud while up to your waist in deep brown water. There is a certain amount of masochistic fun to be had in these predicaments, but not for three weeks continuously.

## IT NEVER RAINS BUT IT POURS...

Dawn at the check-post south of El Golea. It was a bitterly cold morning; the army personnel were drinking black tea and smoking French cigarettes. Breakfast for them was bread and oranges. We waited and waited. And waited. Till 16.00. Finally they told us the bad news, 'Today no convoy'.

Dawn again. A soldier gave us a bottle of Orangina in exchange for a fresh orange. The convoy set off together, but within minutes we were alone in the desert; being hopelessly unable to keep up. In any case there were no police or army in the so-called convoy. Soon it was pouring with rain, so much so that we had the windscreen wipers on all day long. Could this really be the Sahara? So much rain fell that we ended up driving through great torrents of water with huge waves. A day later large pink flowers blossomed in wild profusion, taking full advantage of this unexpected manna from heaven.

At In Salah, the first fuel station was unreachable because of the truck-swallowing mud. The second was slightly better, but with a long line of vehicles attempting to fill up. In the old streets children played happily in the swimming pools made by the unusual precipitation; perhaps some of them had never seen such an event before in their short lives. We camped outside the poshest hotel in town. Inside, the lobby was almost a swimming pool too. The ceiling dripped, and the beautiful carpets had to be moved to a drier part of the building. We watched BBC World and Al Jazeera briefly, before retreating to the inside of our cosy metal box, listening to the 'tap tap tap' on the roof with a comforting sense of security.

No departure date is likely to suit all the optimum weather patterns fully. If you plan to be on a long journey across Africa, it becomes more difficult. Somewhere en route is going to be awkward; you will just have to work around these things at the time. But time is what you might have most of.

# ROUTE OUTLINES

With regard to the actual routes, things change constantly. In the heyday of African overlanding in the late seventies and eighties, almost all the continent's big routes were open, except for those via Angola, Mozambique and southern Sudan at various times. In the early nineties the superb trans-Sahara routes across Algeria closed, due to Islamic insurgents in the north and the Tuareg rebellion in the south. The route into Mauritania opened via Western Sahara, so the trans-Africa remained possible. When the turmoil of Zaïre erupted, combined with instability in the Central African Republic, the routes across the great rainforests of the Congo basin became history.

Yet routes did remain tenuously possible, as is often the way of African travel. Chad and Sudan allowed a trickle of adventurous travellers to cross from Cameroon to Ethiopia a few years ago, but then a new war in Darfur closed that route in 2004. Recently the Nile route through Egypt to Khartoum, so long a big no-go area, has opened. Even more recently, some courageous souls tried to drive south from Cameroon into Gabon, across the two Congos and into Angola, a route that in a short time may prove a reasonably safe option.

For access to Africa, don't dismiss the route across Europe to Istanbul and then south to Egypt via Syria and Jordan, both exceedingly hospitable countries despite the bad images portrayed in the media. Don't go through Israel, though; you will not be able to get into Sudan later. By linking up the different options, almost any type of trip can be contemplated. Over the past 25 years, one route at least has always seemed to be possible;

enough to keep the flickering candle of African travel passion alive. In the end though, the latest circumstances will usually dictate your final choice.

In planning the route you need to be fully informed about the latest political situations in the countries en route. You need to consider if visas for countries you want to visit are being issued. You should definitely consult the various government foreign-travel-advice websites such as the British one at **www.fco.gov.uk**. Of course, if you took complete notice of the information given out in these websites, you might never go anywhere at all. They are by their nature somewhat cautious, over-protective and sometimes out of date. The nanny state is all around; one is not supposed to be this adventurous.

A good example of the difficulties in assessing the risk is illustrated by the current warnings about Chad north of the capital N'djamena, which seem to be absolute in their advice about not travelling anywhere in the whole area. While the Tibesti region is certainly dangerous, the Ennedi area is not, except for the known existence of mines. We are still here to tell the tale and might have missed an incredible experience if we had heeded the FCO warnings. This is not to say we recommend that everyone should go to Chad. Maybe we were lucky that time! Things need to be put into context and, above all, good and reliable local advice must be sought for such areas. Some places in Africa are frankly best avoided by people like us in our own cars, and are better visited with experienced local operators, as we did in both Chad and parts of Niger.

We have set out below in more detail the routes that exist across Africa. We include some details covering the Middle East – a varied and pleasant introduction to the ways of third-world motor travel. A number of options cover the Sahara and West Africa; others concentrate on the west-to-east routes. Outline details are also given about possibilities within the Congo basin, and of course the routes south of Kenya to South Africa, on which political instability is fortunately not an issue. Whether you are planning a short foray into North Africa, a longer trip through West Africa and back via the Sahara or the complete trans-Africa, the planning will re-ignite the dreams that you had when you first decided that this journey was for you.

Of course no trip will ever go exactly to plan. Well, it might, but anyway the travellers and local people along the way are sure to provide you with invaluable up-to-date news about roads, routes, new ideas and safety.

## Note on place names

Confusion inevitably arises between the Democratic Republic of the Congo (DRC) – formerly Zaïre – and the People's Republic of the Congo. For the purposes of this book we have used Democratic Republic of the Congo or DRC for the former and Congo or Congo Brazzaville for the latter.

## Getting to Africa
### Ferry routes

At the beginning or end of your trip, you will probably need to consider the ferry routes from Europe into Africa or vice versa; most will be looking for the cheapest and most convenient routes.

One popular route is **Spain to Morocco** from Algeciras, Málaga or Gibraltar to Ceuta or Tangier. Those with a vehicle or motorbike will probably opt to go via Ceuta, because the city forms part of Spanish Morocco and its tax-free status means that fuel is cheap. It's always a good idea to fill up those jerrycans.

Other popular routes are from **France** (Marseille) **to Morocco or Tunisia**. Ferries to Algeria are currently not possible or safe. From **Italy** good ferries run to **Tunisia**. These go primarily from Genoa, Naples and Trapani (in Sicily) to Tunis. Ferries also connect the Italian ports of Genoa, Livorno and Naples with Palermo, meaning you can visit Sicily on the way without driving all the way down through Italy.

## MAP, WHAT'S THAT?

Where was the road to Khartoum? Maps are a wonderful thing until you realise that a road on a map in northern Sudan is in reality the sand beside the railway, and on which side of the line does it go? This road is a complete figment of Michelin's imagination. We followed the railway line but, even before leaving Wadi Halfa, we were in quite deep sand. More by luck and guesswork than map-reading, we found the way by following the line of telegraph poles alongside the railway tracks. For 200 miles we followed the tracks; occasionally the sand was very deep. We met just one vehicle all day and that was only ten miles out of town. Despite the fact that there is a railway here, which offered some comfort, this route is surprisingly remote and devoid of life.

At Station Four we encountered some workmen preparing the line for the expected train. They were sweeping sand off the tracks, and were not pleased with us as we pulled into the station astride the lines, carefully avoiding the points and steel cables. 'Which way to Khartoum?' They were not amused and directed us out into the deepest sand a hundred metres from the station. Horribly bogged now, we discovered that the low-ratio gears on the Land Rover would not engage. Fortunately some digging and then diff lock got us out. Away from the station, we again headed as close to the railway tracks as possible, sneaking on to the embankment at the next deep sand. The track was surprisingly smooth as the rails were buried by hard sand and the only problem was avoiding touching the lines themselves. It was lucky for us that the train comes only once a week in each direction, as we were stuck on this embankment for many miles with no way off. And today there were no trains, because of a mass wedding party in Wadi Halfa, to which all were invited and no-one could leave.

It was great to camp wild in the desert at last, below some low rocky hills with a tremendous view. Having just parked and made a cup of tea, Bob said to me, 'Look, what's that over there? It looks almost like a train!' 'It *is* a train,' I replied. Thank goodness we were no longer on the lines. It was a large freight train, which was obviously too late for the wedding party!

Ferries were operating from **Greece** and **Turkey to Egypt**. But recent reports suggest that these, if they still exist, are best avoided. In 2004 some people shipping vehicles into Egypt were kept waiting at the dockside by the authorities for more than a few days, one party for two weeks. This may not be a wise option. It may be possible to ship a vehicle from **Malta to Libya**, but this is unlikely to be of any benefit unless you are going to Malta anyway. It's better to ship your vehicle into Tunis, a very well-organised port, and take the excellent road from Tunis to Libya.

It is quite easy to ship a vehicle from Aqaba in **Jordan** to Nuweiba in the **Egyptian** Sinai, making a route possible across Europe through Turkey and Syria to link in with the Nile route to Khartoum.

One final ferry route that might be of some use to those travelling north from **Sudan** to the Middle East is the one from Port Sudan to Jeddah in **Saudi Arabia**. It's shown as route ME2 on the map of trans-Sahara routes on page 15. This cannot be done southbound because of difficulties in obtaining the Saudi transit visa, which is valid only for three days (and is not given to unmarried couples). This visa was issued in Khartoum for direct travel from Jeddah to Jordan only – again for three days. Security issues may affect this option. Do not attempt it during *hajj*, the annual Muslim pilgrimage to Mecca.

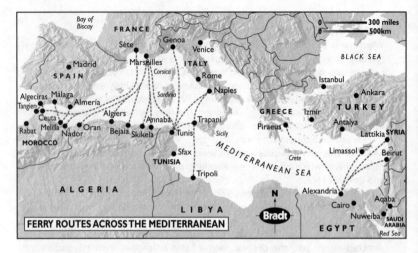

FERRY ROUTES ACROSS THE MEDITERRANEAN

Ferries run daily from Brindisi and Bari in southern **Italy** to Igoumenitsa near Corfu in **Greece**, for those heading to Africa via the Middle East who want to avoid some bad roads in eastern Europe.

Coming back from or going out to **South Africa**, there are roll-on roll-off ferries between Durban and Southampton in the **UK**. These can be arranged through **P&O Ferrymasters**. Further details later.

There are also ferries from **Mombasa**, but we have been told that dealing with the bureaucracy and corruption needs patience, and the costs are extortionate.

## Ferry prices

For the Algeciras-to-Ceuta ferry it is not necessary to book in advance. Shop around when you arrive, though. At most ports, there are sales people representing the major ferry companies who can sell you a ticket there and then. Most ferries running the Spain-to-Morocco route run regular services every 15–20 minutes both ways. A standard ferry crossing from Algeciras to Ceuta usually takes up to 45 minutes. The average price for the short ferry crossings, for example Spain to Morocco/Ceuta for two people in a car, is around US$200 at the time of writing in 2005.

Ferries to Tunisia are cheaper from Italy than France, and the drive to Genoa is almost as quick (allow three days from London). For the best prices these routes should be booked well in advance if possible. They are very heavily booked in summer, but most overlanders will not be going then anyway, unless they are masochists or want a totally mad experience. Return fares are particularly good value, although none is that cheap. The ferries take about 24 hours. Approximate prices are US$800–900 return (within four months).

From Trapani (Sicily) to Tunis the ferry takes about nine hours. This ferry is best booked in advance, but beware: it can be delayed by rough weather at times. It is much cheaper as a cabin is not required.

Note when asking about ferry prices that harbour tax, embarkation fees and GST (VAT) are not always included in the quote. It is safest to add on another 25% to the original quote to get a correct pricing on a route. Some of the ferry companies offer concessions, depending on the season.

## Ferry companies

Below is a list of ferry companies with international representation:

*Spain to Morocco*
**Compañia Trasmediterránea** Head office: Av de Europa 10, Parque Empresarial La Moraleja CP 28108 Alcobendas; tel: +34 91 423 8500; fax: +34 91 423 8555; information and booking: +34 90 245 4645; email: correom@trasmediterranea.es; www.trasmediterranea.es
Offices and agents: *Algeciras* (Cádiz) Recinto del Puerto, s/n, CP 11201; tel: +34 95 658 7517; *Ceuta* Muelle Canonero Dato 6, CP 51001; tel: +34 95 652 2239; *Málaga* Estación Marítima, Recinto del Puerto, Local E1, CP 29016; fax: +34 95 206 1218; *Morocco* Limadet; 13 Av Prince Moulay Abdellah, Tangier; tel: 39 931142; *UK* Southern Ferries; 1st Floor, 179 Piccadilly, London W1V 9DB; tel: 020 7491 4968; fax: 0870 499 1304; email: info@southernferries.co.uk; www.southernferries.co.uk
**Ferrimaroc SA** www.ferrimaroc.com; *UK* email: helpdesk@ferrimaroc.com; *Morocco* Voyage Wasteels SA, Port of Beni Enzar, 62050 Post du Beni Enzar, Nador; tel: 56 348786; fax: 56 348781; and Ferrimaroc Nador SA, BP 96 Beni Enzar, Nador; tel: 56 348100; fax: 56 349520; *Spain* Ferrimaroc Agencias SL, Muelle Ribera s/n, 04002 Almería; tel: +34 95 027 4800; fax: +34 95 027 6366, email: info@ferrimaroc.com

*Italy to Tunisia*
We have personally used both of these agencies successfully. Viamare act as agents for Grandi Navi Veloci and Grimaldi, while Southern Ferries deal with SNCM (French), CTN (Tunisian) and Trasmediterránea (Spanish). Check with them for any changes or updates to ferry schedules and routes.

**Viamare UK Ltd** Graphic House, 2 Sumatra Rd, London NW6 1PU; tel: 020 7431 4560; tel: 0870 410 6040; fax: 020 7431 5456; email: ferries@viamare.com; www.viamare.com
**Southern Ferries** 1st Floor, 179 Piccadilly, London W1V 9DB; tel: 020 7491 4968; fax: 0870 499 1304; email: info@southernferries.co.uk; www.southernferries.co.uk

*France to Morocco or Algeria*
**SNCM Ferryterranee**; BP 90, 13472 Marseilles cedex 2, France; tel: 0891 701 801; tel: +33 4 91 56 32 00; fax: +33 4 91 56 35 86; email: info@sncm.fr; www.sncm.fr

*Greece, Turkey, Middle East to Egypt*
For Greek ferries, look at the following website and further links. At the time of writing in 2005, most ferry services to North Africa were suspended. Email: info@greekislands.gr; www.greekislands.gr.

*International companies*
**MBendi Information Services** PO Box 23498, Claremont 7735, South Africa; tel: 021 671 9889; fax: 021 671 6316, email: MBendi@MBendi.co.za; www.mbendi.co.za

Two general **websites** have information on international ferry companies: www.routesinternational.com and www.ferrycenter.se.

## Overland routes
The following section examines the routes for vehicles and motorcycles primarily. There's information for cyclists in *Planning a Bicycle Trip* on page 30.

*Route NA – Europe, Tunisia, Libya to Egypt*
The quickest route to Egypt from Europe is from Genoa to Tunis and along the Libyan coast to Cairo. These roads are excellent. Formalities at the Libya border have to be handled by a local agent and you have to travel with a Libyan guide in your own vehicle, or accompanying you in his own car. At the moment this cannot be avoided, but at the very least you can learn much about the country and you have someone to

read the Arabic road signs. Along the way, the old part of Tripoli, Roman ruins at Sabratha and Leptis Magna and the solemn war graves at Tobruk are the main attractions. Entering Egypt and dealing with the bureaucracy is a minefield, but everyone will be at pains to welcome you and take a little reward for services rendered. The road to El Alamein, Alexandria and on to Cairo is excellent, if a little busy nearer the capital.

### Route ME1 – Europe, Turkey, Syria and Jordan to Egypt

Using this route via the Middle East, it will take a little longer to reach Egypt than going via Tunisia and Libya directly, but it offers a whole new world of historical attractions, varied scenery and hospitable people. Coming from Europe, you will need a visa for Syria in advance, but Turkey and Jordan issue them at the borders. Going northbound, Syrian visas are easily obtained in Amman. Other considerations are the vehicle taxes charged on the borders of both Syria and Jordan, which can be significant amounts. Fuel, though, is cheap, as a counter to these charges. Campsites do exist, and some hotels will allow parking/camping in their grounds.

From Istanbul any number of excellent roads head to Syria and, with time, a fascinating trip can be made along the Turkish southwest coast. Here are many ancient Greek and Roman attractions, as well as fine beaches and rugged mountains. In central Turkey, not far off the direct route from Ankara to Aleppo in Syria, are the amazing underground churches, settlements and volcanic chimneys of the Cappadocia area near Göreme. In Syria the highlights are Aleppo, with its bazaars and citadel, Crusader castles dotted around the country, the aromatic bazaars of Damascus, and, a little off the route to the east, the Palmyra ruins in the desert. Jordan has some great attractions too, with Petra and Wadi Rum at the top of the list. A ferry links Aqaba in Jordan to the Sinai peninsula in Egypt. All the roads on the way are good throughout.

## Within Africa
### North Africa and the Sahara

North Africa and the Sahara include the following countries: Morocco, Tunisia, Algeria, Libya, Mali, Niger, Mauritania, Chad, Egypt and Sudan. You should plan to cross the Sahara between October and March, when there is less danger from the heat.

### Route S1 – Morocco to Mauritania

This route remains the most popular trans-Saharan route at the moment. The road all the way through Morocco and Western Sahara is tarmac. Within Morocco, main roads are excellent, with Fez, Marrakech, Todra Gorge and the route of the Kasbahs being some of the highlights. Going south, you enter Western Sahara, which is currently administered by Morocco and awaiting a referendum on its status. Laayoune is the nominal capital of Western Sahara and it is possible to camp along the coast. Fuel and better facilities are expected to be available once the new road in Mauritania is open. Until then, be sure to carry enough fuel.

The Morocco/Mauritania border immigration and customs are now at Fort Guergarat. The border area was heavily mined, so you should keep to any marked tracks until the road is completed. The Mauritanian and Moroccan governments have normalised all overland travel northbound into Morocco now. Once in Mauritania, it should be easy to pick up a guide to take you across the desert from Nouadhibou to Nouakchott if the new road is not open. Check with locals when high and low tides take place, as the area is not drivable at high tide. The drive along the beach can be done easily during one low tide. Plan to do this stretch in one go, as there are very few places that allow you to drive off the beach, and high dunes hug most of the coastline. Carry enough fuel for approximately 1,000km (620 miles).

You can also put your vehicle on the longest train in the world to Choum/Atar, from where you can take the tarmac road to Nouakchott. If you take the piste from Nouadhibou to Choum and Atar beside the railway, allow two to three days and keep on the south side of the tracks to avoid possible old landmines. From Atar, the oases of Chinguetti and Ouadane are close by. Note that the piste from Chinguetti direct to Tidjikja south is serious desert motoring, and a guide should be taken.

The road heading east of Nouakchott towards Mali has deteriorated significantly in recent years and is considerably broken, adding a day or so to the driving time. Finally, beware of occasional problems with bandits on the stretch of road from Nema to Bamako across the Mali border.

## Route S2 – Tunisia to Niger

This used to be the main Sahara overland route until early 1993. By 1999 a few intrepid travellers were starting to take it again. Until the kidnapping of 32 westerners in their vehicles in 2003, the route was experiencing a great revival, in which we were able to partake. Sadly once again it is off-limits. In any case, the north of Algeria remained unsafe throughout that time. In case this route becomes possible again, we include details. Another popular route through Algeria was via the eastern oilfields road from Hassi Massoud to Djanet. The scenery is truly spectacular, as the new tarmac road goes close to the amazing Tassili N'Ajjer plateau.

The main trans-Sahara route runs from Tunis to Agadez via Tamanrasset. It is referred to as the Route du Hoggar, after the spectacular mountain range outside Tamanrasset. The total driving distance is approximately 3,800km (2,370 miles) and takes about 12 days, but we would suggest spending longer in order to visit the Hoggar Mountains and enjoy the stunning desert scenery. The road all the way from Tunis via Tozeur, Ouargla and Ghardaia to Tamanrasset is paved, but some sections south of In Salah are pot-holed and uneven.

The road from Tamanrasset to Arlit is a mixture of desert pistes and dunes; real desert driving. New tarmac is slowly being laid northwards from the border at In Guezzam and a short section of tarmac south of Tamanrasset is now breaking up. The scenery is varied and the driving challenging. Some care is needed following the piste, as it is not one single track but often many different routes, sometimes quite a long way apart. Just keep a close eye on the piste and look for occasional marker posts. Be very careful if you leave the main pistes to camp; getting lost cannot be ruled out.

This section is approximately 600km (370 miles) with fuel only occasionally available in In Guezzam, so don't plan on getting any here. (The fuel station manager has several wives, and it is difficult to find out which one he is with if you want to buy fuel!) But seriously, carry enough with you, bearing in mind that your vehicle will use up to 50% more fuel in the sand than on paved roads.

From In Guezzam, the last town in Algeria, there is a section of no-man's-land between border posts, with some deep sand. Going south to the remote desert outpost of Assamaka, the first settlement in Niger, which cannot by any stretch of the imagination be called a town, the track is easy to find. But if you are leaving here and heading north, the route is initially ill-defined, so ask the Customs people. We did not, because we had encountered some rogues there on our way south, but we paid the price by getting stuck out of sight in deep sand for two hours at midday.

The piste to Arlit is mostly well defined, but quite lonely. The road from Arlit to Agadez is known as the Uranium Highway, because of the mines at Arlit, and is paved. Agadez is a superb mud Sahel town with great markets and a famous mosque. Close by are the Aïr Mountains.

The other route from the border at Assamaka to Agadez via Tegguida-n-Tessoum is not paved, hard to follow now and there is no fuel available. It does take you past salt

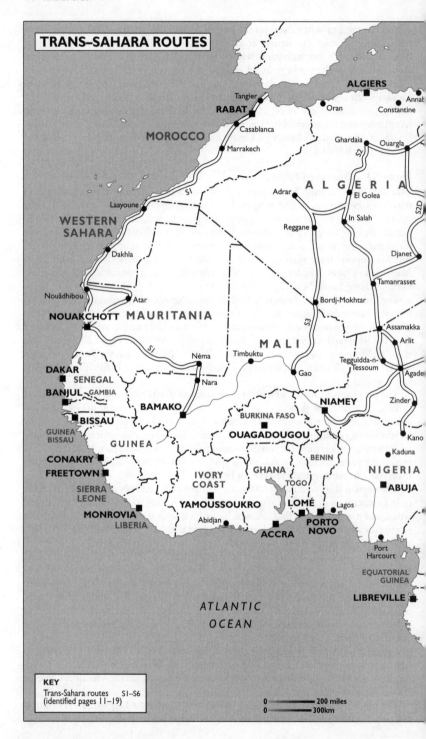

## TRANS–SAHARA ROUTES

**KEY**

Trans-Sahara routes    S1–S6
(identified pages 11–19)

0 ————— 200 miles
0 ————— 300km

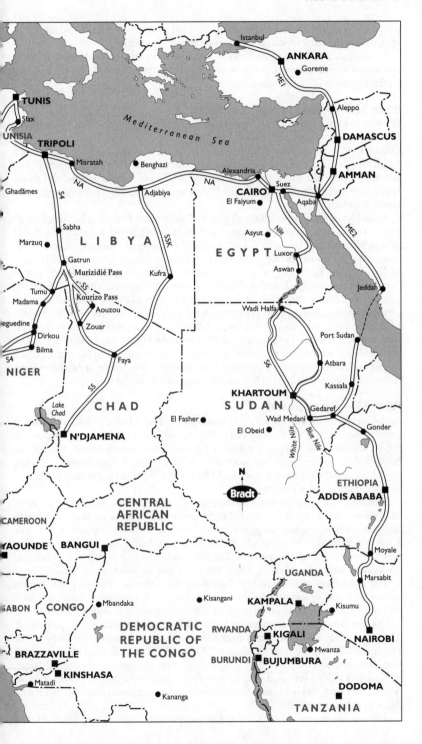

mines and you may be lucky enough to see a salt caravan. This route should not be attempted in the rainy season, as it becomes a muddy quagmire.

From Agadez a mostly tarmac route (with 100 miles of well-marked sandy track) continues through to Zinder. A tarmac road continues on to Kano in Nigeria. The best border to cross at is Matamey/Kongolam.

## Route S2D – Algeria to Niger via Djanet

We will make a brief comment about this alternative route from Tunisia to Niger. From Touggourt a good sealed road runs through the oilfields via Hassi Messoud and Ohanet to In Amenas. After Illizi the road climbs on to the Fadnoun plateau, once a rough area and now crossed easily. A detour to Iherir, a lost canyon, is a must, before the truly spectacular drive along the foot of the Tassili N'Ajjer plateau to Djanet. Leave your vehicle in the campsite in Djanet and go trekking on the plateau; it's a superb experience.

From Djanet the route is almost all piste to Tamanrasset. Fuel must be carried; don't forget to allow extra for some stretches of soft sand that will devour it. Ideally you should travel with more than one vehicle. GPS is advised if you are not with a local guide. This route is not always well defined, with many tracks once you are off the main road north of Djanet from Bordj el Haoues. The military have reoccupied the lonely fort at Serouenout and Mount Telertheba acts as a prominent waymark. Once past here, the piste is more clearly defined to Ideles and Hirafok. From Hirafok a well-defined but extremely rocky, and in one place extremely steep, track climbs into the Hoggar Mountains to the hermitage of Assekrem. A better way is to continue west to the main road, follow it towards Tamanrasset and then go to the Hoggar from there. It will save your vehicle as well as your nerves and is strongly recommended. The better track of the two from Tamanrasset to the Hermitage Foucauld and the viewpoint at Assekrem is the eastern one. From Tamanrasset the route to Niger is the same as route S2.

## Route S3 – Algeria to Mali

Again, because of the kidnapping of 32 westerners in their vehicles in 2003, this route is currently unsafe. But in case it should become possible again, it is included. Known as the Tanezrouft, it was less popular than the S2 route above, mainly because the distance between water and fuel stops was much larger – Adrar to Gao is approximately 1,500km (930 miles) and the unpaved section is 1,320km (820 miles). Fuel is generally available in Reggane, but again don't count on it.

This route was often preferred by those travellers using VW Combis, Citroen 2CVs and motorcycles, as its surface tended to be harder. The road is paved from Adrar to Reggane. South of Reggane, the piste is mostly hard-packed sand and quite fast, with only a few softer spots. The terrain is flat and less varied than the Hoggar route, but nonetheless has a certain remote feel. The Algerian border post is at Borj Mokhtar and the Malian customs is at Tessalit. There was a well here for water.

The last section from Tessalit to Gao along the Vallée du Tilemsi is the hardest section, with areas of soft sand. It too can be confusing, with a number of tracks, but there are some wells and settlements en route. Also it's often impassable during the wet season.

Once in Gao, you can continue on to the Malian capital, Bamako, on a paved road. This route offers some fascinating destinations, such as the Hombori rock towers, the Dogon villages, and the mud mosques at Mopti and Djenné. Heading southeast from Gao, you can follow the river Niger along a scenic route to Niamey, the capital of Niger. This route is at times very sandy, but has now been tarred on the Niger side after Ayorou. A very sandy track also heads west from Bourem, crossing dunes in places, to Timbuktu. Allow two days for this trip.

The total driving time from Adrar to Gao is approximately six to seven days. As with the S2 route, there has been continuing political unrest in the area, particularly in northern Mali, so seek advice before you set out.

## Route S4 – Libya to Niger

Travelling in convoy with at least one other vehicle is essential, and taking a guide from Gatrun to the border is advisable, and currently required by the Libyan government, throughout the country, even in the north. Guides with vehicles are required in Niger as far as Agadez. Remember not to take alcohol into Libya. To get a Libyan visa, you need to have your passport officially translated into Arabic and you also need an invitation letter from a Libyan agency. (See details under *Libya* in *Chapter 8*.)

In May 1995 a peace accord with the Tuareg in Niger came into effect and the situation in northern Niger improved markedly. Isolated banditry is still a possibility, though, and you are advised to enlist the help of, and indeed required by law to link up with, a local tour operator for safety and security reasons. A number of agencies in Agadez operate trips to Bilma, Djado and the Aïr Mountains, and can be contacted by email. See details on page 91.

In Libya, roads south from Tripoli are excellent. A diversion to the Akakus Mountains near Ghat and the dune lakes near Awbari is well worthwhile. The dune lakes must be visited with at least one other vehicle and are only for the experienced; the dunes are seriously big here and potentially extremely dangerous. At the campsite it is possible to hire a 4x4 with driver for the day trip to the lakes if you don't want to risk it yourself! From Ghat there is a route through to Djanet in Algeria, but this is not currently open and is said to be very wild and sandy. From Sebha, paved roads lead to Gatrun and then it is piste to the border at Tumu.

When possible, the most common route from Libya into Niger or vice versa is from Tripoli to Sebha, Gatrun, Tumu, Madama, Seguedine, Dirkou and through the Ténéré Desert direct to Agadez. The route via Bilma and Fashi is serious dune driving and potentially extremely dangerous for the inexperienced. It is therefore not recommended except with a local operator. The total distance is about 1,500km (930 miles), with fuel available at Sebha, Dirkou (mostly) and Agadez. You will need to carry fuel for approximately 1,200km (745 miles). It is easy to lose your way on this route and there are some difficult sandy sections.

Agadez is a great place and should not be missed. It has bustling camel markets, traditional mud architecture and lively colourful people. Its festivals are riotous. South of Agadez, the road to Zinder is not all paved. A fun section of sandy track about a hundred miles long still exists. Allow a day and a half to reach Zinder. Otherwise the roads west to Tahoua, Maradi and Niamey are pretty good, with the odd pot-hole; beware!

## Route S5 – Libya to Chad

The Libya-to-Chad routes are not for the inexperienced. The Tibesti area of northern Chad is very remote and renowned for its landmines and bandits. Sadly it too is currently off-limits. It is one of the most spectacular areas of the Sahara, with volcanoes, crater lakes, hot springs and mountains up to 3,200m (10,500ft) high. The main routes are either Gatrun – Murizidié Pass – Kourizo Pass – Zouar to Faya; or, longer but more scenic, Gatrun – Murizidié Pass – Aozou – Zouar to Faya Largeau.

Routes through the Tibesti are said to be rough, rocky and severely punishing. From Faya to N'djamena, the piste is reasonably easy to follow, but is quite sandy. Fuel is generally available in Faya. Some small settlements such as Moussoro might have diesel drum supplies, but this cannot be guaranteed. It is possible to do these routes in either direction, but getting permission from the Chadians to head north is harder than heading south from Libya. The crossing is about 1,250km (775 miles) via Zouar and an extra 300km (185 miles) if you go via Aozou. Fuel is extremely cheap in Libya, so fill up regularly and particularly in Gatrun.

This route, should it become possible, is not for the faint-hearted. You must be very well equipped, research all the latest information and travel with at least two vehicles. Take a local guide, despite the costs. In fact you will be forced to take a guide anyway to satisfy local etiquette and contribute to the local economy. Even agents in N'djamena do this.

Another distant possibility, only for very experienced Saharan travellers, is to follow a route across eastern Libya from Kufra close to the Egypt–Sudan border (**Route S5K** on the map). A minimum of two vehicles is essential. The remote and little-used piste from Kufra heads around the Ramlat Rabianah sand desert and crosses into Chad north of the famous Ounianga Kebir and Ounianga Serir lakes, both stunning places. Mines are said to be a serious issue on this route near the border area, and normal border formalities do not exist.

From Ounianga Serir an ill-defined piste goes to Fada, passing smaller lakes. From an isolated settlement at Demi, a treacherous piste continues adjacent to the Depression de Mourdi and through some amazing rock formations in the northern Ennedi. After Fada the route via Oum Chalouba to Abéché is fairly obvious. Taking a local guide is essential to smooth a path though the larger settlements. We have met only one couple who have done this complete route, a remarkable achievement, and they were not so young either.

## Route S6 – Egypt to Sudan and Ethiopia

This route is currently (2004–05) the best option for a complete trans-Africa trip by road, avoiding major political hotspots. Sudanese visas are available in Cairo in a few days and were possible to obtain in London, allowing two months for the process. Bear in mind that evidence of having been in Israel renders your passport useless for travel in any other Arab countries. Some travellers who have crossed from Israel into Egypt and onwards have carried two passports, but be careful about this.

Currently the Egyptian authorities require all tourist vehicles, including tourist coaches and private cars, to run in daily convoys from the Red Sea resorts of Hurghada or Safaga to Luxor and south to Aswan. You may stop to stretch your legs and visit the antiquities of Kom Ombo and Idfu within this convoy system for allotted times. Tourists can also drive to Abu Simbel in daily convoys with pre-arranged permits.

It was occasionally possible some years ago to drive to Abu Simbel and catch a pontoon ferry across to Wadi Halfa, but this whole area is run by the military and is effectively off-limits at present. It was suggested that tourists might be allowed to drive directly to Wadi Halfa in future, but that is perhaps hard to imagine when certain vested interests are understandably doing very nicely at present from the ferry arrangements. The route shown on the maps along the Red Sea south from Safaga to Port Sudan is currently not an option, but things could change.

The normal route south from Aswan to Wadi Halfa is via the ferry, which runs once a week each way. Recently this was on Mondays heading south and Wednesdays heading north. The ferry is quite expensive (extortionate if you are the only vehicle wishing to travel) and can be a great deal of hassle. Prices might be fixed, but this is not obvious. Patience, tact, restraint and a sense of humour are needed to deal with Egyptian officials, who know that there is no other route south at present. Sometimes a different barge is used if there are a number of vehicles waiting, but that is rare. Heading north, the ferry can also be expensive and difficult to get on to at Wadi Halfa, but at least the Sudanese are super-friendly as they extract your money.

In Wadi Halfa, be sure to get an alien's registration stamp added to your visa stamp. This is a time-consuming mystery tour and will cost around US$20 per person. (A bank nearby changes cash. Travellers' cheques are not usable in Sudan at present.) From Wadi Halfa to Khartoum there are two routes, following either the Nile or the railway line. The Nile route is now used by all local vehicles, but is initially rough and then sandy. It is said to be hard to follow, particularly near settlements. Once you reach Dongola, where fuel should be available, a new superhighway leads to Omdurman and Khartoum. Allow three days at least.

The route beside the railway is surprisingly isolated and the train only runs slowly once a week in each direction. You must follow the railway or watch for the telegraph poles at all times, otherwise getting lost is a serious possibility. Because there is a lot of very soft sand close to the tracks and even nearby, you might be forced in some sections to drive with your wheels astride the railway lines. We don't imagine the Sudanese railway company approves of this, so try not to be seen doing it near a station. A couple of stations are manned; do remember what day a train is scheduled! Driving on the line is hard but not bumpy, as the line is submerged in hard-packed sand. For your safety, though, try to use the line only as a last resort, and be very careful not to hit the rails with the sidewalls of your tyres.

Allow almost two days to reach Abu Hamed, and don't expect much when you get there. From there another lonely piste, which is indicated by tall metal kilometre markers, leads to Berber, where a tarmac road begins. Fuel can be obtained here and at Atbara. A new desert highway runs to Khartoum east of the Nile and passes close to the famous Pyramids of Meroe, not to be missed. You can camp nearby in the bush; the local people were very friendly to us and got down off their camels to help us change a wheel. Their camels needed no maintenance! Other antiquities along here are hard to find without some local help.

From Khartoum an excellent new tarmac road runs south through the Gezira cotton fields to Wad Medani and on to Gedaref (and to Port Sudan). From Gedaref the once ghastly weather-dependent track to Gallabat and the Ethiopian border is now a rough but all-weather gravel road. On the Ethiopian side there is a reasonable gravel road from Metama to Gonder, a scenic and spectacular drive. From Gonder, unbelievably rough gravel roads lead north to Axum, east to Lalibela and south, with some tarmac later, to Addis Ababa.

## West Africa

Any number of options exist from Mauritania. In the north a good road runs from Atar to Nouakchott. East of Atar are the oasis towns of Chinguetti and Ouadane beyond the Adra plateau. Travelling with a guide and in a convoy of at least two cars, it is possible to drive directly from Chinguetti to Tidjikja on a remote desert piste. This links to the main route into Mali.

Reasonable paved roads head south from Nouakchott to St Louis, Dakar and Banjul. Continuing into Guinea Bissau, roads are steadily improving. In Guinea the main roads close to the capital Conakry are good, but after Dabola are said to be pot-holed further inland. In Mali, Burkina Faso, Ghana, Benin, Togo and Nigeria, main roads are generally good paved routes, but pot-holes soon appear when away from these.

A good road heads south from Zinder to Kano, via Matamey/Kongolam; not the one shown directly south on the Michelin map. The road from Kano, a pleasant place with some old Hausa buildings, is good heading east via Potiskum to northern Cameroon. The road from southern Nigeria into Cameroon has some bad sections after the border to Mamfe and south to Buea.

Cameroon has some excellent roads and some dreadful ones. Those in the north are generally tarred and fairly OK. The road from Ngaoundere to Yaounde is a typical example of a route that springs a surprise. South of Ngaoundere is a relatively good dirt road to Garoua Boulai, which then becomes an amazing but empty (a telltale sign) superhighway to Bertoua. Then suddenly the tarmac ends and a dreadfully corrugated section of 200 miles follows, only improving just before Yaounde. Roads in some areas of southwestern Chad are set to improve, now that oil has been found.

KEY

| West-east routes<br>(identified page 22) | WE1, WE2 |
| Central African routes<br>(identified pages 22–25) | C1, C2<br>E1, E2 |

## West–east routes

Avoid the West African rains. These tend to start around May and last throughout the summer months. They start slightly later the further north you go.

### Route WE1 – Chad to Sudan to Ethiopia

Although this route is at present not possible due to the new conflict in the western Darfur region of Sudan adjacent to the Chad border, the information collected by Charlie and Illya is included in case things improve.

The main route is from N'djamena to Abéché near the Chad border at Adre then to El Geneina (Sudanese border), Nyala, El Fasher, El Obeid, Kosti and Khartoum. From Khartoum it is possible to get to Ethiopia via Gedaref (Sudanese border) and Metema and on to Gonder in Ethiopia. Currently you cannot go via Eritrea, as the border with Ethiopia is closed, and going from Assab south to Djibouti is not advisable without local assistance, if at all.

Leaving from N'djamena and heading to Khartoum will take ten days of straight driving during the dry season. The route via Mongo is said to be better than the main route to Abéché from N'djamena. The route in Sudan is uncomplicated and the tracks are mostly hard-packed sand. There are usually two tracks, one for the Bedford trucks acting as the local taxi service and another for cars. These tracks run parallel to each other and at the best of times you will lose the car tracks while trying to negotiate the vehicle in the deep ruts left behind by the Bedfords.

It is hard to lose your way on the Sudan side and, if in doubt, just follow the railway line or drive on it. A few police checks are evident along the way, but if your paperwork is in order it's an absolute breeze. More often than not we politely had to decline the invitation of lunch at most police checkposts! The hospitality in Sudan is extraordinary. Make sure you get your Sudan visa before entering (either in Ivory Coast, Chad, Ethiopia or Kenya) and get a travel permit stating your route. (See also *Red tape* under *Sudan* in *Chapter 8*.)

### Route WE2 – Central African Republic to Sudan to Kenya

Should southern Sudan ever become safe, and peace talks have now concluded, the old route from Bangui in CAR to Nairobi via Juba might reopen. From Bangassou the route, formerly a rather dreadful narrow track through quite dense dry forest, runs east through Zemio and on to Obo. A number of ferry crossings also made this route slow going. After Juba this was a super but isolated route with varied mountain scenery, acacia scrub inhabited by the interesting Turkana people and friendly villages in the Sudan. Once into Kenya, improved roads via Lokichoggio and Lodwar lead on to Nairobi.

## Central Africa

Central Africa has plenty of rain and mud to slow you down; this is where 4x4 really comes into its own. The easiest time to cross east–west (or vice versa) is in the drier season from about December to February. There is also a 'less wet' season in June/July. The 'rain barriers' set up on roads in CAR during the rainy season could cause you considerable delays. These routes have been closed to travellers since June 1998, but, with the changing political climate in Africa, this challenging route might become accessible once again to overland travel.

### Route C1 – CAR to DRC to Uganda/Rwanda

This was the classic trans-African route, renowned for broken bridges and enormous bog holes. It may be the only time you need your winch, snatch blocks, and full capacity of fuel, not to mention your reserves of inner strength and patience. Ferry river crossings can be a big headache. Operators may need to use your battery to start the ferry, your diesel to run the ferry and your donation in order to begin the process. But this is **why** you planned to see Africa in the first place, remember!

From Ngaoundere in Cameroon, a reasonable dirt road runs to the main border with the Central African Republic at Garoua Boulai/Béloko. Entry from Chad south of Sarh is at Maro and Kabo, but it's unlikely that anyone has done this for years. Once in the Central African Republic (CAR), things deteriorate. Bridges can be down and rain barriers are set up during the wet season to stop vehicles using and damaging the roads. The road used to improve the closer you got to the capital. At present Bangui is not safe for tourists.

There were two routes across Zaïre, now the Democratic Republic of the Congo (DRC). One crossed the Ubangui River directly from Bangui to Zongo and then slipped and slid its muddy way via Gemena, Lisala, Bumba and Buta to Kisangani. Problems concerning security in Zongo used to be avoided by making sure you crossed early in the day and carried on for at least 50km (30 miles) from Zongo before stopping.

The other route involved driving east from Bangui via Sibut and Bambari to Bangassou. Once across the river from Bangassou, a fairly narrow and overgrown road used to head south via Monga, Bondo, Likati and Buta to Kisangani. This route is now apparently much the worse for wear, but might still be preferable to the other one. Another crossing of the Ubangui was at Mobaye, but we have no experience of this. Should these routes open in the near future, try (difficult unless you meet others coming north) to get an accurate picture beforehand in Bangui.

After Kisangani the route used to head east through Bafwasende and Nia Nia into pygmy territory around Ipulu. Overland parties used to go into the forest with the pygmies on hunts and also visit the rare okapi reserve – it may not exist now. The rainforest continued until Komanda and nearby Mount Hoya. Here the route headed along a ridge with spectacular views south to Beni, Butembo and on to Goma via the Virunga National Park. Another little-used and currently very unsafe bad road went north through some grassy, rolling hills around Bunia to Aru and Aba. Some dreadful bridges caused heart-stopping moments before the route crossed into southern Sudan near Yei. A better track continued through superb scenic boulder areas to Juba.

A new road shown on the Michelin map goes southeast from Kisangani to Bukavu and the Rwanda border near Goma. Until the political situation improves in the eastern DRC, we can only guess about this future option. It was also possible to cross into Uganda from Beni some years ago before the troubles. Once in Rwanda the roads are better, but slow going and hilly. Some paved road was built in the late eighties from the Rusumo Falls border into Tanzania around Biharamulo, well before reaching Lake Victoria. The classic route then went through the Serengeti and up on to the Ngorongoro Crater before reaching Nairobi via Arusha.

## Route C2 – Gabon to Congo to DRC to Zambia/Angola

Despite the current problems in the DRC we know of a handful of brave or perhaps foolhardy travellers trying this route, some with vehicles. It is still fraught with gun-toting soldiers, difficult bureaucracy and bad roads – the worst countries being the two Congos. Cameroon and Gabon are fairly stable at the time of writing and thus reasonably safe. Visas for Gabon are expensive.

Heading south from Yaounde, the road is good but hilly tarmac and very pretty, with dense jungle and occasional distant mountain ridges. From Ambam there are two routes. The one under construction heads south from town to the Ntem River that is currently crossed by ferry. Then a wide road heads towards Equatorial Guinea. This soon becomes a dirt track east of the border post of Meyo to Bitam in Gabon. The other route heads east from Ambam on a very narrow muddy track with ageing log bridges. Another much more friendly ferry crosses the river here to Gabon. All formalities were carried out at Bitam in 2003.

Going south in Gabon, the road is a mixture of new tarmac and corrugated gravel. Again the scenery is spectacular. Before Ndjole the road is badly pot-holed, but then to Libreville and Lambaréné it is good. Once across the Ogooue River towards Congo Brazzaville, the roads deteriorate. This was as far as we got in 2003, when an Ebola virus outbreak and political unrest blocked the way. In any case travelling alone is not recommended for quite some time into the future on this route.

The information given in the paragraph below is not firsthand and is included only as an outline. This route was used by some overland companies quite a few years ago. From Kinshasa head southwest towards Lubumbashi via Kikwit, Kananga and Likasi **(Route C2K)**. You had to obtain permits in Kinshasa to cross the mining region. It may also have been possible to put your vehicle on the train at Kananga.

Heading south from Kinshasa into Angola now seems a vague possibility. It was attempted by at least one group in 2004, but they were unable to get visas for Angola. They got as far as Pointe Noire in Congo Brazzaville. Hopefully it will become safer in the not-too-distant future. From Brazzaville you have to cross the river to Kinshasa and then head south into Angola. The infrastructure in much of Angola is said to be in a bad way and mines are a big hazard away from the main routes. The south of the country, closer to Namibia, is said to be slowly opening up.

## East Africa

Hitting the wrong climate in eastern and southern areas is more likely to be a nuisance than a disaster, as the roads tend not to be so bad. Most rain in the east falls between March and June and October to December.

### Route E1 – Ethiopia to Kenya

The simplest and currently most-used route from Ethiopia into Kenya or vice versa is the Moyale to Isiolo road, if it can be described as a road. From Addis Ababa a good sealed road goes via Awasa as far south as Dila before becoming pot-holed, very hilly and slow. After Argya Maryam it improves and is generally good through Yabello and Mega to the border at Moyale.

Once in northern Kenya things are a bit grim, to say the least. The road is shocking and security concerns mean you are advised at the border to take an armed guard. The former convoy system does not seem to be in use at present and banditry is apparently less common. That said, we did hear about one alarming incident, but fortunately no-one was seriously hurt. Before Marsabit the road is dreadful, allowing speeds of no more than 10–15mph. After Marsabit, a veritable haven of civilisation and good food, the road is patchy.

Allow nearly two days to get to Isiolo from Moyale. Local trucks from Moyale now appear to be taking a better, sandier track via Wajir to Nairobi, but this also heads through bandit areas. Local advice must be sought.

Some travellers were going via the Omo region around Arba Minch en route from Addis Ababa to Moyale. On the Kenyan side, going via Lake Turkana might be a possibility, but security concerns were preventing this recently.

### Route E2 – Kenya, Tanzania, Malawi and Mozambique

Once in Nairobi, any number of good roads and routes lead south into Tanzania, the most popular being directly south to Arusha. Heading to Mombasa and south to Tanga, or going via the game parks circuit including Masai Mara, Serengeti and Ngorongoro Crater, are also possible routes. Through Tanzania a good road goes all the way to Mbeya and on into either Zambia or Malawi, on mostly good roads. The road from Arusha south to Mbeya via Dodoma is said to be very rough and quite remote for much of the time.

It may now be possible to cross from Tanzania into Mozambique south of Dar es Salaam, as a new bridge over the Rio Ruvuma at Mtwara was being built, with new roads as far as Pemba. But with the heavy floods of March 2000, the status of roads and bridges could well have changed. Check before trying this, as roads are still bad on the Tanzanian side according to travellers' reports.

After Mbeya a good road heads via Tunduma south into northern Malawi and then along the lake. From Malawi it is perfectly feasible to head south into Mozambique from Blantyre and then to the south via Swaziland. The roads in Mozambique are mostly good, but some sections are breaking up and pot-holes are an issue in some areas. The route has very little traffic, and fuel or any other supplies are sparse, particularly north of Vilanculos. Hassle from traffic police has lessened. From Maputo into Swaziland and on into South Africa, the roads are good. Be vigilant on the South African side of the Swazi border, where car hijackings are said to be a hazard. Signs around here recommend no stopping!

Currently, visiting Zimbabwe may prove difficult, because of economic considerations. Fuel is said to be hardly available and, although there is little evidence that security issues are a major concern, things are not predictable. Further south of Tanzania, the main routes go either directly from Mbeya to Victoria Falls and then through Botswana to South Africa, or into Namibia and down to the Cape. Roads are mainly fine.

## Southern Africa, Botswana and Namibia

With so many varied routes through southern Africa, it is impossible to list them all. The standard of roads is excellent compared with the rest of Africa, and indeed most roads in southern Africa are as good as those in Europe. Roads in Lesotho are the exception, in the mountain areas away from Maseru. Gravel roads in Namibia are generally very well maintained and offer some spectacular drives. The trans-Kalahari route across Botswana from Lobatse to Windhoek via Ghanzi is now paved throughout, as is the Caprivi Strip in the north. Security concerns in South Africa are perhaps, sadly, more of a problem than any road, route or geographical obstacle. Don't camp away from secure sites or backpackers' hostels.

There are a few routes through southern Africa that are 4x4 only and will get you into the unknown. For further information on 4x4 in southern Africa, read *Southern Africa 4X4 Trails* (1997–1998) by Andrew St Pierre White and Gwyn White, or *The Complete Guide to a Four Wheel Drive in Southern Africa* (1998–1999) by Andrew St Pierre White.

# Suggested routes

The following itineraries are listed as suggestions only. A full overland trip from London to Cape Town or vice versa can be done in as little as four months, but taking at least six to eight months would be better. Of course a year would not be too much either, and some people are able to do this.

## Less than six months

If you have only up to six months available, we suggest circular routes along either the north and west coasts of Africa or southern and East Africa. This of course depends on what you want to experience, see and do. Below are some suggestions, but the time scales are limitless. And after so much investment you want to enjoy the fruits of your labours.

### Shorter options

Perhaps as a warm-up or with limited time:
Morocco and Western Sahara; or Italy – Tunisia – Libya – Tunisia; or with longer, Italy – Tunisia – Libya – Egypt – Jordan – Syria – Turkey – Greece. If Algeria improves, then this is a great three-month trip: Spain to Morocco – Mauritania – Mali – Burkina – Niger – Algeria – Tunisia – Italy.

## Route NW – North and West Africa

Spain to Morocco – Mauritania – Senegal and the Gambia – Mali – Burkina Faso – Ghana – Togo – Benin – Nigeria – Niger – Algeria or Libya – Tunisia and back to Italy.

With longer time and improving security, possibly from Nigeria into Cameroon, then across to Chad and Sudan. Then Egypt or Saudi Arabia to Jordan.

## Route SE – southern and East Africa

Cape Town – Namibia – Botswana – Zambia – Zimbabwe – Malawi – Mozambique – Swaziland – Cape Town.

### Longer routes

The routes we have suggested are completely dependent on the political situation at the time:

Currently feasible is: Turkey – Syria – Jordan – Egypt; or Tunisia – Libya – Egypt; then Sudan – Ethiopia – Djibouti – Kenya – Tanzania – Zambia – Namibia – South Africa; or Tanzania – Malawi – Mozambique – Swaziland – South Africa – Lesotho plus Botswana and Namibia.

Currently this is *almost* feasible, depending on the news from Congo and Angola: Morocco – Mauritania – Senegal and the Gambia or direct to Mali – Niger or Burkina – Ghana – Togo – Benin – Nigeria – Cameroon – Gabon – Congo – DRC – Angola – Namibia – South Africa.

In future, when Darfur is safe perhaps, as above then from Mali to Niger – Chad – Sudan – Ethiopia – Kenya – Uganda – Tanzania – Malawi – Zambia – Botswana – Zimbabwe – Mozambique – South Africa.

## Other factors and limitations

Below are some of the parameters that you need to determine: total number of days available, daily travel distance, acceptable range of climate, geography, road condition, level of accommodation, flexibility with food, availability of fuel and water, delays obtaining visas en route, unexpected festivals and even what wildlife you want to see.

Timing is important. Because of the large number of fascinating destinations in Africa, your inclination might be to try to fit too much into too little time. Seven game parks in seven days in a 4x4 can be as gruelling as a European bus tour of seven countries in seven days. Some travellers suggest that quality is better than quantity; but, if you don't want to miss anything, it's amazing what you can pack in with some determination.

Don't be surprised if your planning chart begins to look a complete mess with rows of 'if, then, maybe' conditions for each separate possible itinerary. It's a good idea to use an Excel spreadsheet if you have it, then you can shift the options and dates around quite easily, and view them side-by-side.

Finally, at the end of the trip, what happens to the vehicle to which you could well have become sentimentally attached?

## SHIPPING YOUR VEHICLE
### 4x4 vehicles

If you are planning to ship your vehicle back at the end of the trip (or indeed to start your journey by shipping one out), this can be a major expense. The lowest prices from Mombasa, Dar es Salaam, Accra or Cape Town to Europe are all over US$1,000 for a container (there are a lot of other African countries that also offer freight service but the above are the largest and most popular). Also beware of all the hidden extras; these can add as much as another 50%.

We shipped our vehicle back from Durban through P&O and a local agent. This service is offered about once a month and the vehicle was put on to a ship bringing hundreds of new cars into Europe, to Southampton, Zeebrugge or Hamburg. Vehicles have 'roll-on roll-off' status and are not in containers. This cost US$1,250, plus various port charges each end adding around US$400, and took three weeks.

Shipping a vehicle from Europe to South Africa is reasonably easy, if a little more expensive. We found the shipping companies and agencies fair, even with all the extra costs, which were quoted in advance. For shipping a vehicle to either East or West Africa, hidden costs may be an issue, as problems can occur later at the African ports where red tape is complex and almost certainly some possibly large bribes may be necessary.

It would be advisable to try to find other travellers who want to ship their vehicle, as a container can be shared, depending on the size of the vehicle.

Whether in East, West, central or southern Africa, you will probably need to use a shipping agent. Although this may add to the cost, it should give you peace of mind and save a lot of time.

## Motorbikes
Of course, shipping a bike can be much cheaper – particularly if you share a container. It is even possible to hitch a lift by putting a bike inside a vehicle already being shipped. Airfreight for motorbikes is also pretty reasonable.

## Bicycles
It is generally possible to take a bicycle as luggage on most airlines.

## Websites
The following are good website addresses for shipping lines, agents and costs:

**An Mbendi Profile – African Shipping Industry** www.mbendi.co.za
**Complete online freight services** (international) www.freightquote.com
**P&O Ferrymasters** email: enquiries@poferrymasters.com; www.poferrymasters.com

# STARTING A TRIP FROM SOUTH AFRICA
*Arnout Hemel and Saskia de Jongh*
## Where to buy your vehicle
Whether you buy your vehicle at home or in South Africa, each option has its benefits and disadvantages. Assuming home is Europe or any Western country, it's worth considering the following factors:

### Availability
In South Africa you'll mainly find petrol cars; diesel cars are less common and more expensive. Toyota Hilux and Land Cruisers, Land Rover Series 3 and Defenders are common. South Africans like the outdoors and 4x4, so there is plenty of outdoor equipment.

### Cost
Cars cost about the same in South Africa as in Europe. Equipment is much cheaper (rooftop tents, fridges etc). Labour costs are lower in SA, so it's cheaper to add an extra fuel tank, get the latest things fixed or get your rooftop tent installed.

### Time
The time you need to prepare your vehicle depends on the state of the car and the level of perfection you want to achieve. It can be done in two to three weeks, while some people spend over a year. If you belong to the second category, prepare your car at home! Preparations are easier to plan and you can spend any free hour you have available.

In South Africa you need a safe place to prepare your vehicle to avoid theft. The best option is to find a guesthouse with a parking lot, a spacious campsite or friends with a big home. You may feel that your preparations in South Africa take time from your actual trip. Try to see them as part of your holiday; enjoy the good weather and finish your day with a sundowner and braai!

### Shipping/selling
Unless you make a round trip, there will always be a moment when you have to ship your vehicle or sell it at the end of your trip. Selling a South African car is easy in South Africa; more difficult elsewhere. Shipping in either direction between Europe and South Africa seems relatively straightforward.

## Buying and preparing a car in South Africa
So you have decided to arrange everything in South Africa. Then keep the following things in mind:

### Before you leave home
Check whether your local automobile association issues a *carnet de passage* for a foreign vehicle (normally they do not, but for example the Dutch ANWB does). If they do, it gives you the flexibility to sell the car in your home country as well as in South Africa. Also the process for depositing the money is easier and more reliable.

Check out the web to get an impression of the cars on sale. Two good websites are www.autotrader.co.za and www.ananzi.co.za.

Buy guidebooks and maps. The Michelin series (746, 741 and 745) are very good, or check out MapStudio's *Southern & East Africa Atlas*. Maps are not easy to find in SA. However, detailed 4x4 maps with GPS coordinates for southern Africa are available in Johannesburg and Cape Town. Here you can also find a very interesting book from Getaway Magazine: *Getaway Guide Cape to Cairo*, with a description of the whole trip including GPS coordinates.

Check at your local bank to see if it is possible to transfer money to South Africa. The easiest way is by internet banking, otherwise you can order an international payment. If you want to be on the safe side, arrange a gold card so that you can withdraw money from a local bank in SA (not the cheapest option, but it will work).

### Finding the right car
The best markets to buy a car in South Africa are either Cape Town or Johannesburg. In Cape Town there tend to be more overlanders wanting to sell their cars than in Johannesburg. Recommended places to look are: guesthouses, garages/dealers, special overland equippers, private persons, internet: www.autotrader.co.za.

If you want to be sure that you are buying a good car, you can do a Test & Drive check at one of the AA test stations (www.aa.co.za). The AA test is very thorough.

### Money and paperwork
When you have decided which car to buy, it's a matter of paying for it and getting the paperwork done. Getting money transferred to a South African bank account can be quite a hassle. In 2003 we couldn't easily transfer money from Holland to South Africa through our internet bank accounts. So we withdrew money with our credit cards (maximum €7,500 per card) and paid for our car in cash. This was not the safest option, and we were really glad our backpack full of R100 notes arrived safely at Johannesburg to pay for our Land Rover!

Getting the paperwork done is not too difficult. You just have to complete the following steps:

1) The seller needs to get the car through a roadworthiness test.
2) The buyer and seller need to fill in two copies of the selling papers, which the seller sends off to get the car de-registered from his name. The buyer needs to go to a local municipality office with one copy to buy a licence disc, and to register the car in his/her name. Total costs are less than € 100, but you need an address in South Africa to be registered as a South African road user. Ask the guesthouse where you stay if they will support you. We used the address of friends with whom we were staying.
3) You obtain a *carnet de passage*. This is not necessary if you stay in southern Africa (Mozambique, Namibia, Botswana, Zimbabwe, Zambia, Malawi). If you plan to go to other countries, it's mandatory. Make sure Egypt, Jordan and Syria are on the carnet as you might need to cross them, and many AAs tend to exclude those countries.

## Insurance
Normally when you try to insure your car for an overland trip, you need only third party insurance. If something happens, however, for example if you hit a child in Ethiopia, your third party insurance won't help you much. Whether you are insured or not, you have to pay for the costs (typically in cash US$).

If you want a comprehensive insurance, try Cross Country Consultants (www.allterrain.co.za). They have a modestly priced (€ 60 per month) comprehensive insurance for southern Africa, Kenya, Tanzania and Uganda.

If you are crossing Africa (across the east) all the way from/to Europe, you need roughly the following insurance:

Green Card for Europe up until Morocco, Tunisia and Turkey.
COMESA/Yellow Card: one policy covering third party insurance for Burundi, Djibouti, DRC, Eritrea, Ethiopia, Kenya, Malawi, Rwanda, Sudan, Tanzania, Uganda, Zambia and Zimbabwe.
Third party insurance at all other borders.

## Preparing the car
In South Africa you can find a good selection of spares, tools, accessories, camping equipment and skilled mechanics.

## Tools and spares
Tools are readily available at every hardware store. Spares like oil filters, air filters, points etc can be found around the country at Midas. For more specialised Land Rover spares in the Gauteng area, you can visit Leimer's Land Rovers.

## Camping equipment
South Africa has probably the best selection of outdoor and camping equipment in the world and prices are considerably lower than Europe. You can find the world's best portable fridges (National Luna, Engel), and many rooftop tents originate from South Africa (Eezi Awn, Echo, Howling Moon, Hannibal). Just visit an outdoor store and you will get an idea. When buying equipment, make sure you haggle about the prices (you will get at least 10% discount for paying cash). Rooftop tents can also be bought directly at the factory for great prices.

## Some useful outdoor stores
**Camp World** www.campworld.co.za
**Outdoor Warehouse** www.outdoorwarehouse.co.za
**Makro** www.makro.co.za

One great thing to keep in mind when you go shopping for outdoor equipment is the following: when you leave South Africa and don't intend to return, you can get reimbursed for the VAT paid on all stuff that is not permanently attached to the car and is not consumed (eg: your rooftop tent). All you have to do is keep the original receipt and fill out the forms at the border when you leave South Africa. You must do this within three months of purchasing the goods.

### Accessories
South Africa is also the ideal place for buying car accessories. Hi-lift jack, winch, tyres, fuel jerrycans, long-range fuel tank; you name it, everything is for sale and most of the time the seller will be happy to install it free of charge for you.

### Mechanics
If you need to get some work done on your car, there are many options. In general the mechanics in South Africa are skilled and the labour is cheap compared with Europe. A recommended Toyota mechanic and safari outfitter is Baillies Off-Road (www.baillies.co.za).

### Our own experience
We arrived in South Africa on a one-way ticket with only our backpacks. We stayed for two weeks with friends in Johannesburg. In that period of time, we bought a car (which took two days), built in a long-range tank, rooftop tent and fridge, and bought all our camping equipment (chairs, table, plates, cutlery, boxes, braai), tools and spares.

We paid R50,000 for the car (1984 Land Rover Series 3, LWB, with a new 3.5L V8 petrol engine). We bought it through Autotrader from a private person. We spent another R20,000 on all the equipment. Altogether it cost us about R70,000 (then about €8,500). We rented a car and mobile phone for the first ten days, to make it easy to look for a car and do the shopping while we were preparing our Land Rover Pumba.

Next time we would do it the same way, with the one exception that we would buy a diesel-powered car instead of petrol, as diesel fuel is generally cheaper, easier to handle and the engine needs less maintenance.

## PLANNING A MOTORBIKE TRIP
Much of the planning for a motorbike trip can be based on the above details. The major differences will be in costs, which will be significantly lower. The other main difference concerns route planning. The chosen itinerary will to some extent depend on the quantity of fuel and water your motorbike can carry and how far off the beaten track you feel confident to go. That said, motorbikes are much easier to handle in many situations. They can be carried across rivers on canoes, and put on trucks, buses and even planes. They do offer a greater degree of freedom in many aspects and generally are less worry if they go wrong. They also do not look extravagant and desirable. For much greater detail please see *Motorbike Preparation* on page 68.

## PLANNING A BICYCLE TRIP
*David Mozer of Bicycle Africa Tours*
Those thinking of driving across Africa might be surprised to learn there is an even more adventuresome bunch planning the trip on a bicycle. If you have plenty of time and do not mind the hardship and physical effort, cycling when done intelligently can be the perfect way to see the continent. It certainly brings you into closer contact with both the people and the environment than most other methods. But honour the *caveat* – this means taking into account the geography, weather patterns, political reality, culture, and availability of food and water, as well as being prepared and having the proper equipment.

Just as in Western countries, there is something nicely different, and sometimes inspirational, about arriving almost anywhere in Africa by bicycle. In the cities, bicycles are efficient – even in Africa streets are congested and parking spaces few, which is not a problem with a bicycle.

In the countryside the bicycle is liberating. It reduces your dependency on mechanically questionable, over-crowded and unpredictable public transport. It expands your range over those who walk and it creates more social interaction than is possible from a tourist van or overland truck. As you cycle you are certain to meet people whom you would not meet any other way, generating rich experiences. The physical activity benefits your health and fitness, and the unrestricted access to the environment puts you into the middle of an exciting world that begs exploration.

Even if you don't like a lot of extreme hardship and can settle for seeing a carefully selected area of the continent, you can get the people-to-people benefits of a bike tour in Africa. Because of the flexibility of a bike and the ease with which it integrates with planes, trains, buses and boats, you can start and stop your road adventure almost anywhere you want.

If you are riding coast-to-coast, it goes without saying that you should not dream of such a trip unless you are in good health – cycling across the Sahara or through muddy forest trails can be extremely hard work. Some previous experience of long-distance cycling is vital before setting out. More modest cycling tours in Africa require preparation similar to that which you would need for a similar tour in Europe or North America: a basic level of physical activity in your life, and proper equipment. Of course there are no written rules and attitude can prevail over all else; Christian and Gilly Lee, who contributed to earlier editions of this book, didn't do any cycling at all before they set off on their successful trip from Victoria Station to Victoria Falls.

Bicycle Africa Tours report that they regularly have complete bicycle touring novices and African travel novices on their programmes, who do very well because they have so much enthusiasm for exploring Africa.

In most ways, the fundamentals of long-distance cycling in Africa differ very little from those of long-distance summer cycling in North America or Europe: the hills go up and down; the weather can be wet and dry; the temperature is hot and cold; the humidity varies from high to low; and it seems that regardless of which direction you are going there is a head wind. But, there are also major differences to keep in mind:

- Repair facilities are fewer and farther between, so that the initial quality, ongoing upkeep of your bike and your general self-sufficiency need to be more of a concern. This is covered in the sections on selecting and preparing a bike for travel in remote areas and the bike tools section of the packing list.
- Although there are tens of thousands of kilometres of paved roads in Africa, the proportion of major roads which are unpaved is much higher than in most industrialised countries, and many of the paved roads are deteriorating. The rotating joke for countries that have fallen on hard times is, 'What do you call a driver going in a straight line?' Answer: 'Drunk.' On the other hand, new stretches of roads are being paved each year and the dust is gradually disappearing.
- Cycling in Africa can easily be made more rigorous than is typical of touring in Europe and north America, especially if you are motivated to get off the highways and off the beaten track into the villages. It is there that you will find some of the most interesting scenes the continent has to offer. On any long-distance tour in Africa it is likely that you will find a mix of riding conditions. You will enjoy it a lot more if you prepare appropriately. Important points on this are covered in the relevant sections of this guide.
- Don't expect generic highway feeding. The food will be different. If you keep your expectations of the variety of food modest and learn to like Africa's cuisine, you will find plenty to eat in most areas. Cuisine in Africa is not homogeneous; some is more

elaborate than others. If you are willing to explore, the chances are that you will find some excellent hole-in-the-wall restaurants and great local cooks and dishes. Unless you have heard that a specific area is suffering from famine it probably has adequate, if not abundant, food supplies.

- Quiet and personal privacy may become a luxury.
- Water acquisition may need to be carefully planned. Bottled water, carbonated drinks and beer are not always available in grocery stores, restaurants or bars. When they are, they probably won't be as cold as you would like and the choice will be limited, with a different selection from that in the last town. Even coffee, in countries that export tons of it each year, may not be brewed and sold outside the major cities. If you are drinking water from other sources it may need to be boiled, filtered or treated so that it is a blessing and not a curse.
- There is also an element of truth to some of the myths: toilet facilities may not meet the standards of cleanliness and freshness of the Western service station or may be absent altogether. Smells engulf markets, towns, people and all aspects of life more than in the West.
- Lastly, unless your initial cycling is in Burkina Faso, or a few other select spots where cycling is a popular mass activity, you will quickly note that cycling does not command the status in Africa that it does in China, much of the rest of Asia, or even Europe and North America. This is not a point of concern per se, but may explain some bewildering looks and questions of disbelief. Hold your ground. Cyclists may be in the minority, but Africans are used to minorities and they are willing to bestow respect on deserving innovators.

The watchwords are 'be flexible, be tolerant and plan ahead'.

Bicycle touring may be one of the hardest, but it also is one of the most economical means of travel. The only costs you need to incur are on your bike, visas, food and accommodation. If you eat the local cuisine and camp or stay in rock-bottom guesthouses, you can keep expenses to the absolute minimum. Even at the end of your trip, many airlines will ship your bike back free as part of your luggage (but not all of them, so shop around).

If the idea appeals to you, a good first stop would be to contact the *Internet Guide to Travel in Africa by Bicycle*, www.ibike.org/africaguide, or the Cyclists' Touring Club in the UK (Cotterell House, 69 Meadrow, Godalming, Surrey, GU7 3HS; tel: 01483 417217; fax: 01483 426994; email: cycling@ctc.org.uk).

Once you join the CTC, you get a wide range of services – insurance, technical advice, touring itineraries and travel information. Information sheets are published by the CTC on various aspects of travelling with a bicycle and on specific countries and areas in Africa – including West Africa, South Africa, Seychelles, Malawi, Gambia, Zambia, Zimbabwe, Algeria and Tunisia, Egypt and Sudan, Morocco, and the Sahara. Information is also available for trans-African journeys and those planning round-the-world trips.

No guide to overland travel in Africa would be complete without some reference to cycling – a mode of transport that is more popular than you might imagine. But there are plenty of practical questions that need to be addressed by anyone who has plans for such a trip. So that you learn a minimum of the lessons the hard way, here are some general aspects that are worth considering.

## Constructing the itinerary

Constructing an itinerary, especially for a bike tour, is a multi-faceted project; the desire to see what you want to see, the limitations of daily range, the need for food and lodging and the complications of weather and topography can make it seem like solving a Rubik's cube. Here are some of my approaches and considerations.

## Mileage

Experienced international bicycle travellers find that for a variety of reasons their daily mileage in foreign countries is less than they would typically ride at home. For starters there is a lot to see, and because everything is so different you will want to leave extra time just to look around. It also tends to be the case that everyday chores, small business matters (ie: banking, posting mail and buying supplies), transportation and unfamiliar procedures in a foreign culture generally take longer than similar tasks at home. If you are travelling in a less-developed country, you might need double, triple or quadruple the amount of time you would regularly set aside for these matters.

As a practical tip, it is more comfortable and easier on your health to plan your itinerary with conservative estimates of daily distance, so that most of the bicycling can be done in the morning or late afternoon if necessary. If this is a once-in-a-lifetime opportunity, you want to enjoy the places you go, not merely pass through. Don't overestimate the daily distance you will cover.

## Planning for daylight

Because Africa straddles the Equator, in most of the continent the sun rises at about 06.00 and sets around 18.00 (natural time), plus or minus half an hour, all year round. An excellent, practical and recommended routine on cycling days is to live by the sun. Mostly pack the night before, get up at 06.00, eat breakfast around 06.30 and try to be on the road by 07.00. For the next few hours bicycle, sightsee and stop as necessary to eat and drink. If you don't reach your destination before the midday heat hits, stop from 12.30 to 15.30, eat a good meal, take a siesta, read, write and/or watch the local life. When it starts cooling down, saddle up and finish the day's ride. If you are staying in villages where there is no electricity, it is easy to be in bed by 20.00. You will then get a good ten hours' sleep before you have to confront the journey again.

## Route

There are now thousands of kilometres of excellent paved roads in developing countries. As modernisation continues, new stretches are paved every year. Even unpaved, the laterite (clay) and black cotton soil roads, common in Africa, can be nearly as smooth to ride on as paved roads – when they are dry. When wet, laterite and black cotton soil roads are virtually impossible to ride on. Depending on the situation, they may take from a few hours to several weeks to dry out after the last rains. Washboard, rocky and rutted dirt roads create their own discomfort and fall somewhere between dry and wet laterite roads. It is on the unpaved roads that you tend to find a much more traditional and interesting side of Africa. To best enjoy these areas you need to schedule your visit to correspond with the dry season – though Nature always reserves the right to be spontaneous. Even where the roads have good, all-weather surfaces, you should take note of the prevailing winds for the time of year you plan to travel. The wind can determine the direction of travel. If the route is a loop – *c'est la vie*. If your itinerary involves large changes in elevation, the geography may also be a major influence on your choice of starting and finishing points and your direction of travel.

## Climate

The weather can be an important determinant for the ease and enjoyment of bicycling, especially in less-developed areas. If you have a choice, schedule your travels for the cool, dry season. This varies from month to month and place to place. The cool part of the dry season is usually at the beginning of the dry season, just after the end of the rains. This period has the added advantage that the dust is relatively low, though the high-altitude *harmattan* dust affects West Africa a couple of months into the dry season. In addition to moisture and heat another important factor can be wind – try to keep it on your back.

# Vehicle Selection and Preparation

Once your budget is assessed and you have planned a route, you can think about your biggest expense of all: the vehicle. Don't rush off without careful planning and preparation; it could be a fatal mistake. In any case, planning and preparing is half the fun. Careful planning with an eye for detail will make your trip much more enjoyable and help you to avoid some potential pitfalls later on.

If you are taking your own vehicle, we would recommend a planning period of about a year. You should have your vehicle at least six months or more before you leave, especially if you are doing the preparation work yourself in your spare time. It may sound like a long time, but you will be amazed at just how much preparation is necessary and how many things there are to consider. But don't be put off!

We have divided the planning stages into vehicle, motorbike and bicycle preparation, detailing every requirement before and during your trip.

At the end of the book we have included a checklist which will help you with your planning decisions.

## SELECTING YOUR VEHICLE

The biggest decision is what type of vehicle to choose. Of course all have their advantages and disadvantages.

### Four-wheel drives

This is the best option if you can afford it. Some people suggest that travelling in a vehicle can distance you from the environment you are visiting, cocooning yourself in a self-contained world. This is true only if you allow it to be. The major advantage is that you are free to go more or less anywhere, stop for tea or a snooze any time. With relative comfort and the capacity to carry a fair amount of supplies, this is the best option.

The range of 4x4 is quite varied now, but most are being used on the school run. Of the more suitable models, there is a choice of permanent or part-time 4x4 and, more useful, low and high (normal) ratios for all gears. Some have diff lock and others have varying degrees of automation. Diff lock is when all four wheels are able to rotate without the loss of traction that normally occurs if one wheel is spinning. Diff lock should never be used for normal driving any longer than necessary, as the gears will 'wind up' and create excessive stress on gear components. The other significant factor when choosing a 4x4 is the type of suspension it has. Some have leaf springs, others have coil springs and some have a mix. Coil springs rarely give trouble but can induce a rolling effect. Leaf springs are more stable, but prone to breaking. Is there ever a perfect answer?

### *Petrol or diesel?*

It's hard to see any advantages in taking petrol, so stick with diesel. Diesel engines usually offer superior fuel consumption. Diesel is also safer to carry, unlike petrol, which is lethal once it has been shaken about in hot jerrycans. Diesel engines are also simpler in that they have no points, coils, condensers or distributors, though they do have more complex fuel systems. Make sure your injector pump and injectors have been professionally serviced before you leave. Diesel engines produce high torque at low revs, whereas petrol engines tend to produce maximum torque at high revs, which can be a disadvantage in difficult conditions where wheelspin is a problem.

Most of the 4x4 manufacturers have now moved on to diesel engines that are turbocharged. To gain more power some have inter-coolers. These two systems basically make use of exhaust gases to boost power levels. Being more complicated, they have some disadvantages. Buying such models secondhand can have risks. Ideally you should ask for the servicing record of the vehicle. Wear rates can be higher with faster motion and greater heat generated by these models. Of course the power gains are significant and undoubtedly an advantage in deep sand.

Fuel availability (either diesel or petrol) varies from country to country. As a general rule, however, diesel is cheaper throughout Africa and more readily available than petrol. Vehicles that use unleaded petrol have a definite problem, since such petrol is not available in many countries.

## Short or long wheelbase?

A long wheelbase has the obvious advantage of space. Remember you are most likely planning to live in and on your vehicle for long periods. It will be a close companion, and so will the person you share it with, so you might as well start out with the idea of making it comfortable. With more space a vehicle can be adapted in more ways; more equipment can be stored inside and out of sight. Pickup versions of long-wheelbase vehicles with added rear box units are extremely good for storage capacity. Rear box shells are available; some are rather low. Otherwise, if you are lucky enough to have access to welding and fabricating equipment, you can make your own metal and aluminium-clad box. Some people put custom-made caravan-style boxes on to pickups. Some are quite good; others look unstable and are not ideal in sand dunes.

A short-wheelbase vehicle does not really have the capacity or the convenience. Attaching a trailer to a short wheelbase for extra storage space is a possibility, but we don't recommend it. Towing a trailer can be a severe hindrance in some terrain, particularly sand or mud and over loose, uneven or sloping surfaces. There is potentially some danger when manoeuvring trailers at difficult angles or on sloping muddy roads. A badly loaded trailer can cause instability when cornering and braking. Trailers do spread the load better, but overall are best not considered.

Further information on storage and driving techniques regarding a short-wheelbase vehicle with trailer can be obtained from major 4x4 or trailer outlets. Companies offering 4x4 courses will also be able to assist. For a list of 4x4 clubs, research website www.fourwheeler.com/facts/clublist.html.

## Age and value

Buying the latest model or the most expensive vehicle might be desirable ordinarily, but there is one important factor to consider. Remember that the level and cost of your customs document for the vehicle, the *carnet de passage*, is related to the value of your vehicle. The bond or insurance-cover fees you must arrange before leaving your home country will depend on the value of the vehicle you choose, its age and in some circumstances its initial cost when new. When a country like Egypt charges a 500% mark-up on the assessed value of your vehicle, new or old, it can be a seriously daunting amount to put up as collateral. If you are planning a limited trip and to travel in countries that do not require a carnet, the problem is not an issue.

See *Paperwork* on page 93 urgently about this **before** deciding on the vehicle. Unless you have inherited a lot of money, this effectively means buying an older model, preferably in good condition, and spending some considerable time fixing it up. How old it is depends on your mechanical ability, the time and enthusiasm you have, and the depth of your pocket!

## Vehicle makes
By far the most common 4x4s in Africa are the Land Rover, Toyota Land Cruiser and Toyota Hilux (4x4). You are more likely to find spares and experienced mechanics for these vehicles than any other.

The older models are more common, such as the Land Rover Series III, 90, 110 and Defender, and the 60, 70 and some 80 series of the Land Cruiser and mid-1980s' Hilux. There is generally a good secondhand spares market, but not everywhere. You will also find Land Rover and Toyota dealers in most capital and larger cities, although the stock of spares varies greatly from dealer to dealer. They will sometimes only stock spares for the newer models.

Unless you are a very experienced mechanic, have a very reliable vehicle or can afford to have spares sent out to you, avoid the seriously overcomplicated newer models which bush mechanics will not understand. Go for an older Land Rover, Land Cruiser or Hilux.

The following is a brief rundown of vehicles available and a few of their advantages and disadvantages.

### Land Rover
The ageing Land Rover Series III is probably a bit long in the tooth regarding chassis rust and suspension when buying secondhand. The Series III had leaf-spring suspension with part-time 4x4 and a two-ratio transfer gearbox. Favourites now include the 110 and Defender Land Rover series, which are the most suitable for African roads. Their fairly simple and robust design makes them ideal for the wide variety of difficult conditions. They are available in a long or short wheelbase, with six-cylinder petrol or four-cylinder diesel engines. The smaller 2,286cc engine is rather underpowered. The 2.5 engines are normally aspirated or with turbo-charging and injection – the Tdi series. The later models are more powerful but more complicated. The early 2.5 turbo is best avoided but the following Tdi 200 engine models are quite popular. The later 300 Tdi had some timing belt problems. The very latest Td5 is much more sophisticated; servicing is probably best done by main dealers in African capitals.

The 110 and Defenders have permanent 4x4. With coil springs, they are a joy to drive on rough terrain. This is not to say that even Land Rovers are sufficiently robust to ignore bad conditions. They actually need constant attention and nurturing throughout the journey. Land Rover fans are a very caring, enthusiastic lot, spending happy hours underneath, admiring their steeds, and keeping an eye on the oil leaks and loose bolts.

Guess which vehicle we took?

### Range Rover
This vehicle was designed to bridge the gap between off- and on-road driving. It offers greater comfort than the Land Rover and is an excellent vehicle, but for a trans-African journey it is of fairly limited use. It does not have much in the way of storage capacity and the compensating advantages of its powerful engine and comfortable interior can now be found in the newer Land Rovers.

### Land Rover Discovery
Although it has the same engine, gearbox and axle specifications as the Land Rover Defenders, it has fewer practical advantages. It does have greater comfort, though. It is not common outside southern and eastern Africa. This vehicle has the Tdi 200 or 300 engines, which are now fairly reliable. The gearboxes are still liable to early wear and the shape is not ideal for tinkering with or living in for long periods.

### Toyota Land Cruiser

The Land Cruiser's design is rugged and very reliable, and spare parts are readily available throughout Africa. Toyota is rapidly taking over Africa! Toyota have a rather confusing numbering system for their various Land Cruiser models. To put it simply, they started with the 40 series and worked up to the 80 series in the early 1990s. The FJ prefix denotes a petrol engine and the HJ series diesel engines. Just to confuse you further, BJ refers to the short wheelbase. The engines tend to be large but very reliable and, in particular, the H2 engine (fitted in the HJ 60 series) will go on forever if looked after. The suspension is by solid axle and leaf springs, and the older models are all part-time 4x4 with a two-ratio transfer gearbox. Watch out for chassis rust when buying older secondhand models.

In 1984 Toyota introduced the 70 series. The HJZ75 and HJZ78 are still probably the best models for the Sahara and Africa. The 78 had coil springs fitted to the front and retained leaf springs on the rear, which can mean broken springs if you drive too fast. Toyota's 4-cylinder 3.5 and 6-cylinder 4.2 engines are still the reliable workhorse power units to have. The 80 series came along in 1990 with all coil springs, and the VX models have permanent 4x4. It may be better perhaps to look out for the GX models, which do not have permanent 4x4. The local mechanics tend to be familiar with these earlier vehicles. Toyotas are now made in South Africa but specifications can vary.

www.toyota.com/landcruiser

### Toyota Hilux

The Hilux is available as a double or single cab and with either a 2.2-litre petrol or 2.4/2.8-litre diesel engine. The engines are fine unless you expect to be dune-bashing for most of your trip. It also has part-time 4x4 with a two-ratio transfer gearbox. They are increasingly popular vehicles in Africa and nearly rate up there with Land Cruiser and Land Rover. They are a little easier to roll over on to their roofs if you are not careful, so take particular care when crossing slopes and cornering at speed. If you are considering buying a Hilux pickup, be sure to keep the height as low as possible when designing the rear living/storage area. Following on from the Hilux are the 4Runners. These have part-time 4x4 and a 3-litre turbo diesel engine. The Hilux is still more common at the moment in Africa.

www.toyota.com

### Nissan Patrol

These vehicles have a good reputation in Australia and South Africa and are reported to be very reliable. They are increasingly seen in southern Africa, where spares seem to be available in larger towns. They have coil-spring suspension and part-time 4x4. The later Patrol GR had a 6-cylinder 2.8 turbo diesel engine. The TD42 models have a larger engine. These two versions kept the part-time 4x4. We do not have any direct experience of these vehicles, but their shape and size certainly have no apparent disadvantages.

www.nissanuk.com and www.nissanusa.com

### Mercedes Unimog

The Unimog is popular with some German travellers and it is indeed a wonderful vehicle. It is a powerful 4x4 truck with very high ground clearance and offers a lot of storage space. The living quarters are separate from the driving cab. Although you can buy Unimogs quite cheaply at auction in Germany, costs can really start to mount on the road. The fuel consumption can be very high indeed, and some are petrol. You should test drive the Unimog in various conditions as they can easily tip over in soft sand.

www.unimog.net

### Bedford and other trucks

4x4 **Bedford** trucks, especially ex-British Army models, were much favoured by British-based trans-Africa overland tour companies such as Exodus and Encounter Overland. Bedfords are seriously old and outdated these days. It's not the most suitable vehicle to invest in, unless there are quite a few of you. You would need to carry most parts, spares and tools with you, preferably taking a Bedford expert along too. Very old J6 Bedfords are still used along the desert tracks of the Sudan as transport for the locals (and hardy travellers) who have to sit on top of the loads. In much of the rest of Africa they have now all but disappeared.

Although only suitable in general for larger parties, some Europeans have converted small trucks into quite spacious mobile homes. Both **Mercedes** and **MAN** have 4x4 versions, but preparation costs are high. MAN has the smaller models.

### Jeeps

The Jeep Wrangler is probably a bit small for all the equipment you'll be taking, and the Cherokee range tend to be gas-guzzlers. We met one Dutch couple with a Jeep and, although new, it suffered from suspension problems. Again it is virtually impossible to find even basic spares and is not recommended.

www.jeep.com

### Top of the range

These models are best avoided. That said, for a go-anywhere vehicle there is the Austrian Pinzgauer, which is available in either 4x4 or 6WD – this is a phenomenal vehicle at a phenomenal price. Others include the Land Cruiser Prado models, Isuzu Trooper and Mitsubishi Pajero. You are more likely to find these in supermarket car parks or outside schools in the smart suburbs of London or Sydney than you are crossing Africa. That may be more to do with their price than their off-road ability. More seriously, you will struggle to find a mechanic who can fix them, or any spares outside Europe or South Africa.

### Isuzu Trooper

This is another of the top-of-the-range, undoubtedly comfortable, vehicles. It is reported to suffer from a very sensitive accelerator that may cause difficulty when delicate accelerator work is required. It may also cause excessive wheelspin in sandy and muddy conditions. Some are seen in East and South Africa, but further north it is probably an unwise choice.

www.isuzu.com

### Mitsubishi Pajero

The Pajero is reportedly one of the better top-spec vehicles when it comes to off-road ability, but its front suspension is said to let it down.

www.mitsubishi.com

Some of the above vehicles could be used as your overland vehicle, but you must be able to fix it yourself and carry all the spares you may need. Others may only be suitable if sticking to southern Africa.

### Other vehicles

The following other 4x4 examples are not recommended for remote areas at all and are of limited appeal outside southern Africa. Again do remember that finding spares and mechanics may be a big problem.

## Ford Courier

Ford Courier is a similar type of vehicle to the Toyota Hilux and is similarly available as a single or double cab. It is a part-time 4x4 vehicle with high- and low-range transfer gearbox.

www.ford.com

## Mitsubishi Colt

The Colt is another vehicle in the same vein as the Hilux. It has part-time 4x4 with automatic free-wheel hubs.

www.mitsubishi.com

# Two-wheel drives

Although not really suitable for more adventurous, full-blooded trans-African trips, 2WD vehicles can be used quite happily if you plan your route with care or will be travelling in areas with better roads. Some actually have definite advantages, because of either their comfort or their light weight – the lighter the vehicle, the less power you need to get it through difficult conditions.

It is possible to drive across the Sahara, and even right across Africa, in a vehicle like a VW Combi. Twenty years ago quite a lot of overlanders used these air-cooled models. They provide far more comfort than most 4x4 vehicles. But you have to time the seasons precisely and definitely be prepared to get stuck more often than with a 4x4. Combis are not so good in seriously thick mud, but in harder-packed sand they can be surprisingly effective. However, travelling with another vehicle is highly desirable.

Some smaller 2WD cars can be surprisingly good in all but the muddier sections of central Africa. Citroen 2CVs and Renault 4s are economical on fuel and capable of desert crossings on main tracks with some pushing and cursing. Their lack of ground clearance is a limitation and is a particular problem where rocks poke out of sand – south of Tamanrasset in places, for example, but not so bad south of Reggane on the Tanezrouft route. If you don't mind the lack of space, they could prove a low-cost option for much of the continent where roads are reasonable. Charlie and Illya met someone who had converted his 2CV to adapt to the harsh African conditions and had travelled not only most of the Sahara, but also Zaïre (as it was then known). It is advisable to go with a convoy if you are travelling in a 2WD and wanting to cross the Sahara or any other difficult sections.

## Car hire

There is no need to drive all the way if you are short of time or do not fancy a complete trans-African trip. Much of southern Africa and parts of the east and west are perfectly accessible by 2WD vehicles that can be hired locally. If you want to get off the beaten track once you arrive, you should be able to find more substantial vehicles for hire in some of the major tourist centres. In cities like Windhoek and to some degree Nairobi, for example, it is possible to hire 4x4 vehicles such as Suzuki, Isuzu Troopers and Land Rovers, already kitted out with camping gear, cooking equipment, water containers etc. Hire can be arranged in advance through the Africa Travel Centre.

**The Africa Travel Centre**
*London:* 21 Leigh St, London WC1H 9EW; tel: 0845 450 1520 and 020 7387 1211; fax: 020 7383 7512; email: info@africatravel.co.uk; www.africatravel.co.uk
*South Africa:* PO Box 772, Hurlingham View, 2070 Johannesburg; tel: +27 (0) 11 880 5108; fax: 011 880 5655; email: webmaster@backpackafrica.com; www.backpack.co.za.

# VEHICLE PREPARATION

The range of possibilities for vehicle preparation is obviously enormous – from paying someone else to do the job for you, to having the fun of tackling most of it yourself.

Varying degrees of help are available. A company like UK-based Gumtree Enterprises (tel: 01273 890259; email: gumtree@ukonline.co.uk) can provide a vehicle completely customised to your own requirements. Others will give advice and help so you can prepare your own vehicle. Keeping the vehicle close to the standard is best, and try not to overload it.

Whatever model you have, it is crucial that you should know your vehicle well. This is extremely important if you have not had a hand in getting it ready to leave. Take time to become totally familiar with it before setting off. What follows is a guide to some of the more important issues to bear in mind. Each person will have their own ideas about what is essential and what optional extras are chosen.

The first and most important part of vehicle preparation is to ensure that the basic vehicle is in sound mechanical order. That is before you add on any extras. If you are not a mechanic, you will soon become one! In the meantime, it would be advisable to take it to a garage for a major check/overhaul. This should include the engine, cooling system, fuel system, suspension, gearbox, transfer box, clutch, differentials, brakes, electrics and chassis condition.

Initially take the vehicle on some test drives, then some longer day trips. It is really preferable to take it on a more extended drive, a trip around your own country or further afield, before going to Africa. This applies whether you have some mechanical knowledge or not. If you are already in southern Africa you will be well ahead of the game. Teething troubles are most likely to occur earlier on and many can be ironed out over these initial forays. Try to identify any problems and get them fixed while you still have access to good mechanics. With thorough and conscientious preparation beforehand, the number of problems, and hence headaches, will be limited later most probably to the effects of African conditions.

Make sure as many nuts and threads as possible have been greased before you go; there is nothing worse than rusty nuts on the side of the road.

Despite years of experience, we had a serious problem with our gearbox. This we had sent to a supposedly reputable specialist to be reconditioned beforehand in the UK. But no-one is perfect, and we suffered the consequences. Fortunately we broke down in a more favourable place than we might have done.

Once you have the basic vehicle in good working order, you can start to fit it out for overland travel. From a security angle it is desirable to limit the amount of equipment placed on or around the vehicle. With gear all over, it can look a bit pretentious; it certainly shows a level of wealth undreamed of by most Africans. This in turn might attract petty thieves. The more you keep hidden, the more you blend into the local ambience. Or maybe that is wishful thinking!

However, most of the local people will be curious, welcoming and friendly.

## Factors to consider

The following section details some of the main factors to consider. Again some personal preferences will come into play.

### Sleeping options

You have the following choices: a rooftop tent, sleeping space inside the vehicle, a tent or hotel accommodation. The ultimate choice is obviously dependent on where and for how long you intend to travel.

The option of hotels every night is only a consideration if you are travelling in places like Morocco, Tunisia, Egypt and southern Africa, where towns are frequent and roads good. Although you will find hotels in some places in all countries, you should always be prepared to camp out, as you never know where you might end up.

### Tents

Pitching a tent with a sewn-in mosquito net and groundsheet is the cheapest option, but invariably not convenient. When sleeping on the ground in Africa you will not be alone, as all manner of bugs will find your presence attractive; a camp bed helps, but takes time to set up. Getting tent pegs in can be a bind; sand is too soft, mud too sticky and the Sahel too hard. Isn't life a hassle! Seriously though, when driving for long stretches for a number of days, pitching a tent daily can be a nuisance. Finding suitable rough camps is not so easy in a continent with a rapidly increasing population. Dome tents are better in any event except in tropical downpours. Things do dry fast though.

### Rooftop tents

Most overland vehicles that you see throughout Africa have rooftop tents of various designs. They are the most convenient option. They do not require much space, are quick and easy to put up, and keep you away from people as well as from large and small wildlife. Being well above ground, they afford good ventilation. There is the standard air camper, the folding roof rack tent or the pop-up variety. Any one of these can usually take a double mattress, which stays in the tent as it is folded up and can be fitted to most vehicles. With a little ingenuity, it is possible to pitch any normal robust tent on the roof rack, assuming your rack has a plywood base. This is a cheaper option if you already have a good tent stored away.

### Sleeping inside the vehicle

Even if you have a roof tent, it is a good idea to plan some way of sleeping inside. This can be handy in certain situations, foul wet weather, sandstorms, borders and some rather public places. If you intend to sleep inside the vehicle a lot, try to devise a system that minimises the number of things you need to move when you go to bed. Sleeping inside can sometimes be too hot and ventilation needs to be considered. It is useful to have a multi-purpose platform that can slide in and out, and which lies above the equipment. Part of the platform can double up as a table by attaching legs to it. Sleeping in the vehicle is clearly the most secure option for both you and your belongings. See the diagrams on pages 48–9 for options.

rooftop tent fitted on to roof rack of vehicle

entrance

ladder extended to bull bar or ground

## Roof rack

Roof racks are available in all shapes and sizes and can be used as a low-cost alternative to a rooftop tent by simply adding a sheet of plywood so you can sleep under the stars. If you are adding a plywood sheet, you might consider ways of extending it over the windscreen. The shade offered by this idea will be seriously appreciated under a burning hot sun. This will be perfectly adequate in many situations, but is far from offering a comprehensive solution. Do not overload a roof rack. Most 4x4 vehicles are not built for heavy loads on the roof. Structural parts, like windscreens, also have a habit of cracking under the strain if overloaded. Roof racks should only be used to store light equipment like sand ladders and empty jerrycans. Try to devise a system in the rear of your vehicle that can take as much equipment as possible inside and out of sight. Overloading the roof increases the risk of tipping over on uneven or sandy roads.

## Security

It is surprisingly hard to find good places to camp wild, as much of Africa is populated. That idyllic spot you found may prove to be a much-used track between the local village and its distant well. One hundred percent security is impossible to achieve, but every effort you make is worthwhile. The most important security system will ultimately be your own vigilance. It is worth mentioning here that security concerns and how you plan to camp are linked.

More about this later, under *Accommodation* on page 118.

### Padlocks and hasps

Padlocks should be put on any items mounted outside the vehicle, and may be put on some doors. Avoid any delicate mechanisms such as combination locks, which will very quickly become clogged by the thick dust that will cover your vehicle once it hits the African roads. Also try to buy a set of padlocks with a common key, or it will take forever to find the right one. If you can't do this, paint them different colours. Hasps can be forced, so you should consider some form of internal mechanism to back them up, such as additional locks or bolts.

### Windows

Windows are another problem area. Rubber surrounds in particular are a security hazard, as they can easily be cut away. Metal grilles on windows will help, but they also have the adverse effect of making you look as if you have something worth stealing. A vehicle with fewer windows is more secure. If you intend to sleep in the vehicle, metal grilles covering the windows mean you can sleep with the windows open. Sand ladders can also be mounted and locked over windows.

### Curtains

It is worth putting up curtains, whether or not you intend to sleep inside all the time. They provide instant shade in strong sun and dissuade prying eyes. Simple strips of fabric on curtain stretchers can fit inside the inner roof gulley of most vehicles, or you can fit curtain rails with proper hooks. Bungee cords are useful for many things; curtains, drying washing and holding equipment in place for starters.

### Valuables – safety box

This is tricky. You don't want to be with your vehicle all the time, and carrying vital documents, passport, carnet and cash on your person all the time is not ideal. But leaving them in the vehicle is not ideal either. Bolting in a safe box is one possibility, but don't keep everything in it, just in case the worst happens. It is best to have a few hiding places around the vehicle for spare emergency cash; carry the rest with you in a moneybelt along with your passport. Travellers' cheques are less of a risk, but be extra careful about the carnet. Carrying this around is not great; they are bulky. We tried to find a hiding place behind the spares, but anywhere secure is fine as long as you remember where it is!

It is also advisable to hide copies of documents, as well as travellers' cheque numbers and purchase receipts, in some other area of the vehicle. If staying overnight in a hotel, whether cheap or expensive, take the carnet and main valuables with you before retiring.

## Alarm systems

Some form of alarm system will undoubtedly help, as it should deter a thief from continuing with a break-in. But do not depend on it to safeguard your gear. There is a wide selection of alarm systems available from all accessory shops.

## Bull bars

These are designed to protect the lights and radiator from anything you may hit. Bull bars are optional. However, bearing in mind the amount of general debris on the roads, it may be advisable to fit one. Cows, goats and other animals, including camels in particular, will often stroll out into the middle of the road just as you are passing. The bars can also be used to install mesh to prevent stones breaking your headlights. Additional lights are best placed higher.

## Baffle/bash plate

A baffle plate is a steel plate fitted beneath the vehicle, helping to protect its vulnerable underside from rocks. They can, however, make routine maintenance considerably more awkward. You should consider covering the tie rods on your vehicle, as these are vulnerable. An old tie rod can be bolted on in front of them with a little thought and can even be designed to act as a tow bar. Putting baffle plates under the sump and gearbox is only really worthwhile if you are heading off into the remoter pistes in the Sahara, where rocks are hidden in sand. It is better to drive with caution where potential obstacles exist; get out and check first if in doubt.

## Suspension

The biggest enemy for vehicles in Africa is the state of the roads. That means your suspension is more at risk than anything else. There is a great deal to be said for fitting new springs and shock absorbers all round before setting off. Some people even strengthen the chassis – only a good idea if you are likely to be carrying heavy loads.

Opinion is divided as to which springs are the best. Fitting heavy-duty springs for the additional strains of African roads might sound fine, but African mechanics will often tell you that lighter springs are more supple and less likely to break under the strain. The chassis will be under less vibration too.

If you can afford it, Old Man Emu shock absorbers and springs still have the best reputation throughout Africa. Take plenty of spare rubber bushes, as they will disintegrate with great rapidity on some road surfaces. Some people take poly bushes but, being less supple than rubber, they can induce more vibration. By driving carefully you can reduce the worst effects of rough roads.

## Spare battery and split-charge system

This one is a personal matter. Carrying two batteries is definitely a good idea, especially if you are intending to be out in the wild for long periods. Batteries can fail without warning. The cheapest option is to change the batteries over periodically to keep them charged. It is a bit of a bind, however, and, in storing the second battery, you must ensure it cannot tip over. If you are intending to run other electrical items, like a refrigerator, off your battery, we would suggest a dual battery and split-charge system. This enables the second battery to run other electrical items while the vehicle's main battery stays unaffected.

Fashions change over the best setup for batteries and charging them. Many campervans have a deep-cycle-type second battery like the Willard 722 Pleasure Master (available in South Africa). This is designed to cope with charge and recharge. These batteries are not ideal for starting, though. You might consider having a dry cell, sealed battery as the second battery. A split-charging system ensures both batteries remain charged. Since these need to be in good order, we strongly suggest you seek appropriate advice. As with all things, the more complicated the more risk of problems. Maybe it's easier to change the batteries over manually after all. Don't forget to take some good-quality jump leads anyway.

## Oil cooler

Recommended by many, ignored by many others. Probably a good idea if you are likely to take full advantage of fast roads in the hottest conditions. Less useful if you are in an older vehicle.

## Raised air intake

This is standard on many African 4x4 vehicles, reducing the intake of large quantities of dust and acting as a safeguard if you intend to drive through deep water. It will certainly do no harm to fit one and you could end up saving your engine from damage. The Australian Safari Snorkel is the most popular and available at most off-road outlets. You could also have loads of fun making up your own from old drainpipes! But get it right.

## Axle breathers

Another tip, if you think you are likely to do some deep wading, is to extend your gearbox and axle breathers. These are small air valves, mounted on the top of the axles and gearbox, which allow air to be drawn in or out as the parts heat up and cool down. The problem is that, when you go into deep water, the axles cool quickly and suck in water through the breathers. The easiest way to deal with this is to fix a length of plastic tube over the breather and thread it up into the vehicle. You could make up an extension for the exhaust pipe for dealing with deeper river crossings – a luxury item perhaps.

## Wheel rims

Riveted steel rims should be selected for tougher terrain, as they are more reliable. Magnesium alloy rims are not very convenient because the bead, the part of the rim most often damaged in tougher terrain, cannot be hammered back into place like a steel rim. If you have a puncture repaired by an African, he will usually use a very heavy hammer, often skilfully, to break the bead; that is, to separate the tyre from the rim. Sometimes it's best not to look!

Some older cars are fitted with split rims, which are very convenient when you are repairing your own tyre. Ensure that the tyre is properly deflated before splitting the rim, as air pressure remaining in the tyre could cause an explosion and serious injury. Some people fit a ring of shaped rubber around the inner wheel rim to stop the tube wearing and ripping.

## Tyres

Set off with a completely new set of tyres, including two spares, if you are planning a long trip. Aim to fit the best you can. It will be well worth the extra expense. You will be facing a wide variety of terrain – sand, mud, laterite, rocks and tarmac roads. Good-quality, all-terrain tyres are the best bet. The brand you use is often a very personal choice. Many people opt for the Michelin XZY or the Continental Super All Grips. BF Goodrich tyres are significantly cheaper than the Michelin. There is no way of saying which manufacturer is the better. Tyres need to be suitable for the mixed terrain on a general African trip. Seek advice from experienced enthusiasts if you can.

If you are going only to the Sahara, you may decide to take specialist sand tyres. But nowadays some of the newer tyres are multi-purpose anyway and will be good on sand as well as tarmac and mud. In any case, you can do a great deal to cope with sandy conditions by reducing tyre pressures until you get back on firmer roads.

Keep the least-worn tyre from the old set as an extra spare. The main spare wheel is usually fitted on the rear doors, where the hinges and clamps should be periodically checked and tightened. Sometimes it is fitted under the rear below the fuel tank, which reduces ground clearance, or on the bonnet. Those fitted to the bonnet can be a real nuisance, making the bonnet very heavy to lift and restricting the view. The second spare may well have to be fitted on the roof. In our case we fitted the two spares inside; much better if you have the space.

### Tubed or tubeless tyres?
This is a personal choice; the debate rolls on. Tubed tyres are generally easier to remove from the rim, as the bead does not need to be so tight, but it is possible to fix a puncture in a tubeless tyre without removing it from the rim. We have always used tubed tyres, but many people take tubeless and have no problems. Others do. Tubeless tyres can be repaired from the outside using the 'gluey plug', but, since this method is outlawed in Europe now, getting the kits could be a problem. Surprisingly perhaps, tubeless tyres can be run with low air pressures in sand without many snags. There are pros and cons to each type, but in the end it comes down to personal preference.

### Inner tubes
It is important to carry two or three spare inner tubes, particularly if you are visiting isolated areas where tubes can be found but not necessarily in the correct size or make. It is also preferable to inflate, deflate and re-inflate the tyre once the new tube has been fitted. This will remove twists in the tube, which can cause splits and major blow-outs while driving. This takes a lot of effort in some circumstances so try to be careful, inflating slowly if you do it once only.

### Valves
It is better to fit your tyre with a short-stemmed valve rather than the longer one often stocked by African parts shops and garages. Longer valve stems are more susceptible to breakage, particularly in tough terrain. Always carry some extra valve cores with you. Valves have a habit of flying off into the sunset when being removed to let air out, so beware!

### Extra fuel and water tanks
#### Fuel
In most parts of Africa fuel is actually more readily available than you might think. Unless you aim to go deep into the Sahara or get right away from the normal routes, you should not experience many problems. There are not many places where you will need to go more than 640km (400 miles) without supplies. But you can't always guarantee to get fuel when you expect to, and you may want to take full advantage of cheaper supplies when you have the chance. The final judgement on how much you should carry is always likely to be something of a balancing act. We would recommend a 1,000km (620 miles) capacity. Work out your fuel consumption to determine your desired capacity.

Keep things as simple as possible. The more complex the system, the more things can go wrong. African roads will constantly cause things to shake loose, leak and wear away. Fuel pipes are notorious for shaving and becoming holed, and it's very difficult to find such leaks. The cheapest and simplest option is to take metal jerrycans, available in many places. Unless you are going into remote desert, four will probably suffice, except if your vehicle has a high fuel consumption.

If you really want to avoid filling your vehicle with jerrycans, then you may consider fitting extra tanks, particularly for older models with higher fuel consumption. Land Rovers can be modified to add an extra tank. Be aware though, that you will need to have either an electric pump to transfer the fuel from the extra tank to the main one, or have a two-way fuel valve. Both options can add to the list of things that can go wrong.

You can supplement the standard long-wheelbase, 15-gallon, rear-mounted fuel tank with short-wheelbase 10-gallon tanks under a front seat. That's a total of 35 gallons. Customised tanks with even larger capacities for both fuel and water are also available and can be fitted to most vehicles. Plan to carry as much fuel as possible, but always bear in mind weight restrictions. Fuel and water are the two most important items you need – but they are also incredibly heavy. There is little point in being well prepared if you destroy your suspension or even break your chassis in the process.

## Water

Make sure you carry enough, but beware of overloading. The greater your carrying capacity, the more tempting it becomes to overload your vehicle. Again the cheapest option is to take good-quality plastic jerrycans. These containers also enable you to see quickly how much water is left. You should aim to carry at least 40 to 50 litres, preferably in two or three containers in case one of them leaks. Keep one untreated water can for boiling and cooking, one for treated cleaner water and keep some extra plastic bottled water for drinking as well. Make sure all jerrycans stored inside are held in place securely. These containers can be worked into your general interior plan. Of course there is always something in the way inside; that's life.

A built-in water tank can be more convenient than a vehicle full of jerrycans. However, filling the tank can sometimes be quite awkward. You will need a hose where taps are inconveniently located. And filling tanks from wells is not always plain sailing. Also, tanks need to be drained periodically, as sludge can build up and with it contamination. Keep it simple. All jerrycans can be stored between inside lockers below a sleeping platform, keeping them secured. See diagrams on pages 48 and 49.

If you do use jerrycans, don't put them on the roof when full (never overload your roofrack with heavy items). **Never** have petrol in jerrycans on the roof; it spells double trouble as the sun will soon make it hot and very dangerous.

## Jerrycans

You **must** use metal ones for fuel; **we repeat, storing petrol in plastic jerrycans is dangerous** as it could explode. Do not store water in jerrycans that were previously used for fuel, as the taste never disappears. The number you take will depend on fuel consumption, tank capacity, route, load and how much you plan to take advantage of cheaper fuel supplies when you find them. For water, your route is the most important factor. Long stretches in the open desert will mean you need to carry substantially more.

## Oils

You are likely to get through more oil than in normal conditions – so be prepared. Engine oil is generally available, but some specialised gear oil, and brake and clutch fluid are more difficult to locate. You will find everything you need in the bigger cities like Abidjan or Nairobi, but don't count on it elsewhere. We carried 25 litres of engine oil, in different containers, which gave us two oil changes, ie: one emergency change (broken sump) and one regular change. Try to buy internationally recognised brands of oil, as some local supplies may be substandard.

## Storage

Careful planning of your storage facilities can make all the difference between comfort and a nightmare. Try to achieve a closely packed but accessible arrangement. At all costs avoid having anything loose that can be thrown about in the back. Fitted cupboards and storage space can be built by customising companies, or, if you feel confident, you can do the job yourself. Remember the whole thing can easily get shaken to bits unless it has been well made.

Some kind of modular system is probably the best approach to storage. You need to be able to pull things out quickly, find what you are looking for and repack into the same space you started with. This process is generally a lot harder than it sounds. It can be very useful to split your storage space into compartments and within this into a series of rigid sections or boxes.

Over the years we have found that a locker system works quite well. You can build in sections for spare parts, food supplies, oils, grease etc, spare battery, even valuables. The ways are infinite. Try to keep your toolbox safe but accessible – you'll need it daily for maintenance checks. To make simple lockers you need only a drill, saw and energy, or get the plywood cut by your friendly wood merchant. Before you start, though, consider the width and size of any jerrycans. You will need to work out a basic design first and calculate the sizes – not so easy. It should be possible to keep the jerrycans in place

**SUGGESTIONS FOR VEHICLE LAYOUT**

Roof rack

Storage

Mattress

Table/bed board

Gas cooker

Jerrycans for fuel and water

Storage lockers

Storage lockers

## SOME SUGGESTED VEHICLE DESIGNS

Roof rack and tent

Sand mat

Spare tyre

High-lift jack

Internal storage

One/two spare tyres

Table/bed board

Cooker/gas

Cool box

Storage

Storage

Separators

Jerrycans for fuel and water

Spare parts

Storage

Food locker

Mattress

Raised roof level

Platform for tent

inside sleeping above storage lockers

**LWB Vehicle Pick-up model with home-built rear 'camper'**

between the lockers. Further wooden sheets can be cut to fit between the two lockers to separate fuel and water cans if necessary. It can be fun devising such units.

Using 11mm plywood cut and bolted together with metal angle pieces from a hardware store, one can make a series of compartmentalised lockers. These can have hinged lids attached. Use spring washers on all bolts or they will shake loose quickly. Make two long lockers and fit them in each side of the rear part of the vehicle. The jerrycans need to have good seals as they may need to be lying down. Two or three central plywood sheets can then be put between the two lockers and above the cans. One might be a table and all together can provide a platform on which to sleep. See the diagrams included under vehicle preparation and design suggestions on pages 42 and 48–9.

If you don't have the time or inclination to do the above, then use rigid plastic storage boxes, or even metal flight cases if you can afford them. Elastic bungee cords and canvas or webbing belts are useful for lashing things down. Anything removable on your roof rack should be secured with padlocks. Whatever system you adopt, something that you need will always be at the bottom or in 'the bl..dy locker'!

## Comfort
### Seat covers
The choice of seat covers depends on the seats in the vehicle. If they are plastic, they will be very uncomfortable in the hot sun if they are not covered. Towelling is ideal. With removable covers you have the added advantage of being able to wash out the grime that will inevitably build up. Even if you have fabric-covered seats already, you will appreciate washable covers – you will pick up more dust and grime than you could believe possible!

A set of beaded seat covers is a good option; they help in extreme heat when long hours behind the wheel cause sweat and sores. They also ease your back over long distances.

### Steering-wheel cover
Standard black plastic steering wheels can become extremely hot in direct sunlight and your hands can easily slip. It is advisable to fit some type of non-slip cover before you leave.

### Music
Install a standard tape deck and radio, mounted securely, and bring a selection of tapes/CDs. When driving long distances in a country where you may not understand the local language, a variety of music is irreplaceable. It's a good idea to mount the stereo in the glove compartment and keep tapes in a dustproof box. You may not be able to hear anything over the engine and road noise, but at least when you stop you can relax to your favourite tunes!

We also recommend a shortwave radio, to tune in to the BBC or similar and keep up to date with what is going on around you or further down the line.

### Canopy
Just an optional extra. A canopy will keep you dry during the wet season, and it will also offer shade and a certain amount of privacy. You can either make up your own canopy with strong canvas or vinyl-based material, or have one fitted to your vehicle.

## VEHICLE EQUIPMENT
We all have our own priorities. Deciding what to take and what to leave behind is difficult. You must ask yourself very carefully if you really need it; overloading is your vehicle's worst enemy. With four wheels you will be nothing like as restricted as with a motorbike or bicycle in terms of what you can carry; but still, when your springs start to sag, or worse, to break, you'll regret every extra kilo of unnecessary weight.

Make sure that all equipment is correctly stored and strapped down. If you are carrying a cooker with a gas cylinder, always ensure that it is tightly secured, that both are locked into a base, and that both have been turned off when leaving the vehicle for long periods of time or while driving. Refrigerators should also be secured tightly with straps, but can be kept switched on while driving.

You should have a **fire extinguisher** with you. It is not only compulsory in many countries, but might very well be needed at some point. If your vehicle already has one, make sure that it works properly.

Here are a few of the most important items of equipment you will need to consider.

## Recovery gear

Recovery gear is defined as anything you might need when trying to get yourself out of a difficult situation or rescuing another vehicle.

### Electronic or manual winches

Winches are of limited use and possibly not worth the expense or extra weight. In practically every situation it is easier to be towed out of trouble.

The main advantage of a winch is that it can give you the confidence to explore further off the beaten track, away from roads and tracks used by other vehicles. If you plan to be that adventurous, it would be wiser to team up with at least one other vehicle anyway.

A sensible compromise could be a good hand winch – the best is probably made by Tirfor. Another simple winching technique is to make use of a high-lift jack. If this is chained to the vehicle at one end and to a winching point, such as a tree trunk, at the other, you can slowly pull the vehicle out of trouble. The only drawback with this technique is that you can only winch the length of the jack (1 metre/3 feet) at a time. If you are using a tree as an anchor, use canvas, or the purpose-made anchor straps available at most major equipment outlets, to protect the tree. In general a winch is not your highest priority.

### High-lift jack

The high-lift jack could be one of the most useful tools that you will carry with you. It is indispensable and highly versatile. The classic high-lift jack is the red American-made one, which is simple and reliable. However, there are now numerous other makes on the market that are modelled on the original version and are just as good. Remember to use wooden blocks or some sort of base when jacking the vehicle up. Also ensure that your vehicle is in gear and that the handbrake is on. Older vehicles with heavy-duty bumpers make good jacking points, but you will find that a jacking point may need to be fitted to your vehicle if you have a newer model. If you have to store the jack outside, ensure regular cleaning, as dust can get trapped in the oil. Cover the jack with canvas for further protection.

### Hydraulic jack

Whether or not you have a high-lift jack, you will need a hydraulic jack for smaller jobs; changing springs or lifting the engine to change engine mountings, for example. Make sure you have an assortment of flat and chunky wooden blocks for jacking. Old-style hydraulic jacks are hard to find now, because trolley jacks are the latest preference. These are too bulky and not very good on sand and mud. Hydraulic jacks, made in the Far East, can be bought in many places in Africa, but you might need one before you get there!

shaft

jacking arm

operating lever

lifting pins

foot

base

*High-lift jack*

perforated steel planks

flexible tank tracks

**Sand ladders**

## Sand ladders (Sand mats)

With luck and careful driving you may not need sand ladders at all, but it would be crazy to leave home without them. As well as getting you out of soft sand, they can have other uses, for example on broken bridges and, with extra support, for bridging some holes. Various types of ladders and planks are available, including some made from lightweight alloys. Aluminium alloy ladders are expensive but easier to use. Perforated steel sand ladders are just as good, although a little heavier.

Another type is the flexible variety that looks a little like the tracks from a tank. These do not have to be laid flat like sand mats, so you can save yourself some digging.

Do-it-yourself fans with welding equipment can make ladders from square or round metal tubing. These can be just as effective and are much cheaper.

## Towing points

Ensure you have adequate towing points on your vehicle, usually mounted below the vehicle at the back and front, making sure that they are easily accessible.

## Towing straps

There are two types available; static and kinetic. The kinetic type are basically slightly elastic, flat towing straps, otherwise known as snatch straps. A popular brand is Tuggum. These are specifically designed for pulling other vehicles out of a difficult situation. Snatch straps have a limited life of about 20 tugs and then the line becomes static. You should carry at least two towing straps of either type and sufficient shackles to connect them. Shorter, wider tree straps are also a good idea.

## Shovels

A small shovel may be useful as a companion to the sand ladders. Failing to scoop out sand or dig out mud from around your tyres will result in more strain. Sand can be cleared by hand, but mud is a different kettle of fish! Clearing mud by hand may be fun for five minutes but not for hours.

'D' shackles

bow shackles

**Shackles – the only types that should be used on a vehicle**

For sand, a shovel with a concave blade is better. In mud, a flatter angle is better. Compromise, but take only one. A shovel can be used for rubbish; always burn or bury anything you are planning to leave behind. Be careful not to bury jagged cans or broken glass in game parks where animals may dig up your rubbish and injure themselves. Also be aware that locals can use empty cans for water storage if they are cleanly cut with a tin-opener.

A garden trowel is useful for toilet trips.

## Sleeping gear

You will need a mattress, pillows, duvet or sleeping bag and sheets. A covered duvet or quilt is much more comfortable than a sleeping bag, which over long periods can feel restricted, and proper pillows will make you feel much more at home. If you have limited space, a roll-up mattress and fold-up pillow are useful, and a sleeping bag can be rolled into its cover and easily stored. A three-season bag should be adequate, but some parts of Africa can be very cold. The sleeping bag should be washable. For the cover of your mattress and pillows, use some thick cotton material. A darker colour helps to avoid having to see every speck of the grime you will accumulate! Also see *Hammock* on page 60.

## Mosquito nets

A mosquito net is not an optional item; it could be a lifesaver. Whatever type of sleeping arrangement you have, it is very important that you equip your tent, rooftop tent or sleeping space inside the vehicle with a net. Even if you opt to find local accommodation, it is advisable to carry your own mosquito net. Some places in Africa do provide them, but they are not always in the best condition. Nets can be bought in specialist shops. It is not always easy to find them abroad and/or the choice is limited.

# Lighting

Fluorescent strip lighting is bright, convenient and doesn't put too much strain on the battery. Festoon bulb lights also use little power, but are less bright. Bring some electrical wire in case you need to adapt things, or have a mobile lighting strip as well as normal internal lights. Camping Gaz lights, which run on small canisters, are not a good idea, as the canisters are almost impossible to find and are extremely expensive.

Whatever you do, remember to bring a torch with spare bulbs and batteries. There are some torches available with fluorescent strips.

## Map light

A standard map light which can be attached to the car lighter is very useful when trying to read maps at night. Maybe it's a luxury; a torch would do as well.

# Washing gear
## Portable shower

This isn't essential, but it can make you feel infinitely more human after a long day's drive. The following are available: a plastic bottle, pump-action shower which holds enough water for a seven-minute shower, heating water on the stove to take the chill off in cooler weather; a solar-heated shower which heats four litres in about an hour; or a simple plastic tub with holes and filled with hot water from the kettle!

Of course, unless you are showering fully clothed, you risk providing amusement for the locals or causing some offence; be discreet!

## Portable washing machine (ie: a bucket!)

This idea was suggested by Sue and Steve Marshall, who did a trans-Africa trip in 1996. Use a bucket with a lid as a portable washing machine. Before driving off, fill the bucket with washing detergent, water and dirty clothes and strap it firmly in the vehicle. Remember to put the lid on and make sure it fits securely! The motion of the vehicle will act as a washing machine, leaving you to rinse and hang up the clothes once you've reached your destination. Take a washing line and clothes pegs. A plastic bucket will also have many other uses (like draining the oil or radiator too, but don't tell your better half).

# Table and chairs

These might seem like a luxury, but, depending on how long you intend to travel for, folding chairs and a table are a very good idea. When choosing, remember that they need to last for as long as you need them and will be used on a daily basis. Canvas-covered chairs (some are like director's chairs) have a much longer life and can also be washed regularly.

## Compass and/or Global Positioning System (GPS)

Many travellers today use GPS as a navigational aid. GPS is essential and fun if you are going into really isolated areas like the Sahara, and you can set your coordinates accordingly. Most guidebooks specifically relevant to the Sahara and southern Africa have recorded coordinates of an area.

It is best to hide your GPS when crossing borders. It could be misconstrued as a transmitter and get you into trouble with the security forces. In general you will be quite surprised by how little you actually use either the GPS or a compass.

Silva makes an excellent selection of dash-mounted compasses that are designed specifically for use in a motorised vehicle. Remember that the electrics will throw off a normal compass so if you have a hand-held type stop and walk off a few paces for an accurate reading. Also remember that, without a good map, a GPS or compass is often useless.

## Mobile phone

With ever more sophisticated mobile phone systems, you may well consider taking a satellite phone or normal mobile phone for peace of mind.

Check out www.thuraya.com. It is probably the most common setup.

## Other essential equipment
### Axe or machete
Very useful for chopping wood and hacking through vegetation.

### Warning triangles
In many countries it is compulsory to carry **two**.

### Foot or electric tyre pump
This is an essential item when repairing tyres on the side of the road, or pumping up an airbed. Try using a foot pump in the heat of the African day and you will wish you had purchased a cheap electric pump. They have crocodile clips to attach to your battery. Extra wire may be required with some models.

### Tyre repair kit
Speaks for itself really! But it can be hard to find these days in Europe. Chris Scott suggests in his excellent *Sahara Handbook* (see *Appendix 5*, page 302) taking a bicycle tube to assist when pumping up tubeless tyres in the desert after a puncture. It is used to fill the gap between the tyre and rim before a seal is made under pressure. It should be the same size as the tyre rim.

### Pressure gauge
A good pressure gauge is particularly useful in the desert, where you will be deflating and re-inflating tyres continually.

### Assorted wooden blocks
As mentioned above, these are essential to place under a jack in soft sand or mud.

## Food and cooking
### Water and water purification methods
As discussed under *Storage* in this section, your best bet for carrying water is in 20-litre jerrycans. One of these should be accessible at all times to be easily filled with water. Some plastic containers have a tap, but be aware that it may leak. Any major outdoor equipment retailer can supply them. Traditional nomads carry water in goatskin sacks called *guerbas*. These keep the water remarkably cool, as the skin allows for slow evaporation.

In many parts of the Sahara and wilder regions, you may have to obtain water from local wells. You should be careful not to contaminate them. Wells in places like Niger are often the only source of water and it can be very pure. Getting such water up is an art form in itself. It may sound easy, but have you ever tried throwing an empty bucket 50 feet down a well so that it lands upside down? You will certainly create some amusement for the nomads at these wells. Very likely they will give you a lesson in the art of extracting well water. Wells in the Sahel are a pivotal point for the community and are places of social interaction for all: local villagers, nomads, long-horned cows, goats and occasional tourists. Some wells are astonishingly deep. Often the water is raised in containers attached to exceedingly long ropes and hauled by recalcitrant camels.

Unless you are certain the water is safe, you will need to purify it. The simplest, cheapest and safest option is to boil it. Another popular option is Chloromyn-T. You need only an amount equal to the tip of a matchstick to purify 25 litres. Allow it to work for one or two hours, until the Chloromyn-T has settled. Micropur, Puritabs and iodine are other purification methods. Iodine is an effective purifier but shouldn't be used on a long-term basis as your body absorbs it (see *Health* in *Chapter 4*). Some people use 'filter socks', but no method completely guarantees the killing of all evils that may lurk in the water.

Ideally, you should take a water filter with you, particularly if you are going to be travelling in more remote areas. Cyclists should definitely have one. There are many filters on the market ranging in price from US$50 to US$150. Top of the range are the Katadyne filters used by the Red Cross throughout Africa; though excellent, they are expensive. Mountain Safety Research (MSR) also make a range of filters and Charlie and Illya used the MSR MiniWorks, for which you can also purchase an additional virus filter, costing a total of US$50. See www.msrorg.com.

Suppliers in the UK, South Africa and Australia include:

**First Ascent** Units 4 & 5, Limetree Business Park, Matlock, Derbyshire DE4 3EJ; tel: 01629 580484; fax: 01629 580275; email: info@firstascent.co.uk; www.firstascent.co.uk
**Outward Ventures** 14 Second Av, Claremont, 7700 Cape Town; tel: +27 21 683 3638
**Grant Minervini Agencies** 1 Quinlan Av, St Mary's, South Australia 5042; tel: +61 8 275 1555; fax: +61 8 275 1556; email: info@gmagencies.com.au; www.gmagencies.com.au

## Refrigeration

Refrigerators for vehicles run on either 12V DC, 240V AC or gas; some refrigerators are built to run on all three. If you have the space and money, a fridge might be one of the first luxuries to take. Whether the added cost and space it takes are justified by the cool film and cold drinks it provides is a matter of debate. It is surprising how cold things can keep when buried in the depths of a good locker after a cool night.

Ordinary camping shops can be a good source. Three-way or paraffin types need careful balancing to work properly. The Engel fridge has been recommended as an efficient but expensive option.

The simpler and cheaper option is to have an insulation box. We have managed like this every time; cold drinks can be found in many places along the way. Keeping margarine and yoghurt is a little more difficult. The traditional bush method of wet towels draped over boxes and even bottles is very effective at keeping things cool.

## Cooking equipment

When it comes to cooking, your choice of fuel and equipment depends on how long you intend to be on the road. Bringing vegetables etc to the boil and then leaving them to cook in the hot water will save your valuable fuel, whichever you choose.

## Gas stoves

Gas stoves are the easiest, cleanest and most reliable option. We have always used Camping Gaz, but it is not a complete answer. The bottles are quite small, so we have had to carry at least four. A Camping Gaz (size 907) bottle can be made to last about three to four weeks with very careful usage and easy-to-cook food supplies. We mounted the cooker on a light frame with aluminium windbreaks riveted around three sides. Underneath, in the enclosed area below the cooking level, we kept the gas bottle, pots, pans etc. It is nice for cooking outside but a bit of a pain inside, and it needs securing properly.

The small Camping Gaz cartridges (*cartouches* in French) are almost impossible to find, but refillable gas bottles can be filled in some of the larger towns. Taking two Camping Gaz bottles and later buying a larger butane bottle in Africa might be better. Many local families cook with gas (particularly in the Sahara) and most gas stoves have a choice of regulators to cover a range of gas fuels. On a very long trip, using a purely gas system might have its limitations, but its simplicity is a prime factor. It invariably comes down to personal choice and the routes chosen in the end.

## Petrol stoves

The wide variety of camping stoves available means you can exercise a fair degree of choice, though bikers and cyclists tend to opt for small, lightweight petrol stoves or burners. These can be fussy to light but are fairly reliable, depending on how much you are prepared to spend, though even expensive models can let you down. Several people have recommended Coleman petrol stoves (one, two or three burners) as very reliable, though they are rather bulky and so not suitable for bikers or cyclists.

Disadvantages of petrol ovens are the blackening of pots (though the soot does rub off much more easily if you smear the outside of your pans liberally with soap or washing up liquid before you cook) and smoking when you first light it.

## Kerosene stoves

The Chinese-made kerosene wick stoves can be found almost everywhere in Africa. There is virtually nothing that can go wrong with them, and the small amount of fuel they burn means you can easily carry enough to last until the next source of kerosene. Again they can be a bit messy to operate.

## Open fires

Although open fires are harder to control for cooking, they are an instant focus when camping, particularly when it gets cold at night. Take a small fire grille, self-supporting

---

### COOKING WITH ONE BURNER?

Even if you only have one burner, you don't need to restrict yourself to one-pot meals. Bring your rice or pasta to the boil for a few minutes, then leave to continue cooking in its own heat. You can then make up a basic vegetable sauce, or heat a tin of chicken curry! If you are cooking with meat or beans, start off your rice or pasta about half an hour before you plan to eat and set it aside while you finish off your other dish. Always bring rice or pasta back to the boil and check it is thoroughly cooked before straining.

If you are cooking two dishes you can always prepare them separately and heat them up just before you eat. In time you will get more than skilled at juggling pots. If you find yourself travelling in convoy, meeting up with other travellers in campsites or free camping, you can pool resources and end up with some really adventurous meals. Four one-burner stoves means four hot dishes to share.

preferably. Otherwise you can use a few strategically placed rocks. Nomads use rocks to support pots and cook using very little wood by using the burnt ends of small branches or the charcoal remnants. It's a bit slow though. And remember that rocks aren't available everywhere!

Potatoes and other vegetables, wrapped in foil with a few herbs or spices for extra flavour, can be roasted in no time on an open fire. If you do build a fire, be sensible in dry areas where sparks may set grass or scrub alight. And never cut green wood for a fire, particularly in the desert and Sahel areas or game parks. Africa has enough deforestation problems of its own without your adding to them. If your transport allows you to carry firewood as you go, you can dry it out by lashing it to the roof rack of your vehicle.

Remember from a security point of view that an open fire may be visible for miles.

### Matches/lighter
Matches are available almost everywhere, but it is a good idea to carry a spare box. A couple of lighters are advisable too.

## Cooking utensils
Like everything else, it is best to keep these to a minimum. You will quickly learn to adapt what you have for a whole range of purposes, and cooking on the road is all about using your imagination. Obviously you have more choice with a bigger vehicle. We have used two small stainless-steel cooking pots, which fit inside each other and have flat lids, plus a small non-stick frying pan and kettle. Our food has tended to be simple, though. You might want to be more creative on a long trip. It's a matter of personal expectations, personal requirements and dietary variations. Charlie and Illya used a saucepan which also served as a two-tier steamer, a deep, straight-edged frying pan, and a kettle. Other favourites are pressure cookers, woks and, particularly if you are in a reasonably sized group, cast-iron pots for fires. Pots can be left sitting on an open fire to stew away for hours.

A small Thermos flask is a good idea for easy hot drinks on the way or at borders. Other items needed are a decent sharp knife, a wooden spoon, something to strain boiled pasta or vegetables (unless you have a saucepan and lid that are suitable), a tin-opener, a bottle-opener, Swiss Army knife or Leatherman's knife, vegetable peeler, bread knife and a small chopping board.

Go for enamel or plastic plates and bowls, but plastic or melamine mugs for tea and coffee, as enamel gets frustratingly hot. Plates are best with raised edges, bowls are easier to eat from without a table and safer for runny dishes. Take a plastic box for the cutlery – teaspoons love inaccessible corners in a vehicle. Don't lose the lighter!

## Food to take with you
It is surprising how your taste buds change in Africa. That bottle of salad cream or ketchup you never finish at home might suddenly seem the missing ingredient you are craving. Even if you are planning a short trip, you will not be able to take everything you are going to eat, but it is a good idea to assemble a store box of basics and emergency supplies before you go. It will not take long before you realise what you need to carry, and what can be picked up on the road. As a rough guide, the following food items are mostly available on the road: bottled water, bread, tomatoes, bananas, carrots, garlic, tinned fish, potatoes, eggs, rice, pasta, couscous, cooking oil, spices and dodgy un-fresh meat as well as good fresh meat. Items like margarine, yoghurt, other fruits and vegetables can be found, depending on location and climatic zone. Going south, Nairobi has large supermarkets and further south things are mostly as good in the capitals and larger cities. In West Africa you will find expensive French supermarkets in all the capitals; these have a good but expensive selection. What you don't find are tinned curries, assorted tinned meats, puddings and standby dehydrated meals.

Good basic supplies to take with you include: salt (extra fluid loss through perspiration means you will naturally salt your food more); sugar (even if you do not normally use it – it has a high barter value and sweet tea is great if you are ill and cannot face food); herbs and spices to liven up vegetables; tea and coffee. Take some cereals and muesli for an easy breakfast when bread is not available. Some boil-in-the-bag rice, instant mash and pasta are easy and quick to cook. Tomato puree in tubes, stock cubes, oil in plastic screw-top bottles, cornflour for thickening, dried milk. Small packets of parmesan cheese are a wonderful addition to basic pastas.

Make sure you always have a few days' supply of emergency rations. You never know if you are going to be unavoidably delayed along the way, and you may not find any food en route. We always had enough meals for a week, just in case. Good standby meals are instant potato, dried vegetables/fruit, tinned tuna, tins of meat, peas or beans, long-life cakes, peanut butter, Marmite, Vegemite, jam and/or marmalade, instant desserts etc. The list goes on: mustard, dried mushrooms or onions to liven up pasta or rice dishes, lemon juice in plastic bottles, custard, biscuits or crackers. Boiled sweets are good for when you need a burst of energy, and Kendal Mint Cake when you are flagging (it's a high-glucose bar that goes into the supplies for every major expedition). An indispensable item on all our expeditions has been a homemade Christmas cake; always delicious at any time of year!

Unless you are extremely lucky, there will be times when you will be unable to cook anything hot because the weather, circumstances or fate conspire against you. On these occasions you will feel a lot better for having some provisions that can be turned into a cold meal. For example, a refreshing salad can be made from a tin of tuna in oil, with beans in lemon juice and a freshly chopped onion or tomato.

It all depends on space and weight. With a vehicle you can afford to carry quite a number of tins, some as standby. Sadly, your chocolate won't go far. Take the odd luxurious items such as a bottle of wine, sweets, Christmas pudding and other goodies, specifically for those arduous days when you need to spoil yourself. You can always live on bread and generally bananas. And don't forget those plastic bottles of mayonnaise, ketchup and Branston!

Obviously food that requires longer cooking times will use more fuel, so use open fires if possible when you plan a hearty meal.

## Storing food

We kept our food reserves in a locker, but any vermin and bug-proof containers would do. Choose storage containers with care. Square ones pack better. Rough driving conditions will shake things around so much that jars will literally unscrew themselves, plastic lids will pop off, and tubes of tomato puree will puncture. You can minimise these nightmares by having the right containers in the first place. Pack loose spaces with towels and toilet rolls etc so things do not jump around so much.

Plastic jars and bottles with deep screw tops are best used for storing things like sugar, tea and coffee. Tupperware-style boxes should have very tight seals. Do not buy oil in a flip-top bottle; it can get flipped just when you don't want it to. If you can't get oil with a screw top, then transfer it to a safer container. You are only likely to forget this once! Food storage boxes need to be kept reasonably clean. You will know when it's time for a clean out. Fresh vegetables are best kept out of plastic bags, which make them sweat and start to rot. An open cardboard box is a good idea, or tie them up in a cloth local-style to keep them as dry as you can.

## Washing up

For washing up we used an oblong plastic bowl, which can double up as your personal washbasin. Washing-up liquid, a cloth and a scourer are the essentials. Some travellers wash their dishes in Milton (a gentle disinfectant). Giving all your dishes, cutlery and pots a good clean when hot water becomes available should be sufficient to keep the germs at bay. If you are struggling to clean that burned-on mess at the bottom of the pan, use sand or gritty mud: the best scourers you could ever find.

A drying-up cloth or tea towel is useful. We took one and used it regularly, but it does need frequent washing as it gets really filthy. Some travellers either leave their dishes to dry or flap them vigorously to dry them off. You will see a lot of organised tours doing this, usually to the amusement of onlookers.

## Personal equipment
We have listed a few personal items that we found useful. Remember that overloading a vehicle is easily done, so take care when making your choices.

### Clothes
Take as few as possible; you will not need much once you are on the road. You'll need warm clothing for nights in the desert and in the highlands, and something to keep the rain out is also useful. Otherwise, lightweight cotton is the general rule. Dark and patterned fabrics don't show stains and rips, but can be hotter to wear.

You should also be aware of local dress customs. In some Islamic countries women in particular should take care; even the tops of your arms can be regarded as provocative. Men also should wear long trousers and long-sleeved shirts. To make sure you are not offending anyone, look at what local people are wearing. Their reactions will soon let you know if you have crossed acceptable levels of modesty.

Taking one 'smart' item of clothing helps when having to deal with a very conservative embassy, as in Sudan, or even at a border crossing. With the number of people you meet along the way, you never know to where you might be invited.

### THE 'CLOTHES BOX' (FOR A COUPLE TRAVELLING TOGETHER)
- two pairs of jeans
- two pairs of light cotton trousers
- four T-shirts
- four long-sleeved shirts
- one long skirt
- one long tunic dress for Muslim countries
- one pair of 'smart' trousers
- two swimming costumes
- one wraparound skirt (double up as a towel/sarong)
- two 3–4m-long light cotton scarves (useful to wrap around your head like a Tuareg *cheche* or turban, protecting against sun and wind as well as insects and sunburn)
- two sweatshirts
- two thick sweaters
- two woolly hats
- two sun hats
- two pairs of hiking boots
- two pairs of sandals
- two raincoats or lightweight waterproof jackets
- socks and underwear

## Other items
### Shortwave radio
A shortwave radio with plenty of shortwave bands is great for picking up news from home and about conditions in the countries you may be visiting. We sat alone in the silent vastness of the northern Sudanese desert listening to news about the conflict in Darfur. It is a good idea to take something that is not fixed to the vehicle, for both security and portability.

### Camera
Photographic equipment and photography are discussed in detail elsewhere. See pages 120–1. In addition to your usual camera equipment you might take a Polaroid camera, which can be of real help when wanting to take photos of people. If you first take a photo with a Polaroid and give them that photograph, more often than not they will then be happy for you to take as many pictures as you wish with your usual camera. And the delight of adults and children alike as they watch the picture develop in front of their eyes is an added bonus.

### Fun and games
We found it useful to carry a pack of cards or backgammon, for those lonely nights in the middle of nowhere.

You might also find that it is fun to get into the local games that are played on street corners. The most popular game throughout Africa is a kind of backgammon, most commonly known as *woaley*. It changes its name from country to country, however; other names it goes by are *awalé* in the Ivory Coast, *ayo* in Nigeria, *aju* in Togo and Benin, *ouri* in Senegal, and *aware* in Ghana. Rules of play also change slightly from country to country, so always ask locals before delving into the game.

### Pocket calculator
Useful for working out fuel consumption and exchange rates.

### Hammock
This is a non-essential item, but one that people on long trips recommend. After a hard day's driving, if you are intending to stay a few days, there is nothing like stringing up the hammock and relaxing under the African sun.

### Gifts
It is quite amazing just how important a small supply of inexpensive gifts can be, particularly for children who are desperate to help you fill your jerrycans at wells, guard your vehicle, or give directions. On the other hand, you should never hand out gifts just for the sake of it. Constant handouts can mean that the local economy comes to depend on them, and later travellers will suffer because the same will be expected of them.

There will, however, be occasions when people have greatly helped you, either in deed or in material terms. This is particularly true for overlanders, who have far more than just a backpack to consider. Generosity can be thanked with a simple gift. Pens and postcards of your home country are always welcomed. Other items asked for were magazines or newspapers, cotton and needles (particularly in the Sahara for the local nomadic women), and recycled goods from your own supplies. Empty containers of any kind that can be used to carry water are highly sought after in many areas. You don't need to bring everything with you from home – you can top up your supplies at local markets, thereby helping the local economy too.

However, often your friendship and the chance to swap addresses can be the most appropriate response, but don't make promises you don't intend to keep.

Also see *Giving Something Back to Africa* in *Chapter 7* (page 177).

# SPARES AND TOOLS

Working on your vehicle before you leave will give you some idea of what you are likely to need. Check through your workshop manual or talk to a friendly mechanic or off-road enthusiast to find out if you are missing something essential regarding spares and tools.

In many cases you will be able to limp along to the next big town where spares are available at an inflated price. In general, labour is cheap but parts are expensive. It pays to be as well equipped as possible.

'Murphy's Law' comes into play when you're selecting spare parts; it's always the one bit you didn't include that fails. Too many heavy parts are likely to damage your suspension, but not taking sensible items isn't very wise either. Take more lightweight spares than you think you will need, like gaskets, oil seals or bearings. Some could then be sold or exchanged for heavier parts.

Some places in Africa are better than others for picking up spares. The high cost of imported parts means secondhand spares may be the only viable option. Even official dealers for your vehicle are not guaranteed to have what you need, although they will generally direct you to the best secondhand source. The hammering a vehicle takes on African roads means most sizeable towns have a secondhand yard that can come up either with what you need or with a good alternative.

Having worked for an overland company for many years, and being more mechanically minded than the other drivers, I invariably ended up with the 'knackered' trucks. This sometimes led to problems on the road so I became even more knowledgeable about what could go wrong. Perhaps our list of spare parts reflects this expectation and is more comprehensive than most. You take your choices.

## Spare parts

Deciding what spares to take with you is a bit of a guessing game. What you include is somewhat dependent on the make, model and age of your vehicle, as well as the amount of space available in it. The actual list will also depend on the amount of preparation you have undertaken on the basic vehicle. Did you have a reconditioned injector pump or a new starter? Try to assess beforehand what might go wrong and what spares may be available locally en route.

You should get advice from a good mechanic who may know of typical problems regarding the make and model of your vehicle. Always remember to take all your workshop manuals with you. We have assumed you have a diesel engine.

We've also assumed that you will have the engine, gearboxes and clutch all reconditioned; that is, unless you are on a very tight budget and not too concerned about what happens to your vehicle afterwards. The front and rear axle differential units should be in good order. It's best to have the following parts new or reconditioned: radiator, brake and clutch master cylinders, clutch slave cylinders, brake wheel cylinders, starter, alternator, water pump and brake hoses. Also suspension rubbers, engine mountings, brake pads and fuel lift pump. The injectors and injector pump must be reconditioned and the work done by recommended specialists. Injector pumps rarely go wrong if in good condition, but if they do it's a rather serious matter. Taking a spare would be a good idea if you can find an old version that works, but this is where the costs can rise quickly. In any case all used parts should be kept as spares.

After this you need to take items that you will have to replace as part of a service: oil filters, fuel filters and air filters, unless your vehicle has an oil bath air system. Oil baths are very good in dust and sand and there is no need to carry bulky filters, but most newer models now don't have these. Take as many of these filters as you can fit in: one for every 3,000–4,000 miles, as some local units may not be up to standard. You will have to change these more often than recommended by the makers. How often you change them partly depends on the terrain, dust, sand and temperature, and the quality of your oil. As a bare minimum, carry three of each type you require.

Don't forget all the little extras that save the day like radiator sealer, Araldite glue, bits of metal, string, duct tape, fuses and countless other items.

The following is a list of suggested spares, which should be tailored to your requirements. An asterisk denotes a part for a petrol engine.

## Consumable spares
- 3 oil filters
- 4 fuel filters
- 2 or 3 air filters
- oil (enough for two changes)
- 5 litres of gear box/differential oil (check whether the same oil is used in each)
- grease
- 1 or 2 litres of brake and clutch fluid oil
- 1 litre of radiator coolant (you can use water)

## General spares
- heater plugs/spark plugs★
- 1 spare diesel injector
- set of engine gaskets
- set of all oil seals (wheels, gearbox, engine, differential)
- set of wheel bearings
- set of engine mountings
- set of radiator hoses plus other hoses
- accelerator cable
- 2 fan belts
- set of brake pads
- brake master cylinder rubbers (if old units not serviceable)
- clutch master and slave cylinder rubbers (as above)
- wheel cylinder kit – rubbers (or kit for disc brakes)
- water pump
- lift pump
- suspension rubbers and bushes
- condenser★
- distributor cap★
- contact breaker points★
- spare fuel cap
- spare radiator cap
- U bolts/centre bolts for leaf springs
- main leaf springs (coil springs rarely break with careful driving)
- track rod ends
- clutch plate
- wheel nuts
- water temperature sensor unit
- sump/gearbox drain plugs (the silly things can fall into the sand – not guilty!)
- propshaft UJ
- flexible brake hose
- alternator (better a complete unit or at least the brushes)
- fuses
- light bulbs
- plastic fuel line and connectors

### TIMING CHAINS AND BELTS
Your vehicle timing chain or belt, where there is no reliable service record, should be replaced before departure. Even if it is not causing you any problems before you set off, you could get into big trouble if it were to break while you were on the road.

## Other optional parts
• starter (for remoter areas, Sahara and Congo)
• fan (for seriously remote areas or constantly fording rivers)
• injector pipes
• injector pump (remoter areas, Sahara and Congo)
• injector pump solenoid if applicable (remoter areas, Sahara and Congo)

## Useful bits and pieces
• funnel (make sure it fits the filler of your fuel tank and has a gauze filter)
• jubilee clips
• cable ties
• electrical tape
• electrical wires
• masking/duct tape
• assortment of wire
• assortment of nuts, bolts and washers
• contact adhesive
• 2 metres of fuel hoses (long enough to be used as a siphon)
• flexible 'bathroom' sealant
• instant gasket paste
• rapid Araldite/plastic metal glue
• plastic padding/instant fibreglass
• exhaust repair putty
• gasket paper
• WD40 or Q20
• radiator sealant
• towing eye/cable
• assorted small sheet metal, short drainpiping, square tubing etc
• assorted bits of rubber, inner tube, old stockings – not for evening attire!
• old rags – lots and lots

## Tools
Ensure you pack a good and comprehensive set of tools. Requirements vary from vehicle to vehicle and many jobs need 'special service tools'. However, there are general tools that will cover most jobs and, with a bit of lateral thinking, can be used in place of special service tools.

## Suggested list of tools
• a good set of spanners (imperial or metric as required by your vehicle)
• a good set of sockets with a power bar and ratchet
• extra large sockets (check sizes needed)
• assortment of screwdrivers
• adjustable spanner
• mole wrench (large and small)

- pipe wrench (steelson and adjustable size versions)
- grease gun
- metal and rubber hammers
- torque wrench (essential for all engines)
- pliers (various)
- circlip removers
- multi-size puller
- jump leads for battery
- set of feeler gauges
- hacksaw and spare blades
- multi-meter electrical tester
- flat metal file
- coarse flat file
- small round file
- hand drill and bits (9V cordless drills can be connected directly to your battery)
- tyre levers
- tyre valve tool/valve extractor
- set of Allen keys
- centre punch/assorted punches and metal drifts
- wet and dry sandpaper
- length of pipe (to extend your power bar for those stubborn nuts)
- arc welding rods – a few
- G clamp/small vice to attach to bumper
- magnetic retrieving tool – for when you drop a nut that gets trapped
- plus the hydraulic jack

The lists are not exhaustive; but again space, weight and money determine which extras to take.

## SUPPLIERS AND USEFUL ADDRESSES
### Vehicle manuals
A very good source of information specific to your chosen vehicle is the series of manuals/technical books produced by Haynes. They cover most vehicles. Check them out at www.haynes.co.uk

### Vehicle selection
*Autotrader* **magazine** can be found at major newsagents. It has information on used and new vehicles to sell or buy. Also look in local newspapers.
**Westfield 4x4** Lancaster LA2 OHF, UK; tel: 01524 791698; fax: 01524 792653; email: sales@west-4x4.demon.co.uk; www.west-4x4.demon.co.uk. Spare-part suppliers specific to Mercedes-Benz Type 411 and all makes of Unimogs worldwide.

### Vehicle preparation
#### UK
**Black Diamond Warrington Transmission Centre Ltd** One of the largest independent re-manufacturers of gearboxes, differentials and axles. Nationwide delivery and they speak English, French and German. Unit 2–7, Guardian St, Warrington, Cheshire WA5 1SJ; tel: 01925 416619; fax: 01925 230472; technical hotline: 08457 125914; email: sales@blackdiamond-ltd.co.uk; www.blackdiamond-ltd.co.uk
**Brownchurch Ltd** The largest suppliers of rooftop tents in the UK. Bickley House, 1A Bickley Rd, London E10 7AQ; tel: 020 8556 0011; fax: 020 8556 0033; email: sales@brownchurch.co.uk; www.brownchurch.co.uk

**Essential Overland Preparation** Email: info@allisport.com; www.allisport.com
**Gumtree Enterprises** (specialists in Land Rovers) Fallbrook Workshop, Plumpton, Lewes, East Sussex BN7 3AH; tel: 01273 890259; email: gumtree@ukonline.co.uk
**Footloose 4X4** Tel: 01780 784781; www.footloose4X4.com
**Formula 4X4 Ltd** Stafford Rd, Stone, Staffs; tel: 01785 811211; fax: 01785 817788; email: info@formula4x4.com; www.formula4x4.com
**Mantec Services** Unit 4, Haunchwood Park Drive, Nuneaton, Warks; tel: 0247 639 5368; fax: 0247 639 5369; email: sales@ mantec.co.uk
**Superwinch** (worldwide suppliers of winches and recovery gear) based in Devon; www.superwinch.com

## South Africa
**Avnic Trading** (suppliers of Garmin GPS 11 Plus); PO Box 532, Lanseria 1748, Johannesburg; tel: 011 704 6147; fax: 011 704 6151; www.avnic.co.za
**Brakhah 4X4** (specialist vehicle equipment centre) Centurion, Pretoria; tel: (012) 661 0583; fax: (012) 661 1481; email: anton@brakhah.co.za or johan@brakhah.co.za; www.brakhah.co.za
**Outdoor Warehouse** (specialists in outdoor equipment) Randburg, Johannesburg; tel: 011 792 8331/6818. Also in: Pretoria; tel: (012) 661 0505; Durban; tel: 031 579 1950/70; Cape Town; tel: 021 948 6221.
**Safari Centre** (the best-known and longest-established 4x4 outfitter) Main Rd, Bryanston, Johannesburg; tel: 011 465 3817; fax: 011 465 2639; email: bryanston@safaricentre.co.za; www.safaricentre.co.za. Branches also at Menlyn (email: menlyn@safaricentre.co.za), Windhoek (email: windhoek@safaricentre.co.za) and Umhlanga (email: gateway@safaricentre.co.za).

## Off-road driving courses
### UK
**David Bowyer's Off-Road Centre** East Foldhay, Zeal Monachorum, Crediton, Devon EX17 6DH; tel: 01363 82666; fax: 01363 82782; email: sales@davidbowyer.com; www.davidbowyer.com
**The Ian Wright Off-Road Driving Centre** Ian Wright Organisation, Ashtree Farm, Teston Rd, West Malling, Kent ME19 5RL; tel: 01732 529511; fax: 01732 529513; www.ianwrightorg.com
**Lee James 4X4** (countrywide) The Garage Workshops, Nottingham Rd, Oxton, Notts NG25 0SE; tel: 08453 309830; www.leejames4x4.cwc.net

## South Africa
**Safari Centre** offers off-road driving training and guided trails (see above).

## Off-road websites
**www.4x4mag.co.uk** Internet magazine – particularly good classified section on used vehicles.
**www.4x4offroad.co.uk** Of general interest regarding off-road issues.
**www.4xforum.co.za** Offering information on all aspects of four-wheel driving in Africa.

## Other
**Expedition Advisory Centre** (Royal Geographical Society) Kensington Gore, London SW7 2AR; tel: 020 7581 2057
**Africa Travel Centre** 4 Medway Court, Leigh St, London WC1H 9QX; tel: 020 7387 1211
**Nomad** 3–4 Turnpike Lane, London N8 0PX; tel: 020 8889 7014; fax: 020 8889 9529

# MOTORBIKE SELECTION
*Alex Marr and David Lambeth*
For those prepared to sacrifice comfort and space, travelling by motorbike offers a very exciting alternative. Although frequently physically demanding, most bikes also give the traveller an unparalleled freedom to explore off-the-beaten-track Africa. A bike can cope

in a number of situations that a 4x4 vehicle cannot. Whether crossing rivers by canoe, negotiating narrow, rocky climbs or simply weaving a line along a badly pot-holed road, two wheels beats four nearly every time.

Another factor, often overlooked, is that bikes are not perceived by locals as great symbols of wealth (unlike cars) and they tend to be friendlier as a result. It helps at checkpoints and border crossings too – there is something about turning up at a remote road control tired and dirty that generates a sort of sympathetic admiration in all but the most heartless of officials. Someone getting out of a shiny new Land Cruiser is a lot more likely to be invited to participate in some underhand redistribution of wealth.

Of course, travelling by bike has its downside. It's hard to convince yourself it's a good way to travel if you get a puncture in a thunderstorm the day after you've had your tool kit stolen. Also note that bikes are not allowed into any national parks in Africa and must be left behind while you make alternative arrangements.

## Makes and models

In virtually all of Africa a bike with some degree of off-road capability is essential. Two-stroke bikes are not suitable for long trips, as they are generally small, impractical and unreliable. These days there is a myriad four-stroke bikes which are given an 'off-road' label by the manufacturers. The degree of 'off-roadability' varies enormously, ranging from superlight enduro bikes (designed for racing), which can tackle virtually any terrain, to large twin-cylinder bikes which are given trendy off-road styling but are really more designed for touring in comfort in easy conditions. The large middle ground is made up by versatile 'trailbikes' offering varying degrees of compromise between comfort, features, weight and off-roadability.

Just to confuse the issue, note that trailbikes are often called 'enduros' in Germany and are also sometimes referred to as 'dualsport bikes', particularly in America. What the British call enduro bikes – for competition use – tend to be called 'hard enduros' in Germany.

Listed below is a non-exhaustive selection of models which a fairly adventurous traveller who is not content with sticking to the main roads could consider. As with 4x4 vehicles, buying the latest models is not a good idea.

### Yamaha

The legendary reliability and unsophisticated engines of the XT500, and subsequently the XT600, meant Yamaha were the most popular overland bikes from the 1970s to the 1990s. The XT600 Ténéré models, with their 27-litre tank and bulletproof simplicity, were for a long time *the* bike to use in Africa. Discontinued in 1991, they are rarer, but there are still those who would never use anything else. Unfortunately, finding decent secondhand models can be a problem. One big advantage of their popularity is that a number of XTs are still found in Africa, having been sold by overlanders at the end of their trips, and scavenging spares is a reasonable possibility. If you do choose a 600 Ténéré, the best by far is the 1988–91 twin-headlamp electric-start-only 3AJ model. The earlier kick-only and kick-and-electric models suffer from some serious engine and gearbox problems.

The more recent electric-start XT600E is another good option, available new until early 2005 and can easily be 'Ténérised' with the addition of a large tank, a good screen and an 18in rear wheel. The best model is the 1996 onwards 4PT version with a rev counter and right-hand-side clutch actuator. The XTZ660 Ténéré, a water-cooled, 5-valve single, is a little over-complicated for overlanding, but worth a look if a good 600 can't be found. The XTZ750 Super Ténéré is Yamaha's twin-cylinder offering. It is a bit of a monster, but reliable and a good option for 2-up travel.

The TT600s are truer off-roaders than the XT, but are more limited in availability.

They are a good choice but good ones can be hard to find as they are not imported officially into some countries and have often been used hard off road. The best are the TT600E and RE models. Both use the electric-start XT motor in a high-spec chassis and have a proper high-output generator.

Yamaha's four-stroke WR range, which in 1998 revolutionised the four-stroke competition scene, is a superlight bike, but as a high-revving out-and-out racer it is hardly designed with luggage-carrying in mind. It is an unlikely choice and definitely not suitable for those doing long distances on tarmac, but it may suit someone travelling light and regularly in very tough conditions. If you do choose a WR, go for the electric-start 450.

More recently the XT660R has arrived on the scene, but with their more sophisticated electronics these models are probably best left to enthusiasts in Europe, where repairs and failures can easily be sorted.

## Honda

The Honda XR600, and since 1996 the XR400, are extremely robust off-roaders and utterly dependable. Offering the usual Honda high standard of quality, they are an excellent choice, with no frills – air-cooled and no electric start, not even an ignition key. Comfortable they may not be, but they are built to last. Partly as a result of their use in desert rallies, a good range of accessories, such as large tanks, are available (see below).

The XR650L is a more street-legal version of the XR600 with the Dominator electric-start motor and a high-output generator (but over 20kg/44lb heavier) with a high seat that suits tall riders. The NX650 Dominator is slightly more road-orientated, but also a good candidate if fitted with an 18in rear wheel. Many high-mileage or overheated examples suffer from exhaust valve seats falling out – be careful! A good XL/XR/Dominator engine should make no rattling noises at all, hot or cold.

The all-new Honda XR650R replaced the XR600 in 2000. With an aluminium frame and compact engine, this is an incredibly light bike for the power it produces, weighing in at under 130kg (285lb). It looks to have all the makings of a good overlander, but only time will tell if it is as reliable as its ancestor.

The Transalp and Africa Twin are comfortable, larger, twin-cylinder bikes, but because of their weight most people would consider them to be too cumbersome for a trans-Africa trip. Note that they also have expensive fairings, which would almost certainly not withstand the rigours of African travel.

## Suzuki

The long-established DR350 and DR650, simple air- and oil-cooled machines, have their fair share of fans, the smaller version having a reasonably low seat and being particularly popular with female riders. Unfortunately, the 650 has a 17-inch rear wheel. The new DR400 was introduced in 2000, with a water-cooled motor which comes in both kick- and electric-start versions. Just for the record, there was a 750/800 single version.

## Kawasaki

Not so frequently seen in Africa, the water-cooled KLX range (300 and 650cc) are very capable off-roaders, although, as with the DR, the larger model takes a 17-inch rear. The KLR650 is heavier and more road-orientated. These models are popular in the US, so check out the internet for more info. I consider the KLR/KLX range a little over complicated for overlanding, with its twin cams, water cooling and twin-balance shafts.

## KTM

The R640 'Adventure' is the closest you can get these days to a dedicated overlander's bike. With a 28-litre tank, twin tripmeters and options like side panniers, this bike is almost ready to go straight from the crate. However, they are expensive and there are question marks over engine vibrations and long-term reliability. One to consider for the more affluent 'must have' overlander could be a retired 660 Rallye. It's hugely expensive new (£15k), but built to endure the Dakar and more. It has 60-litre fuel capacity, and top-spec suspension, wheels and chassis, and comes with a full navigation equipment setup. The 660 LC4 motor also seems now to have become reliable, while remaining simple to maintain and repair. You have four separate fuel tanks, so you could use one for water storage. The later models made after 2001 have better fuel consumption and a generally smoother response.

## BMW
The F650GS/Dakar is BMW's single-cylinder trailbike, but at over 190kg (420lb) it is more at home on the road.

The GS series of large twin-cylinder bikes have been available throughout Africa for years. These creamy-smooth, shaft-driven machines are a pleasure to ride on the road, but for most people their sheer weight makes them a real handful in tough-going terrain. Even so, the latest R1200GS is certainly marketed as a real off-road machine and the GSs will probably never lose their faithful band of supporters, who will continue to manhandle them around the continent for years to come. Needless to say they are not cheap, and a massive range of equally expensive accessories is available from a number of German manufacturers.

### Which to choose?
Your choice of bike depends upon a number of factors: ·

- Your mechanical knowledge. Don't choose a bike you can't fix, because you WILL have to fix it at some point. You must at least be able to carry out basic servicing. Go and do a short mechanics' course and take your bike to work on while learning.
- Your intended route. Generally speaking, the harder the terrain the more suitable a lighter bike will be. For example someone crossing central Africa in the rainy season would have a gruelling, if not impossible, time on an Africa Twin. At the other extreme, if you are going to be cruising around southern Africa, most of the time on tarmac roads, you may find a Honda XR400 slow and uncomfortable.
- Your size. Those short on leg-length will not enjoy the comparatively high seat of an XR650L. Also very important for those travelling alone in remote areas, you need to be able to pick the bike up on your own – and you have to be pretty strong to right a fully loaded XTZ750 lying on its side in a pile of mud. Try it before you go – if you can't manage it, choose a smaller bike or get down to the gym!
- The availability of extra equipment, such as large tanks and luggage carriers. Yamaha XTs, Honda XRs and BMWs are the most popular overland bikes and so offer the best choice in this respect.
- How much the standard bike has to be modified – especially important for those people short on time or not mechanically inclined.
- Your budget.

## MOTORBIKE PREPARATION
*Alex Marr and David Lambeth*
Thorough pre-trip preparation is the key to a successful time in Africa. Cutting corners at this stage will result in problems en route and you can almost guarantee that they will occur in the most remote and inconvenient places. As well as having a mechanically sound engine and chassis, considerable thought should be given to any peripheral items, such as mounting racks for luggage, fuel, water, tools and spares. These are the things that are going to break or cause problems.

Whatever bike you use, it goes without saying that it should be given a thorough mechanical overhaul before you leave. At the very least, you should start with new oil, filters (air, oil and fuel), spark plugs, chain, sprockets, clutch, tyres, inner tubes, brake pads and cables. Items which you know are going to get considerable wear, such as the non-engine bearings (wheel, swingarm, steering), should be thoroughly checked. It would be prudent to fit new ones before you leave. Whether or not you go for a complete engine strip-down depends on the age of the bike, how long you have owned it yourself and its general condition.

## Tools

It is a good idea at this stage to think about what tools you intend to take with you. With a view to keeping things as light as possible, select the smallest number of the best-quality tools you think you will need on the trip and prepare the bike confining yourself to using only these tools. It will soon become obvious what you do and don't need. Try to keep your tools in a dedicated, solidly mounted, waterproof, lockable toolbox.

## Bike modifications/additions

How you go about modifying the bike really depends on the length and intended route of your trip. When planning a trans-continental trip, for example, the following essential points need to be addressed.

### Fuel and water tanks

Generally speaking the ideal size for a fuel tank is around 25–30 litres. This is a good compromise between not being overly heavy or bulky and giving a decent range, around 500–600km (300–380 miles) for most bikes. This will be sufficient in all but a few circumstances. Realistically you are more likely to be constrained by what large tanks are available for your particular bike. Companies like Acerbis, IMS and Aqualine make large plastic tanks for a wide range of off-road bikes, though most of them tend to be slightly small, in the 18–24-litre range. The extra capacity can be achieved using side- or rear-mounted small auxiliary fuel tanks or cheap 10-litre jerrycans. Always fit transparent fuel filters to all your fuel lines. You can then see when you have contamination early enough to do something about it.

It's worth pointing out that in areas where you actually need more fuel than this, such as certain parts of the Sahara, for safety reasons you are more than likely going to be travelling with at least one other vehicle (a 4x4 or truck) which will be able to carry extra fuel in jerrycans or plastic containers for you.

For a long trip in the desert you will also need a considerable amount of water, say 20 litres, which just adds to the difficulty of carrying fuel on your bike. If there is no extra vehicle and if you don't have jerrycans to carry extra fuel, you can usually find cheap plastic containers which can be disposed of after transferring the fuel into your main tank. Another way is to use water 'bags', such as those made by Ortlieb, or flat foldable emergency fuel bags. They are very resilient and are fine for carrying fuel for short periods – and of course they take up very little space when not in use.

### Hard luggage

There are essentially two ways of carrying your gear, and the debate among experienced overlanders will continue forever about which is the better system! Hard luggage usually involves mounting hard aluminium side-boxes at the rear of the bike on to some sort of steel rack attached to the mainframe and subframe. This method is very popular in Germany and a number of companies manufacture the equipment.

Aluminium boxes have two big advantages over soft luggage; they are waterproof and they offer a much greater degree of security from theft. However, they are also heavy and unwieldy and annoyingly hard to mend if they break in a crash. You can find steel welders everywhere in Africa, but specialist aluminium welders are rare. Over time, friction on the aluminium creates a dark-grey dust, which means clothes and other sensitive items have to be kept covered. Tough fabric inner bags will prevent this problem and ease removal of contents. Tools and spares can be kept low in the boxes under a false bottom for protection.

## Soft luggage

Soft material side-panniers (Cordura, leather or similar) are also fitted at the rear side. Unless the contents are very light, they cannot just be thrown over; some sort of frame is needed to support the weight and resist constant abrasive movement and fatigue.

Much cheaper and lighter, soft luggage is most people's choice on a short trip. Actually, good-quality panniers are surprisingly hard-wearing and, provided they are well supported, should easily last a long trip. If damaged, they can easily be repaired with stitching. The obvious disadvantages are that they get wet in the rain and it is easier for people to pinch things from them. It is also harder to access the contents easily through a single zip on the top.

Whatever method you choose, it is very important to keep the weight as low down and as between the axles as possible. If the bike's centre of gravity is too high or too far back, it makes riding in difficult conditions, such as soft sand, even harder.

For my long trip on an XR400, I settled on a compromise of soft panniers at the sides and a small, lockable, 100% waterproof, aluminium topbox for camera, films, important documents, etc. This was designed so a spare rear tyre could fit perfectly around it. I had a waterproof Sealine drybag for camping gear sitting across the rear seat and panniers. I found this system worked very well. The key was fabricating a very strong steel framework which provided support and transferred a lot of the weight on to the mainframe. It also meant I could strap a 10-litre jerrycan under either pannier. The non-waterproof factor was not such a problem; I generally tried to avoid rainy seasons, but when it was wet I kept my clothes in dustbin liners. Maybe I was just lucky, but I never found security a big issue; in 23 African countries I never had anything stolen.

Within the luggage, it is important to protect all your belongings from the constant vibrations they will receive. Most things can be neatly stored in small Tupperware boxes and clothes within plastic bags. Apart from the main luggage, lightweight items can also be secured in front of the headlight.

Most riders also carry either a tankbag or a small rucksack for essential items which need to be accessed quickly. Kriega, based in the UK, produce some exceptionally well-designed and unusually comfortable overland-specific backpacks.

## Tyres

One important point to realise is that trailbikes which take anything other than a 53cm (21in) front and a 45cm (18in) rear tyre will have a restricted choice.

On a long trip, tyre choice requires careful thought, mainly because sourcing decent tyres in Africa (apart from some places in southern Africa) is a perennial headache. Tyres are always available in big cities, but they tend to be rather narrow and of light construction for small-capacity bikes. With a bit of persistence you can usually find something, but in West and central Africa, generally speaking, it is very difficult.

Ultra-knobbly motocross tyres offer the best grip in rough terrain, but they are not really practical because of their very limited life, particularly when ridden on tarmac, which is more often than you think. A better choice in tough conditions are tyres like Michelin Desert, Pirelli MT21 or Metzeler Karoo. They have much harder-wearing knobbles, which are spaced closer together and consequently have a much longer life, although they still wear fast on the road.

More versatile 'trail tyres' – such as Metzeler Sahara, Avon Gripster and Dunlop Trailmax – with a broader, shallower tread pattern, are generally a good compromise, offering a longer life and an acceptable amount of grip in sandy or stony conditions; they are not so good in mud, however.

For those entering North Africa and crossing the Sahara, it is best to leave southern Europe with a pair of new Michelin Desert tyres and to carry a spare at the rear, space permitting.

For ultimate puncture and pinch resistance you can do no better than use Bridgestone's Ultra Heavy Duty inner tubes, lubricated with Michelin mousse gel and treated with a puncture-resisting 'slime' type product.

Good tyres are of little use if your rims and spokes are about to part company. Make sure your wheels are true and that your spokes are tight and the nipples are free to be adjusted.

A rim lock on each wheel is a good idea and will stop the tyre creeping round and ripping out the air valve when running at low pressures in difficult conditions.

## Miscellaneous

Other essential modifications are:

- A bash plate, to protect the crankcase from flying stones.
- An O-ring (or X-ring) chain. Stronger than normal chains, the inside of the links is constantly lubricated, increasing longevity. Try to stick with DID as you will find it easier to find spare links. Always use a rivet link rather than a clip as clips can come free with time. Use genuine steel, not alloy, sprockets. They last a lot longer and are stronger.
- Good-quality, alloy-reinforced handguards, which protect your levers in a fall.

Desirable modifications include:

- Fitting an oil-temperature gauge, and for those bikes with a small oil-cooler (or none at all) replacing it with a larger unit.
- For those who intend using a GPS (global positioning system), a power lead and some sort of mounting bracket on the handlebars is necessary.
- Bland looks. The less new and shiny a bike looks, the better. Removing stickers from new bikes helps.

# Spare parts

For those who have never travelled in Africa, one of the problems is not knowing in advance what spares you are likely to be able to pick up on the way. Generally speaking, very little is available for large bikes north of South Africa. In some large capitals you may find basic items, like oil filters for popular models, but not much more; there simply isn't the demand. In the more westernised capitals like Harare, Windhoek, Nairobi and most of South Africa, you will find more choice, especially non-model-specific items such as tyres and chains.

What spares you take with you is a compromise between trying to cover all eventualities (the wrong approach), and taking as little as you can get away with (the right one). Only take what there is a good chance you will probably need. This may sound naïvely optimistic, but it is really a case of logical risk evaluation. If you have a fundamentally good bike, well prepared and properly looked after, it is pretty unlikely that anything serious mechanically will go wrong – and if it does, how can you possibly know what it is going to be and plan for it? If the worst does happen in the middle of nowhere, you will be able to get your bike to the nearest town eventually – although you may have to hire help and it will take a while – where you can try to repair it. You may need the right spares to be couriered out from your home country and you should be able to convince customs that, as you'll be exporting the spares again as part of your bike, you should not have to pay any duty. It is a good idea to have some arrangement set up in advance with your local dealer back home in case this is required.

## TOOLS AND SPARES LIST

- spare rear tyre
- front and rear heavy-duty inner tubes
- good-quality puncture repair kit with lots of patches
- small mountain bike pump
- a few spare spokes
- connecting links for chain
- clutch lever
- brake lever
- clutch cable
- throttle cable(s)
- air filter
- three oil filters
- fuel filter
- two spark plugs
- fuel hose and jubilee clips
- bulbs and fuses
- electrical wire and connectors
- assorted nuts, bolts and washers
- main gaskets

- duct tape
- assorted cable ties (lots)
- spare bungee rope/straps
- instant gasket
- silicon sealant
- epoxy glue
- liquid steel
- Loctite (for nut threads)
- small tub of grease
- about one litre of engine oil (for top up and oiling air filter)
- standard small toolkit (combination spanners, 3/8 inch drive ratchet + relevant sockets, screwdrivers)
- Leatherman's or Swiss Army knife
- feeler gauges
- file
- spark plug spanner
- tyre levers
- repair manual

Much more likely problems concern luggage carriers etc, so lots of bodge-it items such as glue, duct tape and plenty of cable ties are invaluable for temporary repairs.

## Clothing

Choice of riding gear is yet another compromise; protection versus practicality. While some degree of protection against a crash is essential, don't underestimate the amount of time you'll be off the bike, walking around villages or cities. A strong Cordura enduro jacket with built-in shoulder and elbow pads is a good choice. A simple spine protector with a waistband provides back support and protection without being too restrictive or uncomfortable.

Most riders use full-length motocross-style boots – an excellent safety measure – although some people find them too cumbersome when not actually riding and prefer the flexibility of normal strong walking boots which cover the ankle. This is something of a risk, given how vulnerable feet and legs are in the event of a crash, but again it boils down to personal preference.

As with the bike, the blander you look the better. Unfortunately nearly all off-road gear these days is distinctly unbland.

## Helmet
Off-road-style helmets with a peak and requiring goggles (which are easily lost) are best in dusty conditions, but normal road helmets are usually more comfortable and offer better all-round vision, though the visor can become scratched after a while.

## Camping
### Tents
A lightweight tent, sleeping bag and mosquito net are essential. Some sort of mattress is highly desirable. Thermarest make one that can be packed to an incredibly small size.

### Stove
A high-quality petrol stove (such as MSR) is the most practical way to cook.

### Water
A camelback-style water system (a hose coming from a 'bladder' on your back) can be very useful when you need to drink often in hot and difficult conditions.

A filter bag (made of a material such as Millbank cloth) is the most space-economic method of filtering.

### Personal items
Clothes, hygiene, books, etc are of course subjective things, but it is really a question of common sense based on the available space. Most people take far too much at the start of a long trip. A good general rule is to sort out what you would like to take with you and then halve it.

## Further information
Contact David Lambeth, Rally and Overland on 01892 853913.

### Books
*Adventure Motorcycling Handbook* by Chris Scott
*Afrika-Motorrad-Reisen* by Bernd Tesch, a German biker who has ridden right across Africa on several occasions, and has his own website (see below).
*Desert Biking* by Chris Scott

### Magazines
*Trailbike and Enduro Magazine* (TBM). A UK-based monthly publication with up-to-date information on the latest trailbikes. For information and subscriptions, tel/fax: 080 8840 4760 or 5066.

### Websites
A mass of enlightening information is available from the following websites (and their links), dedicated to overland motorcycle travel:

www.adventure-motorcycling.com
www.berndtesch.de
www.horizonsunlimited.com

*For luggage and accessories*
www.acerbis.com
www.touratech.de
www.wunderlich.de
www.xr-only.com
www.kriega.com
www.metalmule.com
www.coreuk.co.uk

# BICYCLE SELECTION AND PREPARATION
*David Mozer of Bicycle Africa Tours*
## Types of bicycle

Most people cycling across Africa use mountain bikes, although some do still prefer touring, and hybrid (or cross-bikes) are also possibilities.

I have a preference for mountain bikes (MTBs) over touring bikes for most excursions in Africa. The MTB is versatile, durable, stable and the disadvantages are few. I have found that once the bike is loaded with gear, a couple of extra kilograms in the frame are immaterial. The tyres and wheels are probably more of a factor, because that is where you'll find a lot of the extra weight. But for most excursions in Africa you won't want to give up the fat tyres.

In my opinion the hybrids, or cross-bikes, are crossed the wrong way. Instead of narrow tyres and straight bars, I would select fat tyres and drop bars as a better cross. The fat tyres increase stability and the drop bars increase control and the number of hand positions, as well as reduce wind resistance. This is especially useful if you know you will be doing some big mileage on paved roads, but also some challenging terrain on dirt roads. With narrow tyres you lose stability. The straight bar also tends to raise the centre of gravity, which further diminishes control. If you are looking for less rolling resistance and straight bars, put narrower tyres on an MTB.

If you already have an MTB and want to increase your grip options, two come to mind. Get some bar extenders (there is quite a wide variety available), or replace the whole handlebar assembly with the setup you prefer. I have put drop-bars on an MTB with good results.

There are many good mountain bikes on the market and the choice comes down to personal preference. Though their names are different, many are made in the same factory, with the same inputs. Basically you get what you pay for. A rule of thumb is to pay enough to get what you feel you need.

## Selecting your bicycle
### Frames

In addition to the geometry and size of the frame, there are other important factors: the size (diameter and thickness) of tubing; the quality of workmanship; the kind of metal; and the size of wheel that the frame uses. Many of these factors play more of a role in how comfortable the bicycle is to ride than how durable it is under normal use. Under normal conditions there is little or no performance difference between frames with high-top tubes (men's bikes) and slanted-top tubes (women's bikes).

Generally, new models have more efficient frame geometry than older bikes. Once you have the right style you probably won't have to worry too much about the specifics of the frame angles. In considering the kind, size and quality of the tubing, it is not necessary to get sucked too far up-market. Low-end bicycles, above the lower mass-market levels, simply don't fall apart very often.

Our advice is to not overlook the cost effectiveness and advantages of the solid US$300 bike with a frame of a weldable metal (chrome-moly steel). In the unlikely event that it should break, you usually don't have to go far to find someone who can fix it in some fashion. I have seen steel frames brazed over a blacksmith's bed of coals! On the other hand be wary of expensive frames made of materials or assembled with adhesive that might be weakened by vibration. I have seen expensive bikes shake apart even on 'paved' roads. Aluminium frames have the same problem of being difficult to repair if they break in a remote area.

An important variable dictated by the frame is wheel and tyre size. Not all frames use the same size of wheel and not all wheels have the same selection of tyres. For remote areas consider a frame with a wheel that takes a sturdy tyre.

Collectively, in terms of geometry, tubing, tyre availability and workmanship, this suggests a modest MTB as a starting point.

## Size

A bicycle that is too big or too small for the user can be a safety hazard. Bicycles are sized, in inches or centimetres, by the measurement along the seat tube from the top tube to the bottom bracket (theoretically, it varies by brand). The final determination of a safe size comes when the bicyclist straddles the top tube, stands with both feet flat on the ground, and checks the clearance between the top tube and his/her crotch. The recommended clearance depends on the type of riding you will be doing – 3–5cm (1–2in) for road riding and double that for off-road riding. Your crotch and 7.5cm (3in) below it is a fixed distance above the ground, but because the bottom bracket isn't the same distance above the ground on all bicycles and 'sizing' varies by brand, the 'right size' may be different from bicycle to bicycle. Typically, people use MTBs 5–10cm (2–3in) smaller than they use touring bicycles.

# Preparing and maintaining your bicycle
## Speeds

Once upon a time there were only single-speed bikes, then there were three speeds, and that expanded to five, ten, 12, 15, 18, 21, 24 and 27 speeds. Is there a difference? Sometimes. Is it important? Sometimes. Between one, three, five, ten and 15 speeds there are functional differences that can be important. In a flat area, with short trip distances and no loads, a one-speed might be sufficient and cost effective. In hilly terrain, on rough roads, over long distances and/or when hauling a load, 15 speeds are advantageous. Each additional chainring (front gear) you combine with a basic five-gear freewheel cluster (the rear gears) creates a substantial increase in the range of gear ratios. It's the 'range' that is important! The same is not true for changing from a five-, six-, seven- or eight-gear freewheel. The incremental difference between speeds is smaller, but the range is usually unchanged. At the efficiency level that most people ride, the benefits from reducing increments between gears is not measurable. In fact, the fancy freewheels can cause new problems.

## Freewheels, hubs and axles

There are two systems for attaching the gears to the rear hub; traditional threaded freewheel units which screw on to the hub, and rear hubs with built-in freehub mechanisms that use cog cassettes. These are not interchangeable. To change from one system to the other you must change the hub, which requires rebuilding the entire wheel. In terms of remote-area maintenance, the main significance of this is on the rear axle. Mountain bike rear hubs with screw-on freewheels generally use an axle similar to those on Chinese bicycles (and local knockoffs) found around the world. If you break this axle you can get a replacement axle almost anywhere. Good luck finding an axle for a freehub.

If your freewheel should self-destruct you are more likely to be able to find a fill-in freewheel than cog cassettes.

Traditional hubs are available with solid nutted axles or hollow quick-release axles. Unless you need to take a wheel off frequently, solid axles are an economical and practical choice. Hollow axles can be replaced with solid axles and vice-versa.

Hub bearings can be loose or sealed. Loose bearings may require adjusting (use standard-size bearings) and can be serviced and rebuilt easily with a set of cone wrenches. Sealed bearing hubs are difficult to service and require special parts and tools.

## Protecting freewheels and hubs from dust, grit and rain

Usually the manufacturer's instructions tell you to lubricate most of the ball bearings on a bicycle (the headset, bottom bracket and hubs) with grease, but to lubricate the freewheel with light machine oil. In some extreme climates and cycling conditions it also may be practical to protect the bearings in your freewheel by packing them with grease.

If you are cycling in conditions where dust or a lot of water are likely to get into the freewheel you should consider packing your freewheel with grease. This is done by screwing a fitting (freewheel grease injector, US$25) on to the back of the freewheel. It has an 'O' ring so it seals against the back. You then use a grease gun to pump grease into the injector. The injector directs the grease into the freewheel. When the chamber of the freewheel is full, grease will begin to come out of the front of the freewheel.

Problems can be created from doing this, so care is necessary. (This could be more of a problem when installing the grease in a cold climate. We have never had a problem during any of our activities in the tropics.) First a description of a freewheel: a traditional freewheel is essentially two frustums (cones with the top cut off by a plane parallel to the base), one nested in the other. There is a race and a ring of ball bearings at each end of the frustums to keep the two pieces evenly spaced and able to rotate independently. The outer frustum is grooved and threaded on the outside to support the gears and the inside is notched all the way around. The inside frustum screws on to the rear hub and has spring-loaded teeth sticking out of it. The springs are very small and not particularly strong. When a bicycle is coasting the teeth slip over the notches and this creates the familiar clicking sound. When the bike is pedalled the notches come up to the teeth and engage them, pulling the rear wheel along.

When you pack a freewheel the entire space between the frustums is filled with grease. As you ride the bike the bearings and the teeth carve out a path for themselves within the chamber of grease. Within their 'chambers' they are protected from dust and moisture. The potential problem lies in the strength of the small springs behind the teeth and the stiffness of the grease. If the grease is too stiff the teeth may not extend fully and may break off. You need to use a soft grease in the freewheel and start off coasting and riding easily after you pack the bearings. It will help if you do the process in warm weather.

On hubs (usually older) where the dust cap doesn't rotate with the axle, you can keep foreign material out of your bearings by wrapping the exposed part of the cone with a pipe cleaner and then twisting the two ends back on each other so that it fits snugly. This technique can also be used on the bottom bracket.

## Chains

It used to be that all chains more or less fitted all bicycles. No longer! The new seven-speed freewheels require narrower chains, and some of these chains require their own special tools, replacement rivets and service techniques for maintenance and repair. The high-tech chains are hard to repair if they fail on the road. Unless you have a certified mechanic working on your bike you may want to stay away from some of the advanced technology. You will maintain more options if you stay with five- or six-cog freewheels and the standard chains that fit these assemblies.

An ongoing concern for chains is lubrication. Africa is dusty. If you over-oil your chain will get caked up. And once you get into the desert you will have to run dry as oil quickly attracts sand and this will destroy even the very best equipment.

## Derailleurs

Derailleurs are now built to close tolerances so that a specific movement of the shiftlever moves the derailleur to a specific gear (indexing). To use this system the derailleur and shifter have to be matched. Generally, most models of derailleurs from one manufacturer are interchangeable. The main differences between the derailleurs within one manufacturer are weight, price and quality. As the weight goes down the price goes up. But a higher price doesn't necessarily mean better quality. Grams are shaved by using more plastic or alloy metals, but this can also compromise strength. Generally at the level of performance at which MTBs are ridden a few ounces of weight is not as important as durability. Unless you are certain of their durability, derailleurs with plastic parts should be avoided. For remote locations, a high-quality, all-metal derailleur can be sufficient and is preferable. To continue to use an index system, any replacements should be the same brand as the original equipment. Whatever you use, if you go far enough on bad roads it will take a beating.

## Gear shifters

For years gear shifters have been disks with a lever sticking out. The shift lever rotates through a continuous range of settings. To shift gears, the user moves the lever to the desired setting and the disk stays in place by friction. Any shifter would work with any derailleur. Engineers have now calculated the distance the disk needs to rotate for a specific derailleur to shift gears and have put stops (indexing) at these locations on the shifters. As long as the index systems continued to use over-the-bar shifters with both 'index' and 'friction' modes, even if the system came out of calibration from cable stretch or some other reason, you could switch to friction mode and things would work. Even if you needed to replace the derailleur with an incompatible model, you could move a lever, release the indexing, return to the friction system and continue on your way.

The world is no longer as interchangeable. The latest 'advance' is grip shifters which twist, and two-lever, under-bar ratchet systems (eg: 'rapid-fire' or 'express-shifting'). Just push a lever to ratchet up a gear, push another lever to release down a gear. Neither system offers a friction option. To work, the systems must be calibrated. If the derailleur breaks and you can't get a compatible replacement, the shifter is useless. Furthermore, the shifters are virtually impossible to repair. The best thing about a broken ratchet shifter is the opportunity to replace it with a dual-mode, over-the-bar shifter. 'Grip shifters' don't protrude out from the handlebars as far and have fewer moving parts to jam and break, so they are less prone to malfunction. But they are still single mode. If you are selecting a new bike, shifting systems with a friction mode alternative are highly recommended. Short of this, grip shifters are the choice.

## Bottom brackets

The bottom bracket is the mechanism inside the frame, between the two crank arms that hold the pedals. There are bottom brackets with sealed bearings and bottom brackets with free-bearings. The former is more expensive and harder to service. In contrast, the latter can be serviced worldwide and the bearings are available in many remote areas, assuming there are bicycles in the area.

## Brakes

It is said that a bicycle will always stop – brakes just let you determine where. If you want that choice, choose your brakes carefully. The heavier the loads and the more downhill, the stronger the brakes need to be. Among the strongest type of brakes are cantilever, v-brakes, u-brakes, roller-cam and drum brakes.

Drum brakes are expensive and usually found only on tandems. V-brakes, u-brakes and roller-cam brakes have tended to be problematic and clog with mud very fast under those conditions. The most cost-effective brakes on the market today are cantilever brakes. The simplest designs use a standard brake cable from the brake lever to the cable hanger between the brakes. Standard brake cables are widely available. The more unique part of cantilever brakes is the way the two sides are connected. The simplest use a straddle-cable between the brakes, with a fixed anchor at one end and an adjustable cable-pinching plate on the other. These can be repaired with a short piece of standard brake cable.

## Wheels and spokes

There are alloy rims and steel rims. Alloy rims are more effective when wet, easier to keep true and easier to tap dents out of, but they dent more easily. Steel rims are strong, but they are dangerous in wet weather and when they start having problems they can be tough to get true.

Spokes are available in different gauges. The standard ones are 15g spokes, but 14g spokes are stronger. Double-butted 14/15/14 spokes are strong and light. The preferred material for spokes is stainless steel.

## Tyres

One of the major features of MTBs is their durable wheels and tyres. The wheel is a small diameter and the rim is wider, so they are stronger, more trouble free and more stable than comparable touring bike wheels. The beefy tyres on MTBs are also relatively trouble free and if properly inflated they are very effective at protecting the rims from dents. The wider the tyre the higher the rolling resistance, so if you will be doing a lot of riding on smooth roads this is a drawback. If you will be cycling on both paved and unpaved surfaces, consider combination knobby tyres with a solid raised centre bead. The centre bead makes easier rolling on paved roads and the knobby tread will help you in the dirt.

Though the supply line for good tyres may be long, the longer life, less down time and additional versatility usually make them a good choice. MTB tyres are becoming more widely available in Africa's large cities. With a little planning ahead it is not hard to keep a sufficient number of spares on hand.

The price bears very little relation to suitability. Cheaper, gum-walled tyres can be better than skin walls at taking the weight on bad roads. On desert pistes deflate your tyres so they bulge, increasing the surface area in contact with the ground. Skin walls invariably split under this kind of treatment. Tyres with little tread proved to be the best at sitting on top of the sand – Chan Sheng and Michelin road tyres are particularly good.

## Inner tubes

Inner tubes can be made out of a variety of materials and there are at least three types of valves. Airless tubes are also available. The construction material of pneumatic tubes may affect its puncture resistance and will determine what type of glue and patches you need to repair a puncture. The most common inner tube material is butyl rubber, which can be repaired with the glue and patches found in patch kits around the world.

'Thornproof' tubes are probably better labelled 'puncture resistant'. They are usually two to six times as expensive as regular tubes. Puncture-resistant tubes can be made of extra-thick butyl rubber, or of totally different materials, such as polyurethane plastic. When this punctures it requires its own special patch kit (twice as expensive as kits for butyl tubes). Combination latex/butyl tubes are an expensive hybrid (eight times the price of regular butyl) that can be patched with a standard patch kit.

Puncture-resistant tubes may be of the greatest advantage where there is a lot of glass or short, sharp objects on the road. If there are no sharp objects on the route all tubes are about equal. If you have long thorns to contend with, the best thing to do is avoid them!

Automobile tyres and tubes and most US bicycles use a 'schraeder valve'. European cyclists often use a 'presta valve'. The Chinese bikes use a third type of valve. One solution to the valve issue is to make sure that every bicycle has a pump that fits the valve of the tubes on that bicycle. A little more coverage can be gained by using one of the pumps that can be switched from schraeder to presta. If schraeder valves are used, make sure that every pump for automobiles can also be used to inflate the bicycle's tyres.

Airless tubes solve some problems, but they offer a harsher ride, are six to ten times as expensive as regular tubes, at least twice as heavy, have twice the rolling resistance and don't carry heavy loads well. It is still probably most practical, for remote sites, to use butyl compound tubes that are repairable.

## Tube protectors
Some people praise tube protector strips. I know of several cases where the edge of the strips wore a line of holes in the tube, causing unrepairable punctures. For off-pavement riding, there is no final decision on the effectiveness of protective strips. I have never used them in Africa and have only rarely had problems with a flat that I think a tube protector would have prevented.

## Pedals and toe-clips
If you are likely to be dismounting in dirt (anything from dust to mud) it is best to stay away from any pedals that have hardware on the bottom of your shoes that can clog. This pretty much eliminates cleats and clipless pedals. Conventional pedals give you the flexibility to use multi-purpose shoes, which cut down on the number of pairs of shoes you will have to pack.

You can gain some efficiency as you pedal by using toe-clips. If you are trying them for the first time, or don't have a high level of confidence, don't tighten the straps initially nor when you are in urban traffic, sand, mud, rocks and other technical situations.

## Saddles
You are going to have an intimate relationship with your saddle; get one that is comfortable. Those that are too narrow or too wide may not support your pelvic bones properly or comfortably. Spring saddles will have you bouncing about all day. Gushy soft and rock hard can also leave you constantly searching for a comfortable way to sit. If you are not used to riding a bike, almost any saddle will leave you sore to begin with. Gel covers on saddles help to reduce saddle soreness, along with a comprehensive application of Vaseline or something similar over the relevant parts of your body!

The angle of the seat and what you wear also play a role in saddle comfort. Thick seams and bunched clothing between you and your saddle quickly take their toll. Wear padded cycling shorts, which are designed to be worn without underwear.

## Accessories
The best advice on accessories is, be sure they are strong enough to take the beating they are sure to get. And, attach them securely. If accessories fail while in use it may not be fatal, but it can be very frustrating. Buy equipment that is properly designed and sufficiently durable for its intended use. One way to minimise lost screws is to apply Loctite (medium strength) or tyre patch cement to the threads before bolting on racks and cages.

## Racks and packs
Do not carry anything on your back in a rucksack or backpack. Your back will ache very quickly and you will overheat sooner. Even water packs can be a problem for some

people, though they have their advocates. Waistpacks (bumbags) are more manageable, but can still be annoying. I like the versatility of a waistpack, but rig it to handlebars while I am riding.

To carry large loads you need a sturdy rack and saddlebags (panniers). Racks and packs can wear fast and screws loosen quickly when rattled about on a daily basis. Choose racks and packs that are sturdy and stable enough to handle the conditions they will be subjected to. The weak points on racks tend to be the welds and eyelets. The weak points on panniers tend to be where the hooks screw into the backing.

Bicycles travel best if the weight of any load is distributed evenly and kept low. Four slim packs, two front and two rear, are better than two giant bulging ones. If you are travelling with only a moderate amount of baggage (say 10kg/22lb) you can get by with just a rear rack and medium-size panniers on each side. If the weight is too heavy in the rear the front wheel becomes hard to handle and you will expend extra energy trying to keep the bike under control. For heavy loads split the weight between front and rear.

There are two choices for strength with lighter weights: racks made with aluminium rod or with steel alloy tubing. I have seen a lot of aluminium racks break and they tend to be hard to fix. I have never seen a steel alloy tubing rack break, though if it did it would be easier to get it repaired.

The best mount is to screw the rack directly on to the frame. Look for a frame with rack braze-ons on the seat-stays and threaded eyelets on the axle drop-outs. If you expect to be riding on roads, trails or streambeds with high rocks or roots DO NOT USE low-rider racks. Low-riders will give your packs more of a beating than on racks that hold them higher. And if one of those rocks or roots gets hold of your pannier you may take a beating as well.

If you will be travelling on rough roads, it is preferable that the attaching system for the packs consists of strong hooks and non-stretch webbing straps with buckles or Velcro fasteners. Packs with suspension systems that rely solely on elastic cords and springs can bounce off when you hit bumps and pot-holes. Similar advice applies for attaching articles to the top of the rack: you will have more flexibility and fewer problems if you use non-elastic nylon webbing straps with buckles instead of elastic straps, shock cords or bungee cords. Webbing is also lighter.

Handlebar bags, frame packs or waistpacks are not essential, but they are very convenient for cameras, snacks, sun lotion, notepads, etc. As they sit so high, you don't want to carry too much weight in a handlebar bag.

The advice on water-bottle cages is the same as for racks; they should be sturdy enough to handle the conditions they will be subjected to. It's best if they mount into braze-ons on the frame.

### Fenders and kickstands

Fenders and kickstands can be more of a disadvantage than an advantage: on trains, planes, buses and during the course of a normal day, fenders get knocked out of alignment. They are inconvenient to detach, reattach and keep adjusted. In dry weather they keep a little sand off the chain. In rain they will keep you happy and stop the chain from being washed, but if you ride off paved roads, they can quickly clog with mud and become a major aggravation.

If you have a rear rack, a less fragile (although less thorough) protection is available from snap-on commercial products which can be fitted to the top of the rack. Alternatively, you can improvise by cutting up a 1.5-litre water bottle and taping it on to the racks to provide a splash guard which keeps body, drive train and baggage drier.

The disadvantage of kickstands is that they are often not designed to support the weight of a loaded touring bike. If your bike is going to be fully loaded most of the time most kickstands are not worth the bother.

## Mirrors

Rear-view mirrors are not a substitute for good cycling technique, but they are useful. They tend to lead a rough life on tour. Whether they are attached to the handlebar, helmets or glasses, they tend to get a good bashing and have a short life span.

## Lights

Every effort should be made to stay off the roads at night. A disproportionate number of accidents happen at night, and they are often fatal. If you have to be on the road after dark, lights and reflectors are essential. Plan ahead for your lighting system. If you don't expect to be riding at night much, you won't need a particularly elaborate system.

There is a choice of four kinds of power source. In ascending order of initial cost, they are: battery, generator, rechargeable battery, and combo generator/rechargeable battery. Prices can range from US$2 to US$100. Your budget, location and pattern of use will dictate which is the best system for you.

A versatile solution is to use a headlamp. These strap around your helmet or head and provide hands-free light on or off the bike. If you decide on battery power, choose a model that uses batteries that are easily replaced ('D' is most common worldwide). Remember that rechargeable batteries need an electrical current or a solar cell to recharge.

## Locks

It seems that the further you are from the New-York-style cities of the world, the less sophisticated the bike thieves, the rarer the bolt cutters and the less need there is for heavy locks and chains. While on tour, my bike is usually loaded and conspicuous, securely stored at the hotel, or left for only a few minutes while I run an errand. In the latter cases I lock it. I use a rather ordinary lock and long cable. The long cable is attached to a fixed object to prevent snatch-and-ride.

## Tools and spare parts

To fully enjoy the self-sufficiency and independence that a bicycle can provide, you need to carry a few tools and spare parts. They do not add much weight and could prevent you from having to push your bike on a long walk or having a long wait for a taxi. Select the tools and spare parts you need to do basic adjustments and maintenance on your bicycle and any special tools if your bicycle has esoteric components.

For a long solo trip, or any kind of group trip when supply lines could be long, bring enough tools and spare parts to be able to completely overhaul your bike and repair everything, short of a broken frame or rim. Essentially turn yourself into a mini-portable bike shop! If you are in a group of fewer than ten, usually only one set of these tools needs to be brought on a trip. The group leader or their designate is responsible for organising this kit, and other participants need not worry about these items.

If you should need a spare part or tool sent to you in an emergency, DHL and other worldwide package services are now available in most African capitals and many other major African cities. You will need a contact back home who can buy a replacement part and send it out via courier. Unfortunately, the shipping is not cheap.

## Water

Dehydration can hit very quickly. Feeling thirsty is not a good indication; by then you could well be in serious trouble already. Basically there is no substitute for drinking plenty of water in a timely manner.

## Water bottles

It is essential to take a water bottle on every trip. In hot weather you will be drinking a litre of water or more every 15km (10 miles). For long trips you need a large water supply, such as water bags. Be sure you have sufficient water capacity for the kind of travel you plan. Safe drinking water is getting increasingly available in Africa, but it is still problematic. It is also possible that some areas have no water during the dry seasons. Even when there is water you may find the pump that you expect to use is broken.

A tip is to use white-coloured water bottles as the water inside doesn't heat up quite as much.

### Water purification

A heavy, relatively expensive and high-tech option is to carry a filtering water pump. There are several brands of differing quality available, priced from US$30 to US$200. If you don't have a filter and are out of water, a few water purification tablets can save your life. Carry some on every trip. However, I don't like to rely on them too much because they can 'purify' your system in the same way that they purify the water – some of the organisms they kill are beneficial. You don't want a purified intestinal tract.

## Food and cooking utensils

Even if you start the day with a good breakfast and full of energy, as the day goes on you will burn it up. If you do not eat again, the calories will be consumed and you will reach a state of hypoglycaemia, or low blood sugar. It can hit you very quickly and leave you dead in your tracks. On any trip have extra food with you at all times. It needs to provide not just quick, but also sustainable, energy. Breads, local pastries, biscuits and bananas are widely available and are good choices. You should carry emergency packets of dried food for times of need. The dehydrated meals available from camping and outdoor shops are expensive, none too generous in size and do not offer much in the way of choice, so unless you are rich with a small appetite and not particularly interested in food, you will have to look at alternatives. Good buys, particularly if weight is a problem, are packet soups, packets of instant Chinese noodles and other dried 'instant' food.

There's a wide range of lightweight billycan sets, though if you go for collapsible pots and pans pay particular attention to handles and how they clip or hook on. If some plastic slot-on handles chip you will never get them to stay put again.

## Personal equipment
### Helmets and gloves

Many sports present a risk of head injury. Bicycling definitely has this hazard and warrants precaution. Scrapes and broken bones heal, but scrambled brains may not. Helmets won't prevent an accident but they can reduce the severity of the consequence. Compared with the lifetime cost of a head injury or even death, the cost of wearing a helmet is small. I know of several crashes in remote locations of Africa where the cyclist's helmet took a hard hit and the cyclist rode on. None of these cases involved an automobile.

In sun a helmet also serves to protect your head, which significantly reduces fatigue.

The value of gloves is similar to that of a helmet. Gloves don't prevent accidents but they can reduce injuries, such as the amount of gravel embedded in your palms. They are also invaluable in reducing road vibration.

### Clothing

On extended tours all clothing – and bodies – get really filthy as there can be a long time between washing opportunities. Perhaps the hardest aspect of travelling by bike is going for two weeks at a time without a decent wash – sweating every day in the same smelly clothes. As the trip progresses, it is easy to get increasingly sloppy about things, for example cycling in flip-flops after shoes become too smelly and start falling apart. Leather gloves get forgotten for the same reasons.

In choosing your clothes consider comfort, visibility and social standards. You can never make yourself too visible as a cyclist. Brightly coloured cotton T-shirts work well. Special cycling shorts have padding in the crotch, relatively long legs and no heavy inseams. Leather in cycling shorts is less durable than shorts with towelling or synthetic material.

If you are going to be cycling at dawn, dusk or at night, an oversize, long-sleeved white shirt is an excellent item. It can be slipped on over anything and does not take up much space. A long-sleeved shirt also doubles during the day as protection from the sun. By covering your arms, you will reduce the amount of moisture you lose (for more information see *Health* in *Chapter 4*). Worn separately or together, a medium-weight sweater (or pile jacket) and nylon wind jacket will prepare you for a variety of changes in temperature and weather conditions. A pair of loose trousers or a wraparound skirt that can be slipped on over your cycling shorts will make you more presentable.

You can get shoes specially designed for cycling, but they tend to be uncomfortable to walk in. If you have a pair of shoes that you can cycle in without getting cramp in your feet and also walk in, then they are probably fine for general bicycle touring. As a rule cheaper athletic shoes have stiffer soles, so are better for cycling. If your feet get cramp using multi-purpose shoes to cycle in then you will need to have two pairs of shoes.

Dust and exhaust are another problem. The irritation from exhaust can be the worst. When pollutants reach a choking level a bandana over the mouth and nose helps considerably.

## Sunglasses

If you are used to sunglasses, you will want to wear them most days. They will not only protect your eyes from the sun but also keep dust out of your eyes and reduce eye-fatigue from the drying wind. **Do not** wear sunglasses with side blinders. They restrict peripheral vision, which is very important if you have to manoeuvre in traffic or swerve to avoid a hazard. In the afternoon, just when you are ready to take off your sunglasses, a new irritant appears: gnats and small bugs. If you are going to be riding at dusk, it is worth buying a pair of glasses with clear lenses.

## First-aid kit

When people are in unfamiliar surroundings they can receive more injuries than usual. A lot of these are cuts and scrapes. Carry a first-aid kit and be able to give minor first aid. Prompt attention to even the smallest scratch is very important.

For an extended tour you should also prepare a medicine kit with prescription medicine and remedies for headaches, colds, upset stomachs, allergies and other common ailments. If possible get pills in 'blister packs' or individually packaged forms. Bulk-packed pills tend to vibrate into dust on long cycle tours. If you take a prescription drug, carry a duplicate prescription that gives the generic name.

## Camping equipment

You only need camping gear if you are going to camp. If you are taking a tent and/or stove, make sure you have all the pieces before you leave.

One of the problems with camping on a cycling tour is the security of your belongings – you're pretty much tied to your camp. A second problem is when it rains in Africa, it generally rains buckets, so no tent is going to be as nice as the simplest hotel room. When it is not the rainy season, what you really need, included in many hotel rooms, is a free-standing bug net.

The most practical of these is made by Long Road Travel Supplies (111 Avenida Drive, Berkeley, CA 94708, USA; tel: 800 359 6040 (USA or Canada) or 510 540 4763 (USA only); fax: 510 540 0652 (USA only); email: sales@longroad.com; www.longroad.com).

## SUGGESTED CYCLE KIT LIST
### Spares and tools
- panniers eg: Overlander by Carradice
- two spare tyres
- ten inner tubes
- a puncture-repair kit
- cables
- brake pads
- grease and oil
- bearings
- wires and straps
- pliers
- a set of Allen keys
- cable cutter
- spoke tensioner
- a set of spanners
- screwdriver
- bottom bracket tensioner
- front bearing spanner
- spokes
- box of nuts and bolts, etc
- chain link extractor
- toothbrush

### Medical
- rehydration mix and spoon
- gauzes, bandages and creams
- suture kit
- anti-malaria tablets
- antibiotics
- eye ointment
- Paracetamol
- tooth repair kit

### Water
- two Travelwell military water purifiers
- two ten-litre water bags

### Cooking
- Coleman's multi-fuel cooker
- two spoons
- two plastic bowls
- two plastic cups
- a saucepan
- a penknife

### Camping equipment
- a tent
- two sleeping mats
- two sleeping bags
- nylon string
- a towel
- a torch

### Miscellaneous
- two whistles (as a warning and signal)
- binoculars
- a compass
- a camera

If you either take a tent or plan to sleep under the stars in your bug net, it is useful (if not essential!) to have a dedicated ground cloth, ie: a piece of plastic, a woven mat, an old sheet, etc.

To self-cater you need not only a cooker, but also the pots, pans and utensils to use with it. You will also need space to carry some staples that you will need frequently but won't want to buy for every meal, like cooking oil, salt, pepper, sugar and spices.

The most versatile stoves are multi-fuel designs. Mountain Safety Research (MSR) make one that is highly regarded. You will need a safe container for carrying fuel. Sigg bottles work well for this. Make sure you have enough fuel storage capacity to last between fuelling points.

## Other items for bicycle touring
Depending on your plans there are a number of other special items worth taking:

- If staying in local houses or small guesthouses that don't necessarily provide linen, take sheets and a towel.
- If travelling in the cold season or at altitude, you might want to take a sleeping bag or blanket as well as the above.

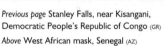

*Previous page* Stanley Falls, near Kisangani, Democratic People's Republic of Congo (GR)

*Above* West African mask, Senegal (AZ)

*Above right* Women collecting water from the pump, Nigeria (GR)

*Below* Tuareg making tea in the Sahara, near Timbuktu, Mali (AZ)

- Rubber thongs or flip-flops are good for those slimy loos.
- Business cards are useful to impress officials and honour requests for your address.
- Extra passport photos are good for gifts and if bureaucracy invents an unexpected new form or you need to apply for an additional visa.
- Binoculars are good in game parks but otherwise they are just extra weight.
- Camera, film and batteries because some may be hard or expensive to obtain en route.
- Reading material helps to pass the time at borders etc.

# Other tips for cyclists
## Accommodation and food
If you plan to stay overnight outside major cities and tourist destinations, which is the norm for bicycle tourists, it is usually difficult to plan your accommodation too specifically without the help of a travel consultant who has been there. In small towns and villages you may find you have no choice at all. You will get to stay in the best – and probably only – hotel in town. Where there is a choice it is often determined by price, so your selection will be dictated by your budget.

Many budget African hotels have only a few rooms and beds, so if you are travelling with a large group your choices may already be narrowed and the group may exceed the capacity of a village hotel. While camping is an option, we tend not to camp for a combination of reasons: you have to carry more gear (both shelter and cooking) or include a support vehicle (which negates much of any savings); setting up and taking down a camp uses time that is better spent on being more involved in seeing Africa; camping tends to be on the outskirts of towns and separated from the community.

I prefer to be more immersed in the village. The modest cost of most accommodation and meals does more to help the village economy and may be no more expensive than camping. Furthermore, many parts of Africa don't lend themselves to camping and there can be more security problems. Meal planning is similarly influenced by budget and by the availability of markets, cooking facilities and restaurants. In rural areas selection may be so limited as to constitute no choice. But if you are in an area where any Africans are travelling cooked food is usually available.

## Seeing wildlife
One of the best experiences is seeing free-range animals from the freedom of a bicycle seat. If you know where to look it is possible to see a wide variety of wildlife and birdlife from a bicycle, but with the continuing encroachment on wildlife habitats by man this is further and further away from inhabited areas.

If you choose to search for wildlife, be selective about your objectives. These are wild animals and when threatened can be very dangerous. They have their own ideas on how to handle intrusions into their personal space. I have seen baboons and elephants from a bicycle in Burkina Faso, Togo and Zimbabwe, watched giraffes, zebras and gazelles in Kenya and Cameroon and enjoyed monkeys jumping overhead in Ghana and Liberia. I once heard the growl of a lion while on a bicycle and an elephant has chased me – not a relaxing experience.

Without an experienced guide **do not** go in search of cape buffalo, lions, elephants or rhinos by bicycle or on foot. Most countries help you with this by not allowing bicycles or foot travel in the major game parks. To see the big game you will have to store your bike and get into vans for a day or two. Unless you pre-arrange it, you will not find transport for game drives waiting at the park entrance. Usually game-watching safaris begin from major cities, so you need to plan accordingly.

# Organised Tours

If you have limited time and money, then an organised overland trip may be the best choice for you. Of course, you will need to sacrifice a degree of independence and be prepared to live and travel with a large group. However, there are quite a few compensations.

There will be none of the planning, preparation and expense involved in getting your own vehicle. No carnets, no spare parts to worry about, no engines to overhaul and definitely no greasy hands to clean. There will be none of the hassles in dealing with border officials; you can just lie back while some other mug – the driver's mat – deals with the cantankerous officials. If you are so inclined, you can enjoy the mesmerising lethargy induced by long hours in the truck, while the countries roll by. You can enjoy the camaraderie of like-minded travellers. You might fall in love! Some of you may already be wondering why you would want to take your own vehicle.

Of course there is a downside to everything. You will have to put up with long hours in the back, covered in dust, sitting next to the obnoxious member of the group you can't stand. Despite some pretence of democracy, you will definitely have less input when the driver dictates that safety, security and the well-being of the group take precedence. You will have to muck in with the daily chores, buying group food, cooking and, dare we say it, washing up 20 people's plates and mugs, as well as the black pots and pans. You will definitely have to push the truck out of sand and probably have to dig it out of thick sticky mud. You might fall out with your better half or significant other. Does this sound like fun?

Let's look more closely at why you might take this overland expedition. There is little pre-planning to do. The company will brief you about things like visas, vaccinations, insurance and what to pack for the trip. All you need to do is be on time for departure. There are trips to suit all budgets. The company will be familiar with the routes, security, daily planning, good places to camp and where to get water, fuel and food. The driver will have done most, if not all, of the trip at least once before and will know the best choices.

Those who do choose an organised tour will probably never realise just how much they have been protected from African bureaucracy. Unless the group is very large, border crossings are likely to be quicker than for those learning the ropes as they go along. Most trucks operate some kind of rota system, giving those not on cooking duty time to explore at the end of the day. Tasks can be more efficiently divided and shared out. Travelling independently, you have to deal with all the daily tasks of guarding the vehicle, motor maintenance, shopping, pitching camp, making a fire, purifying water, cooking, cleaning and so on. On a group overland trip, costs such as fuel, equipment, spares, carnets and insurance are spread across a much larger group.

Security is one of the most significant differences between the two options. The biggest headache for independent travellers is the need for constant vigilance over their vehicle and its contents. This can make it difficult to get away from the vehicle, perhaps reducing the possibilities for hiking and visiting more inaccessible spots. With an organised tour, there are more people to ensure a permanent security rota, allowing members to leave their gear behind and take off by foot, canoe, train or bus. Individuals can generally leave the tour at any time and travel independently (at their own expense) to a pre-arranged rendezvous point.

So what are the disadvantages of organised trips? First is the lack of independence, which is why most of us consider doing a trip to Africa in the first place. The routes will be pre-designated and changing them can risk disagreement within the group. The leader will generally permit a measure of democracy, perhaps allowing the trip to deviate a little from the published route; but this isn't the same thing as finding a particularly nice beach and deciding to hang around for a week or so, deciding to miss some countries out altogether or to take a completely different route from the one originally planned. Only independent travel gives you absolute freedom.

Despite the common interest of crossing Africa, there is no guarantee that the members of the group will get along. On a six-month trip the group dynamics would be a university degree subject in its own right. Groups with a good cross-section of participants often work surprisingly well, but then again you could be on the trip that just never gels. You are very unlikely to be landed with an entire group that you can't stand. Although perhaps – no, we won't go there! It's mostly about some team effort. You don't need to be caged in with the group all the time.

Mixing with the local people is all part of the routine, but perhaps making genuine friendships is more difficult. When a truck comes into town, the people will react very differently from the way they might react to a solitary Land Rover. Then again, coming into town in a solitary Land Rover might not be so relaxing either. So many decisions! Better let someone else make them and relax on an organised tour, or just go to the Maldives instead!

## The routes

There are many trips to choose from, from short two-week tours in Morocco to the original trans-African expeditions. Many of the routes are the same as those outlined earlier. For years the favourite routes were across the Sahara via Tamanrasset to Nigeria and then across CAR and Zaïre to Nairobi before continuing south to Johannesburg.

Most companies who still operate trans-Africa will take the route from Morocco via Mauritania and through much of West Africa. However, with persistent problems in the Congo, groups have to fly to Nairobi, usually from Accra in Ghana, Douala in Cameroon or Libreville in Gabon. Another truck will then be waiting in Nairobi, where the trip will continue around East Africa before continuing south. The eastern Nile route has opened up over the last couple of years and a few companies are now running trips each way between Cairo and southern Africa via Ethiopia. It is possible to link these with extensions into the Middle East and Asia. A limited number of shorter trips now operate in West Africa, but costs are higher and some visas take more time to obtain. A few operators have recently run new trips in Libya and Tunisia.

Currently there is a boom in overland truck travel between Nairobi and Cape Town, either by routes through Malawi and Mozambique, or west through Zambia to Victoria Falls and Namibia. These shorter tours allow you to fly into a region for a few weeks and get a taste of it in a concentrated burst. Shorter expeditions also mean you can add them into your schedule once you arrive in a particular area, so giving you even greater freedom of movement. An organised tour could easily fit in with other parts of your journey by combining it with a hired car. Often, as one region closes off, others open up; that's the beauty and intrigue of Africa.

Throughout East and southern Africa there are now a number of good local operators. Smaller companies in South Africa (and previously in Zimbabwe) now offer a variety of expeditions, including South Africa, Mozambique, Namibia and Botswana. Local tours can respond to changing conditions much faster than the London-based operations, perhaps providing a more interesting trip. The downside is that you have no way of assessing the quality of their operation until you arrive, and you probably have no 'come back' options if you have a major complaint.

## What to expect

Of course, the way in which the tours are organised varies from company to company. They will generally organise briefing sessions to introduce themselves and explain how the trip will work, the everyday practicalities and precisely what you need to arrange in advance in the way of documents, vaccinations and so on. They will usually also offer or suggest a comprehensive insurance policy, essential for any form of travel. Don't leave without it.

Most tour operators aim to make the experience feel as close to independent travel as possible. As mentioned, there will be a fairly democratic approach to deciding on day-to-day details. Members of the group will normally set up a rota to cope with all the daily chores, especially cooking and security. Before leaving, most trucks will be partially stocked with food supplies, but most fresh items will be bought locally and shopping will generally be the responsibility of those on cooking duty for the day.

Even where a company provides a cook as part of its team, you will be expected to help out with much of the actual work, with the cook acting more as an adviser.

Participants will also be expected to volunteer for additional jobs such as stores, fire-lighting, water purification, security, first aid and rubbish collection. These vary from company to company and according to the number of people on the trip. Many drivers will also suggest the option of setting up a bar, which tends to be a popular job!

You will normally pay a deposit on booking. Most companies ask for a kitty at the beginning of the trip to cover food and other communal expenses, but others include this within the overall cost of the trip. Some companies only include transport; others will cover camping, game park fees and other admission charges. It is important to be clear what **is** and what **is not** included in the basic price. A few companies add a 'Local Payment' in addition to the main charges. This may cover direct costs en route such as national park entrance fees, etc. Remember to add in the cost of any airfares when you are budgeting for your trip. These will not be included in the tour operators' cost.

You will generally have to supply your own bedding, but tents are normally provided. Sleeping is generally in shared, two-person tents. Check the availability of camp beds and mosquito nets, as most do not supply these.

Most companies use Bedford, MAN or Mercedes trucks, customised with their own seating configuration. They have very different layouts, but all of them can accommodate a group of around 18 to 24 people. South African companies often use Japanese models; some are very well designed.

A few trucks pack luggage and tents into a separate trailer, making more space in the truck itself. It is worth checking out the seating design of trucks in which you are thinking of travelling. Has it been organised simply to fit in the greatest number of bodies, or does it look relatively comfortable with a decent view? Does it offer forward-facing or inward-facing seats? The various companies offer different combinations. You will be spending a long time in that truck, so you ought to be quite sure you are happy with the layout.

Your drivers/leaders are the ones who can make your trip that bit better, but remember their job is an incredibly demanding one. They have also to be a motor mechanic, a diplomat, an actor, a social worker, an expert on everything and a friend to everyone. Most companies have extensive training programmes for their drivers, including both workshop experience and travelling with another leader/driver.

Some companies also provide couriers or cooks. On a short journey a good all-round leader/driver should be adequate. On a longer trip a second team member is invaluable in order to help with visas and bureaucracy, dealing with the paperwork, and helping out with the driving and mechanics.

### SPIES IN THE DANAKIL

We'd been driving for hours, with nowhere to pull off the side of the new tarmac road, when we saw a small dirt track off to the left. That would have to do. A tin of Sainsbury's vegetable salad from our emergency reserves, and a cup of tea.

Halfway through our drinks, a plain white Toyota pulled up behind us. Five men got out, with large guns at the ready. That's it, we are going to be robbed, it's finally going to happen. We said our Salaams, and Good Mornings in case they weren't Muslims. Bob shook hands with them and I nodded my head respectfully from the interior of the vehicle. No-one spoke English, but it was intimated that we should drink up and get back on the road immediately. Wow, was this scary? They could have smiled a bit. Well, we hadn't been robbed yet. 'Police,' they claimed, but it was not in any way obvious. Local warlords, more likely.

With our adrenaline levels at an all-time high, we gulped down the remains of our tea and got on to the main road, where we stopped at the next settlement, a small scruffy collection of permanent but temporary-looking shacks called houses. At the pharmacy, the only proper shop in town, the man spoke English and translated. We were obviously international spies. Even spies have to stop for tea. It was all quite absurd, but no-one demanded any money and, after further consultations, the episode was closed. We couldn't possibly really be spies – no, they drink alcohol, shaken not stirred, not tea!

Needless to say, we did not stop again on the side of the road until we reached a fuel station.

## Choosing a tour

You can pay anything from £2,000 to £5,000 for a full trans-African trip, but the variations between them are not just a matter of cost. The range of choices offered can be quite bewildering. Make sure that you find out exactly what is included in the price and how the trip is organised.

As with most things, the general rule is that the more you pay the more you get. The cheaper end of the market can also tend to have less experienced leaders/drivers and use older and less dependable vehicles, though this is not always the case. Leaders/drivers with the larger operators keep in constant touch with full-time staff back at base, who can help out in the event of problems or emergencies.

One-off expeditions and budget trips are less secure when the going gets tough, but may offer a different style of trip. You might have to accept the possibility that the truck may break down more frequently, but this is not always the case. Anyone can break down in any place!

## Other options

For some parts of Africa it can be more beneficial to take shorter trips with local operators, most of whom will have representatives in Europe and elsewhere. Travelling with the European operator affords you the benefit of more financial security, of course. These shorter expedition options apply in particular to the Sahara, parts of West Africa and most of southern Africa. Two weeks or three weeks in the Sahara to places such as Mauritania, Mali, the Ténéré in Niger, Ennedi in Chad, Tassili N'Ajjer/Hoggar in Algeria are best done with specialist operators, who have experienced local guides and who travel with at least two 4x4 vehicles. Morocco, Libya, Egypt, Tunisia, Kenya, Ethiopia and Namibia are other countries where local trips have a lot to offer.

The boxed story above may perhaps be a good reason to join an organised tour if you are a little nervous!

# Overland operators
## Based in the UK

**Acacia Adventure Holidays** Tel: 020 7706 4700; email: info@acacia-africa.com; www.acacia-africa.com. Operating since the 1980s, originally as an overland company. Now a more varied programme, including safaris, trekking, diving and short overland.

**Africa in Focus** Tel: 01803 770956; email: africainfocus@yahoo.co.uk; www.africa-in-focus.com. Photographic specialist trips, mostly in southern Africa.

**Africa Travel Centre** Tel: 020 7387 1211 and (in UK) 0845 450 1520; fax: 020 7383 7512; email: sales@africatravel.co.uk; www.africatravel.co.uk. Offers a wide range of long and short overland options including truck tours, rail tours, self-drive in southern Africa, camping and coach tours, motorbike safaris, balloon safaris and game lodge safaris. Because the Africa Travel Centre represents a range of companies it can be a good place to start when shopping around for a trip that suits you.

**African Trails** Tel: 01772 330907; email: sales@africantrails.co.uk. Has been running trips since 1980 with one driver and courier. No age limit quoted – most passengers 18–35. Seats face inwards. Also offers Kenya/Tanzania game parks tour, and shorter trips in southern Africa. Nairobi to Cape Town.

**Bukima Africa** Tel: 0870 7572230; email: adventure@bukima.com; www.bukima.com. Offers overland and small group adventure in Africa from 7 days to 15 weeks.

**Dragoman** Tel: 0870 499 4484; email: wd@dragoman.co.uk; www.dragoman.com. Running trips for 16 years, using uniquely designed 16-ton Mercedes trucks with a crew of two. Seats face forward. Offers a very wide range of long and shorter tours in most of Africa. Also run trips which feature visits to community projects helping local people to maintain their culture and benefit from tourism.

**Encounter Overland** (now part of Dragoman) Tel: 0870 499 4485; email: wd@encounter.co.uk; www.encounter.co.uk. Over 30 years' experience running overland trips and safaris throughout Africa. Vehicles all 4x4 with inward-facing seats. Operate expedition-type trips with only one leader/driver, so 'passengers' must be willing to participate fully. Age guideline 18–45; most in their 20s and 30s.

**Exodus** Tel: 0870 240 5550; email: sales@exodus.co.uk; www.exodus.co.uk. Company with 30 years' experience using Mercedes trucks. Age range 17–45 on trips of 2–11 weeks, mostly in East and southern Africa. Mixed seating. Phone for dates of slide shows held once a fortnight in London.

**Expedition World** Tel: 01243 789264; email: sianpj@hotmail.com; www.expeditionworld.com. A small specialist company with a particular interest in trips to the Sahara (Algeria, Niger, Libya and Chad) plus Asia Overland for oldies.

**Explore Africa** Tel: 01633 880224; fax: 01633 882128. Company with 18 years' experience using Bedford trucks, with a crew of two on longer trips. Age range is 18–35. Older passengers accepted if 'young at heart'.

**Explore Worldwide** Tel: 0870 333 4001; fax: 01252 760001; email: res@exploreworldwide.com; www.explore.co.uk. Small group holidays using a mix of hotels, lodges and camping in North Africa, Kenya, Tanzania, Uganda, Malawi, Zimbabwe, Zambia, Botswana and Namibia.

**Guerba Adventure and Discovery Holidays** Tel: 01373 858956; www.guerba.com. Running overland expeditions and shorter safaris for over 20 years. Uses Mercedes trucks with inward-facing seats and three crew. Offers a wide range of treks, safaris in East and southern Africa, lodge safaris and 4x4 tours with comfort-added camping and no camp chores.

**Kumuka Expeditions** Tel: 0800 068 8855; www.kumuka.com. Overland adventures for independent-minded travellers from 14 days to 9 weeks.

**Nomadic Expeditions** Tel: 0870 220 1718; www.nomadic.co.uk

**Oasis Overland** Tel: 01963 363400; email: travel@oasisoverland.co.uk; www.oasisoverland.co.uk. Small company offering tours in Africa (also the Middle East and South America). Uses Scania and Leyland trucks with a driver/mechanic and courier. Seats face inwards. Passenger ages generally 18–40. Trips from 3 weeks to 7 months.

**On the Go Tours** Tel: 020 7371 1113; email: info@onthegotours.com; www.onthegotours.com
**Overland Club** Tel: 0800 731 8841 (Freephone) or 01740 623633; email:
info@overlandclub.com. Budget camping expeditions throughout Africa from two weeks to 26
weeks, for those who are free spirited and have a passion to experience the real Africa. 'Africa All
The Way' UK to Cape Town via West Africa 26 weeks £1,600 + £400 kitty.
**Phoenix Expeditions** Tel: 01509 881818; fax: 01509 881822; www.phoenixexpeditions.co.uk.
Camping safaris and expeditions for the adventurous budget traveller. Transport is in custom-built
Scania or Bedford safari vehicles with the expertise of a tour leader and driver/mechanic. Trips 2 to
11 weeks in East and southern Africa.

## Other overland companies worldwide

Many of the UK-based companies (above) also have representatives in Nairobi, Harare
and South Africa, as well as in Australia and the US. There are also other expedition
companies worldwide. Here are some to look out for:

**The Adventure Center** 1311 63rd St, Suite 200, Emeryville, CA 94608, USA; tel: 800 227 8747;
email: tripinfo@adventurecenter.com.
**Trek Holidays Canada** Toll free: 888 456 3522; *Calgary* tel: 403 283 6115; *Vancouver* tel: 604 734
1066; *Edmonton* Westcan Treks; tel: 780 439 0024.

## Based in South Africa

There are many companies offering specialist overland tours specific only to southern
Africa, with representation in South Africa only. You will need to shop around and your
best bet is to visit a local travel agent for further information. Here are a few of these
companies:

**Affordable Adventures** PO Box 1008, Sunninghill, 2157 Johannesburg; tel: 011 465 9168; fax:
011 467 3913; mob: 083 325 7218; email: info@affordableadventures.co.za;
www.affordableadventures.co.za
**Africa Tours** Pretoria; tel: (012) 333 7110; email: dat@global.co.za; www.destination.co.za
**Drifters Adventours** PO Box 4712, Cresta, Johannesburg 2118; tel: 011 888 1160; fax: 011 888
1020; email: drifters@drifters.co.za; www.drifters.co.za
**Felix Unite** tel: 021 425 5181; email: info@felixunite.com; www.felixunite.com
**Harvey World Travel** Hermanus; tel: 028 313 0526
**Karibu Safari** Natal; tel: 031 563 9774; or Johannesburg; tel: 011 462 6414; email:
karibu@karibu.co.za; www.karibu.co.za
**Umkulu Adventures** Tel: 021 853 7952; fax: 021 853 0153; email: umkulu@iafrica.com;
www.umkulu.co.za. A budget operator.
**Wildlife Africa** Tel/fax: 011 782 3410; email: info@wildlifeafrica.co.za; www.wildlifeafrica.co.za

## Based in Tanzania

**Swala Safaris** Arusha; tel: +255 37 250 8424; www.swalasafaris.com

# Practicalities

## PAPERWORK
### Passports

Make sure you have plenty of spare pages in your passport! Most visas will take up a whole page each, and sometimes the whole of the opposite page for entry and exit stamps when you reach the country. Some African countries are extremely 'stamp happy', and use up a lot of space. You may come across checkpoints where all your documents will be scrutinised and your passport stamped, sometimes over and over again. Some countries, like Egypt and Libya, put details of you and your vehicle in your passport as well as in the carnet (see below).

If you have dual nationality it may be worth taking both passports, as some visas may be cheaper for different nationalities. However this can sometimes give you more problems at borders where you need to produce both passports. Some officials may act very suspiciously over a person holding two passports. Remember you will not be allowed into certain countries if your passport has an Israeli stamp in it. Be aware too that a border stamp could imply a visit to Israel. This can happen at the Egyptian border south of Eilat, even where no Israeli stamps are shown in the passport.

### Passport photos

You will find when applying for visas that a lot of embassies demand two, and sometimes three, passport photos to attach to your visa application. We suggest you take around 30 passport photos with you; if you need more, it is relatively cheap to have your passport photo taken in most capital cities of Africa.

## Carnet de passage (carnet)
### What is the carnet?

The *carnet* is an essential and expensive document for everyone taking a vehicle (including a motorbike) across Africa. It is effectively the passport for the vehicle. Carnets are issued by national motoring organisations, eg: the RAC in the UK. This document allows you to import a vehicle into a country temporarily without paying customs duty – which in some cases can be many times its actual value.

Different countries have different regulations on the issue of carnets. Unfortunately, however, you cannot just shop around on the international markets, unless you go to the trouble of re-registering your vehicle. The carnet must be issued by an authority in the country where the vehicle is registered.

Although a carnet is likely to come in useful everywhere, it is not absolutely essential in North and West Africa. If you do not have a carnet here, a *laissez-passer* will be issued when you enter the country, for a small fee. You should be able to cover most of western and southern Africa without a carnet. In central and East African countries, a carnet is essential.

The existence of carnets is the main factor that makes selling a vehicle at the end of your journey far more difficult than you might think. When you sell, you have to get your carnet discharged by the local Customs. This means the import duty will need to be paid before the deal can go through. Make sure that all the paperwork is correctly processed, or you could face a large bill later on. If you do sell without discharging your carnet, the insurance company is still entitled to recoup the duty from you.

### How do I get a carnet and how much does it cost?

To obtain a carnet in the UK, you should contact Ms Sue Collins at the RAC (Royal Automobile Club). The address is RAC Motoring Services, Great Park Road, Bradley Stoke, Bristol, BS32 4QN; tel: 01454 208000 ext 33837; email: sjcollins@rac.co.uk; www.rac.co.uk. The cost of the carnet (around £75) depends on the number of pages you require, but is minor compared with the cost of the bond. You should make absolutely sure your carnet has been validated for all the countries you have requested. Customs officers will check carefully to ensure their country is listed. You may as well play safe and request absolutely every country you may possibly wish to visit – the number of countries covered does not affect the cost.

You will need either to lodge a bond equivalent to several times the current value of the vehicle, or to take out a special insurance policy to cover this amount. The bond required is one-and-a-half times the value of the vehicle for most countries, but up to five times the value for Egypt. For this reason, you should value the vehicle as low as possible. Current valuations can be obtained from motoring magazines – go for the lowest option.

If you lodge a cash bond, you must send a cheque for the full amount to the RAC, who will hold the money until you return the carnet correctly processed to them at the end of your trip. The money will be returned to you without interest.

If you go for the insurance option, insurance is available from Campbell Irvine Ltd (43 Earls Court Road, London W8 6EJ; tel: 020 7937 6981; fax: 020 7938 2250). There is no refund of the insurance premium.

At the time of our trip, carnets were no longer issued by the AA in the UK, but for reference, and in case the situation changes, their address is Automobile Association (UK), Fanum House, Basingstoke, Hampshire RG21 4EA; tel: 0870 600 0371; international tel: +44 191 223 7071; email: customer.services@theAA.com; www.theAA.co.uk.

### How is the carnet used en route?

The carnet is a large booklet containing a number of pages that are identical (except for the page numbers). Each page has three sections with details of the vehicle such as chassis number etc. Details about the owner are also shown. When you enter a country the Customs officer should stamp, remove and keep the third section. The first section should also be stamped in the entry part as a record. When you leave the country the second section should be stamped, removed and kept by the Customs. The official should also stamp the exit part on the first section, which provides a record for you and the motoring association who issued the carnet.

The idea of this is that the main Customs departments in the countries you visit will collect the two matching halves. If the two halves are not collected they will claim Customs duty through the issuing authority. (One might ponder how long these pieces of paper take to find their way to the central Customs of some countries!) It is therefore vital that you collect a complete set of entry and exit stamps – if you don't get an exit stamp for a country where you got an entry stamp, you could be in big trouble later on. It could also cost you a lot of money, because the carnet may not be cleared.

## International certificate for motor vehicles

Known as a *carte grise* (grey card) wherever French is spoken – even though it is white! – it costs around £10, and is a vital investment. Available from motoring organisations, it provides an official-looking summary of the details and serial numbers of your vehicle. In fact we were always asked to produce the original registration document for our vehicle, but it is definitely advisable to have both close at hand at every border, police checkpost or rain barrier you come across.

## Insurance
### Medical and personal belongings
Medical insurance is essential. Shop around for a good deal, as prices and cover can vary substantially. Travel insurance policies generally include some cover for personal belongings – but this is unlikely to include theft from a vehicle.

### Vehicle
Comprehensive vehicle insurance is less important. You can try to get insurance through Campbell Irvine, 43 Earls Court, Kensington, London, W8 6EJ; tel: 020 7937 6981. They are experienced in meeting the insurance needs of overlanders, though it is almost impossible nowadays to insure a vehicle for anywhere in Africa through a British insurance company. Currently a British comprehensive insurance policy should cover you for travel within most of Europe – check the back of your certificate.

Third-party vehicle insurance is not available in advance for most areas. It is both advisable and compulsory (policed to varying degrees) to buy third-party insurance locally. Once you reach Niger or Mali it is possible to buy a single policy which will cover you for the whole of West Africa. Similarly, you can get another single policy covering Central CFA countries (Cameroon, Chad, Central African Republic, Equatorial Guinea, Gabon and Congo). In Kenya, you can buy a policy to cover almost the whole of southern Africa, except Mozambique, though it may be marked as covered on the policy. Third-party insurance certificates are available at the border in some countries, including Zimbabwe and Zambia.

## International driving licence
These are available from national motoring organisations (such as the AA or RAC) on production of a current driving licence. You must get your international licence in the country where your licence was issued.

## Personal references
References can be useful if you are up against big bureaucratic problems. A reference from a bank or other financial representative can be used to prove that you will not be stranded through lack of funds. A character reference may also be helpful if you are in a tight corner. If at all possible, also get a character reference translated into French.

## MONEY
From a security point of view it makes sense to take most of your money as travellers' cheques, but in fact in many places they are worse than useless. In northern Africa, if you can change them at all, you will almost certainly get a far worse rate than for cash.

Generally you should take as much hard currency in cash as you feel you can safely carry. At borders you will often want to change a small amount of money before you get to a bank or official moneychanger where you can check the current correct rates. You may also wish to take advantage of changing money on the street (a decision for each individual to make – be extremely careful if you do). Some banks will not change travellers' cheques. In some areas there may be no banks at all and you may have to rely on changing money with local traders. One bank in Cameroon actually sent us to the man 'behind the onion sellers', who they said would give us a much better rate! Some countries will demand payment for certain services in hard currency.

It is worth bringing both small and large denomination notes with you. Be aware though that there are a number of fake US$100 bills in circulation; most banks will not accept them because of this. But if you are using a moneychanger, he will usually prefer larger notes such as US$50 or €50. Small notes are useful when you have to pay low charges in hard currency – otherwise you end up getting your change in local money. Bring a mix of currencies to take advantage of swings in exchange rates. You will also find that only certain currencies will be acceptable in some countries. The two most important currencies to carry are US dollars and euros. The dollar is the international currency of exchange, but in some banks in West Africa, particularly in small towns, euros are the only currency accepted.

Also make sure you have either euros or CFA francs with you when crossing the Sahara into Niger or Mali, as you must have these to pay various charges at the border. CFA (Communauté Fiscalière de l'Afrique de l'Ouest) is the common currency of the West African Monetary Unit. There are two CFAs – the West African CFA and the Central African CFA. They are not interchangeable, though they do have the same value. The latter is used in Cameroon, the Central African Republic (CAR), Chad, Congo, Equatorial Guinea and Gabon.

If you have travellers' cheques, make sure you carry your original purchase receipt, as many banks in Africa will not exchange them without it. You are not supposed to carry it with your travellers' cheques (for security), so, assuming you are travelling with someone else, you can carry theirs and they can carry yours. It's best to carry a photocopy and to keep the original securely elsewhere, hidden in the vehicle.

You do not necessarily need to take all the money you are likely to need. American Express cardholders can buy US$1,000 worth of travellers' cheques at any of their offices with a cheque guaranteed by an Amex card. It is sometimes even possible to buy hard currency with your credit and debit cards (shop around – different banks in the same town will have different rules). With the increasing number of ATMs (hole-in-the-wall cash machines) around the world, you can also withdraw money in local currency in many places in many countries.

You can also have money wired to a bank in Africa, although it can take some time – sometimes up to 12 days! If you have someone to take care of your financial affairs back home, they should be able to help to transfer funds if necessary – for example, quickly (but quite expensively) by either Western Union or Moneygram, both of which are increasingly represented throughout Africa. For peace of mind it's best to arrange for all your regular outgoings to be paid by direct debit while you're away, with that same someone perhaps checking your bank statements to ensure all is in order.

We recommend you to find a relatively safe place in the vehicle to hide some money – a mixture of hard currency and local currency of the country you are travelling in – just in case you are unfortunate enough to be robbed. But do remember where you have hidden it!

## VISAS

It will save you a lot of time en route if you can get visas for the first few countries you'll be visiting at the start of your trip, as well as any visas that are difficult to obtain in Africa. Libya, Sudan and Nigeria are notoriously difficult to get and are well worth getting before you leave. Even if they run out before you arrive, at least you have something in your passport and that may just make the difference. For Libya, though, you need an Arabic translation of your passport and an invitation from a Libyan travel agency, who must send a guide to escort you throughout your stay in the country.

For other countries, depending on the route you take and the time you intend to spend in Africa, more often than not your visa will have expired by the time you have arrived in that country.

It is also not necessarily a good idea to get every visa before you leave, as the political situation in Africa is forever changing and by the time you intend to visit that

## A VISA SAGA

Some things never change! It took six weeks to get a Sudan visa in 2004; but what happened on an overland trip to Africa in 1976? Some snippets from the diary...

### Bangui January 3

Crossed the Ubangui River, only to be turned back by the Zaïre Immigration. (The great Zaïre expedition falters before it's begun.)

Now trying for the Sudan visa, but the ambassador is a very bored fellow from Khartoum and has other ideas; he wants to wine and dine our girls before a visa is remotely possible. It's a good job the whole truck isn't loaded with females, or we'd never get out of here. Of course our CAR visa will expire before we get the Sudan one.

Managed a day trip down to the Congo border – that's another version of Zaïre run from Brazzaville not Kinshasa. That's if anyone is running Zaïre, with Mobutu Sese Seko Sese Banga Waza etc etc partying here in Bangui with Big Daddy Idi Amin and Emperor Bokassa.

Our co-driver and one client have succumbed to hepatitis and both had to fly out to Paris.

### January 9

Looks like the Sudanese Ambassador is getting bored with our girls; not that anything underhand appears to be going on. Encounter Overland, another party, are here now for visas, so they have become more interesting for the fellow. We might be out of here tomorrow with visas.

specific country, it might not be safe or convenient. Clearly, if you are cycling, travelling will take a lot longer than in a vehicle, making visa validity and timing even more important.

On both our recent expeditions we were able to get visas for all of the northern African countries in advance (down to and including Ethiopia and Gabon). Just be sure to make it clear when you intend to visit and they will normally post-date the visa. But be careful – we arrived in Ethiopia one day before our visa was issued, which caused some consternation at the border. Most visas are issued as you go, from embassies in capital cities or consulates in larger towns. Consulates are often a better bet as embassies can sometimes take several days to process an application – which can mean an enforced lengthy stay in an expensive city if you have several visas to get.

Generally speaking you should be able to pick up a visa in the capital of a neighbouring country – but do not rely on it. For example, there is no Cameroon consulate in N'Djamena, Chad, despite being only a few kilometres from the border. Major cities – Dakar, Abidjan, Nairobi, Dar es Salaam and Harare – have embassies for most other African states. Addis Ababa has the most representation when it comes to embassies and consulates, because of Ethiopia's early involvement with the OAU (Organisation of African Unity) and UNECA (United Nations Economic Commission of Africa) in 1958; most countries have some type of representation there. The moral: if all else fails, go to Addis Ababa.

If you can, write to the embassies of those countries you intend to visit several months before you leave, asking for information on the latest entry requirements (you can also pick up some interesting background material and tourist information from them). Where there is no embassy in your country, write to the nearest embassy. Nowadays you can often get this information from their website, and download visa application forms.

## Visa agencies

It is often easier, and indeed cheaper if you live outside the capital, to get your visas via a specialist visa agency. They will send a courier with your passport to the various embassies, saving you time and effort, and of course money if you are still at work. They may ask you to download the visa application forms from their website, or from the websites of the countries concerned. You then simply complete the forms and send them, together with a cheque and the relevant photographs, and of course your passport, to the agency by registered post. Then you can sit back and get on with the vehicle construction and design! Two visa agencies we can personally recommend are:

**Travcour** Tempo House, 15 Falcon Rd, Battersea, London SW11 2PJ; tel: 020 7223 5295; fax: 020 7738 2617; email: amanda@travcour.com; www.travcour.com

**Home Visas** 84 rue du Dôme, 92100 Boulogne Billancourt, France; tel: 01 46 21 80 40; fax: 01 46 21 01 15; email: contact@homevisas.com; www.homevisas.com

## Visa requirements

Specific visa requirements vary according to nationality. Most requirements for European travellers have now been harmonised – apart from special arrangements for UK travellers in most Commonwealth countries and similar arrangements for French nationals in former French colonies. Other travellers, such as those from Australia, New Zealand and the USA, will have different requirements. If in doubt, contact your own embassy for further information.

There are many varying factors that need to be considered when applying for a visa. Firstly, costs can vary considerably from one country to the next, depending on your nationality and where you applied for your visa. On reaching a certain border, even though your embassy, and every guidebook, has told you that you are exempt from needing a visa, you may find that you will still have to pay to have your entry stamped in your passport. This is true when it comes to most Commonwealth nationals. It is a good idea to ask other travellers or locals about the latest status on visa applications for the next country you're visiting. Remember that you may need a valid Yellow Fever vaccination certificate in order to obtain some visas.

## EMBASSIES AND CONSULATES

Below is a list of African embassies and consulates in the UK, South Africa, USA and Australia. A good website for further information is www.embassyworld.com, or try www.yellowpages.co.za for South African embassies. Note that the details below can change without notice and we recommend you to check these websites for up-to-date information.

You can also check the British Foreign Office website, **www.fco.gov.uk**, travel advice section, which lists the relevant London embassy or consulate for each country. The French equivalent is www.diplomatie.fr/voyageurs and the German is www.auswaertiges-amt.de.

### African embassies and consulates in the UK

**Algeria** (embassy) 54 Holland Park, London W11 3RS; tel: 020 7221 7800; (consulate) 6 Hyde Park Gate, London SW7 5EW; tel: 020 7589 6885

**Angola** 22 Dorset St, London W1U 6QY; tel: 020 7299 9850; fax: 020 7486 9397

**Benin** Dolphin House, 16 The Broadway, Stanmore, Middlesex HA7 4DW; tel: 020 8954 8800; fax: 020 8954 8844

**Botswana** 6 Stratford Pl, London W1C 1AY; tel: 020 7499 0031 and 020 7647 1000

**Cameroon** 84 Holland Park, London W11 3SB; tel: 020 7727 0771–3; fax: 020 7792 9353

**Cape Verde** 18–20 Stanley St, Liverpool L1 6AF; tel: 0151 236 0206; fax: 0151 255 1314

## UK EMBASSY ADDRESSES

Embassy addresses and telephone numbers in the UK are regularly updated and published by HMSO in *The London Diplomatic List* (ISBN 0 11 591746 2). The closest embassy in Europe is normally given for countries which have no embassy in the UK.

**Congo** The Arena, 24 Southwark Bridge Rd, London SE1 9HF; tel: 020 7922 0695
**Democratic Republic of the Congo** (embassy) 281 Gray's Inn Rd, London WC1X 8QF; tel: 020 7278 9825; fax: 020 7278 8497; (consulate) 2 Lowndes St, London SW1X 9ET; tel: 020 7235 9719
**Egypt** 26 South St, London W1Y 6DD; tel: 020 7499 2401; fax: 020 7491 1542
**Eritrea** 96 White Lion St, London N1 9PF; tel: 020 7713 0096; fax: 020 7713 0161
**Ethiopia** 17 Prince's Gate, London SW7 1PZ; tel: 020 7589 7212–5
**Gabon** 27 Elvaston Pl, London SW7 5NL; tel: 020 7823 9986; fax: 020 7584 0047
**The Gambia** 57 Kensington Ct, London W8 5DG; tel: 020 7937 6316–8; fax: 020 7937 9095
**Ghana** 13 Belgrave Sq, London SW1X 8PN; tel: 020 7235 4142; fax: 020 7245 9552
**Guinea** 20 Upper Grosvenor St, London W1K 7PB; tel: 020 7409 3279
**Ivory Coast** 2 Upper Belgrave St, London SW1X 8BJ; tel: 020 7201 9601
**Kenya** 45 Portland Pl London W1N 4AS; tel: 020 7636 2371–5
**Lesotho** 7 Chesham Pl, London SW1 8HN; tel: 020 7235 5686; fax: 020 7235 5023
**Liberia** 23 Fitzroy Sq, London W1T 6EW; tel: 020 7388 5489
**Libya** 61–62 Ennismore Gdns, London SW7 1NH; tel: 020 7589 6120; fax: 020 7589 6087
**Malawi** 33 Grosvenor St, London W1K 4QT; tel: 020 7491 4172–7
**Mauritania** 8 Carlos Pl, Mayfair, London W1K 3AS; tel: 020 7478 9323; fax: 020 7478 9339
**Morocco** 49 Queen's Gate Gdns, London SW7 5NE; tel: 020 7581 5001–4; fax: 020 7225 3862
**Mozambique** 21 Fitzroy Sqe, London W1T 6EL; tel: 020 7383 3800; fax: 020 7383 3801
**Namibia** 5 Chandos St, London W1G 9DW; tel: 020 7636 6244; fax: 020 7637 5694
**Nigeria** (embassy) Nigeria House, 9 Northumberland Av, London WC2N 5BX; tel: 020 7839 1244; fax: 020 7839 8746; (consulate) 56–57 Fleet St, London EC4Y 1JU; tel: 020 7353 3776
**Rwanda** 120–122 Seymour St, London W1H 1NR; tel: 020 7224 9832; fax: 020 7724 8642
**Senegal** 39 Marloes Rd, London W8 6LA; tel: 020 7938 4048; fax: 020 7938 2546
**Sierra Leone** Oxford Circus House, 245 Oxford St, London W1D 2LX; tel: 020 7287 9884; fax: 020 7734 3822
**South Africa** South Africa House, Trafalgar Sq, London WC2N 5DP; tel: 020 7930 4488; fax: 020 7321 0835
**Sudan** 3 Cleveland Row, London SW1A 1DD; tel: 020 7839 8080; fax: 020 7839 7560
**Swaziland** 20 Buckingham Gate, London SW1E 6LB; tel: 020 7630 6611; fax: 020 7630 6564
**Tanzania** 43 Hertford St, London W1J 7DB; tel: 020 7499 8951–4; fax: 020 7491 9321
**Tunisia** 29 Prince's Gate, London SW7 1QG; tel: 020 7584 8117; fax: 020 7225 2884
**Uganda** Uganda House, 58–59 Trafalgar Sq, London WC2N 5DX; tel: 020 7839 5783; fax: 020 7839 8925
**Zambia** 2 Palace Gate, London W8 5NG; tel: 020 7589 6655; fax: 020 7581 1353
**Zimbabwe** Zimbabwe House, 429 Strand, London WC2R 0JR; tel: 020 7836 7755; fax: 020 7379 1167

## African embassies and consulates in France and Belgium

**Burkina Faso** 16 Pl Guy d'Arezzo, 1180 Brussels, Belgium; tel: 02 345 99 12
**Burundi** Sq Marie Louise 46, 1040 Brussels, Belgium; tel: 02 230 45 35
**Central African Republic** 30 Rue des Perchamps, 75016 Paris, France; tel: 01 42 24 42 56
**Chad** Bd Lambermont 52, 1030 Brussels, Belgium; tel: 02 215 19 75

**Djibouti** 26 Rue Emile Ménier, 75116 Paris, France; tel: 01 47 27 49 22
**Equatorial Guinea** 29 Bd de Courcelles, 75800 Paris, France; tel: 06 61 40 14 01; fax: 01 42 25 23 12
**Guinea Bissau** 94 Rue St Lazare, Paris, France; tel: 01 45 26 18 51
**Mali** Av Molière 487, 1050 Brussels, Belgium; tel: 02 345 74 32; fax: 02 344 57 00
**Niger** 154 Rue de Longchamp, 75116 Paris, France; tel: 01 45 04 80 60
**Rwanda** Av des Fleurs 1, 1150 Brussels, Belgium; tel: 02 763 07 38; fax: 02 763 07 53; also 12 Rue Jadin, 75017 Paris, France; tel: 01 47 66 54 20; fax: 01 42 27 74 69

## African embassies and consulates in South Africa

**Algeria** 348 Hill St, Hatfield, Pretoria 0083; tel: 012 342 5074
**Angola** 153 Oliver St, Brooklyn, Pretoria; tel: 012 342 0049
**Botswana** 24 Amos St, Colbyn, Pretoria; tel: 012 430 9640
**Burundi** 1090 Arcadia St, Hatfield, Pretoria; tel: 012 342 4881
**Congo** 960 Arcadia St, Hatfield, Pretoria; tel: 012 342 5508
**Democratic Republic of the Congo** 960 Arcadia St, Hatfield, Pretoria; tel: 012 342 5508
**Egypt** 270 Bourke St, Muckleneuk, Pretoria; tel: 012 343 1590
**Ghana** Pretoria; tel: 012 342 5847
**Ivory Coast** Hatfield, Pretoria 0083; tel: 012 342 6913
**Kenya** 302 Brooks St, Menlo Park, Pretoria; tel: 012 342 5066
**Lesotho** 1 T Edison St, Pretoria; tel: 012 460 7640
**Malawi** 209 Bauhinia Rd, Waterkloof Heights, Pretoria; tel: 012 347 6899
**Mali** Hatfield, Pretoria 0083; tel: 012 342 7464
**Morocco** Pretoria; tel: 012 343 0230
**Mozambique** 529 Edmund St, Arcadia, Pretoria; tel: 011 336 1819
**Nigeria** 142 Oudeberg Rd, Waterkloof Heights, Pretoria; tel: 012 347 3011
**Rwanda** 1090 Arcadia St, Hatfield, Pretoria 0083; tel: 012 342 1740; fax: 012 342 1743
**Sudan** 1203 Pretorius St, Hatfield, Pretoria; tel: 012 342 0599
**Swaziland** 715 Government Av, Arcadia, Pretoria; tel: 012 344 1917
**Tanzania** 822 George Av, Arcadia, Pretoria; tel: 012 342 4371
**Zambia** 570 Ziervogel St, Arcadia, Pretoria; tel: 012 326 1847
**Zimbabwe** 798 Merton Av, Arcadia, Pretoria; tel: 012 342 5125; fax: 012 342 5126

## African embassies and consulates in the USA

**Algeria** 2118 Kalorama Rd, NW, Washington DC, 20008; tel: 202 265 2800; fax: 202 667 2174
**Angola** 866 United Nations Pl, Suite 552, New York, 10017; tel: 212 861 5656
**Benin** 2737 Cathedral Av, NW, Washington DC, 20008; tel: 202 232 6656–8; fax: 265 1996
**Botswana** 3400 International Dr, Suite 7M, NW, Washington DC, 20008; tel: 202 244 4990/1; fax: 202 244 4164
**Burkina Faso** 2340 Massachusetts Av, NW, Washington DC, 20008; tel: 202 332 5577/6895; fax: 202 667 1882
**Burundi** Suite 212, 2233 Wisconsin Av, NW, Washington DC, 20007; tel: 202 342 2574; fax: 202 342 2578
**Cameroon** 2349 Massachusetts Av, NW, Washington DC, 20008; tel: 202 265 8790–4; fax: 202 387 3826
**Cape Verde** 3145 Massachusetts Av, NW, Washington DC, 20007; tel: 202 965 6820; fax: 202 965 1207
**Central African Republic** 1618 22nd St, NW, Washington DC, 20008; tel: 202 483 7800/1; fax: 332 9893
**Chad** 2002 R St, NW, Washington DC, 20009; tel: 202 462 4009; fax: 202 265 1937
**Congo** 1800 New Hampshire Av, NW, Washington DC, 20009; tel: 202 234 7690–1; fax: 202 237 0748

**Democratic Republic of the Congo** 4891 Colorado Av, NW, Washington DC, 20011; tel: 202 726 5500; fax: 202 726 1860

**Djibouti** Suite 515, 1156 15th St, NW, Washington DC, 20005; tel: 202 331 0270; fax: 202 331 0302

**Egypt** 3521 International Court, NW, Washington DC, 20008; tel: 202 895 5400; fax: 202 244 4319/5131. Consular section: tel: 202 966 6342

**Equatorial Guinea** Suite 405, 2522 K St, NW, Washington DC, 20005; tel: 202 393 0525; fax: 202 393 0348

**Eritrea** 1708 New Hampshire Av, NW, Washington DC, 20009; tel: 202 319 1991; fax: 202 319 1304

**Ethiopia** 2134 Kalorama Rd, NW, Washington DC, 20008; tel: 202 234 2281/2; fax: 202 238 7950

**Gabon** Suite 200, 2034 20th St, NW, Washington DC, 20009; tel: 202 797 1000; fax: 202 332 0668

**Gambia** 820 Second Av, 9th Floor, New York 10017; tel: 212 949 6640; fax: 212 808 4975

**Ghana** 19 E 47th St, New York 10017; tel: 212 832 1300

**Guinea** 2112 Leroy Pl, NW, Washington DC, 20008; tel: 202 483 9420; fax: 202 483 8688

**Guinea Bissau** 1511 K St, NW, Washington DC, 20005; tel: 202 347 3950; fax: 202 347 3954

**Ivory Coast** 2424 Massachusetts Av, NW, Washington DC, 20008; tel: 202 797 0300

**Kenya** 2249 R St, NW, Washington DC, 20008; tel: 202 387 6101; fax: 202 462 3829

**Lesotho** 2511 Massachusetts Av, NW, Washington DC, 20008; tel: 202 797 5533–6; fax: 202 234 6815

**Liberia** 5201 16th St, NW, Washington DC, 20011; tel: 202 723 0440

**Malawi** 2408 Massachusetts Av, NW, Washington DC, 20008; tel: 202 797 1007

**Mali** 2130 R St, NW, Washington DC, 20008; tel: 202 332 2249 or 939 8950

**Mauritania** 2129 Leroy Pl, NW, Washington DC, 20008; tel: 202 232 5700; fax: 202 232 5701

**Morocco** 1601 21st St, NW, Washington DC, 20009; tel: 202 462 7979–82; fax: 202 265 0161

**Mozambique** Suite 570, 1990 M St, NW, Washington DC, 20036; tel: 202 293 7146; fax: 202 835 0245

**Namibia** 1605 New Hampshire Av, NW, Washington DC, 20009; tel: 202 986 0540; fax: 202 986 0443

**Niger** 2204 R St, NW, Washington DC, 20008; tel: 202 483 4224–7; fax: 202 483 3169

**Nigeria** 3519 International Court, NW, Washington DC, 20008; tel: 202 822 1500

**Rwanda** 1714 New Hampshire Av, NW, Washington DC, 20009; tel: 202 232 2882; fax: 202 232 4544

**Senegal** 2112 Wyoming Av, NW, Washington DC, 20008; tel: 202 234 0540/1; fax: 202 293 4198

**South Africa** 3051 Massachusetts Av, NW, Washington DC, 20008; tel: 202 232 4400; fax: 202 265 1607

**Sudan** 2210 Massachusetts Av, NW, Washington DC, 20008; tel: 202 338 8565–70; fax: 202 667 2406

**Swaziland** 3400 International Drive, Suite 3M, NW, Washington DC, 20008; tel: 202 362 6683–5; fax: 244 8059

**Tanzania** 2139 R St, NW, Washington DC, 20008; tel: 202 939 6125; fax: 202 797 7408

**Togo** 2208 Massachusetts Av, NW, Washington DC, 20008; tel: 202 234 4212; fax: 202 232 3190

**Tunisia** 1515 Massachusetts Av, NW, Washington DC, 20005; tel: 202 862 1850

**Uganda** 5909 16th St, NW, Washington DC, 20011; tel: 202 726 7100–2 or 202 726 0416

**Zambia** 2419 Massachusetts Av, NW, Washington DC, 20008; tel: 202 265 9717–9; fax: 202 332 0826

**Zimbabwe** 1608 New Hampshire Av, NW, Washington DC, 20009; tel: 202 332 7100; fax: 202 483 9326

# African embassies and consulates in Australia

**Botswana** 52 Culgoa Circuit, O'Malley, ACT 2606; tel: 026 290 7500

**Cameroon** PO Box 150, Wahroonga, NSW 2076; tel: 029 989 8414

**Egypt** 1 Darwin Av, Yarralumla, ACT, 2600; tel: 026 273 4437; fax: 026 273 4279
**Eritrea** 16 Bulwarra Close, O'Malley, ACT 2606; tel: 026 290 1991; fax: 026 286 8902
**Ethiopia** 38 Johnston St, Fitzroy, Victoria, 3065, PO Box 2088; tel: 039 417 3419
**Kenya** 3rd Floor QBE Building, 33–35 Ainslie Av, Canberra, ACT 2601, GPO Box 1990,
Canberra City, ACT 2601; tel: 026 247 4788; fax: 026 257 6613
**Lesotho** 294 Old South Head Rd, Watsons Bay, NSW 2030; tel: 029 398 3798; fax: 029 247 6384
**Nigeria** 26 Guilfoyle St, Yarralumla, ACT 2600, PO Box 241, Civic Square, ACT 2608; tel: 026
282 7411; fax: 026 282 8471
**South Africa** Corner State Circle and Rhodes Pl, Yarralumla, ACT 2600; tel: 026 273 2424; fax:
026 273 3543
**Zimbabwe** 11 Culgoa Circuit, O'Malley, ACT 2606; tel: 026 286 2281; fax: 026 290 1680

# HEALTH
*with Dr Jane Wilson-Howarth and Dr Felicity Nicholson*

Nomad Pharmacy in the UK supply all organised tours with their medical kits and are
experts in what you will need when travelling in Africa. You can choose from a mini-kit
or full truck kit. A full medical kit from Nomad Pharmacy costs about US$500 (3–4
Wellington Terrace, Turnpike Lane, London N8 0PX; tel: 020 8889 7014).

We would also suggest that you go over your previous medical history with your local
GP and take the appropriate medication with you. Hopefully you won't be needing it –
but better be safe than sorry.

For women travellers it's important to carry all relevant medication regarding vaginal
infections. See elsewhere for more detailed information on health and women's issues.

The medical kit list on pages 294–7 includes everything we think you might need, but
this does not necessarily mean that every item needs to be taken with you. The list should
be discussed with either your local GP or a travel clinic, who can advise you on what you
are more likely to need. Malaria, bilharzia, diarrhoea of varying kinds, constipation, skin
infections, flu and irritable eyes and ears from the dust are the problems you need to
consider. Most of the travellers we spoke to while on the road had suffered from at least
one of these.

It is also a good idea to attend a first-aid course for your own safety and security. In
terms of intravenous (IV) treatment, it's best not to undertake this unless you are a
qualified medic, doctor or nurse. Most travel kits include IV treatment packs as many
medical institutions in Africa do not have these supplies. If you are seriously injured you
should always take all of your own medical equipment with you. Medical staff in Africa
do not find this offensive and in fact welcome good equipment.

Carry a medical self-help book with you. The one most travellers carry is *Where
there is no doctor – a village health care handbook* by David Werner, Carol Truman and Jane
Maxwell. This book can be ordered through amazon.co.uk and is also available at
Nomad Pharmacy. There are many other choices of self-help books, so you should
shop around and take whichever one suits your needs. You may also find it useful to
ask your local pharmacy for a copy of the BNF (*British National Formulary*). This book
documents all the medicines available in Britain and their prescribed doses for the
relevant diseases. It is updated every few months so you should be able to get a
recently expired copy.

# Before you go
## Vaccinations

To ensure a healthy trip to Africa check on your immunisation status. You must be up to
date on **tetanus** (ten-yearly), **polio** (ten-yearly), **diphtheria** (ten-yearly), **hepatitis A**
and **typhoid**. For many parts of Africa vaccinations against **yellow fever**, **meningitis**,
**hepatitis B** and **rabies** are also needed. The majority of travellers are advised to be

vaccinated against hepatitis A with a hepatitis A vaccine (eg: Havrix Monodose, Avaxim). One dose of vaccine lasts for one year and can be boosted to give protection for up to 20 years. The vaccine can also be used close to the time of departure and has replaced gamma globulin, which should no longer be used.

The newer typhoid vaccines last for three years and are about 85% effective. You should have this unless you are leaving within a few days for a trip of a week or less, when the vaccine would not be effective in time.

Oral cholera vaccine (Dukoral) is now available in the UK and is recommended for extended trips to West Africa or for shorter trips in areas of extremely poor hygiene. Older travellers or those with chronic health problems may also be recommended to take the vaccine. A primary course (adults and children over six years old) consists of two doses of vaccine taken between one and six weeks apart, the scond dose being taken at least a week before entering the infected area. The vaccine gives good protection for up to two years. Even if the cholera vaccine is not recommended you may be required to produce a cholera exemption certificate when crossing land borders in sub-Saharan Africa and it may also be required by individual countries (eg: Tanzania, Zanzibar and Uganda). Cholera certificates can be obtained from your local travel clinic who are aware of the obstacles you might face in Africa.

Hepatitis B vaccination should be considered for longer trips (two months or more) or for those working in situations where risk of contact with blood is increased. Three injections are ideal, which can be given over a minimum of 21 days prior to travel.

Vaccination against tuberculosis is also advised for trips of two months or more and should be taken at least six weeks before departure.

Go to a travel clinic a couple of months before departure to arrange all these.

## Malaria prevention

There is no vaccine against malaria, but using prophylactic drugs and preventing mosquito bites will considerably reduce the risk of contracting it. Seek professional advice for the best anti-malarial drugs to take. Mefloquine (Lariam) is the most effective prophylactic agent for most countries in sub-Saharan Africa. If this drug is suggested and you have never used it before then you should start two to three weeks before departure to check that it suits you. About 25% of people will experience some side effects but these are nearly always not serious. Stop immediately if it seems to cause depression or anxiety, visual or hearing disturbances, fits, severe headaches or changes in heart rhythm. Anyone who is pregnant, has been treated for depression or psychiatric problems, has diabetes controlled by oral therapy, is epileptic (or has suffered fits in the past) or has a close blood relative who is epileptic should not take mefloquine. Malarone is considered to be an effective alternative to Lariam. However, this drug is expensive and is therefore better for shorter trips. Malarone need only be started one to two days before arrival into a malarial area. It is taken daily and is continued for seven days after leaving the area. It is currently licensed in the UK for trips up to three months. It is also available in paediatric form for children under 40 kg. It is prescribed by weight so it is helpful to know how much your children weigh.

The antibiotic doxycycline (100mg daily) is considered to be a viable alternative when Lariam or Malarone cannot be used. (It also has the coincidental benefit of providing some protection against tummy bugs.) Like Malarone it need only be started one to two days before arrival, it is taken daily but needs to be continued for four weeks after leaving the malarial area. It may also be used by travellers with epilepsy, unlike Lariam, although the antiepileptic therapy may make it less effective. Users are warned that allergic skin reactions in sunlight can occur in about 1–3% of people. The drug should be stopped if this happens. Women using the oral contraceptive should use an additional method of protection for the first four weeks when using doxycycline.

All prophylactic agents should be taken with or after the evening meal, washed down with plenty of fluid and continued for the recommended time after leaving Africa. Chloroquine (Nivaquine, Avloclor) and proguanil (Paludrine) are considered to be ineffective in sub-Saharan Africa and are only ever used now as a last resort.

There is no malaria above 3,000m; at intermediate altitudes (1,800–3,000m) there is a low but finite risk. Much of South Africa is free from the disease, although it is a risk in some parts; elsewhere the risk to travellers is great. It is unwise to travel to malarial areas of Africa when pregnant or with children: the risk of malaria is considerable and such travellers are likely to succumb rapidly to the disease.

Whether or not you are taking anti-malaria tablets, it is important to protect yourself from mosquito bites, so keep your repellent stick or roll-on to hand at all times. Some travellers carry a course of malaria treatment with them. Self treatment is not without risks and diagnosing malaria is not necessarily easy, which is why consulting a doctor is the best option. If you are going somewhere remote in an area where malaria is a high risk, you probably have to assume that any high fever for more than a few hours is due to malaria. At present Malarone is considered the best treatment, but this will depend on whether you are taking prophylactic anti-malarial tablets and if so which ones. It is always wise to check for up-to-date advice before purchasing any malarial medication. Current experts differ on the costs and benefits of self-treatment, but agree that it may lead to people taking drugs they do not need. Discuss your trip with a specialist to determine your particular needs and risks.

Be aware that no prophylactic is 100% protective, but those on prophylactics who are unlucky enough to catch malaria are less likely to get rapidly into serious trouble. See also page 108.

### Personal matters

Remember to have a dental check before you leave home. Read *Safe sex* on page 107; if you'll be using a coil, get it fitted at least six weeks before departure. Take whatever tampons you may need initially; see page 108. Finally, see the advice about multivitamins under *Weight loss and gain* (page 107).

## Travel clinics and health information

A full list of current travel clinic websites worldwide is available on www.istm.org/. For other journey preparation information, consult www.tripprep.com. Information about various medications may be found on www.emedicine.com.

## UK

**Berkeley Travel Clinic** 32 Berkeley St, London W1J 8EL (near Green Park tube station); tel: 020 7629 6233

**British Airways Travel Clinic and Immunisation Service** There are two BA clinics in London, both on tel: 0845 600 2236; www.ba.com/travelclinics. Appointments only Mon–Fri 09.00–16.30 at 101 Cheapside, London EC2V 6DT; or walk-in service Mon–Fri 09.30–17.30, Sat 10.00–16.00 at 213 Piccadilly, London W1J 9HQ. Apart from providing inoculations and malaria prevention, they sell a variety of health-related goods.

**Cambridge Travel Clinic** 48a Mill Rd, Cambridge CB1 2AS; tel: 01223 367362; email: enquiries@cambridgetravelclinic.co.uk; www.cambridgetravelclinic.co.uk. Open Tue–Fri 12.00–19.00, Sat 10.00–16.00.

**Edinburgh Travel Clinic** Regional Infectious Diseases Unit, Ward 41 OPD, Western General Hospital, Crewe Rd South, Edinburgh EH4 2UX; tel: 0131 537 2822; www.link.med.ed.ac.uk/ridu. Travel helpline 0906 589 0380) open weekdays 09.00–12.00. Provides inoculations and anti-malarial prophylaxis and advises on travel-related health risks.

**Fleet Street Travel Clinic** 29 Fleet St, London EC4Y 1AA; tel: 020 7353 5678; www.fleetstreetclinic.com. Vaccinations, travel products and latest advice.

**Hospital for Tropical Diseases Travel Clinic** Mortimer Market Building, Capper St (off Tottenham Ct Rd), London WC1E 6AU; tel: 020 7388 9600; www.thehtd.org. Offers consultations and advice, and is able to provide all necessary drugs and vaccines for travellers. Runs a healthline 0906 133 7733 for country-specific information and health hazards. Also stocks nets, water-purification equipment and personal protection measures.

**Interhealth Worldwide** Partnership House, 157 Waterloo Rd, London SE1 8US; tel: 020 7902 9000; www.interhealth.org.uk. Competitively priced, one-stop travel health service. All profits go to their affiliated company, InterHealth, which provides health care for overseas workers on Christian projects.

**MASTA** (Medical Advisory Service for Travellers Abroad) London School of Hygiene and Tropical Medicine, Keppel St, London WC1 7HT; tel: 0906 550 1402; www.masta.org. Individually tailored health briefs available for a fee, with up-to-date information on how to stay healthy, inoculations and what to bring. There are currently 30 MASTA pre-travel clinics in Britain. Call 0870 241 6843 or check online for the nearest. Clinics also sell malaria prophylaxis memory cards, treatment kits, bednets, net treatment kits.

**NHS travel website** www.fitfortravel.scot.nhs.uk, provides country-by-country advice on immunisation and malaria, plus details of recent developments, and a list of relevant health organisations.

**Nomad Travel Store/Clinic** 3–4 Wellington Terrace, Turnpike Lane, London N8 0PX; tel: 020 8889 7014; travel-health line (office hours only) 0906 863 3414; email: sales@nomadtravel.co.uk; www.nomadtravel.co.uk. Also at 40 Bernard St, London WC1N 1LJ; tel: 020 7833 4114; 52 Grosvenor Gardens, London SW1W 0AG; tel: 020 7823 5823; and 43 Queens Rd, Bristol BS8 1QH; tel: 0117 922 6567. For health advice, equipment such as mosquito nets and other anti-bug devices, and an excellent range of adventure travel gear.

**Trailfinders Travel Clinic** 194 Kensington High St, London W8 7RG; tel: 020 7938 3999; www.trailfinders.com/clinic.htm

**Travelpharm** The Travelpharm website, www.travelpharm.com, offers up-to-date guidance on travel-related health and has a range of medications available through their online mini-pharmacy.

## Irish Republic

**Tropical Medical Bureau** Grafton Street Medical Centre, Grafton Buildings, 34 Grafton St, Dublin 2; tel: 1 671 9200; www.tmb.ie. A useful website specific to tropical destinations. Also check website for locations of other bureaux throughout Ireland.

## USA

**Centers for Disease Control** 1600 Clifton Rd, Atlanta, GA 30333; tel: 800 311 3435; travellers' health hotline 888 232 3299; www.cdc.gov/travel. The central source of travel information in the USA. The invaluable *Health Information for International Travel*, published annually, is available from the Division of Quarantine at this address.

**Connaught Laboratories** PO Box 187, Swiftwater, PA 18370; tel: 800 822 2463. They will send a free list of specialist tropical-medicine physicians in your state.

**IAMAT** (International Association for Medical Assistance to Travelers) 1623 Military Rd, 279, Niagara Falls, NY14304-1745; tel: 716 754 4883; email: info@iamat.org; www.iamat.org. A non-profit organisation that provides lists of English-speaking doctors abroad.

**International Medicine Center** 920 Frostwood Drive, Suite 670, Houston, TX 77024; tel: 713 550 2000; www.traveldoc.com.

## Canada

**IAMAT** Suite 1, 1287 St Clair Av W, Toronto, Ontario M6E 1B8; tel: 416 652 0137; www.iamat.org

**TMVC** (Travel Doctors Group) Sulphur Springs Rd, Ancaster, Ontario; tel: 905 648 1112; www.tmvc-group.com

## Australia, New Zealand, Singapore

**TMVC** Tel: 1300 65 88 44; www.tmvc.com.au. Twenty-three clinics in Australia, New Zealand and Singapore including:

*Auckland* Canterbury Arcade, 170 Queen St, Auckland; tel: 9 373 3531

*Brisbane* 6th floor, 247 Adelaide St, Brisbane, QLD 4000; tel: 7 3221 9066

*Melbourne* 393 Little Bourke St, 2nd floor, Melbourne, VIC 3000; tel: 3 9602 5788

*Sydney* Dymocks Building, 7th Floor, 428 George St, Sydney, NSW 2000; tel: 2 9221 7133

**IAMAT** PO Box 5049, Christchurch 5, New Zealand; www.iamat.org

## South Africa

**Glaxo Wellcome** Experts in malarial prophylactics. PO Box 3388, Halfway House, Johannesburg 1685; tel: 011 403 3586

**SAA-Netcare Travel Clinics** Private Bag X34, Benmore 2010; www.travelclinic.co.za. Clinics throughout South Africa.

**TMVC** 113 DF Malan Drive, Roosevelt Park, Johannesburg; tel: 011 888 7488; www.tmvc.com.au. Consult the website for details of eight other clinics in South Africa.

## Switzerland

**IAMAT** 57 Chemin des Voirets, 1212 Grand Lancy, Geneva; www.iamat.org

# In Africa
## Health, food and hygiene

This is one area where it can be difficult to strike the right balance between justified concern and outright paranoia. A lot of common problems can be avoided by being sensible about hygiene. There will, of course, be times when you are more or less dependent on local standards of hygiene. Some health guides for travellers visiting out-of-the-way places will frighten you half to death. Basically you will find your own levels of hygiene and personal care – and even then your standards will vary according to the different conditions you find yourself in. Most of the time all you need is common sense.

Do not hesitate to see a doctor or take advantage of medical insurance cover if you think there is something really wrong with you. Some countries have perfectly adequate hospitals and health clinics; some facilities are so basic they will make you cringe. Trust your judgement, but do not assume that health care will be bad just because it is African – after all, the doctors there are far more accustomed to tropical diseases than are those at home.

### Water sterilisation

If you drink contaminated water, you will probably get sick, so try to drink from safe sources. Water should have been brought to the boil, passed through a good bacteriological filter or purified with iodine. Chlorine tablets (eg: Puritabs) are also adequate, although theoretically less effective and they taste nastier.

If you buy mineral water, make sure the bottle is properly sealed. Some mineral water has been found to be contaminated in many developing countries and may be no safer than tap water.

### Hygiene

One of the main problems you will face is being able to keep clean with only a limited amount of water after a hard day's driving with sweat, dust and sand clinging to every part of your body. Following the advice below will also help prevent dysentery:

• Carry a small, compact flannel with you and use a minimal amount of water, but still wipe the day's activities from your body.

- Disinfectant soap, like Dettol, can be found throughout Africa.
- Always wash your hands after visiting the local market and handling raw meat and vegetables, as well as before eating or drinking.
- When using a cutting board or any other surface to cut meat or vegetables, always use one side for meat and the other for vegetables.
- Wash any vegetables you want to eat raw in potassium permanganate or Milton, and always peel fruit before eating.
- When there is plenty of water available, give all your cutlery a good wash in hot water just to sterilise everything. This is a general rule in terms of clothing, too, but often not possible, unless you are intending to boil loads of water.

## Day-to-day health issues
### Weight loss and gain
Travelling independently can cause weight loss and, while some lose weight, others gain it. Constipation is a common problem among women, particularly on organised tours. You are much less likely to lose weight on an organised truck tour. In fact, the high quality of the three square meals per day, as well as the lack of activity, sitting and driving all day, mean you are more likely to put on the pounds rather than lose them. Remember to bring some laxatives with you. If you find yourself losing weight, three square meals, if at all possible, should keep the weight loss under control and a multivitamin supplement will ensure your body gets any vitamins missing from your diet. Buy them before you leave home.

### Dental care
Toothpaste and toothbrushes are available in cities, but err on the side of caution and take everything you are likely to need. When you see some of the African versions of toothbrushes you'll be glad you did! Oil of cloves is good for numbing toothache, though of course it will not solve any real problems.

### Safe sex
Travel is a time when we may enjoy sexual adventures, especially when alcohol reduces inhibitions. Remember the risks of sexually transmitted infection are high, whether you have sexual intercourse with fellow travellers or with locals. About 40% of HIV infections in British heterosexuals are acquired abroad. Use condoms or femidoms. If you notice any genital ulcers or discharge get treatment promptly.

Condoms are usually extremely difficult to get hold of in Africa, though there is reputed to be a black-market stall in Abidjan that sells nothing else. And can they be trusted not to burst at that critical moment? Generally you would be advised to bring what you are likely to need – and more. In the more remote areas, thorough searches at border posts which concentrate on your washbags and medical box do so for a reason. Presumably the opportunity to relieve travellers of the odd three-pack of condoms is regarded as one of the perks of the job.

If you are only having sexual intercourse with your regular partner, condoms are not your only choice of contraception.

If you are taking the pill, you should refer to the guidance set out on the packet for storage (normally in a cool, dry place) and follow it carefully.

If you decide on a coil, it must be fitted at least six weeks before you leave, to check you are not at risk from infection or expulsion. Some women experience heavy and painful periods with a coil.

You can also use a cap, which can be sterilised easily in a mug with an ordinary water-purifying tablet. But you should think about the number of times you will be using communal toilet facilities or washing in the open air before making a decision to rely only on your cap while you are away.

## QUICK TICK REMOVAL

African ticks are not the prolific disease transmitters they are in the Americas, but they may occasionally spread disease. Lyme disease has now been recorded in Africa, and tick-bite fever also occurs. This is a mild, flu-like illness, but still worth avoiding. If you get the tick off whole and promptly the chances of disease transmission are reduced to a minimum.

Manoeuvre your finger and thumb so that you can pinch the tick's mouthparts, as close to your skin as possible, and slowly and steadily pull away at right angles to your skin. This often hurts. Jerking or twisting will increase the chances of damaging the tick, which in turn increases the chances of disease transmission, as well as leaving the mouthparts behind. Once the tick is off, dowse the little wound with alcohol (local spirit, whisky or similar are excellent) or iodine. An area of spreading redness around the bite site, or a rash or fever coming on a few days or more after the bite, should stimulate a trip to a doctor.

One other possibility is to have an injectable contraceptive (Depo-Provera) which will last for two or more months. Side effects can include irregular periods, or no periods at all – not necessarily a disadvantage on the road. Fertility can also be delayed for a year after the last injection. Another disadvantage could be needing another injection when you are miles away from anywhere.

If you are thinking of changing your normal method of contraception talk this over in plenty of time with your doctor.

### Tampons and sanitary towels

You will be able to buy tampons and sanitary towels in most big towns in West Africa and more easily in East and southern Africa. Problem areas are North Africa, desert and other remote areas like the Congo and Central African Republic. Take enough supplies to get you through early problem areas and you will be able to stock up later on. If you have a definite brand preference and lots of spare space it's a good idea to bring extra supplies.

It might also be worth considering a re-usable menstrual sponge, though if you have not used one before make sure you practise before you leave so you know exactly what is involved.

### Avoiding insect bites
### Mosquitoes

It is crucial to avoid mosquito bites between dusk and dawn. As the sun is going down, put on long clothes and apply repellent on any exposed flesh. This will protect you from malaria, elephantiasis and a range of nasty insect-borne viruses. Malaria mosquitoes are voracious and hunt at ankle-level, so it is worth applying repellent under socks too. Sleep under a permethrin-treated bednet or in an air-conditioned room. During the day it is wise to wear long, loose (preferably 100% cotton) clothes if you are going through scrubby country; this will keep ticks off and also tsetse and day-biting *Aedes* mosquitoes, which may spread dengue and yellow fever.

### Tsetse fly

Tsetse flies hurt when they bite and are attracted to the colour blue. Locals will advise on where they are a problem and where they transmit sleeping sickness.

### Blackfly

Minute pestilential biting blackflies spread river blindness in some parts of Africa between map co-ordinates 190°N and 170°S. The disease is caught close to fast-flowing rivers as flies breed there and the larvae live in rapids. The flies bite during the day but long trousers tucked into socks will help keep them off. Citronella-based natural repellents do not work against them.

## Tumbu flies or putsi

Tumbu flies or putsi are a problem in areas of East, West and southern Africa where the climate is hot and humid. The adult fly lays her eggs on the soil or on drying laundry and when the eggs come into contact with human flesh (when you put on clothes or lie on a bed) they hatch and bury themselves under the skin. Here they form a crop of 'boils', each of which hatches a grub after about eight days, when the inflammation will settle down. In putsi areas either dry your clothes and sheets within a screened house, or dry them in direct sunshine until they are crisp, or iron them.

## Jiggers or sandfleas

Jiggers or sandfleas are another kind of flesh-feaster. They latch on if you walk barefoot in contaminated places, and set up home under the skin of the foot, usually at the side of a toenail where they cause a painful, boil-like swelling. These need picking out by a local expert; if the distended flea bursts during eviction the wound should be dowsed in spirit, alcohol or kerosene, otherwise more jiggers will infest you.

## Common medical problems
### Travellers' diarrhoea

At least half of those travelling to the tropics or the developing world will suffer from a bout of travellers' diarrhoea. The newer you are to exotic travel, the more likely you will be to suffer. By taking precautions against travellers' diarrhoea you will also avoid typhoid, cholera, hepatitis, dysentery, worms, etc.

### TREATING TRAVELLERS' DIARRHOEA
*Dr Jane Wilson-Howarth*

It is dehydration which makes you feel awful during a bout of diarrhoea and the most important part of treatment is drinking lots of clear fluids. Sachets of oral rehydration salts give the perfect biochemical mix to replace all that is pouring out of your bottom, but unfortunately they don't taste nice. Any dilute mixture of sugar and salt in water will do you good, so if you like Coke or squash, drink that with a three-finger pinch of salt added to each glass. Otherwise make a solution of a four-finger scoop of sugar with a three-finger pinch of salt in a glass of water. Or add eight level teaspoons of sugar (18g) and one level teaspoon of salt (3g) to one litre (five cups) of safe water. A squeeze of lemon or orange juice improves the taste and adds potassium, which is also lost during diarrhoea.

Drink two large glasses after every bowel movement; more if you are thirsty. If you are not eating properly (or at all), you need to drink three litres of water a day plus whatever is departing from you. If you feel like eating, have a bland, high-carbohydrate diet. Heavy greasy foods will probably give you stomach cramps. If the diarrhoea is bad, or you are passing blood or slime, or if you have a fever, you will probably need antibiotics in addition to fluid replacement. Wherever possible seek medical advice before starting antibiotics. If this is not possible then a three-day course of ciprofloxacin (50mg twice a day) or norfloxacin is appropriate.

If the diarrhoea is greasy and bulky and is accompanied by eggy burps, the likely cause is giardia (see overleaf).

Travellers' diarrhoea and the other faecal-oral diseases come from getting other people's faeces in your mouth. This most often happens from cooks not washing their hands after a trip to the toilet, but, even if the restaurant cook does not understand basic hygiene, you will be safe if your food has been properly cooked and arrives piping hot. The maxim to remind you what you can safely eat is: PEEL IT, BOIL IT, COOK IT OR FORGET IT. This means that fruit you have washed and peeled yourself and hot food should be safe, but raw food, cold cooked food, salad and fruit which have been prepared by others, ice-cream and ice are all risky. Foods kept lukewarm in hotel buffets are usually time bombs waiting to explode!

## Giardia
Giardia is a type of diarrhoea or intestinal disorder caused by a parasite present in contaminated water. The symptoms are stomach cramps, nausea, bloated stomach, watery, foul-smelling diarrhoea and 'eggy' burps. Giardia can occur a few weeks after you have been exposed to the parasite and symptoms can disappear for a few days and then return – this can go on for a few weeks. Giardia is basically a form of amoebic dysentery and is best treated with tinidazole (2g in one dose repeated seven days later if symptoms persist).

## Bilharzia or schistosomiasis
### with thanks to Dr Vaughan Southgate of the Natural History Museum, London
Bilharzia or schistosomiasis is a disease which commonly afflicts the rural poor of the tropics, who repeatedly acquire more and more of these nasty little worm-lodgers. Infected travellers and expatriates generally suffer fewer problems because symptoms will encourage them to seek prompt treatment and they are also exposed to fewer parasites. However, it is still an unpleasant problem that is worth avoiding.

The parasites digest their way through your skin when you wade, bathe or even shower in infested fresh water. Unfortunately many African lakes, including Lake Malawi, and also rivers and irrigation canals, carry a risk of bilharzia. In 1995, two-thirds of expatriates living in Malawi had evidence on blood testing of having encountered bilharzia, and 75% of a group of people scuba-diving off Cape Maclear in Lake Malawi for only about a week acquired the disease. The most risky shores will be close to places where infected people use water, where they wash clothes, etc. Winds disperse the cercariae, though, so they can be blown some distance, perhaps up to 200m from where they entered the water.

### AVOIDING BILHARZIA
- If you are bathing, swimming, paddling or wading in fresh water which you think may carry a bilharzia risk, try to get out of the water within ten minutes.
- Dry off thoroughly with a towel: rub vigorously.
- Avoid bathing or paddling on shores within 200m of villages or places where people use the water a great deal, especially reedy shores or where there is lots of water weed.
- Cover yourself with DEET insect repellent before swimming to protect you.
- If your bathing water comes from a risky source try to ensure that the water is taken from the lake in the early morning and stored snail-free, otherwise it should be filtered, or Dettol or Cresol added.
- Bathing early in the morning is safer than bathing in the last half of the day.
- If you think that you have been exposed to bilharzia parasites, arrange a screening blood test (your GP can do this) more than six weeks after your last possible contact with suspect water.

Scuba-diving off a boat into deep offshore water should be a low-risk activity, but showering in lake water or paddling along a reedy lakeshore near a village carries a high risk of acquiring bilharzia. Although absence of early symptoms does not necessarily mean there is no infection, infected people usually notice symptoms two or more weeks after penetration. Travellers and expatriates will probably experience a fever and often a wheezy cough; local residents do not usually have symptoms. There is now a very good blood test which, if done six weeks or more after likely exposure, will determine whether or not parasites are going to cause problems and the infection can be treated. While treatment generally remains effective, there are treatment failures for reasons that are not yet fully understood; retreatment seems to work fine and it is not known if some drug resistance is developing.

Since bilharzia can be a nasty illness, prevention is better than cure, and it is wise to avoid bathing in high-risk areas.

## Skin infections

Any mosquito bite or small nick in the skin gives an opportunity for bacteria to foil the body's usually excellent defences; it will surprise many travellers how quickly skin infections start in warm humid climates and it is essential to clean and cover even the slightest wound. Creams are not as effective as a good drying antiseptic such as dilute iodine, potassium permanganate (a few crystals in half a cup of water), or crystal (or gentian) violet. At least one of these should be available in most towns.

If the wound starts to throb or becomes red and the redness starts to spread, or the wound oozes, and especially if you develop a fever, antibiotics will probably be needed; flucloxacillin (250mg four times a day) or cloxacillin (500mg four times a day). For those allergic to penicillin, erythromycin (500mg twice a day) for five days should help. See a doctor if the symptoms do not start to improve in 48 hours.

Fungal infections also get a hold easily in hot, moist climates, so wear 100% cotton socks and underwear and shower frequently. An itchy rash in the groin or flaking between the toes is likely to be a fungal infection. This needs treatment with an antifungal cream such as Canesten (clotrimazole); if this is not available try Whitfield's ointment (compound benzoic acid ointment) or crystal violet (although this will turn you purple!).

## Prickly heat

A fine pimply rash on the trunk is likely to be heat rash; cool showers, dabbing (not rubbing) dry, and talc will help; if it's bad you may need to check into an air-conditioned hotel room for a while. Slowing down to a relaxed schedule, wearing only loose, baggy 100% cotton clothes and sleeping naked under a fan will reduce the problem.

## Damage from the sun

The incidence of skin cancer is rocketing as Caucasians are travelling more and spending more time exposing themselves to the sun. Keep out of the sun during the middle of the day and, if you must expose yourself to it, build up gradually from 20 minutes per day. Be especially careful of sun reflecting off water, and wear a T-shirt and lots of waterproof SPF 15 or higher suncream when swimming; snorkelling often leads to scorched backs of the thighs, so wear bermuda shorts. Sun exposure ages the skin and makes people prematurely wrinkly; cover up with long loose clothes and wear a hat whenever you can.

## Foot damage

If you wear old plimsolls or flip-flops on the beach you will avoid getting coral, urchin spines or venomous fish spines in your feet. If you do tread on a venomous fish, soak the foot in hot (but not scalding) water until some time after the pain subsides; this may mean 20–30 minutes' immersion in all. Take the foot out of the water to top it up, to

## SNAKES

Snakes rarely attack unless provoked, and bites are unusual among travellers. You are less likely to get bitten if you wear strong shoes and long trousers when in the bush. Most snakes are harmless, and even venomous species will only dispense venom in about half of their bites. If bitten, therefore, you are unlikely to have received venom; keeping this fact in mind may help you to stay calm!

Many so-called 'first-aid' techniques do more harm than good. Cutting into the wound is harmful; tourniquets are dangerous; suction and electrical inactivation devices do not work. The only treatment is anti-venom.

If you think you have been bitten by a venomous snake, follow this advice:

- Try to keep calm – it is likely that no venom has been dispensed
- Prevent movement of the bitten limb by applying a splint
- Keep the bitten limb BELOW heart height to slow the spread of any venom
- If you have a crepe bandage, bind up as much of the bitten limb as you can, but release the bandage every half-hour
- Evacuate to a hospital which has anti-venom.

Here's what NOT to do:

- NEVER give aspirin; paracetamol is safe
- NEVER cut or suck the wound
- DO NOT apply ice-packs
- DO NOT apply potassium permanganate

If the offending snake can be captured without risk of someone else being bitten, take it to show the doctor – but beware since even a decapitated head is able to dispense venom in a reflex bite.

prevent scalding. If the pain returns re-immerse the foot. Once the venom has been heat-inactivated, get a doctor to check and remove any bits of fish spines in the wound.

### Meningitis

This is a particularly nasty disease, as it can kill within hours of the first symptoms appearing. Usually it starts as a thumping headache and high fever; there may be a blotchy rash too. The tetravalent vaccine (eg: Mengivax ACWY) protects against meningococcal A C W135 and Y strains of bacteria, which cause the serious forms of meningitis. It is recommended for most of sub-Saharan Africa, but specific advice should be sought. Other forms of meningitis exist (usually viral), but there are no vaccines available for these. Local papers normally report localised outbreaks. If you have a severe headache and fever, go to a doctor immediately.

### Rabies

Rabies may be carried by all mammals (beware the village dogs and small monkeys that are used to being fed in the parks) and is passed on to humans through a bite, a scratch or a lick of an open wound. You must always assume that any animal is rabid (unless personally known to you) and medical help should be sought as soon as is practicably possible. In the interim, scrub the wound thoroughly with soap and bottled/boiled water for five minutes, then pour on a strong iodine or alcohol solution. This can help to prevent the rabies virus from entering the body and will guard against wound infections, including tetanus. The decision whether or not to have the highly effective rabies vaccine will depend on the nature of your trip. It is definitely advised if you intend to handle animals, or you are likely to be more than 24 hours away from medical help.

Ideally three pre-exposure doses should be taken over a minimum 21-day period.

If you are bitten by any animal, treatment should be given as soon as possible. At least two post-bite rabies injections are needed, even by immunised people. Those who have not been immunised will need a full course of injections together with rabies immunoglobulin (RIG), but this product is expensive (around US$800) and may be hard to come by. This is another reason why pre-exposure vaccination should be encouraged in travellers who are planning to visit more remote areas. Treatment should be given as soon as possible, but it is never too late to seek help as the incubation period for rabies can be very long. Bites closer to the brain are always more serious. Remember if you contract rabies, mortality is 100% and death from rabies is probably one of the worst ways to go!

### Treating local people
You may be asked to provide medical help. Many local villagers believe that every white person is a doctor, perhaps because most travellers carry a significant amount of medicine with them.

Aspirin is particularly useful, as it is unlikely to harm anyone and is often seen as a cure for everything. Vitamin pills also enjoy a legendary status. NEVER hand out antibiotics carelessly, as you risk making someone seriously ill if you give them an inadequate dose or they fail to complete a course. Take care, too, when administering eye-drops or bandaging sores, as infection is very easily passed on. If there is a local doctor nearby, it is better to send a person with these sorts of ailments to them. He or she will be there to continue treatment long after you have gone. If you do have some medical background, bear in mind that the local health post may be poorly equipped and may appreciate some of your surplus supplies.

## On your return
### Health checks
If you suspect you may have caught bilharzia, for example, you should certainly see a doctor when you return to your own country. This also obviously applies if you contracted malaria on your trip, or if you fall ill after you have come home. Remember to complete your course of malaria prophylaxis.

## Further reading
Self-prescribing has its hazards, so if you are going anywhere very remote, consider taking a health guidebook. Here are some we recommend:

*Bugs, Bites & Bowels* by Jane Wilson-Howarth (Cadogan, 1999). For adult health matters.
*Your Child Abroad: A travel health guide* by Jane Wilson-Howarth and Matthew Ellis (Bradt Travel Guides, 2005). For those travelling with children.
*Where there is no doctor – a village health care handbook* by David Werner, Carol Truman and Jane Maxwell (Macmillan Heinemann, 1993).

## SECURITY

> The black people possess some admirable qualities. They are seldom unjust and have a greater abhorrence of injustice than any other people. There is complete security in their country. Neither traveller nor inhabitant in it has anything to fear from robbers or men of violence. They do not confiscate the property of any white man who dies in that country, even if it be uncounted wealth. They are careful to observe the hours of prayer, and assiduous in attending them in congregations and in bringing up their children to them.
>
> Ibn Battuta, the Moroccan traveller,1352; translated H A R Gibb

Remember that there are hundreds of thousands of visitors to Africa every year and only a small percentage may have a bad experience. Realistically, that person could well have had a similar experience at home or taken unnecessary risks.

## Personal

With day-to-day security issues, you will need to make your own judgement on the situation and act accordingly, using common sense. Africa is generally a safe place to travel and, more often than not, you will be surprised by the kindness and hospitality of the African people; respect it. When walking around towns or cities, always look as though you know where you are going and stick to busy roads rather than isolated alleys. As always, dress respectfully and do not flash money, cameras and jewellery around. Moneybelts next to your body are the best way to carry cash and other valuables when away from your vehicle. If in any way you do feel threatened by a situation, drive away or find the nearest local police station or security guard. When people in Africa have so little, looking rich will not help your security situation.

## Vehicle

As you travel and meet other travellers, you will undoubtedly hear horror stories of oranges filled with nails being flung under your car, ripped tyres, hostage situations – put it all into perspective, as these are usually isolated incidents.

Lock everything up at night. Some travellers even have chains and locks to wrap around possessions, so they don't have to pack the vehicle up every evening.

Locking yourself in your vehicle at night is generally not necessary, but judge each situation for yourself. Do always lock and put everything away before leaving your vehicle. If you are on a motorbike or cycling, many campsites and backpackers' hostels have secure areas for you to lock your valuables. We did not carry our passports or other important documents on us all the time, only when we left the vehicle unattended.

## Wild animals

Out in the bush, and particularly in areas where there are significant numbers of wildlife, there can be a danger from wild animals. Even when they are not a physical danger, monkeys can, for example, become very attached to your windscreen wipers, which can prove a great inconvenience.

In general the chances of encountering hostile animals is low. Nearly all instances of animal attacks occur when animals are surprised, protecting their young or where the animal perceives a danger to itself.

Avoiding these situations is nearly always a simple matter of exercising care and attention. Drivers already have protection in their vehicles but spooking elephants and other large animals in game parks should be avoided. Be careful around waterholes, particularly at dusk when more animals come to drink. Most accidents occur where hippo are bathing near waterholes; watch out also for buffalo. Crocodiles are another possible risk in some areas, but rangers will be aware of these problem places. Attacks on humans by the big cats are very rare. Hyenas may scurry about close to a camping area, but present no threat in the daytime. Monkeys can be a real pest in some campsites, and you should be wary of inquisitive warthogs. Since all visitors to the big parks with private vehicles have to camp in designated areas, the risks are minimised. That said, it is unwise to leave the confines of a tent or vehicle after dark. Plan ahead for that night-time loo stop.

Obviously those hiking or watching game on foot are more at risk. There are some minimal risks on the lower slopes of the big mountains, Mount Kenya, Kilimanjaro, the Ruwenzoris and other remote hilly regions. Never run from a wild beast; in the event of any danger try to get into the protection of trees. Hikers should be aware that there are dangerous snakes, and should be particularly careful in thick undergrowth and tall grasses. Fortunately most snakes, and indeed most animals, will be long gone before the approach of a human.

> The most dangerous animal in Africa, exponentially a greater threat than anything mentioned above, is the anopheles mosquito, which carries the malaria parasite. Humans, particularly when behind a steering wheel, run them a close second!

> Philip Briggs, *Tanzania: The Bradt Travel Guide*

For more details on aspects of security, see the following pages: *Vehicle* page 43, *Bike* page 69.

## WOMEN'S ISSUES

> Within this enclosed women's world, so to say, behind the walls and fortifications of it, I felt the presence of a great ideal, without which the garrison would not have carried on so gallantly; the ideal of a Millennium when women were to reign supreme in the world. The old mother at such times would take on a new shape, and sit enthroned as a massive dark symbol of that mighty female deity who had existed in old ages, before the time of the prophet's God. Of her they never lost sight, but they were, before all, practical people with an eye on the needs of the moment and with infinite readiness of resource.

> Karen Blixen, *Out of Africa*

We didn't often come across women, or for that matter men, travelling on their own. A lot of single women were either backpacking in loose groups or joining organised tours. I am sure that there are hundreds of travellers who have done Africa on their own, but

### WANGARI MAATHAI: NOBEL PEACE PRIZE LAUREATE 2004

It was a lively and colourful ceremony when Wangari Maathai was awarded the Nobel Peace Prize in Oslo in December 2004, with vibrant singing and dancing bringing alive the black-suited observers.

She was the first African woman to win the prize since it began in 1901. The prize was awarded to her for setting up the Green Belt Movement in Kenya. As part of this project, over 30 million trees have been planted across Africa. An environmentalist, she links environmental issues with women's rights, democracy, development and peace. Each is interdependent on the others. If we don't take care of our environment, how can we take care of each other?

Now an MP since the change of government in Kenya two years ago, she has in the past been subject to police brutality, and has spent time in prison. She instigated the planting of trees in parks to demand the release of political prisoners; trees symbolising the struggle for democracy.

Her main theme is that the environment is a reflection of government; first we must heal the earth's environmental wounds, then in the process our own wounds will be healed. We must remember that we belong to a larger family of life. Humanity must shift to a new level of consciousness. We must shed fear and give hope – now!

With Wangari Maathai's shining example, there is indeed hope for Africa.

we did find that those who had started out on their own would hitch up with other travellers on a variety of transport. This was often the case where a country, particularly certain borders or specific routes, had a dodgy reputation. The previous authors met a mother and daughter who were driving across the African continent and had successfully completed most of Africa without any hitches. It did help that the daughter was a professional auto-mechanic!

## Knowing your vehicle

An important difference for women travellers is in weight distribution on the vehicle. Rather than carrying 20-litre jerry cans, it is a good idea to carry 10-litre cans, which are easier to lift off the vehicle. Toolboxes should be smaller and sparingly distributed, once again making them easier to lift. Tyres could be kept inside the vehicle, rather than on top of the vehicle, so they are easier to access.

For women travellers everything else we have discussed regarding driving, biking or cycling through Africa is the same. One concern might be mechanical knowledge of your choice of transport, but then most men who drive the African continent have not much knowledge before departure either. After only a few months on the road, everyone will begin to learn very quickly the ins and outs of their vehicle, motorbike or bicycle. A helping hand is never far away in Africa and, although in more isolated areas you could run into problems, someone will always appear eventually (except perhaps if you get lost in the Sahara. Be especially careful here and try to drive with at least one other vehicle).

It would be a good idea to do a 4x4 course and drive the vehicle or bike as often as possible. Even with a team of man and woman, it is best to learn, listen and get involved as much as you can. Your male counterpart might fall ill and be completely dependent on your skills to get you from A to B.

## Attitudes to women

If you are a woman travelling on your own, your only other concern is going to be the mentality of the African people. Women are seen as having a specific role within the community, and in our eyes this may seem inferior. Remember that this has been part of their culture for centuries. Although not strictly true for every country you visit in Africa, many border posts, banks and embassies are usually run and staffed entirely by men. If you are travelling with a male, it is sometimes best to let the man do most of the talking. Obviously, if you are a woman travelling on your own, you have no choice but to communicate with whoever might be there. Be polite and respectful and you should have no problems.

When travelling through more isolated areas of Africa you will often see men lounging under the acacia trees, enjoying the shade, while the women are doing all the work; collecting water, reaping the fields, cooking, looking after the children and generally running around making sure home and family are looked after. Men are supposedly the financial providers within the community and often seem to do little else. But how do they provide the finances if they spend all their time lounging about under trees?

Most African women (or at least those who initially had the opportunity to attend school) never complete school and start to help around the house as soon as they are able. It is also rare to see children playing. Girls in particular have to start helping around the house at a very young age. We were delighted whenever we came across children just playing with sticks and stones, or swimming and splashing around.

Through their indoctrination into helping the community at such a young age, women are usually very isolated within this community and will speak only the local tongue, even when their male counterparts speak either French or English. Thus you will find that you will mostly communicate with men.

If you have been invited to somebody's home, the women will often provide the meal and then disappear, eating with the family in the kitchen. This is particularly so in Algeria and other Muslim countries. In that case women are perhaps privileged, because a male guest is only allowed into the guestroom, just next to the front door. If he were to venture into the rest of the house he might see the women of the house without their head coverings, and that would never do. As a woman, I was allowed everywhere in the house; the kitchen, living room, the television room etc. Where we had a common language, I could communicate with the women and the men equally.

Women are also often shy in communicating with an outsider and are not used to being asked for an opinion, their lives revolving around their day-to-day responsibilities and survival. Their attitude may come across as – 'a European woman, what does she know? She is barren, no children, not married, driving this car, no home ...' This attitude is quite common and you should certainly not take offence. If time permits and you have the opportunity, it can make entertaining conversation between yourself and the local women. We can only learn from one another.

Some of the greatest fun can be had at markets. In some Arab countries it is the men who trade, but often it is a woman's world. Sometimes having walked for miles with their wares on their backs and heads, they transform a dust bowl into a riot of colour, smells and sounds. Children trace your every footstep, shouts offer you the local brew, food, cloth or even a sheep for sale ... you'll need plenty of patience and time to barter for whatever you want to buy.

Sometimes you'll experience African life as just a rest under the awning of a market stall, laughing and shouting with the women. You may never really learn much about African women, their joys and fears, laughter and tears. Just relax and enjoy the unspoken shared moments together. You'll have a lot in common.

## How to dress

It is very important to dress in accordance with the social norms in the countries you are passing through, to avoid giving offence and indeed to feel more comfortable in the heat yourself. There are reasons for their choice of clothing beyond religious ones. In North Africa, it is best to cover up in loose tops which hang below your bottom, with loose trousers below. Long sleeves are advisable, again not only for religious reasons but because you will be protected from the sun.

I have always worn a long Pakistani tunic-style dress when in North Africa, over Rohan or Regatta trousers, giving the advantage of lots of zipped pockets with the added security that no-one else can see them. Dressing down, as you might call it, also goes a long way to avoiding sexual harassment by African men, particularly in Muslim countries. Again, this is dependent on the area you are travelling in and can take many forms. You may be followed, laughed at, constantly touched, hissed or whistled at, usually innocently, but it can become uncomfortable and annoying.

When you're driving, you will probably be most comfortable in trousers, as a skirt can too easily get torn or caught on some protruding part of the vehicle; there's always something sticking out and waiting to catch you! I usually wore a loose long-sleeved shirt with the sleeves partly rolled up, and a scarf over my hair, tied Tuareg-style in a turban, to stop it blowing constantly in my eyes in the unavoidable wind. It also helps to keep some of the sand out of your hair, a special problem if it's long. I would sometimes wear a T-shirt when driving, but would always cover my arms when in towns or villages in Muslim countries.

Some European women in Africa prefer to wear a wraparound skirt, T-shirt and headband. Just be discreet.

Sometimes young women come off organised tours in their shorts and tight sleeveless or strapless tops, and you can see the reaction of the women – often tittering behind closed palms – and men, usually gawping in astonishment. This does not mean that you can never wear shorts, tank tops, bikinis or swimming costumes, just be very aware of your environment and what the other women are wearing.

Much of southern Africa is pretty relaxed when it comes to clothing, but again this is dependent on the area you are visiting. Most of the rest of Africa, however, is conservative and should be respected accordingly.

If you are a woman travelling on your own, and you find that a particular town, city or even country is becoming a little overbearing regarding the attention of the opposite sex, you could either find other travelling companions, or use a guide (you'll have to shop around) who will often keep the masses at bay, or leave town. No travel is worth getting hurt. Egypt and Morocco can be particularly intensive regarding sexual harassment, though I did not ever feel threatened, just irritated by the constant hassle of touts wanting to sell their wares at inflated prices.

## Avoiding harassment

Sexual harassment is not isolated to single women. Even if you're travelling with a male companion, he could be asked by an Arab man whether he can perform liberties with you. Or whether he will sell you for a certain number of camels! It is unfortunate that Arab men, particularly Muslims, tend to think that Western women are promiscuous and ready to jump into bed with any man at the drop of a hat. It is best just to try to ignore such a situation and state a firm 'no'.

There are certain things you can do to minimise sexual harassment:

- Dress is the most obvious – do not flaunt yourself and dress conservatively. Your own personal experience in Africa will be so much more fulfilling, with both men and women.
- A wedding ring is often helpful in Africa. If you are being hassled, refer to your husband as often as you can, even if you don't have one!
- Avoid eye contact and ignore all rude comments. If you are feeling threatened in any way, walk to the nearest public café and ask the owner for his or her help in getting a taxi home.
- Always know where you are and stick to busy roads rather than isolated alleyways.

## ACCOMMODATION

In Africa you will always be able to find a place to stay, whether it be with the local community, a hotel, bed & breakfast, pension, mission, youth hostel, backpackers' hostel, campsite, or just sleeping in the bush or desert.

One of the more enticing reasons for driving, cycling or biking through Africa is the fascination of meeting other cultures and tribes in the context of Africa, its open spaces, beautiful scenery and often complete isolation from the outside world. Opportunities will arise for you to sleep out in the bush, something that you may come to love, giving you freedom to move as you please. However well you have prepared in advance, carrying adequate amounts of water and food with you, there will come a time when you will need to depend on a village for water and basic supplies. The general rule which applies is *respect the culture and leave nothing behind but your footprints.*

If bush sleeping is not your cup of tea, or you cannot find anywhere where you feel comfortable and undisturbed, more conventional accommodation is available throughout the continent. In some parts of Africa, such as the east coast, there are plenty of lodgings along the coast, while in central Africa you will need to find your own accommodation for the night. Along the west coast, some countries accommodate campers while others offer nothing but hotels.

Outside major cities in places like the Congo and Central African Republic, you are unlikely to find any type of accommodation unless you are lucky enough to come across

## EST-CE QUE C'EST LA LOIRE?

Morning comes and we cross the river to Gabon. Gabon too has its good bits of road and its strange aboriginal villages. The pygmies are not far from here, but we don't see any. The road becomes a rutted dirt highway through the magnificent trees of the equatorial forest. Later camping is a problem, with few places. Finally we stop to cook, but a local appears from nowhere and suggests that camping here is not a good idea; there are too many monkeys or elephants, but maybe it's too many inquisitive villagers. We don't really know; it's a bit forbidding.

We drive on and on into the dark night; the road brushes through thick bamboo forest. After hours some lights appear; it is 21.00, we are in Ndjole, a town on the banks of the wide Ogooue River. We can't believe our eyes as we pull up outside the Auberge St Hubert. The building could be anywhere along the banks of the Loire in France, except it's hot, muggy and the cicadas are deafening. Inside we are greeted by 'Madame la Propriétaire' and some expatriate French guests. We have a beer and find ourselves discussing the state of the country with the expats. One is en route to Franceville on business; the other is out from the capital Libreville. Our room temporarily transports us to France, to a small hotel, a little tatty, a bit smoky and with rather tacky curtains. It could be in Amboise or Blois on the banks of the Loire.

a mission. Throughout southern Africa you will find a plethora of choices, except perhaps that idyllic wild bush camping spot that you longed for.

For more specific information about hotels, guesthouses etc, see *Where to Stay* in *Chapter 6* page 151 and *Chapter 8, A–Z Country Guide*.

# POST AND TELECOMMUNICATIONS

All over Africa, any reasonable-sized settlement will have a post office and a telephone. The question is whether the phone is working. Some systems are so old you wonder how they manage to get a line! And often they don't, or you may get cut off midstream. Now internet access is available in the most unlikely places, as well as the larger towns and cities. Of course they may not always be online, sometimes they are very slow and sometimes they are expensive; but they are always a good means of communication.

## Post

In every capital city and larger town there is a post office with post, telephone, fax, poste restante and courier services.

### Poste restante

Poste restante is a postal service available at the main post office of almost every capital city. It is a general address to which family and friends can send post. Letters and parcels are kept for up to four weeks, and some form of identification will be needed for collection. You may also have to pay to collect it. All post is kept in alphabetical order. Make sure that your name is marked clearly in bold, black capital letters, underlining the first letter of either your surname or your first name. This will make it a lot easier to collect. For example: Joe **B**loggs, c/o Poste Restante, Central Post Office, Gonder (town as required), Ethiopia (country as required). Note that for all French-speaking countries you need to write 'PIT' instead of 'Poste Restante'.

## PHOTOGRAPHY
*Ariadne Van Zandbergen*
Your Africa trip will most likely be a once-in-a-lifetime experience, and while photography might seem like a minor detail among your other preparations, a small amount of forethought will help you take the best advantage of the many photographic opportunities that will come your way.

**Equipment** The simpler the camera, the less there is to go wrong – complex electronic gadgetry can be sensitive to rain, dust and heat. For landscapes and portraits, a solidly built manual-focus camera will be adequate. An auto-focus camera will, however, focus with greater precision than any person can hope to on a regular basis, which is particularly useful for moving subjects, such as animals.

For most purposes, the combination of 28–70 and 70–300 or similar magnification zoom lenses will be ideal. A higher magnification than 300 is useful for wildlife but very expensive; for a small loss of quality, teleconverters are a cheap way to get around this: a 300 lens with a 1.4x converter becomes 420mm, and with a 2x it becomes 600mm.

It is possible to buy one lens that covers the full range from 28–300, but such lenses are generally of inferior quality and bulky by comparison to a 28–70 when shooting at low magnifications.

The best way to protect equipment from dust, heat, water, vibrations and bumps is to store it in a Pelican case (any camera shop can order one). On foot, a backpack-style camera bag is more convenient and less likely to attract attention than a normal camera bag. Or use an ex-Army canvas bag – a metal case for the inside can be made with an old 5-litre oilcan, and with foam padding this makes an excellent, strong and inconspicuous camera bag. A tripod will allow you to photograph on foot in low light conditions. I cannot overstate the importance of supporting your camera on a beanbag when you photograph wildlife from a car – you can make this yourself from strong fabric, and fill it with beans or rice.

**Film** For those using traditional cameras, print film is the preference of most casual photographers, slide film of professionals, serious amateurs, and anybody else who hopes to have pictures published. Slide film now is more expensive to buy, and also much more expensive to develop, as digital photography is taking over a lot of the market.

Most serious photographers working outdoors in Africa favour Fujichrome slide film, in particular Sensia 100, Provia 100 (the professional equivalent to Sensia) or Velvia 50. Slow films (ie: those with a low ASA (ISO) rating) produce sharper and less grainy images than fast films. Velvia 50 is extremely fine grained and shows stunning colour saturation; it is the film I normally use in soft, even light or overcast weather. For hand-held photography in low light, Sensia or Provia 100 is preferable because it allows you to work at faster shutter speeds. 100 ASA film is more tolerant of contrast, and thus preferable in harsh light.

For print photography, a combination of 100 or 200 ASA film should be ideal. It is advisable to stick to recognised brands. Fujicolor produces excellent print films, with the Superia 100 and 200 recommended.

It is important that you try to develop your film as soon as possible, but avoid developing print film outside major cities, and slide films anywhere but South Africa and Nairobi. One solution is to post or courier film home every few weeks.

**Some basics** The automatic programmes provided with many cameras are limited in the sense that the camera cannot think, but only make calculations. A better investment than any amount of electronic wizardry would be to buy or borrow a photographic manual for beginners and get to grips with such basics as the relationship between aperture and shutter speed.

Beginners should also note that a low shutter speed can result in camera shake and therefore a blurred image. For hand-held photographs of static subjects using a low magnification lens (eg: 28–70), select a shutter speed of at least 1/60th of a second. For lenses of higher magnification, the rule of thumb is that the shutter speed should be at least the inverse of the magnification (for instance, a speed of 1/300 or faster on a 300-magnification lens). You can use lower shutter speeds with a tripod or beanbag.

Most modern cameras include a reliable built-in light meter, and give users the choice of three types of metering: matrix, centre-weighted or spot metering. You will need to understand how these different systems work to make proper use of them.

**Dust and heat** Dust and heat are a constant problem in Africa. Keep your equipment in a sealed bag, stow films in an airtight container (such as a small cooler bag) and avoid changing film in dusty conditions. Bring a cleaning kit and take care of your equipment. Regularly clean the inside of your camera with a small brush or air blower. A small grain of dirt inside your camera can scratch a whole film.

**Light** The light in Africa is much harsher than in Europe or North America, which is why the most striking outdoor photographs are often taken during the hour or two of 'golden light' after dawn and before sunset. Shooting in low light may enforce the use of very low shutter speeds, when a tripod or beanbag will be required to avoid camera shake. With careful handling, side-lighting and backlighting can produce stunning effects in soft light and at sunrise or sunset.

Generally, however, it is best to shoot with the sun behind you, which means most buildings and landscapes are essentially a 'morning shot' or 'afternoon shot'. If you spend a bit of time in one place, you'll improve your results by planning the best time to take pictures of static subjects (a compass can come in handy).

When photographing people or animals in the harsh midday sun, images taken in light but even shade are likely to look better than those taken in direct sunlight or patchy shade, since the latter conditions create high contrast. Avoid photographing a shaded subject against a sunlit background, which also creates contrast. Fill-in flash is essential to capture facial detail of dark-skinned people in harsh or patchy light.

**Protocol** Attitudes to photography vary greatly from one country to the next, and travellers should take heed of local sensibilities. As a rule, it is considered offensive to photograph people without asking first. Some people will refuse, some will agree enthusiastically, while others will expect a small payment. Even the most willing subject will often pose stiffly when a camera is pointed at them; relax them by making a joke, and take a few shots in quick succession to improve the odds of capturing a natural pose.

In most parts of Africa, official attitudes towards photographing government installations have relaxed over the last decade, but this too varies from one country to the next – be circumspect about pulling out your camera at border posts, near military installations and on bridges.

The success rate of actually receiving a poste-restante letter or parcel depends on the individual country, and do remember that it can take at least two to three weeks for a letter to get to its final destination.

If you are collecting a parcel, it usually needs to go through an arduous Customs check. It is advisable to indicate that the parcel contains old clothes and food, rather than new goods, otherwise you may have to pay duty.

If you're sending letters home, ask the cashier to frank all the stamps in front of you, as there are plenty of stories about stamps being removed from letters which then never reach their destination.

### Alternative mail services

A good and perhaps easier and safer alternative to post offices is that offered by American Express offices. Anyone carrying an Amex card or their travellers' cheques is entitled to use the company's offices worldwide as a mailing address. This service is free. A booklet is available from American Express (Amex House, Edward Street, Brighton BN2 1YL; tel: 01273 693555) giving a complete list of its offices' addresses around the world.

## Telecommunications

Fax, telephone and email facilities are widely available now, often even in the smallest towns. All capital cities and most larger towns will have public fax, telephone and internet facilities, so there is no excuse not to keep in touch!

All these facilities obviously rely on the individual country's telecommunications network, the quality of which varies greatly. An overseas call is often clearer and easier to make than one to a neighbouring town, as overseas calls are routed via satellite.

Telephone calls and faxes to Europe (the international telephone code for the UK is +44, and for the US, +1) typically cost US$3–10 per minute, which can be much the same as an hour on the internet. It is well worth setting up an internet email account before you leave, so that you can check and send emails on any computer without incurring high phone charges.

The French cultural centres in francophone countries and the British Council often have email facilities open to the public, but they can be more expensive than the local internet cafés. Remember that computer viruses are much more of a problem when using public facilities, so do warn the recipients to virus-check all the mail you send them.

# Part Two

## On The Road

# Your Vehicle

Departure day, and hopefully you are ready for the road; Africa is waiting!

This section provides you with some useful information about driving in Africa: recovery techniques and an overview of daily maintenance, breakdown and repairs. It also deals with African bureaucracy and the challenges you will face along the way.

## DRIVING TECHNIQUES

We aim to give you an insight into the different conditions you can expect to encounter and the best way to tackle them.

Become familiar with the 4x4 capability of your vehicle. Does it have permanent or selectable four-wheel drive? Does it have differential lock, and how can this be used to your advantage? Does it have freewheel hubs or not? All this information will be in the vehicle handbook and is essential knowledge, helping to prevent you getting stuck in difficult terrain.

Driving in Africa can be hot and exhausting. Conditions are harsh and days can be unavoidably long. It is preferable to share the driving and the experiences as much as possible. Do not drive at night unless it is completely unavoidable. With cattle and people straying on to the roads during the hours of darkness, there is constant danger. Many African vehicles have either pathetically poor or blindingly brilliant lights stuck on full beam. Some loads are wider than the vehicles and can be invisible at night.

Be very careful when you first reach the continent and watch out for the local drivers. Some car drivers drive phenomenally fast, including those share-taxis that have 11 people crammed inside and screech around corners with bald tyres! Buses are not always much slower, and are equally overloaded. The African travelling public have a lot to put up with.

You need to anticipate the driver's actions; many do not do the obvious. In fact expecting the unexpected should become second nature. Some vehicles are grossly overloaded; many don't have mirrors. Even when fitted, mirrors may not be used. You will soon learn how Africans drive!

Remember that a lot of African roads are quiet most of the time, and therefore people will not be alert for vehicles passing. This means you must drive **very slowly** through villages and towns; children run out unexpectedly, and women with heavy waterpots on their heads may not be looking out for traffic. If you should be so unfortunate as to knock someone down, it will always be your fault, whatever the circumstances. Animals are also a potential threat much of the time. Camels in particular, with their noses high in the air, seem oblivious to other road users.

Although some main roads are mostly good, there is always the possible threat at any time of large unmarked pot-holes; uncovered manholes aren't totally unknown and surfaces can be suddenly rough. With so many different road surfaces, gravel tracks, sandy pistes and muddy holes, driving in Africa can be great fun. But don't get carried away by the thrill of the moment; Africa will punish you severely. Always drive with great caution.

Keep to a moderate speed, even on the open road. We never drove anywhere over 80km/h (50mph); at this speed you can anticipate and react to obstacles and bad sections of road. A slower speed also helps to reduce wear and tear and is more economical on fuel. In sand and on bad roads and tracks it is preferable to coax the vehicle to go in the right direction rather than to fight the wheel and risk damage. Take it easy, be vigilant.

The benefits of walking through an obstacle before driving through should never be underestimated, particularly when faced with deep soft sand, water, mud holes and rocks. The chances of getting stuck or causing major damage because of an unseen object can be greatly reduced. Finally, keep your thumbs out of the steering wheel rim on rough roads, because hitting even small objects can make the steering wheel kick back, enough to bruise or even break them.

The three main conditions you will face are sand, mud and corrugations. Each requires a different technique and presents its own set of problems. Many main roads in Africa are not in such a bad condition (with the exception of much of central Africa, Ethiopia and northern Kenya). Going trans-Africa you will inevitably encounter one or all of the following situations depending on where and when you go.

## Sand

Driving on sand can initially be daunting, but within a short time you will be able to pick out the different types of conditions that sand presents. It can be hard-packed, quite fast, smooth with some resistance, or seriously soft and deep. In between are countless variations. Sand can change abruptly from one condition to another; be very careful until you get a feel for it. Driving across sand dunes is potentially dangerous and needs extreme care. Vehicles can easily roll over in dune country. Never drive on a dune at any angle other than straight on and straight down. They have a habit of forming with hollow zones that cannot be seen. Consider a reconnaissance walk on any daunting sand dune sections. Most main desert routes avoid dunes of any significance. If you intend to follow sandy pistes for some days it will pay to let some air out of all your tyres. With flatter tyres a greater surface area exists, enabling the vehicle to float more above the sand. The effect this practice has on your mobility is immediately noticeable. Make sure your tyres are built for this, and have a gauge to check the pressure. Most dual-purpose tyres can be run around 1.5 bar (approximately 21psi in sand). Keep a check on tyre temperatures frequently in sand if the pressures are low. Try to run them with the highest practical pressure for the conditions, unless there is no choice.

It's amazing how well a 4x4 vehicle copes in most sand. The key is momentum. Using high-range 4x4 is generally more appropriate for most desert crossings. We used low-range only when we could see a particularly soft patch ahead or we were already stuck. It varies with the vehicle you have. Big throaty Toyotas have less likelihood of getting bogged. When you see a section that you feel needs low-range, give yourself plenty of room for the approach. Try to get into a suitable gear, probably low-range third, before you hit the soft sand. This will give you the momentum you need; try to change down smoothly to avoid losing it. Changing gear too suddenly in soft sand can bring you to a stop as quickly as braking. If you can change gear successfully, you can retain some momentum and avoid getting stuck. It takes some practice though. After a while it becomes a bit of a challenge trying to avoid getting bogged, especially if you are in convoy with experienced Sahara drivers, including the locals. Avoid becoming over-confident, enjoy the adrenalin rushes and highs of desert driving, and act carefully; you'll have endless fun!

But we digress. Try not to use the brakes, as you will build up a wall of sand in front of your tyres, making it harder to get moving. If you have to stop, look for a harder area and just take your foot slowly off the accelerator. If you feel yourself getting stuck, try 'waggling' the steering wheel from side to side; this helps to reduce the build-up of sand. When you do come to a halt, drop the clutch immediately and check the situation. Sometime reversing out back to solid ground is possible and sufficient. Using excess power to get moving could seriously damage your vehicle, even snapping a drive shaft. In any case too much wheelspin will just make it worse, getting you bogged even more deeply.

Once bogged, you have more strenuous options. Often scooping away the sand from in front of and around the sides of all the wheels will be enough to get started. If not, and your vehicle has diff-lock, then engage it, select your low ratio, first or second, and try to engage the clutch smoothly, edging forward until you gain momentum. Sand should also be removed from anywhere underneath if the vehicle is very deeply dug in.

If this fails, then it's out with the sand ladders or sandmats. Two will often be enough, but they must be well dug in and as level as possible. Placing them in front of the rear wheels is usually best. Watch out behind as ladders can be pushed forcibly backwards once motion is gained. Having your better half, whoever that may be, add some weight by pushing will also help, but they must be prepared to leap quickly out of harm's way as soon as you start to move. It can also happen that the sand ladders disappear below the surface of the sand, leaving no trace on top. If this is the case, it is obviously useful to have a person there to tell you where to dig for them! Sometimes it is possible to select reverse and sail out backwards. If you are unfortunate enough to be stuck in soft sand on an upward slope you may be in for a long slow session using your two ladders, or more if you have them. Once moving, don't stop until you are on a harder surface or on a downward slope. Don't forget to walk back and retrieve your sand ladders.

Driving on a good sandy piste is a rare experience these days, and one to be enjoyed.

## Mud

Mud can invariably be worse than sand and, on a very bad section, hours can be spent extracting any vehicle except a bicycle, and your shoes too! Avoiding the main rainy seasons generally means avoiding the worst mud sections. However, be very careful driving on damp mud roads, particularly those in tropical rainforests that have exaggerated cambers. It is all too easy to start sliding sideways towards often-deep ditch areas. Take these sections very, very gently, probably in your lowest gear.

A number of mud roads in Cameroon, CAR and DRC have quite steep hills, and going down these when sticky can also be a little hair-raising. Again use a low gear and crawl down. Always drive into a slide; turn the wheel into the wayward direction.

When you see a muddy section ahead, stop and engage 4x4. Select the appropriate gear before hitting the bad section. For vehicles with large engines, third-gear low-range or first-gear high-range is appropriate, and for smaller engines second-gear low-range. Don't head off thinking your speed will do the trick: this is just going to make things worse in most cases. Avoid wheelspin; it will just make you bog down deeper. When the wheels start to spin, ease off the accelerator until you pick up more traction, then accelerate gently, trying to avoid more wheelspin. Once you appear to be stuck, you'd better get out and assess the situation.

So now what? You could have a cup of tea if it's too bad. Then again, you could try reversing slightly. If you are not badly bogged, this might work. If not, then it's out with the shovel. Digging tropical mud can be rather tiring, so that tea may well be needed sometime soon. There are no quick ways out of this predicament. You need to clear away as much mud as possible. This can mean crawling about underneath to cut away compacted mud and even removing higher central mounds of the road itself. Using your sand ladder, jacks and wooden blocks may all be necessary, as well as utilising available resources like logs, rocks and bits of plank. You might have to fill in the road here and there, using whatever materials are to hand. Fortunately most muddy sections don't go on for miles, except in the Congo. Ho ho ho!

When you encounter a water-filled bog hole, or even long sections of flooded track, always stop. Walk through the hole first, and locate any logs or rocks that are often put in the hole by other drivers. These can do serious damage to the underside of your vehicle. Nine times out of ten it is better to drive through the middle of deep bog holes rather than to try to skirt round them. It is often muddier on the edges. You could end up sliding sideways into the hole, get stuck or, even worse, possibly overturn. Mud can be fun, but it can also be dangerous in certain situations.

## Corrugations

Corrugations are probably the most irritating and most common driving obstacle in Africa. Many roads in Africa are basically carved out of the existing terrain by grading machines. Some are excellent, but many more have not seen a grader since the day they were made or the last colonial left! Some are gravel, some hard-packed laterite (the red dusty ones); some are black murram, which is dreadful after rain. All these sorts of roads can develop corrugations: continuous ripples on the surface. They can occur after a soft section, where previous vehicles have taken the opportunity to speed up. Unfortunately they can often go on for hours at a stretch and can shake a vehicle to pieces. Invariably there is no ideal way to approach these frustrating sections. Sometimes there are other tracks beside the main route which are better.

With fairly regular corrugations, there seems to be an optimum speed at which to drive. This can often be disconcertingly fast and is potentially very dangerous. Beware! The vehicle tends to float over the bumps, doing immense damage to the suspension and also making the steering very light. It is very easy to lose control and clatter off the road. Also you may be going along at an apparently reasonable rate when the nature of the corrugations changes and the vehicle vibrates alarmingly, shuddering to a halt with tremendous shaking. In fact it's sometimes hard to slow down, as the vibration is so intense. Under these circumstances there is nothing to do but crawl along, hoping the torment will end soon. Going slowly will probably save time in the end, as speeding over corrugations invariably causes your vehicle to retaliate by breaking a spring or something else.

Once in the Cameroon jungle our engine stopped abruptly. No, it wasn't fuel problems, nor any of the obvious problems, but a loose electrical connection on the injector pump solenoid, shaken apart.

## Vehicle river crossings

On most trips in Africa, having to drive through very deep water is not very common. That said, a flash flood in the Sahara or a raging torrent in the mountains can be encountered. The first thing to do is nothing. Park your vehicle well back and assess the hazards; crossing any torrent is potentially a very real risk. Invariably with seriously deep water the only action is to wait. Have a cup of tea.

Assuming it's safe and not too deep, walking through the water first is a must. Check for variable depth, large rocks and soft areas. If the depth of water is below the level of your radiator, fan and alternator you can fairly safely proceed slowly, trying to avoid creating any big waves as you go. Always keep a constant speed and do not change gear; correct gear selection is essential. Don't stall the engine. If you do, attempting to restart it could cause even more damage. Water and mud may have been sucked into the engine via the exhaust, which means you have a major job on your hands. So basically don't take the risk in the first place.

Recovering from this mess will probably involve other vehicles, unless you have the luxury of a winch. In deeper water you could take off the fan belt to prevent damage to the fan blades. At worst the fan can be smashed by small stones and churned-up gravel and the radiator might object as well. Another suggestion, which we have not tried, is to place a foot mat over the radiator. This is said to create a larger bow wave and larger draw down in the engine bay, hopefully keeping more of the engine out of the water.

Frankly the best options, if they exist, are to find another way or wait, unless you have any serious reasons for rushing on. We once waited three days for a river to subside, so have enough food and water on board in case. Don't even consider driving into deep water if you haven't prepared your vehicle properly (see *Chapter 2, Vehicle Preparation*). You will literally be landed in even deeper water.

# RECOVERY TECHNIQUES

With luck and sensible driving, you may not need to use recovery techniques too often. Some of the recovery methods have already been touched on in brief within the driving section. Below are some further points to consider. Getting stuck invariably happens when it's hot, windy or raining. Having the right equipment is the first step. Having extra equipment can make it easier. But taking every conceivable aid may in the end be the cause of your getting stuck in the first place, because of the weight factor.

How you go about extricating your vehicle from a tricky spot depends on what you are stuck in. What equipment you are carrying, what is available locally (manpower, other vehicles, logs etc) and the availability of anchorage points need to be considered. In almost all situations a certain amount of digging, common sense and hard work will be required. The following ideas about recovery techniques can be adapted as conditions dictate.

## Sand ladders

As we have mentioned above, and to summarise again, sand ladders (or sandmats) are most often used to get out of deep sand, but can also be used in mud, as a jacking plate for high-lift jacks and for repairing holes in damaged bridges. They can also be dangerous, especially in sand, where wheels throw them backwards. Removing the sand from around all the wheels, and from the chassis if the vehicle is grounded, is the first step. The mats should then be placed, the flatter the better, in front of the wheels with the least traction. Drive on to the mats and try to get as much speed up as possible. Do not stop until you are on a firm surface again. Sandmats can also be very useful when negotiating rotten log bridges in Congo, but again ensure they are secured in place before making any tentative advances.

## High-lift jack

Although we have not carried a high-lift jack, we would strongly recommend it to save time and energy. Always remember to put a jacking plate under it before jacking in soft ground conditions. This could be a sandmat, pieces of wood or a spare tyre. Two useful tips for recovering a vehicle with a high-lift jack are 'jack and pack' and 'jack and push'.

In *jack and pack*, the high-lift jack is used to lift the wheels clear of the ground so that material such as rocks, wood, sand ladders etc can be packed under the wheels to increase traction. This method is useful when the vehicle is bogged up to its chassis in mud. The *jack and push* method involves jacking the vehicle from the front or rear, so that both the wheels are off the ground. The vehicle is then pushed sideways off the jack. This method is useful when the vehicle is stuck in deep muddy ruts or grounded on a central ridge.

The high-lift jack can also be used as a winch, but it is limited to a pull the length of the jack before the whole assembly has to be reset. With all high-lift jack operations, it is important to remember always to leave the jack with the handle in the upright position when unattended.

If you do not have a high-lift jack you will probably have to spend more time getting 'de-bogged'. You can use your hydraulic jack, jacking plates, blocks of wood, spare wheels and any materials found around the site. Good luck!

## Winching

You will probably not be in a situation all that often where using a winch is the best solution. A winch could be useful if you are able to consider crossing the Congo, where there are trees and some roads have steep gradients and nasty, car-eating deep ditches. Winches are not much use in sand. When thinking about winching, you need to consider suitable anchoring points.

A natural anchor might be anything that is strong enough to take the strain, ie: trees, pretty large boulders or rocks. Making your own anchors, from spare wheels or sand ladders stuck vertically in the ground, should only be considered when nothing else is available, as they can be potentially quite dangerous. These methods usually require a lot of effort. The spare wheel or sand ladder must be very well dug in, more so in sand. Be careful how you attach the anchor strap. Try using a bar behind the tyre or sand ladders. Cable eye clamps are another method. The direction of pull needs to be as straight and as low to the ground as possible; you will need to dig a trench for the strap to lie in.

A snatch block is another winching accessory. It is basically a heavy-duty, single-line pulley and can be used to double the pulling force by attaching it to an anchor point, then passing the winch cable through the snatch block and back to the vehicle. A snatch block can also be used to change the direction of pull when using another vehicle to winch you out.

Winches are potentially very dangerous. Whenever winching or towing, always ensure that the cable is securely fastened at both ends and all onlookers are well clear. This is very important in case the cable snaps or your anchor breaks. One person should co-ordinate the recovery and operate the winch and everyone else should stay well back while the cable is under tension. A heavy mat or blanket can also be placed over the cable to help stop it lashing if it snaps.

## Using another vehicle

If you are travelling in convoy, many of the obstacles can be surmounted rather more easily. Using a cable between vehicles is the main method, but again be warned about snapping cables. Anchor points must be carefully considered, to limit any breakages. Also be very careful when using cables in mud, and especially if any local truck needs help.

## MAINTENANCE, BREAKDOWNS AND REPAIRS

Above all, the key phrase to remember here is 'regular maintenance prevents breakdowns'. This cannot be stressed enough. Dusty conditions, extreme temperatures, contaminated fuel and bad roads all take their toll.

Consult the manufacturer's handbook for service intervals as a start, and then consider the conditions you are subjecting your vehicle to. More frequent checks will be necessary for sure. For example, desert driving means air and fuel filters will get clogged up more quickly. If you do a lot of wading, gearbox and differential oils will become contaminated and you can pick up a tank of dirty fuel just about anywhere in Africa.

The tables following are a guideline for maintenance and inspection intervals. Changing all filters more often will help prevent breakdowns. It may seem like overkill to suggest checking something like the wheel nuts every day, but the constant vibrations from corrugated roads mean that they can loosen themselves at a frightening rate. These things happen!

## Regular maintenance

You should get into the habit of checking certain things each day. Start by looking at oil and water levels, keeping both topped up without fail. Check the levels of hydraulic fluid for the brakes and clutch. Any noticeable drop will tell you that a problem may be developing. As you go around the vehicle, look at the wheel nuts, suspension fixtures, nuts, bolts and springs. As you go, watch for any telltale drops of oil and hydraulic fluid around the wheels. It pays to crawl underneath at least once a day and look for any

## INSPECTION SCHEDULE
### Daily inspection
*Check every day* **before starting** *the engine:*
Check for fluid leaks on the ground
Check for oil leaks around the engine
Engine oil level
Radiator water level
Brake and clutch fluid levels
Fan belt tension
Spark plugs leads secure
Tightness of wheel nuts
Tyres visual check
Check for fluid/oil leaks around the wheels
Suspension – look for loose nuts and bolts
Shock absorbers visual check
Check for any other obvious loose nuts
General inspection of undercarriage and springs (daily when on rough roads)

### After starting check
Water temperature
Oil pressure

### Every three or four days
*These items should be looked at more frequently when on rough roads, and less on good roads*
Engine mountings
Exhaust system
Tyre pressures
Clean air filter – dust bowl or pre-filter if in dusty conditions
Drain plugs – check they're not loose
Spring U-bolt/nuts and spring centre bolt
Any movement between spring leaves
Cracks in coils or leaf springs
Rubbing of main leaf against the hangers
Check for any rubbing fuel lines, pipes and wires

### Weekly inspection
Battery acid level and corrosion of battery leads
Gearbox, transfer box and differential oil levels *
Check steering box oil
Check swivel housing oil/grease level *
Steering damper
Air-cleaner oil bath – clean when in constant sand and dust
Brake cylinders and brake hoses

* On old Land Rovers some of these may need to be looked at more often!

changes; things coming loose, exhaust, wires, fractured mountings, fuel pipes touching and wearing. Water leaks often show up in the morning. Put a spanner on all the vital steering and suspension nuts regularly and fix any minor problems immediately.

If you have a mental imprint of how your vehicle should look, you will be able to spot any potential problems far more quickly and easily. Toilet stops or lunch breaks are a good time to have a quick walk-around and carry out the following checks:

- Check underneath for signs of leakage and loose nuts
- Visual check of hubs for signs of oil or brake fluid leakage
- Feel wheel hubs for abnormally high temperature – could indicate a worn bearing
- Feel the tyres for abnormally high temperature – could indicate low tyre pressure

## Common problems
### Vibration damage
It may seem obvious, but inattention to the small things leads to bigger difficulties. With continually rough roads, the effects of vibrations are the most common problem. Nuts and bolts need constant attention. Failure to do these checks will lead to potentially serious problems. Take time to look after the results of vibration.

### Leaks
Also invariably an effect of vibration; watch for weeping water hoses, brake pipes and fuel lines. Keep a screwdriver handy for those loose jubilee clips. More seriously, watch for leaks from the radiator.

### Suspension
Suspension problems are an ever-present threat with the poor state of the roads. Careful driving and constant vigilance can reduce breakages. Fitting new springs on older vehicles before you set out is a good idea. Newer vehicles with coil springs are generally less trouble than those with leaf springs.

The chassis could crack if it was not in good condition before leaving. Older models are more prone to this. Most that are already in good condition will be fine if you take it steadily. It shouldn't be necessary to strengthen the chassis as a rule; this can distort things if not done professionally.

Many suspension problems can be prevented by careful maintenance. Check your suspension nuts are tight. Loose U-bolts can lead to the leaf springs slipping against the axle and eventually to a broken centre-bolt. When this happens the axle can then move fore or aft relative to the chassis and serious damage may follow. You will see a high number of trucks and buses 'going sideways' or 'crabbing' as a result of a skewed rear axle. Africans are not ones to worry over these potentially fatal matters.

### Tyres
Your tyres represent a considerable expense. Punctures are inevitable, but tyre damage is also a constant threat in Africa. Be vigilant when running your tyres at lower pressure, when they are more prone to damage from rocks and stones in sand. Stay away from sharp rocks, sticks and particularly the acacia thorns found under shady trees. Once back on a hard surface, be sure to pump them up or they'll rapidly overheat.

Keep a close watch for tyres going down slowly. Punctures are the main hazard. Be careful to ensure the vehicle is stable before removing wheels; use wooden blocks. It's an obvious point, but in the heat of the moment things happen. Some can be repaired locally, but keep a careful watch on the job; some are done well, others very badly. If in doubt, do it yourself. You need at least two levers for this. When deflating a partially soft tyre be careful to stop the valve flying into the sand or mud; they have minds of their own. Breaking the bead between the tyre and the metal rim is the worst part. Soapy water can be used as a lubricant on stubborn tyres when levering. One way to

*Above* Gabbra hut, Kenya (AZ)

*Left* Sand dunes, Algeria (GR)

*Below left* Initiation ceremony,
Senegal (AZ)

*Below right* Falani woman,
Niger (GR)

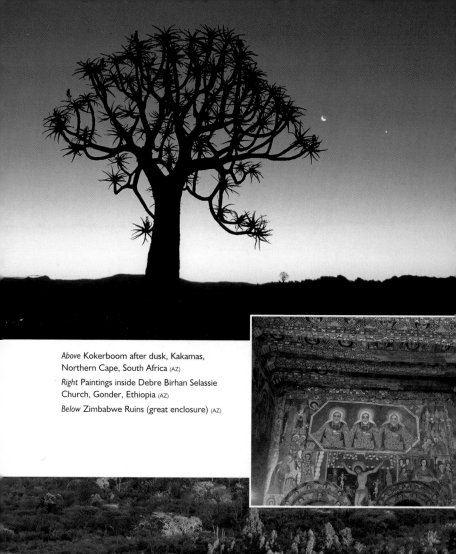

*Above* Kokerboom after dusk, Kakamas, Northern Cape, South Africa (AZ)

*Right* Paintings inside Debre Birhan Selassie Church, Gonder, Ethiopia (AZ)

*Below* Zimbabwe Ruins (great enclosure) (AZ)

### ANOTHER PUNCTURE!

At the least these tyre problems meant interaction with the local people. It's quite easy to breeze by, cocooned in your own vehicle, passing villages. Passing people, whose lives are so different, clinically isolated from them by the very thing that gives you the freedom to see these places and people. Wherever we repaired our tyres, someone would speak English and ask us many things; sometimes we were offered cold drinks. The Sudanese have retained their great sense of self-respect; there was no blatant hassling, just a gentle friendliness and curiosity. In the meantime the media are making out the country is full of terrorists. What is the truth of the Darfur rebellion and humanitarian crisis? It is hard to know the true picture as a traveller.

break the bead is by jacking the tyre down away from the rim using the front bumper, if it's solid, or part of the chassis as the top jacking point. Be careful not to damage the tyre; use a wooden block if necessary. Africans often drive over the tyre to break the bead, but this can cause damage. If repairing a tube, be sure to scratch and roughen the tube well, using a hacksaw blade. Once the repair has been done, take great care not to trap small stones, sand, grit or flakes of rust between the tube and tyre, otherwise another puncture could result very soon. A good dusting of talcum powder between tube and tyre can help lessen the friction between the two and reduce further troubles. It also pays to use graphite around the rim/tyre seal when installing new tyres before departure.

Be careful not to stand over a tyre when it is being blown up, in case it does not bed in properly. Carry a comprehensive selection of patches and repair material. It is also worth having tyre (rather than tube) patches to repair any large holes in the tyre itself. Tubeless tyres need special repair plugs. Old tubes can be cut for use as temporary liners if the tyre has sustained internal damage.

## Fuel

The poor quality of some fuel means your fuel filter is likely to get blocked more often than normal. It is a good idea to rinse the fuel tank before leaving, to get rid of any sludge that may be in the bottom, and flush the filter on the bottom of the pick-up (if fitted). This may not be necessary if your vehicle has been driven solely in countries with good fuel.

While on the road, clean out the sediment bowl regularly and change filters at the first sign of spluttering or loss of power from the engine. Filter your fuel through a fine gauze or cloth when filling the tank if you suspect it might be dirty.

If you have an apparent blockage in the fuel line, you can disconnect the pipe before the lift pump and blow through it. An obstruction can be located in this way; a short length of slightly larger pipe may be of use to avoid getting the fuel near your mouth. Keep an eye on the fuel lines; they can wear quite fast on bad roads. Also ensure that you can repair sections if necessary by taking spare pipe and joining links with ferals. In the event of a serious fuel feed problem in the lines or a leaking/damaged tank, a temporary fix can be made using your spare fuel lines fed from a jerrycan or small plastic container.

## Electrical faults

Electrical faults can be more puzzling than straightforward mechanical failures. You need to understand the basic principles first. All electrical systems involve a complete circuit for the flow of power. A logical analysis needs to be made before any drastic

## MAINTENANCE SCHEDULE
Check the manuals for your particular model first.

| Item | Maintenance Interval | |
|---|---|---|
| Diesel engine oil | 6,000km (4,000 miles) | More frequently if doing a lot of low-range driving as mileage ceases to relate to engine hours |
| Petrol engine oil | 9,000km (5,500 miles) | |
| Diesel oil filters | 5,000km (3,500 miles) | |
| Petrol oil filters | 9,000km (5,500 miles) | |
| Diesel fuel filters | 5,000km (3,500 miles) | Loss of power can be due to clogged filters from bad fuel |
| Petrol fuel filters | 9,000km (5,500 miles) | Loss of power can be due to clogged filters from bad fuel |
| Sediment bowl | 10,000km (6,000 miles) | On diesels inspect regularly |
| Air filters | 10,000km (6,000 miles) | Oil bath and re-usable types, clean with every oil change |
| Gearbox and transfer-box oil | 15,000km (9,000 miles) | |
| Differential oil | 15,000km (9,000 miles) | |
| Set tappets | 10,000km (6,000 miles) | See manuals, it may be a longer distance |
| Set timing | 10,000km (6,000 miles) | See manual |
| Change spark plugs | 20,000km (12,000 miles) | |
| Greasing | Every two weeks or after every wade | |
| Injector pump | See manual, as some need small top-ups | |
| Windscreen | Washer reservoir – as needed | |

action is taken. The problem with wiring is that many wires are well hidden, in looms and difficult to access. Vehicle electrical wiring is exposed to extremely unfavourable conditions: heat, vibration and chemical attack. Look for loose or corroded connections and broken or chafed wires, especially where the wires pass through holes in the bodywork or are subject to vibration. Fuses often blow as a result of such problems.

All vehicles have one pole of the battery 'earthed' and connected to the vehicle bodywork. Nearly all modern vehicles have a negative (-) earth terminal. Electrical current flows through the component and back to the battery via the metal bodywork. If a component mounting is loose or corroded, or if a good path back to the battery is not available, the circuit will be incomplete and malfunction will occur. The engine and/or gearbox are earthed by means of flexible metal straps to the body or subframe. If these straps are loose or missing, problems may result; the starter motor may not turn sufficiently, ignition may fail and the alternator may not recharge the batteries. Sometimes the straps do not make a good contact to the chassis and the contact points need cleaning with emery paper. Various other electrical components – wiper motors, bulb holders, etc – are also earthed directly by their mountings.

Assuming that the earth return is satisfactory, electrical faults will be due either to component malfunction or to defects in the supply wires. For example, if the starter is faulty or not activating, the cause could be the solenoid, the brushes inside or the wires linking it to the ignition, or even the battery leads. When wires are broken or cracked internally, this will result in an incomplete circuit. Sometimes wires become bare and the current is earthed on to bodywork, resulting in a short circuit. Most short circuits will blow a fuse. If not, the result could be burning of the wire insulation, more short-circuiting or, at worst, a fire. This is why it is inadvisable to bypass persistently blowing fuses with silver foil or wire. A good way to check out elusive problems is to bypass the suspect wire or component temporarily, using a length of wire with a crocodile clip or suitable connector at each end. A 12-Volt test lamp can be used to verify the presence of supply voltage at various points along the wire and the break can be isolated.

## Tackling hidden problems

With so many moving parts and extra strain, you will be very lucky to escape all mechanical difficulties. Some failures are obvious and can be located visually: oil leaks, water leaks, brake-pipe fractures, cracked exhaust, loose wheel nuts and so on. Others are not so simple. Some problems can be investigated by listening or smelling: hot rubber, piston rings or broken valve springs clicking, exhaust loose etc. The worst problems are the hidden ones: hot engine, squeaking brakes, wheel noises, knocking suspension noises and other mysterious rumblings.

You can consult the manufacturer's manual first to see if the symptoms are indicated. Familiarity with your vehicle and personal experience are the best tools in checking out elusive problems. Try to think through exactly what is happening, and then try to isolate the problem with a few checks if possible. Clutch and gearbox noises are very hard to isolate, and often little can be done but soldier on.

Jumping up and down on the front bumper or a rear step and listening for any taps can sometimes locate suspension knocks. Squeaking brakes might be worn pads or, quite often, grit in the brake drum. It could be the wheel bearing too, but touching a hub for heat may help decide this. Some noises are worse on bad surfaces; others vibrate intermittently, suggesting less serious snags. With any new noise that is constant you must diagnose the problem as soon as possible. Engine noises and overheating are of prime concern.

With an overheating engine there is an obvious symptom, but the cause may be due to a number of defects.

Here is an example. The water temperature light comes on; your engine is overheating not long after starting off. You need to understand what is happening so you can start eliminating possible causes:

- The engine is hot. Too much heat is retained or not enough lost, maybe both
- Heat goes into the engine through burning fuel and friction from moving parts
- Heat leaves the engine from the radiator via the cooling water, exhaust, oil and airflow over the engine

Check each of these and eliminate possible causes. The most likely cause is connected with the radiator and water system: a failure to lose heat. Water leaks are the first problem to look for and the easiest. The fan belt may have broken, although you can usually hear this happen. Is there an oil leak from the engine? Can you see oil weeping from gasket joints? If none of these seems to be the cause, it could be the heat sensor; even a wire problem is a remote possibility. Check out the following:

- Less airflow over the engine – a defective fan or a clogged radiator – or even the vehicle moving too slowly in the wrong gear

- Reduced cooling from the radiator – water leaks, cracked rubber hoses, faulty thermostat, blocked radiator pipe, low coolant, faulty water pump
- Check that it isn't simply a faulty radiator cap. Unimogs in particular have a complicated cap pressure system
- Reduced cooling due to blown head gasket, or worse, cracked head

Sometimes when a vehicle is ploughing through soft sand for long periods the engine will get hot because it's doing a lot more work at slow speed. Friction can be generated because of low oil. Low oil reduces the cooling ability of the oil. Oil more normally used in cold climates may be too 'thin'. Using heavier-duty oil in hot places may be preferred, but be sure to warm the engine up first thing before driving off.

## General fault diagnosis

Most common faults are caused by bad maintenance, defective parts, poorly installed parts, bad lubrication, blockages and sometimes just plain bad luck. In general, if a vehicle is prepared thoroughly beforehand, most troubles develop as a result of outside factors. Things shake loose, things touch moving parts, other items get too hot and so on. In general things do not suddenly fail. Many problems that develop take time to become obvious; eg: a wheel bearing overheated by a sticking brake shoe. Major mechanical failures in particular are usually preceded by characteristic symptoms over hundreds of kilometres, for example the badly set up or worn thrust bearing in the gearbox that sounded slightly different. Components which do occasionally fail without warning are often small and easily carried in the vehicle, such as the thermostat or the ignition solenoid. Of course larger items – the starter, the lift pump or the alternator – do wear out; it's best to get new ones before you leave.

The first step is to decide where to begin the investigation. Often this is clear. Sometimes a fault can be apparently cured, only to recur. Often the key is observation, finding a problem before it becomes serious, and afterwards looking closely to make sure it has been fixed. Daily inspections can reveal potential hazards ahead. Sit down, have a cup of tea, smoke if you need to; a calm and logical approach is far more satisfactory in the long run. Take into account any warning signs or abnormalities that may have been noticeable in the period preceding the fault – power loss, high or low gauge readings, unusual noises or smells, etc – and remember that the failure of components such as fuses may point to some other underlying fault.

Whatever the fault, certain basic principles apply:

- Verify the fault. This is simply a matter of being sure that you know what the symptoms are before starting work. Don't rely on other people's assessments.
- Don't overlook the obvious. For example, in cases where the vehicle won't start, is there fuel in the tank? If an electrical fault is indicated, look for loose or broken wires before digging out the test gear.
- Cure the disease not the symptom. Replacing a flat battery with a fully charged one will get you back on the road, but if the underlying cause is not attended to, the new battery will go flat too.

Take nothing for granted. A 'new' component may itself be defective (particularly if it's been rattling round in the back for months), and it's a mistake to leave components out of a fault diagnosis just because they were recently fitted. When you do finally diagnose a fault, you will probably realise it was there before the problem.

Whatever the problem, you will need to sit down and think through as many possible causes for the fault as you can. Below is a series of suggestions for fault-finding. Similar trouble-shooting lists can be found in most manuals.

The following are some of the more likely problems:

## Starting problems

These include any problems when starting, and also a partial or complete failure to turn the engine:

- Flat battery (recharge, use jump leads or push start)
- Flat battery caused by loose fan belt – re-tension
- Flat battery caused by loose or faulty alternator
- Battery terminals corroded or loose connection
- Battery earth to body defective – could be engine/starter strap
- Starter brushes, solenoid fault or loose or broken wiring
- Ignition/starter switch faults
- A corroded main earth lead – needs cleaning
- Insufficient power transmitting – engine fails to turn over
- Starter motor pinion sticking
- Flywheel gear teeth damaged or worn
- Starter motor mounting bolts loose

## Fuel supply problems

These include when the engine turns over but fails to start, fails to run cleanly, or runs briefly before cutting out:

- No fuel in tank
- Lift pump failure
- Air in the line due to leaks and damage
- Blocked fuel filters
- Blocked outlet in the tank; blowing down the line might clear this
- Fractured fuel line joints
- Blocked air breather hole in fuel tank filler cap
- Injector pump failure – oh dear, seek specialist advice

## Main engine problems

These include when the engine turns normally but will not start, an engine that will not run properly and when it cuts out or overheats:

- No fuel in tank
- Other fuel system fault – air leak
- Fuel starvation – engine fires but will not run cleanly – blocked filters
- Injector pump fault/leaking pipes/broken injector nozzle
- Poor piston chamber compression
- Ignition warning light illuminated (no charge)
- Air leaks at inlet manifold
- Major mechanical failure, eg: camshaft drive, timing chain, head gasket
- Serious overheating – engine cuts out, as above, radiator etc
- Overheating, slack or broken fan belt – adjust or renew

## Other engine problems

If there is a whistling or wheezing noise:

- Leaking manifold gasket
- Blown or leaking head gasket
- Leaking air pipes or air compressor
- Cracked exhaust pipe or leaking joints

If you hear any tapping, rattling or knocking sounds from the engine itself or close by:

- Incorrect valve clearance
- Valves and camshaft worn
- Worn or stretched timing chain
- Broken piston ring (usually a clicking or ticking noise)
- Inappropriate mechanical contact (eg: fan blades)
- Worn or loose fan belt
- Peripheral component fault, ie: generator, water pump, etc
- Big-end bearings worn (a regular heavy knocking, may be less under load)
- Main bearings worn (rumbling and/or knocking, may be worse under load)
- Piston slack in chamber (often more noticeable when cold)

**Note** Do not add cold water to an overheated engine, as damage may result.

### Ignition and warning lights

If the oil gauge reads low, or the warning light is illuminated with the engine running, it may be one of the following problems. A low oil-pressure warning in a high-mileage engine on tick-over is not necessarily a cause for concern. However a sudden pressure loss at higher speed is far more significant. But it could be the gauge or warning light sender, and not in the engine.

- Low oil level
- Incorrect grade of oil
- Oil filter clogged or bypass valve defective
- Oil pressure failure valve defective
- Oil light/bulb defective
- Oil pump loose
- Oil pick-up strainer clogged
- Oil pump worn
- Defective oil gauge or sender unit
- Wire to sender unit earthed
- Overheating engine
- Worn main or big-end bearings

Other warning lights are illuminated:

- Low oil level
- Coolant loss due to leaking, internal or external, damaged hoses
- Low brake/clutch fluid
- Defective thermostat
- Binding brakes
- Clogged radiator, externally or internally
- Flat or non-charging battery/alternator fault

### Other faults – clutch, brakes and axles etc

- Clutch slipping – worn clutch plate or weak pressure-plate springs
- Clutch erratic or heavy – master cylinder or slave cylinder rubbers worn
- Clutch failure – fluid loss from master or slave cylinder, or pipes
- Wheel noise – worn or damaged bearings, brake drum grooved, loose wheel nuts
- Squealing brakes – brake pads worn or damaged
- Squealing or grating noise from wheel – grit or small stones trapped in disc brake
- Soft brake or clutch pedal – air in hydraulic fluid, hydraulic fluid leaking
- Deep grinding axle noises – low differential oil
- Knocking driveshaft – defective or worn UJ, or loose nuts
- Hot brakes – badly adjusted, worn pads or loose brake shoes

- Hot wheels – badly adjusted or worn bearings, leaking hub seals
- Poor braking – hydraulic fluid or hub bearing oil seeping on to brake pads
- Poor braking – badly adjusted brakes
- Steering knocks – loose or worn track rod ends, bent track rod
- Steering erratic – loose wheel nuts, worn ball joint bearings/kingpins
- Loud exhaust – loose nuts on exhaust joints, holed silencer, loose manifold
- Sagging springs – cracked leaf spring/s
- Loud knocking from suspension – worn or damaged shock absorber rubbers
- Other suspension noises – damaged shock absorbers, loose nuts
- Skewed motion – broken spring centre bolt
- Driver's aching back – driving too far or too fast, or old age!

### Electrical faults
- Battery/ignition faults – as above under engine
- Lights fail – blown fuses, bulbs blown, loose wiring
- Indicator lights – bulbs, loose wire, fuses
- Engine cuts out – loose wiring on injector pump solenoid
- Any failure of electric units, wiper-motor, horn etc – fuses, loose wires
- Starter motor jams on – disconnect battery leads quickly and repair starter motor
- Petrol engines' electrical faults – condenser, points, distributor cap, and plugs
- Too much static electricity – driver's hair standing on end from African road users!

## Roadside repairs

Sooner or later African gremlins will decide it's your turn for a spot of bother. Something will fail or break on your vehicle and, of course, you may well be a long way from the nearest mechanical help, however basic. Now is the time for that quiet moment, in the hope of some enlightening inspiration.

Invariably some improvisations will not work or will work only partly, but patience and thinking around a problem will usually bring a viable solution, whether permanent or temporary. Keep ideas simple. This is the time for inspirational initiatives and inventive attitudes.

Assuming that you are carrying most or all of the items listed below as sundry accessories, you can often fix some quite daunting problems. It is often possible to make temporary improvised repairs. Sometimes it is better to bypass the main problem and work on a simpler solution: one that can be sorted out later where facilities exist.

A good example is where you have a brake problem. The wheel cylinder is leaking brake fluid and needs to be replaced or have new rubbers. It's late afternoon, you can't camp anywhere and this could be a long job. You might encounter difficulties removing a tight brake drum, or perhaps the nuts holding the wheel cylinder are corroded and not happy to come loose. Better then perhaps to disconnect the brake pipe leading to the mischievous wheel cylinder and block it off.

This could be done in quite a few ways, using jubilee clips, spare fuel line joints, clamps on the rubber section, other miscellaneous plastic pipe, even a fuel line nut and some old tube rubber cut to act as a seal and then screwed on to a jointed part of the line. Once you reach somewhere to park up for a while, you can fix it properly yourself with parts, or try the local mechanic. African bush mechanics have some amazing tricks up their sleeves. But then of course most bush mechanics don't have sleeves!

Here are some useful tips and suggestions.

### Starter failure

Pushing is the obvious choice, but there may not be any or enough pushers about. If there is an ignition/starter electrical problem, it's possible on some starters to shortcut the

## MISSION IMPROBABLE
This story is set in the east of the Central African Republic, on an overland trip on which Bob was a client. Most organised overland trips today are a little less fraught, but some of the happenings may not be so dissimilar. From the diary ...

### Bahr al Ghazal, southern Sudan, January 26 1976
Left Bangui then spent three days in Bangassou with brake trouble and officialdom delays. Drove on to Obo, road shocking; it's really an overgrown track and ferries not working. Delayed by a broke back spring. Next day a tooth came off the crown wheel on the back axle and made a neat hole in the diff cover. Also a tyre blew.

Just past Obo the second diff blew. With the rest of the party setting up camp in the bush for some time, the driver, Nick, Dave and I set off to look for parts in Wau, 300 miles on in the Sudan. No traffic at all, so we had to walk the 40 miles to the border, mostly in the cool of the night until some villagers warned us about large animals with big hungry mouths and fluffy, but not cuddly, manes. Ate stale bread and shared some tins of fish for two nights and a day. Spent the second night in a village, some locals invited us into their little thatched mud house. It was quite something – we were offered food and some straw matting; such hospitality, a pity about the bugs in the night, though.

We hitched from the border to Wau on the top of an old Bedford truck, overloaded with a boisterous host of passengers clinging to sacks of grain over every bump of the dirt road. It was hell under the burning sun, stomach cramps threatening at any moment. (A great story to relate from the comfort of leafy England later – you know, great white ashen-faced hunter explores the Sudan by exotic lorry.)

### Wau, Sudan, January 27
Dave took Nick, who was very ill, off to Khartoum by plane. I found a Bedford pinion but no crown-wheel. Later I found a complete axle in the customs house, but they weren't going to part with that. A few haggard-looking travellers arrived on the train from Khartoum, a five-day trip. Slept in the police station courtyard with other travellers. No beds, just sand and no spare parts.

ignition/starter pre-solenoid by using a screwdriver across the terminal of the starter. Be careful though, as it can spark a lot if the connection is not right, and at worst the screwdriver might try to weld itself to a terminal. In case the earth is poor, you can also use jump leads from the battery to another earth point.

Some older vehicles still have starting-handle holes behind the number plates; it's worth a check before you leave. A starting handle might be a saver in a remote desert. Be very careful using these, as they can backfire and break your arm at worst. It is also said that you can jack up a rear wheel and, using a length of rope wrapped around the wheel, pull this to rotate the wheel. We have never tried it. It sounds rather hard and won't work on vehicles with permanent 4x4. Try it if you're bored of waiting for help to arrive.

### Damaged rubber suspension/shock absorber bushes
These could be replaced by using an old tyre tube cut into many small discs with a hole punched or cut out. Add as many discs as necessary. Africans sell strong bushes made of old tyres; they last much longer than the genuine spares. They won't pass an English MOT test though. Temporary fixes can be done using string wrapped around damaged bushes to get a tight wad.

## Tuesday February 3
Back at the stricken truck the locals had been bringing food, water was found a mile away. The camp was set out with loos, a cold store on the evaporation principle, a summerhouse with mosquito nets all round, and a shaded area of poles and leaves. Early next day, Aussie Dave and Kiwi Mike set out to walk to Obo, where a mission was rumoured to exist. Next day they arrived back with a big Unimog from the mission. They proposed to tow the truck back to the mission.

## Thursday February 5
An amazing day – replaced the old Bedford axle with an abandoned Mercedes one. Had to replace one bearing; luckily the truck's one was exactly the same. The mission blokes welded the truck propshaft on to the new axle with the only electricity and welding gear between Bangui and Juba. The brakes didn't really work and we had to put four discarded bald Land Rover tyres on the wheels. The girls kept us all plied with great fruit salads, pineapples, papaya, bananas and lemon juice.

## En route February 10
Departed from the mission, full of trepidation. Nearly came off the road where some terrible rock steps in the track barred the route. Had to camp and use rocks next morning to build the road up under the truck. It took six hours to get 50 yards. Had a puncture afterwards, but got the tyre off using a screwdriver, hammer and jack handle. Used one of the two patches left and later got stuck in a mud hole for hours. Met some tourists going west; our notoriety has spread along the bush telegraph – 'So you're the lot who've been stuck in the bush for four weeks.'

Crossed into Sudan, all the officials were most helpful, they could hardly believe their eyes with the truck a good two feet lower at the back than the front. Had another puncture; we seem to be on three rear wheels longer than four.

## Nairobi, Kenya, February 24 1976
Finally pulled into the big city. Ate almost continuously for three days; mostly bacon, eggs and cake at the Thorn Tree Café.

## Leaking water hoses
These can be temporarily fixed with wire/duck tape reinforced with old tube rubber and large jubilee clips. But you ought to be carrying spare hoses anyway.

## Broken throttle cable or pedal
Tie a piece of cord or electrical wire around the injector pump or carburettor arm and pass it through the window. We once did this on an Indian motor-rickshaw on the way to Delhi Airport and managed to co-ordinate the gear changes with the large Sikh driver. After we'd barely made it to the airport in time, the flight was then cancelled anyway!

## Loose exhaust, broken mounts or holes
Wire can be used to secure a loose exhaust pipe and make temporary mountings on to a suitable anchor point on the chassis. A hole in the exhaust can be patched from old food cans and wire or jubilee clips. Dum dum exhaust paste is a good standby; it hardens fast.

## Broken radiator cowling
Wire can be used to secure a loose or broken cowling mount, but take care the fan is not touching.

### Radiator holed or damaged
Soap, softened with a little water, will temporarily fix the leak. Other methods are to put an egg into the radiator water, but it's better to use proper 'radseal' available from any motor factor trader. Araldite can also be used to seal a badly leaking radiator with limited damage. Otherwise, in cases of severe damage, it is possible to block off any leaking channels or part of the radiator that is damaged.

### Cracked or leaking fuel tank
Fuel tank leaks can be reduced or cured by using plastic padding or Araldite. The tank needs to be drained first to ensure the surfaces are dry and free from oily diesel. Fuel lines are best repaired properly by carrying the necessary pieces and joints.

### Broken main leaf or coil spring
Insert one or more wooden blocks between the axle and chassis. They need to be securely held in place with rope etc. Any largish lump of rubber might do the trick – always assuming that you can find a largish lump of rubber in the first place! A spare tyre, in certain situations, might work, but it would need to be well secured and away from brake lines, propshafts and other moving parts. Where some leaf springs have broken, you can insert small wooden blocks, bits of flat metal or any other suitable filler, and then bind the springs up as tightly as possible with thin nylon rope.

### Damaged propshaft or UJ
Best to have a spare UJ. Otherwise remove the broken shaft and continue in 4x4. Take care though, as all the torque from the engine is now being transferred through one shaft that is not designed for this. It's fine on part-time 4x4 vehicles only. On permanent 4x4 vehicles it may not work where there is a transfer box differential. Using the diff lock will overcome this problem, but don't drive fast or for too long without releasing the wind-up by jacking the vehicle up periodically.

### Clutch not functioning
Start the engine in the lowest gear and change gear by matching the engine and road speeds. Otherwise crawl on using whatever gears you can get moving in.

### Differential or pinion broken
On some vehicles the front and rear differentials and pinions are interchangeable. Check your workshop manual to see if it's the case with your specific vehicle. If they are interchangeable and your rear is damaged, swap the front units to the back to maintain rear-wheel drive. This is advised only as a last resort. You need to reset the crown-wheel and pinion backlash and interface gaps. Normally this is done using a special gauge, but it's possible to get a reasonable match using instant gasket squeezed on to the pinion interface gear. Rotate the pinion; it will leave marks on the crown-wheel. Some manuals have a sample diagram showing the pattern required. Again this applies to part-time 4x4. See above for permanent 4x4.

### Sticking thermostat
Remove the thermostat, but then let the engine warm up for longer.

### Leaking heater hoses
You can use another piece of hose and jubilee clips to isolate and bypass the troubling leak.

### Sump or differential holes
Use plastic padding, Araldite or epoxy metal glue and, if necessary, a small sheet of metal for repair. Again all surfaces need to be free from oil before starting the repairs.

## Track rod sheared

Sounds unlikely, but it happened on a Bedford truck in Amboseli National Park in Kenya. Bind the rod up using any clamps, jubilee clips, nylon rope and a length of piping or a strong metal bar and hope the nearest welder is close by. Bent rods should be hammered back as well as possible.

## Damaged bolt or nut threads

All stripped bolts are best replaced if accessible. Try Araldite where possible as a temporary fix. Nut threads on such things as clutch slave cylinders are prone to damage and can be awkward to fix. Threads on exhaust manifold nuts and studs often strip easily because the nuts are softer. Try metal epoxy glues, or use wire as a quick fix.

## Piston ring breaks/damage

God forbid, but known suggestions that have worked in remote areas on an ancient 6-cylinder Bedford Truck are to remove the damaged piston and seal the piston chamber with a very tightly fitting, fashioned piece of wood. This blocks oil from the sump. The injector pipe to the affected chamber needs to be disconnected, as you don't want diesel in the oil system. This can be re-routed using a plastic pipe into a reservoir, or diesel will spray everywhere. We haven't actually tried this and it can only be a desperate last resort!

We did once have a Bedford Truck aluminium piston welded and turned down with new ring grooves in Turkey. The welder was amazingly skilled.

## Tyres damaged

When the last spare has blown and you are desperate, it is said to be possible to fill a tyre with sand for a limited distance. Otherwise you can use old tubes to line damaged tyres. Africans even stitch up old tyres or bolt them together and use them again. There are no vehicle safety regulations; if it works it's OK!

# Other repairs etc
## Extreme heat

It is possible to do a limited number of repairs using heat and your battery. Apparently, in a worst-case scenario, you can use your battery and arc-welding rods to effect simple repairs. We haven't tried it. Repairing metal brake pipes or loosening press-fitted parts can be done using an air pump or compressor to superheat charcoals. Pump air down a metal pipe into the fire to generate the higher temperature a repair might require. However, none of these techniques should necessarily be your first course of action. Keep it simple. Normally it's better to effect a temporary cure and get along to a decent workshop if you can.

## Degreasing

A 50/50 mixture of diesel and washing-up liquid makes an excellent degreaser for pre-cleaning very dirty areas – rinse off with water after several minutes.

## Old oil

It is prudent to keep old oil both for extra insurance against sudden loss through damage and for ecological reasons. In a worst case, it can be filtered and used until a new source is found.

## Suggested bush spares

- tub of assorted nuts, bolts and washers
- self-tapping screws
- duct tape and electrical tape

- cable ties in various sizes
- contact adhesive (spray-on contact is very quick and easy)
- Araldite and/or plastic metal epoxy glue
- superglue
- gasket cement
- radiator sealant
- plastic padding
- old bicycle/car inner tube
- wire or bicycle spokes
- thin gardening wire
- long piece of chain or steel cable
- small length of lighter chain
- plastic from oil tubs or similar containers
- pieces of sheet metal/aluminium sheet
- small pieces of plywood
- metal strips/old pipe/square tubing
- lots of assorted jubilee clips/clamps
- various lengths of electrical wire
- assorted small springs (throttle, clutch etc)
- various lengths of nylon rope/string/small rope
- ladies' nylon tights, for temporary filters or fan belt (you should be carrying a couple of spare fan belts anyway)
- assorted driver relaxants, tea, chair, hammock etc etc!

# MOTORBIKE DRIVING TECHNIQUES AND REPAIRS
*Alex Marr and David Lambeth*

Once on the road, the two most important things are undoubtedly keeping your air filter clean (in very dusty conditions this can be necessary every day) and performing regular oil changes (around every 2,000km/1,200 miles). Sponge air filters can be washed in petrol, dried, soaked in engine oil and the excess squeezed out.

Other frequent checks should include chain tension, spoke tension and tightness of nuts and bolts (nylock nuts help, as does Loctite thread-locking fluid).

There is a long-running debate as to whether you should lubricate your chain in very dusty and sandy conditions. From direct experience gained from thousands of miles of desert racing events, I believe that a chain will always last longer if lubricated. The rubber O or X rings in a modern chain need to be kept moist to be able to seal the internal lubricant. When run dry, a chain can get very hot, and the rings can dry out and split. Sand is also very salty and lubricant can help to protect the chain and sprockets from corrosion.

## Riding in difficult conditions
### Sand

Reducing tyre pressures considerably – as low as 8psi – increases the surface area of the tyre in contact with the sand and makes riding a lot easier. However, if the sand is in stretches alternating with rocky terrain, do not reduce tyre pressure too much, as you risk a puncture on the rocks. In really deep sand which has been rutted by other vehicles, it can be easier to just move through at walking pace, paddling along with your feet until you feel in control enough to ride properly. If you feel the rear wheel getting bogged down, it is best to dismount immediately and push, simultaneously applying gentle engine power. If you do get completely bogged down, slowly start moving the bike from side to side until it is free enough to be lifted out of the hole. This may require removing the luggage and, if it happens often, a sense of humour is very helpful!

## KHARTOUM

And so to Khartoum; the name conjures up visions of the exotic. We camped at the Blue Nile Sailing Club, basically a large car park next to the river. The shower worked, and after three days in the desert that was truly essential! There was also a pleasant green lawn with shady trees, where we met some fellow travellers – Ina and Alex, who were planning to cycle across Africa over a period of two to three years. But they had already been on the road for over a year, and were about to fly back to Germany for a couple of weeks so Alex could sort out his tax returns. They must be a little crazy! Even crazier than us, we thought!

Then another white man arrived with just a tiny bag of personal possessions. He was Reinhardt, in the process of shipping his vehicle from Aqaba to Port Sudan to avoid getting a carnet for Egypt. He planned to drive his almost-new Land Rover into the desert and make a film following the progress of a particular tribe of Sudanese nomads throughout the year. On the vehicle, at least when it left Aqaba, was all his expensive camera equipment, not to mention sleeping bags and other essentials for life in the desert. How much would remain when it arrived in Port Sudan? His girlfriend was due to fly out to Khartoum at the weekend, then they would take the weekly public bus to Port Sudan and wait for the ship to arrive. To get back to Europe, he was planning to ship the vehicle to Jeddah in Saudi Arabia, but, not being married to his girlfriend, she could not get a visa to travel through Saudi with him, so would have to fly to Aqaba and wait for him there. The whole thing sounded far too much hassle…

*Mirror, Mirror on the wall,*
*Who is the craziest of them all?*
*Cyclists, motorcyclists or car drivers?*

## Mud

A real nightmare with a heavy bike; deep mud can mean you lose almost all grip and control over the bike. Stop before really bad sections and choose the best route; sometimes there is an easier way round the edges or side. Check the depth of water-filled sections before riding through.

### River crossings

The golden rule is to walk through first, checking the depth and the state of the bottom. Riding on large, rounded mossy rocks in deep water is going to have only one result!

In high-risk situations it is better to push the bike through, taking the luggage off first if necessary. If the bike is going to fall over in the water, make sure you switch the engine off first.

## Punctures

Everyone should know how to mend punctures. It is not difficult, but does require technique and practice – make sure you do the practising at home before you leave! Using heavy-duty inner tubes significantly reduces the chance of punctures. Check regularly for thorns, nails and sharp stones in the tyre carcass even if you don't have a puncture. Get them out as soon as possible so that there is less chance of them slowly working through to the inner tube.

## BICYCLE TROUBLESHOOTING

There are a few on-the-road problems that may arise for cyclists, including the possibility of numb hands. Should this happen, check the angle of the tilt on your seat or the direction of the bend of your handlebars and adjust as necessary.

Faced with unexpected noises, try the following:

- Click (only when pedalling) – make sure crank arms and pedals are screwed on tight. Make sure crank arms are not hitting the derailleur cage, the wire on your derailleur, or kick stand
- Click or rubbing sound (even when you don't pedal) – check for deformed rim hitting brake pad, broken spoke or broken axle
- Rattle – check for loose screws all the way around on racks, water bottle cages or other screw-on accessories

# Day-to-Day Issues

## BUREAUCRACY

Bureaucracy proliferates around the world, and our own country is no exception. In fact, given that it was the British who perfected the art of bureaucracy that now persists in its ex-colonies, who are we to blame the Africans? But in Africa bureaucracy can sometimes be encountered at its most intense, and we give some guidelines as to how to deal with it below.

There are a few golden rules to remember: be patient, stay calm and keep smiling. There will be times when this is easier said than done, but remember that you have time on your side. Make a cup of tea for yourself, and offer one to the officials too. This will help you to relax, and make them realise you're not going to be rushed into something you don't want to do. It can be a useful way of getting through a tricky border or check post, so make sure you have a spare cup or two available for such an eventuality.

African red tape is something that may drive you crazy in the short term, but after the event you will probably be amused at the memory. It is sure to enliven your dinner party conversations for years to come! If you are travelling with a vehicle or motorbike, you are almost certainly going to have to deal with officialdom and talk your way through Africa. Always be friendly and polite, even when you feel you are getting nowhere. African bureaucrats are no different from any others, in that they will not want to lose face. Be patient and kind and you will eventually get there. Be rude and you may spend the night there!

## BORDERS AND POLICE CHECKS

Borders and police checks vary from country to country. Some border crossings will take hours, with a tedious amount of paperwork, while others have an easy and convenient system that doesn't take long at all. Never underestimate the systems of African border posts and always allow enough time to cross from one country into another. But bear in mind that things sometimes move faster when they are about to close, and you can often park safely at the Customs post for the night, so that you're ready for a quick getaway in the morning.

It is worth seeking advice from other travellers who have recently crossed a specific border. Most border crossings will involve first Immigration and then Customs, where your vehicle or bike will be cleared; your carnet will be stamped in or out, your international vehicle certificate and driver's licence will be checked. Vehicle insurance

### SIGN ON THE WALL AT THE IMMIGRATION SHED IN ASSAMAKA

However hard life is, approach it with humour and courage

An apt description of this unbelievable place!

## DJIBOUTI – A BORDER CROSSING

Just before the border with Djibouti, the road suddenly cascaded down a fantastic volcanic wall, the remains of a long-extinct caldera with dark brooding lava cliffs and a brilliant white-and-pink dried-out lake bed. This salt lake stretched into the dark, almost blue, mountains beyond. It was lunchtime at the border, even though it was now well past two o'clock. The Ethiopian immigration officers were very helpful, but Customs were not to be found. Eventually a soldier sheepishly took us to one of many rusting cabins, old cargo containers and railway carriages. Here in air-conditioned comfort sat the elusive Customs crew, cross-legged and chewing away to take their minds off the sweltering heat outside. Qat is a plant which resembles the privet hedge from an English country garden. That's how every guidebook describes it, and we cannot better the description. As the sun hits its strongest period, that is the time for the whole of the Horn of Africa and neighbouring Yemen to start the daily ritual of munching and chewing qat. Nothing can disturb this ritual; well, almost nothing. Exceptions are apparently made when a foreign tourist appears on the scene, such a rare occurrence is this.

usually needs to be purchased, and there may be a police or military check on the vehicle. In Libya and Egypt you have to have local numberplates attached, and of course you have to pay for these. In fact in Egypt they even crawled around under the vehicle looking for the chassis number, which is engraved into the chassis next to the front wheel. We didn't know where it was until they showed us. Luckily it was the same as on the carnet, otherwise who knows what might have happened. There may also be an import tax or fuel tax to pay. But with a carnet you do not have to pay import duty, so don't let anyone talk you into doing so. Keeping on top of all this can become a major occupation, but remember – be patient, stay calm and keep smiling!

Police or military checks are apparent not only at every border crossing, but often also on the outskirts of towns and sometimes in the middle of nowhere. The officials may just want to relieve the boredom and say 'hello', or they may insist on seeing everything you have, but the latter is rare nowadays. We personally had no serious problems at any border posts on our last two trips in 2003 and 2004, but the previous authors reported that some bikers in southern Ethiopia ended up at a border post for three days while every one of their items was meticulously searched, regardless of gifts offered. You may be lucky. In Nigeria, which has a terrible reputation for police corruption, we were stopped at nearly every roadside check post, but they simply said 'Good morning, how are you? Have a safe journey.'

Receipts for administration fees are not uncommon; in this case the request is probably genuine. In fact when we left Arlit in Niger we had to pay a road toll for the first tarmac road we had been on for several days. After our experiences at the Assamaka border and then the police station in town, we said we were not going to pay any more money, but the policeman looked at us very apologetically and said 'It's not for me, Sir, it's for the road,' as he gave us a genuine receipt. We felt very embarrassed at not having trusted him.

The best advice we can give is to play it by ear. It is up to you how to handle it if you are asked for money. Sometimes a cigarette (buy some to give away even if you don't smoke) or a pen and a smile is enough – sometimes a smile alone will suffice. Unfortunately, some travellers and tourists in the past have given in too easily to requests for money or gifts. Some officials now expect that you will pay or give a gift. If you can get away with it, it's best not to hand anything over, except for a smile and a handshake!

Do remember that often the police and military, especially in more remote areas, are not paid regularly by the government. Some of them also perform important services, for example restricting access to dangerous or remote areas. They may be totally dependent on donations from tourists as well as the local community, so don't always just refuse to pay; consider their situation and be fair. Assamaka (Niger) is a particular case in point.

# VISAS AND MONEY

Whenever you arrive in a large African town, particularly a capital city, you will probably have a long list of things that need doing: fixing the vehicle, buying spares, changing money, getting visas, making phone calls, sending and receiving emails, collecting post, replacing food supplies, etc. These will probably take longer than you think!

Visa applications can be a waiting game, taking from 24 hours up to three days (the exception is a Sudan visa – it took us six weeks in London, the previous authors three months! But we heard you could get it in a week or less in Cairo). Visiting a bank can take a whole day, if not longer. Trying to find somewhere to change travellers' cheques is a nightmare in most countries (impossible in Sudan); in others, particularly in southern Africa, it is easier and you'll get a better rate than for cash. If you have five things you want to get done on a particular day, you may be lucky to get through two. But you never know. Just relax and slow down into the pace of Africa.

## Visas

See *Visas* in *Chapter 4* (page 96) for information about which visas to get before leaving home.

Once in Africa you are dependent on the capital cities and the embassies represented therein. Not every country has an embassy in every African country, but with some careful planning, depending on where you want to go next, you'll be able to get your visa within a day or two. Some visas can take weeks, but that is very unusual. Try to get your visas where it is the least hassle, perhaps when you are staying a few days somewhere in any case. It is best to apply for a visa as soon as you arrive in town, as it may take longer than expected to be issued.

Filling out the application forms can be time-consuming and involve lots of paperwork. Most embassies have specific opening times for visa applications, so check beforehand. Some embassies demand letters from your embassy, called a 'Letter of Introduction'. This is literally a form of introduction from one embassy to another; a really unnecessary form of bureaucracy, since your passport proves your nationality. These letters usually take 24 hours to process and vary in price, costing anything between US$20 and US$50, depending on the embassy. Sometimes your own letter typed on official-looking letterhead notepaper may suffice.

Photographs, one, two or three depending on the country, need to be attached to the visa application. Passport photos are useful not only for visa applications, but also for other documentation that you may need for a specific country, such as photo permits.

When you apply for a visa it is useful to know the name of a hotel in the country you are proposing to visit. It may help if you can say you're staying at the Sheraton or another respectable hotel, rather than a backpackers' hostel or campsite. Visa costs can vary from US$10 to US$100 depending on your nationality and the country you are visiting.

Visa requirements for different countries and different nationalities alter regularly, and it's unlikely that they'll all remain unchanged throughout the life of this book. Always check beforehand. Some East African countries will issue visas at the border, but in the rest of Africa you almost certainly need to obtain one before you arrive. If in doubt, get it in advance. Your embassy or other travellers can give current advice.

The same applies to most francophone countries (ie: ex-French colonies). Visas for these can sometimes be obtained from a French embassy. Check with your nearest

> ### CUSTOMS AGAIN
> The next morning was spent finding the central Customs, though with some apprehension. We had not been issued with the green papers at the Ethiopian Galafi border; the man with the key to the paper cupboard was simply not 'in station'. Here in Addis no-one seemed keen to rectify this, and all from the boss down insisted the border at Moyale could sort it out. Then, to leave the compound, we needed another piece of paper. 'How did this car get in here?' exclaimed the big man. 'We drove it in here an hour ago.' 'No, no, you cannot have done it, isn't it, where is your gate pass?' The gate men seemed to think the Land Rover was new and had somehow avoided Customs duty, being in this Customs zone. It was finally sorted out at the mention of the big boss and the carnet showing our entry at Galafi.

French embassy or consulate for the current list of countries for which they issue visas, as it seems to change frequently. The following countries are relevant: Benin, Burkina Faso, Cameroon, Central African Republic (CAR), Chad, Congo, Ivory Coast, Equatorial Guinea, Gabon, Mali, Niger, Senegal and Togo. Several of these have embassies or consulates in the UK; for others you will have to send your passport to Paris or get the visa en route.

Some border guards will ask to see a receipt for the visa. You cannot be certain whether this is a genuine requirement, or simply an excuse to ask for money. Try to get a receipt from the embassy or ask them to write the amount paid for the visa in your passport with an official stamp next to it.

## Money on the road

> Finance is the art of passing currency from hand to hand until it finally disappears.
>
> Robert W Sarnoff

## Currency declaration forms

Some countries require you to fill in a declaration on entering, saying exactly how much foreign exchange you are bringing in and whether it is in cash or travellers' cheques. If so, all your money might be counted out in front of you and listed on the form. You cannot change any money at a bank without this form. On leaving the country your leftover money, change receipts and declaration form should all tie up – don't get caught out!

Make sure you have hidden some money in a safe place, not only so you can perhaps get a better rate, but also so you can change money even if there is no bank around or open. This can often happen!

### Cashing money on the road

The best option is to take a mixture of euros, US dollars and pounds sterling, in small and large denominations. For more information on suggested amounts and types of currency to take, see *Money* in *Chapter 4* (page 95).

Finding a bank or somebody to change hard currency is hardly ever a problem, but travellers' cheques are another matter. Most travellers carry them for security, but they can be almost impossible to change. If you're lucky, you might find a bank or bureau de change which will accept them. Some campsites and backpackers', mostly in the south, will change travellers' cheques for you and sometimes even accept travellers' cheques as payment. But generally speaking cash is best.

Changing money, like visa applications, can be time-consuming and filled with paperwork. Some banks are computerised and changing money is a simple process, while others need to go through all sorts of hassles before you see the cash. Always check opening and closing times of banks and leave plenty of time to change money, particularly in Arab countries where the opening hours vary between 08.30 and 09.00 – like in the Sudan – or 09.00 and 10.00. Though guidebooks may state that banks are open from 09.00 to 11.00, it is better to go earlier rather than later, even if you do have to wait for the attendant to have tea and say good morning to everyone. Remember that Friday is usually a holiday in Arab countries.

Most banks in Africa will charge a commission for changing travellers' cheques. Rates and commissions vary widely (from 1% to 10%) from bank to bank, so it is worth shopping around to ensure you get the best rate. It is also advisable to check where your next bank will be and change enough money accordingly.

In Sudan it is not possible to change travellers' cheques, although it is possible to change US dollars cash.

Credit and debit cards can be convenient in southern Africa and parts of East Africa. ATMs are now fairly widely available in larger towns and you can get your cash on the spot. But some countries have no facilities for plastic cards at all.

# WHERE TO STAY
See general information under *Accommodation* in *Chapter 4*.

## Hotels
Hotels are plentiful in most parts of Africa, though many of them do not come close to what we would call a hotel. But then nor do the prices. In some places they are run by the local community with no star structure at all, while in southern Africa, the east coast, parts of the west coast and parts of North Africa, there is one- to five-star accommodation.

In many African countries, and particularly in the capitals, you will find a Hilton or Sheraton, a temporary escape from the third world to the first and the so-called civilisation that you are trying to evade and forget for a while. Such hotels can be a great place to relax and recover your energies when you have been on the road for some time. They usually offer all sorts of amenities, normally at roughly European rates. However, we were exceptionally lucky in Djibouti, when the manager of the Sheraton offered us a room for a very reasonable rate at 17.00; we had been looking for hours for somewhere safe to camp. We used every minute of our air-conditioned comfort before check-out the next day!

'Hotels' in African terms can often be just the bare minimum, so always ask to see the room and negotiate the rate before booking yourself in. If you have your own vehicle, make sure that the hotel has a secure parking area; some hotels will allow guests to keep motorbikes in their rooms.

In many of the French-speaking countries along the west coast, you will struggle to find campsites or hostels, particularly in the larger towns, and you may have to depend on the kindness of a hotel manager to let you stay in his parking lot and use the hotel facilities. In fact we found that many of the hotels in Africa would allow us to sleep in the car park and use a room for shower and toilet facilities. It may not work every time in the Hilton or Sheraton, but it's worth asking and explaining that you're driving across Africa. Often the novelty value of such a trip may inspire sympathy as well as incredulity and wonder.

## Bed and breakfast
B&Bs are mostly found in southern Africa and along the east coast. Often quaint and family run, they offer a wonderful opportunity to relax and get information on what to

do, or not to do, in that specific town or country. Most B&Bs belong to the National Hotel Association and/or are accredited by the tourist board, Automobile Association or various guidebooks. They are usually reasonably priced, around US$15 to US$25 for a double room.

Tourist information offices should be able to supply you with a list of B&Bs in the area and relevant prices.

## Pensions

Perhaps if you're driving across wildest and deepest, darkest Africa, you won't be in need of a pension! But let's be serious … Pensions are similar to B&Bs, but are specific to the French-speaking countries such as Chad, Ivory Coast, Mali and Niger and are often run by a family; they are abundant in Morocco. Most of the pensions we experienced were economical, clean and well run. They are often also a wonderful introduction to the local community, usually offering an abundance of information about the town and surrounding areas. Most pensions cost between US$8 and US$15 for a double room.

## Missions

Throughout Africa, missions, hospitals and aid organisations will often let you camp in their grounds or even offer you a room. Some will expect a small fee, others a large one – either way, a donation based on current camping rates is always welcome.

Missions can be found in nearly every country in Africa. Unfortunately some travellers have abused their hospitality and so those that follow after them are not always welcome. You won't find yourself being turned away by every mission, but it is more and more difficult to depend on them. Most missionaries adhere to strict rules and regulations in terms of curfews, shower time, kitchen and leisure time. If you don't want to keep to such rules, find alternative accommodation; others coming after you may like to use the opportunity, even if you don't.

## Youth hostels

Youth hostels are located in most capitals and other large cities. They are often the most convenient and cheapest places for a lone traveller, but two people travelling together can usually get a double room for the same price and greater privacy elsewhere. Some are spartan, with night-time curfews, daytime closing and no cooking facilities, often lacking in privacy and overrun by school groups. Others, however, are conveniently located and hassle-free, offering a wonderful opportunity to meet other travellers.

### MONKEY BUSINESS

South of Addis a good road drops down from the highlands into the Great Rift Valley of East Africa. We passed a lone Japanese cyclist in this road – we will never know his story. The lakes of the Rift are famous for their birdlife and pleasant scenes. We were surprised how dry the area just out of Addis was, with dusty plains of acacia and bush. On each side of the valley the land rose to distant heights. Awasa is one of the more developed towns, with a superb hotel on the lakeside. Massive shady trees offered a cool retreat in the gardens, while flocks of colourful birds skimmed low over the lake. Vivid blue-bottomed monkeys looked inquisitively at the discarded icing off our last remaining piece of Christmas cake; the icing had become discoloured with aluminium dust, which seems to get everywhere in the back lockers, but the cake itself was still delicious! And the monkeys seemed to enjoy the icing too, once they dared to taste it! So much so that we had to keep the windows of our room firmly shut.

### ANOTHER DAY, ANOTHER CONVOY...

Still in a convoy we visited the magnificent temples and ruins of Idfu and Kom Ombo on the way. Idfu was magnificent, stunning, despite the hordes of day-trippers and silly prices at the tea stand. As soon as we hit Aswan the armed escort melted away into the chaos. The perennial problem: where will we stay here? No campsite, no hotel with safe parking. No lonely oasis, no shady delightful palmeries to hide in, just concrete and walled compounds. We had harboured a notion of camping in the lush gardens of the Old Cataract Hotel; well, it had been possible 20 years ago according to an ancient guidebook. Now, we could not even get into the hotel grounds without paying an entrance fee. Death on the Nile. Choking by mass tourism and choking by security concerns, the death knell of the independent traveller.

## Backpackers' hostels

Backpackers' hostels are found mostly in southern Africa and along the east coast, with an occasional one dotted along the west coast and in North Africa. They are economical, ranging from US$8 to US$15 for a single room, and often you can camp in the courtyard or garden. They offer a huge variety of information on what to do around town, and are a good place to meet up with other travellers.

## Campsites

You will often find that your day revolves around finding a good spot to stay for the evening, if not for a day or two. Along the more frequented Africa overland routes, there are campsites at fairly regular intervals. Major towns and out-of-the-way places will often have a site, but, if you're intending to do a loop around West Africa, you may struggle to find any at all. Campsites are not common in Libya, Sudan, Ethiopia, Cameroon or Gabon. Sites vary from one- to five-star ratings, and prices will usually vary from US$3 to US$8.

Most campsites are visited on the recommendation of other travellers. They also give you the opportunity to meet other travellers, do some maintenance and repairs to your vehicle and catch up on all the other odd jobs that you might have been neglecting. Campsites are often a great source of information regarding vehicle repairs; where to go and who to see. Sometimes they even have their own individual mechanic, a sort of Mr Fix-It and perhaps an ex-driver for one of the tour companies. Information on some of the main campsites is included under individual countries in *Chapter 8*.

## Bush sleeping

Don't miss it! It is an indescribably wonderful experience to sleep out in the bush, listening to the cicadas whispering, or rather chattering at high volume, in the stillness of the night. Or to sleep out in the Sahara, where nothing at all disturbs the silence, and you can hear your own heartbeat. Watching the stars and pondering the immensity of the universe.

For your own security, the less visible you are from the road, the better; unfortunately, not everyone in this world is friendly and you don't want the wrong kind of person to find you alone in an isolated spot. But trying to steer away from prying eyes can often prove difficult. Find a spot earlier rather than later, as problems tend to multiply once it gets dark; then you can't see where you're going, whereas anyone else who might be around can see your headlights for miles. Having spotted an area, try to make sure that no other drivers or villagers are watching when you turn off. This is easier said than done, as villages tend to develop alongside a country's road network.

## THE MEN OF THE NIGHT

South of Tamanrasset and the broken rocky remnants of the Hoggar Mountains, the road becomes open desert, with many pistes. The tracks cross plains dotted with isolated craggy outcrops of boulders, destroyed by heat and cold, smashed by gripping winds and sandstorms, slowly decomposing to sand.

We camped close to the border with Niger. On the roof of the vehicle, we slept intermittently. A cool breeze rustled the plastic bag behind our pillows. The stars were amazing. A large eerie shadow was cast by a 150-foot tower of rock erupting vertically upwards from the warm sands. Sentinels of similar rock towers marched across the desert in the black of the night. Suddenly the headlights of the leading car brushed the Land Rover, and a convoy of two vehicles came to a halt some short distance away. Too stunned to be afraid, we peered out from below the bedding, not daring to breathe. A group of men in turbans got out of the vehicles. Leaping around and shouting, they seemed to be arguing. Then another car came past us. This was it; bandits, kidnappers, smugglers, whoever they were, we were sitting ducks and might as well pretend to be asleep.

After what seemed like an eternity, they drove off into the darkness of the night, leaving us waiting for our hearts to slow down again. Perhaps our crummy old Land Rover wasn't worth the bother!

At In Guezzam, the Tabaski festival was under way, the diesel station was closed and everyone was dressed in their finest robes and colourful cheches. Sheep were nervously corralled in pens awaiting their fate. 'We cannot find the fuel pump man; he is with one of his wives!' However we were invited to partake in the celebrations at the police station. After much delay, large plates appeared loaded with freshly grilled lamb and salad. All we could offer in return was a McVitie's chocolate cake, which went down very well with the local officers. 'What about the men we saw last night?' we asked. 'Oh, they're just smugglers, cigarettes, you know. We don't have any bandits here, you are quite safe.'

Make sure that you respect the bush and be aware of the environment around you. If the surrounding area is particularly dry and there is a gale, don't light a fire. It would in any case make you extremely visible for miles around. Leave only your footprints in the sand, bury only biodegradable products. Do not bury any goods in national parks. Animals will usually dig them up and could cause major damage to themselves, if not the environment. It's best to carry all your rubbish with you until you find an appropriate place to discard it.

In Congo, Gabon or any other tropical rainforest area, bush sleeping can be very difficult, with solid vegetation right up to the sides of the road, and wild animals on the prowl at night. One option, often the only one, is to find one of the 'gravel pits' that have been dug out for material to build the road. Such pits are few and far between and may often contain large pools of water, making mosquito nets absolutely essential. You are also almost guaranteed to have visitors, as they're frequently sited close to a village. It can also be hard to find a spot for bush camping in South Africa, Botswana, Namibia or Zimbabwe, as almost all land is fenced off. In North Africa you can generally camp in palmeries (palm groves), but as these are privately owned you should ask permission if possible.

The other option is to find a village and ask if you may camp there. It is all too easy to forget that we are guests in the communities through which we are driving. Where there are a few roads or tracks the population is likely to be concentrated along them. In this case, try to find the head of the village and ask permission to camp. A small gift of appreciation such as a bottle of Coke, pens or cigarettes is often welcomed. Even empty plastic water bottles are useful. Villagers are by nature curious, as we are of them, and you may feel a little intimidated by ogling adults and children. Mostly they are just friendly, though, and would like to communicate with you. A sense of humour, or being able to play a musical instrument, drawing or just communicating in some way or another usually helps to ease the situation, and is one of the better ways of getting to know a particular tribe, culture or village.

Remember that the vast majority of people in the world are friendly; if you didn't believe that, you would have stayed at home. By taking reasonable precautions, you can have a fantastic experience out in the bush.

# FOOD AND DRINK
## Let's go local

Going local is inexpensive and can be great fun. All of Africa's countries have their own unique meals and local brews. Some can be an acquired taste, others will be something you want to eat over and over again, and a few you will hope never to taste again. For the local flavour of the day go to the markets, street vendors, restaurants or local cafés. But do be cautious about the standard of hygiene. Avoid fresh uncooked salads and fruit you haven't prepared yourself. You can't always choose where to stop the car in an emergency!

Each African country has its own beer, often brewed and bottled locally. In addition to this are fermented ricewater, honey beer, millet beer and all sorts of other local delicacies brewed up 24 hours a day. In some Muslim countries, alcohol is prohibited, so be careful about this.

In most African cultures, people eat with their hands. If you are invited into somebody's home, they will often offer you their one spoon or any other cutlery that might be available. If this does not happen, there is just one golden rule you need to remember; always eat with your right hand. The left hand is used for all other dirty business.

If you are unsure about how to react to a specific situation, watch what others do. In some cultures, they will only begin eating once you have started. Ask to wash your hands before a meal, then help yourself. Often your insecurity and any mishap in eating with your hands can break the ice; it's your turn to be the entertainment!

### ETHIOPIA IN A NUTSHELL
Another day, another shocking road, but what superb scenery. We climbed to the roof of Africa and then plunged down the eastern escarpment into the green and semi-tropical paradise called Woldiya. Another scruffy town, but at least the hotel here was a haven of peace. Two foreign aid workers sat nearby as we slumped down in sumptuous armchairs. They seemed to be solving all of Ethiopia's problems over a cold beer or two, such reassurance. Later they left in their latest Toyota Land Cruiser with its radio aerial strung high over the bonnet and roof. Could we find any carrots in the market? Plenty of bright green water carriers and washing powder everywhere, but food? No chance. What do they eat in this country? We eventually discovered that the hotel had its own bakery and huge vegetable gardens behind the building. Here was a veritable Garden of Eden with carrots, tomatoes, avocados, coffee, papayas ... So why couldn't anyone except this enterprising manager of the hotel grow food? Again we had little or no sleep, all night a great wailing of Coptic prayer drowned out the faintly lethargic crickets and cicadas.

## SOME LOCAL DELICACIES – TO TRY OR NOT TO TRY!
Charlie Shackell and Illya Bracht

### Egypt
**Stella** (local beer)

**Alwa turki** Turkish-style coffee and a great energy booster, particularly with large amounts of sugar

**Molokhiyya** A soup made by stewing leafy vegetables with rice, garlic and chicken or beef broth. Do not be put off by its appearance.

**Grilled samak** (fish) Served by the kilogram and chosen by you. Usually includes salad, bread and dips like tahina (sesame spread with olive oil, garlic and lemon) and baba ghanoug (a mix of aubergine and tahina).

**Gibna beyda** (white cheese like feta) or **gibna rumi** (hard, sharp yellow-white cheese)

### Ethiopia
**Tej** A very potent honey beer that you will either hate or love!

**Coffee ceremony** A must; be ready to experience a caffeine overdrive!

**Shiro wot** Vegetable stew, great for vegetarians, and eaten by Ethiopians during religious fasting

**Doro wot** Hot chicken stew served on the famous injera bread

**Injera** Flatbread, generally made to cover a table. Food is placed on top for communal meals. Not to everyone's taste; can be quite sour.

**Kitfo** Raw meat with yellow pepper (mitmita)

Coffee shops serve fresh coffee, fruit juice and cakes.

### Ghana
**Apateche** Traditional firewater found everywhere. Try it!

**Star** (local beer)

**Shitor din** Traditional dark chilli sambal

**Palava sauce** 'Palava' means 'trouble'; this is a variation of vegetable and meat stew

### Ivory Coast
**Attiéké** Grated manioc served with fish and pepper sauce

**Maquis** Chicken with onion and tomatoes

**Rice and offal balls** A great delicacy

### Kenya
**Tusker** (local beer)

**Irio** Corn mash and maize which most Kenyans think is dull, but it's worth a try

**N'Dizi** Swahili for bananas, wrapped in groundnut. Crunchy n'dizi is self-explanatory.

### Morocco
**Green tea** Very sweet, served with fresh peppermint leaves

**Tagine** with chicken and prunes: a stew cooked in the traditional tagine bowl and said to be one of the oldest recipes in Africa

### Niger
**Green tea** Traditionally brewed up by Tuaregs over an open fire in very small teapots

## Local produce
In much of Africa you'll have no problem finding local produce at markets or from street vendors. Onions, garlic and tomatoes are nearly always available. Goat, mutton and chicken are also readily available, and fish is plentiful near rivers and on the coast. Many other fruits and vegetables can be found according to the country's economy and the

**Fresh camels' milk** – like a warm milkshake and not to everyone's taste
**Goat's cheese** – a Tuareg delicacy and delicious if you're a lover of cheese; should be accompanied by dried prunes
**Tuareg bread** – baked in the sand

## Nigeria
**Lager Star** (local beer)
**Gari foto** Based on the root vegetable of the African diet
**Gari** Like rice, the base for many dishes
**Okra soup** – looks like slime but never say no to a new experience!
**Kyimkying** – West African kebabs and great street food, but not recommended by the local expat community

## Southern Africa
**Castle** (local beer)
**Red wines** from Cape Town
**Amarula** A liquor made up from the amarula tree, which bears a fruit that elephants particularly like to eat
**Biltong** Dried game, not to everyone's taste
**Bobotie** A Malay dish served in southern Africa
**Boerewors** A type of sausage, delicious grilled over an open fire

## Sudan
**Guava juice** A must if you like guavas, freshly squeezed, served out of enormous cooler boxes
**Fuul** Fava beans with oil, lemon, salt, meat, eggs and onions
**Ta'amiyya** Deep-fried ground chick peas – very 'moreish'!

## Tanzania
**Amstel** (local beer)
**Chapati ya n'dizi tamu** Banana fritters, common throughout Africa
**Chilled banana cream** Good, depending on its freshness
**Mboga ya maboga** Pumpkin leaves and flowers in cream
**Plantain or banana chips**

## Tunisia
**Brik** A thin, crisp, pastry envelope filled with egg, cheese or meat. If you choose egg, bite carefully – the yolk may spurt out!

## Zimbabwe
**Black Label** (local beer)
**Nhopi dovi** Like pumpkin
**Sadza** Like the West African banku, the East African ugali, Zambian ntsima or South African 'mealie-meal', sadza is a stiff, steamed dumpling made from white maize flour. It is regarded as Zimbabwe's national dish.

season. But food is not always so easy to find, so make sure you always have some emergency supplies of tinned food with you. For example, in some parts of Ethiopia we found only garlic for sale along the roadside; in one town there was no food for sale in the shops, but the hotel we camped at had a wonderful orchard where our carrots were picked fresh from the ground while we waited. See box on page 155.

It can be great fun haggling and bartering your way through smiling vendors, each protesting that their produce is the freshest, nicest and cheapest. Visit a few stalls and ask around, so you can get a feel for prices and always keep in mind the average local income. Sometimes you will be ripped off, but if you are happy to pay the price asked, then pay it! Most supermarkets have local produce, but at an increased cost, as many of the products are imported from neighbouring countries, or even from Europe.

## Supermarkets

Most capital cities in Africa have a supermarket or two, from well stocked to nearly empty. Local shops, often only a hole in the wall or a table set up on the pavement, have basic goods like toothpaste, toilet paper, margarine and other odds and ends. One hole-in-the-wall shop in Omdurman, Khartoum, had an amazing array of goods, which I browsed through while Bob was getting a puncture fixed next door. Orange juice, Egyptian fava beans, clean loose sugar…

For more luxurious items such as fresh cheese and chocolate, you will need to shop in large supermarket chains, like the Nakomat or Uchumi in Nairobi, which are found in most East African countries. If you have a favourite brand, take enough to last your entire trip, although this is only possible if you have your own vehicle.

## International restaurants

There will come a time when you are tired of eating locally or cooking for yourself. Perhaps there is a special occasion on the horizon. Cuisine from all over the world can be found throughout Africa, particularly in the capitals, from Chinese to Italian, Indian to Lebanese, pizzas to hamburgers. The restaurants cater to every need and every pocket. Some are based on European prices, while others are more affordable. Ask other travellers or wherever you are staying for advice on restaurants in the area. Most campsites and backpackers' hostels also offer basic international meals.

## Water

There is a saying in Agadez, Niger, that once you have tasted the water you will always want to return! In Agadez, the artesian wells are thousands of years old and the water is pure, coming deep out of the ground. It is checked regularly too. But this is not always the case everywhere, and it's better to be safe than sorry; better to spend time purifying the water than be sick for days in your vehicle, or worse, on your bicycle.

You must respect local water sources. Water, especially clean water, is one of the most important commodities in Africa. Never do anything to a well that might contaminate it, such as throwing anything into it, or washing yourself or your clothes close by. This is particularly important in Arab countries, where water is also used for prayer.

Obtaining water and the amount you need to carry depends on the time of year you are travelling, where you are and how dedicated you are to washing both yourself and

### AN ODE TO COCA-COLA
Charlie Shackell and Illya Bracht
Coca-Cola is not only a great thirst quencher, but you will find it wherever you go. In the middle of nowhere, desolate and isolated, without a doubt a hut will appear that is selling Coca-Cola! It's not only good for tummy upsets or dehydration, but also great for cooking.

If you have a very tough piece of meat, boil it up in Coca-Cola for an hour or so and you are guaranteed to have a tender piece of meat. Coca-Cola is indeed the real thing!

## THE PANTOMIME SEASON IN ASWAN

To get to Sudan is not easy, first the visa then the ferry across Lake Nasser. Sunday morning in Aswan. Oh yes we can, oh no we can't. The ferry does go on Monday, but will there be enough cargo to attach the barge? Wait till Monday.

Monday morning bright and early we arrived at the high dam. Four hours later we were still at the high dam and nervous with anticipation. We were dealing with Mohammed; they are all called Mohammed. Yes, there is enough cargo; no, there isn't enough cargo. There aren't any other foreign devils with cars, so it's not looking too optimistic. We sit, and sit. How much are we willing to pay for this once-a-week mayhem? Can we consider coming back next week? What about driving back to Cairo? No more convoys, please! It's going to be pay up, Wadi Halfa or bust. The game is played out all day.

The Sudanese cargo manager, Mahmoud, seems to be the one who pulls the strings, although he claims he is consulting with a higher authority in the building conveniently out of sight. The first Mohammed seems to be on the sidelines, but his cut must surely be in the pie somewhere. More cargo arrives and it looks promising. It's all an illusion, but it's conducted with a great air of honourable pretence on both sides. They say they really are sorry that there isn't enough cargo and we'll have to pay more. Of course we are totally over a barrel, and pretend that it's really too much, we'll have to drive all the way back to London. What a shame.

Two pm and a deal is done. It's outrageous but it's better than going back to Cairo in a convoy. Four pm and we are still waiting to be loaded. There is so much cargo there is barely room for the Land Rover. A barge crammed with potatoes, tomatoes, cans of cooking oil and much else is lashed to the side of the main ferry. Finally we drive the Land Rover up two wobbly planks on to the deck of this narrow barge, without driving straight off the other side. The brakes mercifully stop us ploughing into the lake. They take us proudly to our cabin... What a heap of … and this is the new ferry. The communal toilets have already overflowed and are awash with eight inches of water, or whatever. In order to use them, you must stay above floor level on raised bulkheads and stand in the dark, hoping that your aim is straight and accurate. Judging by the state of the paintwork around the hole, the men are not very skilled.

your clothes. Drinking is more important than washing when water is scarce or unavailable. Remember also that your radiator may be thirsty or, in the worst case, spring a leak. Never waste water, especially when you're on the road.

In the desert at the hottest time of year you should allow six to eight litres a day intake per person, and even in January or February you will easily get through two or three. It is absolutely vital to drink as much as you need, as you could run into serious problems if you do not. If your urine becomes concentrated in colour, you could be heading for trouble. A good guide is that you should urinate often and it should be clear.

Cyclists will face the greatest difficulties in terms of how much they can carry, and motorcyclists will also be restricted by weight. It is best to stick to the more major desert routes, where water is more likely to be available from other travellers. Cyclists will need a good filter because they are less able to carry supplies of good water and will be more likely to rely on poorer sources. If water is not clear in any way, filter before purifying it. We drank either bottled mineral water, or boiled water that locals would drink straight from the tap. Very rarely and only in parts of the Sahara, we drank water straight from the source without purification. Other travellers have recommended Chloromyn T.

For more information see *Water* in *Chapter 2* (page 47) and *Health* in *Chapter 4* (page 106).

In general, wherever there is a village you will find a source of water. Open bodies of water, streams, lakes, etc are probably going to be contaminated and should be treated with caution. If you take water from an open source, always purify it, preferably by boiling. Water from the tap can vary in quality; the best advice is to ask the locals if they drink it straight. Then purify it anyway just in case. When faced with a village well, use some common sense. If people are washing nearby or the toilets are close, then don't trust it. Even if you are at a remote desert well which is well maintained and covered, you should still purify the water before drinking it; there may well be a dead goat or camel down there!

## Soft drinks, beer and spirits

A cold refreshing beer under a fading African sky is bliss after a hot day on the road. Except in North Africa, beer and local spirits are generally easy to find. Local beers at local prices are nearly always pleasant, and of varying levels of alcohol content. Imported spirits can be found in most capital cities at European prices. In Arab countries, where alcohol is often banned, don't try to smuggle any in. You could end up in prison or worse. Soft drinks can be found almost everywhere and Coke or Pepsi are always available.

## SHOPPING

Wherever you travel in Africa, the following are some of the local products and crafts available: weaving and cloth; sculpture; masks; silver crosses from Agadez, Niger; other jewellery; wood carvings; papyrus paintings from Egypt.

# Part Three

## Africa: The Guide

# Bradt Travel Guides

*Africa Overland* Siân Pritchard-Jones / Bob Gibbons
*Albania* Gillian Gloyer
*Amazon, The* Roger Harris/Peter Hutchison
*Antarctica: A Guide to the Wildlife*
  Tony Soper/Dafila Scott
*Arctic: A Guide to Coastal Wildlife*
  Tony Soper/Dan Powell
*Armenia with Nagorno Karabagh* Nicholas
  Holding
*Azores* David Sayers
*Baghdad* Catherine Arnold
*Baltic Capitals: Tallinn, Riga, Vilnius, Kaliningrad*
  Neil Taylor et al
*Bosnia & Herzegovina* Tim Clancy
*Botswana: Okavango, Chobe, Northern Kalahari*
  Chris McIntyre
*British Isles: Wildlife of Coastal Waters*
  Tony Soper/Dan Powell
*Budapest* Adrian Phillips/Jo Scotchmer
*Cameroon* Ben West
*Canary Islands* Lucy Corne
*Cape Verde Islands* Aisling Irwin/
  Colum Wilson
*Cayman Islands* Tricia Hayne
*Chile* Tim Burford
*Chile & Argentina: Trekking Guide*
  Tim Burford
*Cork* Linda Fallon
*Costa Rica* Larissa Banting
*Croatia* Piers Letcher
*Cyprus* see *North Cyprus*
*Dubrovnik* Piers Letcher
*Eccentric America* Jan Friedman
*Eccentric Britain* Benedict le Vay
*Eccentric California* Jan Friedman
*Eccentric Edinburgh* Benedict le Vay
*Eccentric France* Piers Letcher
*Eccentric London* Benedict le Vay
*Eccentric Oxford* Benedict le Vay
*Ecuador: Climbing & Hiking in*
  Rob Rachowiecki/Mark Thurber
*Eritrea* Edward Denison/Edward Paice
*Estonia* Neil Taylor
*Ethiopia* Philip Briggs
*Falkland Islands* Will Wagstaff
*Faroe Islands* James Proctor
*Gabon, São Tome & Principe* Sophie Warne
*Galápagos Wildlife* David Horwell/Pete Oxford
*Gambia, The* Craig Emms/Linda Barnett
*Georgia* Tim Burford
*Ghana* Philip Briggs
*Hungary* Adrian Phillips/Jo Scotchmer
*Iran* Patricia L Baker
*Iraq* Karen Dabrowska
*Kabul Mini Guide* Dominic Medley/
  Jude Barrand

*Kenya* Claire Foottit
*Kiev* Andrew Evans
*Latvia* Stephen Baister/Chris Patrick
*Lille Mini Guide* Laurence Phillips
*Lithuania* Gordon McLachlan
*Ljubljana* Robin & Jenny McKelvie
*Macedonia* Thammy Evans
*Madagascar* Hilary Bradt
*Madagascar Wildlife* Nick Garbutt/
  Hilary Bradt/Derek Schuurman
*Malawi* Philip Briggs
*Maldives* Royston Ellis
*Mali* Ross Velton
*Mauritius, Rodrigues & Réunion* Royston Ellis/
  Alex Richards/Derek Schuurman
*Mongolia* Jane Blunden
*Montenegro* Annalisa Rellie
*Mozambique* Philip Briggs/Ross Velton
*Namibia* Chris McIntyre
*Nigeria* Lizzie Williams
*North Cyprus* Diana Darke
*North Korea* Robert Willoughby
*Palestine, with Jerusalem* Henry Stedman
*Panama* Sarah Woods
*Paris, Lille & Brussels: Eurostar Cities*
  Laurence Phillips
*Peru & Bolivia: Backpacking and Trekking*
  Hilary Bradt/Kathy Jarvis
*Riga* Stephen Baister/Chris Patrick
*River Thames, In the Footsteps of the Famous*
  Paul Goldsack
*Rwanda* Janice Booth/Philip Briggs
*St Helena, Ascension, Tristan da Cunha*
  Sue Steiner
*Serbia* Laurence Mitchell
*Seychelles* Lyn Mair/Lynnath Beckley
*Slovenia* Robin & Jenny McKelvie
*South Africa: Budget Travel Guide* Paul Ash
*Southern African Wildlife* Mike Unwin
*Spitsbergen* Andreas Umbreit
*Sri Lanka* Royston Ellis
*Sudan* Paul Clammer
*Switzerland: Rail, Road, Lake* Anthony Lambert
*Tallinn* Neil Taylor
*Tanzania* Philip Briggs
*Tasmania* Matthew Brace
*Tibet* Michael Buckley
*Uganda* Philip Briggs
*Ukraine* Andrew Evans
*USA by Rail* John Pitt
*Venezuela* Hilary Dunsterville Branch
*Vilnius* Gordon McLachlan/Neil Taylor
*Your Child Abroad*
  Dr Jane Wilson-Howarth/Dr Matthew Ellis
*Zambia* Chris McIntyre
*Zanzibar* David Else

## Bradt Travel Guides Ltd
+44 (0)1753 893444    www.bradtguides.com

# Background

## GEOGRAPHY, VEGETATION AND CLIMATE

In this section is a brief outline of the main physical features of Africa. All of the north, from the Mediterranean to the 25 degree latitude, is *desert*. It is amazingly varied and has the mountainous areas of the Hoggar, Tassili, Tibesti and Ennedi. South of the desert is the transitional zone known as the *sahel*. This is a region of hardy fine grasses, sandy sparse scrub, acacia trees and limited low tree cover. Moving south, these scrub areas become steadily thicker bush, with very striking baobab trees. This whole transitional area is known as *savanna*, a wooded zone with tall grasses that becomes steadily denser. Finally, around the Equator are luxuriant thick *rainforests* with tall trees and dark undergrowth. Heading into the southern hemisphere, the vegetation has similar patterns in reverse, but the desert is confined to the western region of Namibia. South Africa is generally classified as a Mediterranean climatic zone, but with variations depending on altitude. East Africa and Ethiopia present the other main variations, where altitude is the dominant influence on the landscape and vegetation.

Africa's climate has gone through many changes. It is thought that most of Africa and indeed Europe had a wet and warm period between 13000BC and 9000BC. After this the climate became drier, but there is strong evidence from rock art that most of the Sahara area was fertile with herders and some sedentary groups. Some of the rock art of the Tassili plateau in Algeria/Libya, the Tibesti and Ennedi mountains in Chad is thought to be as old as 7,000 years. The desertification of the north to form the Sahara steadily expanded from around 3000BC. Climatic changes are still in progress in Africa today, as the Sahara steadily moves southwards. The droughts of the 1980s bear witness to this.

## NATURAL HISTORY AND CONSERVATION

Detailed examination of this vast topic is beyond the remit of this guide. Suffice to say that any extended trip across the continent will encompass all the major natural features it has to offer. Apart from the well-known safari parks in East and southern Africa, there are many new and amazingly diverse additions to the conservation list. Almost every country in Africa, whether desert, savanna, rainforest or mountain region, has set aside areas of significant natural habitat, many with attendant wildlife. Increasingly Africa is embracing the new forms of tourism: eco-tourism, wildlife preservation and conservation, cultural tourism and village development through small tourist initiatives. Botswana, Namibia, Tanzania, Kenya, Uganda and Gabon in particular have made great efforts towards conservation. It is no longer enough to chase around game parks or climb high mountains without giving something back. Endangered species are now at the forefront of conservation. That said, there are still serious problems. The most intractable are along the DRC/Uganda/Rwanda border, where political instability and saving the mountain gorillas are conflicting interests. In years to come, the need to preserve the continent's natural attractions will always be tempered by the need to eradicate poverty and increase economic development. Protecting nature will hopefully be seen in future as a means of protecting the planet and aiding human development.

## *DJIBOUTI – LAND OF EXTREMES*

In the morning, bleary-eyed and tetchy from the long drive, we headed for Lake Assal nearby. The scenery was again stunning. The road snaked over broken lava fields and past currently dormant volcanic cones. Most were not large, but the sheer number of old cones was breathtaking and somewhat sinister. Lake Assal, although only ten miles from the sea, is below sea level and separated from the sea only by the lava fields. The heat was already stifling by 08.00. The brilliant blue lake is surrounded by the walls of an ancient cauldron, multicoloured but mostly dark and jagged. Around the lake is an almost fluorescent white collar of super- brilliant crystalline deposits. The road descended into this vast cauldron of colour and seemingly dead wasteland.

Yet life is found here too. Small antelopes hop agilely across the rough landscape, tentatively watching the intruders. Distant flamingos gather around the shore. Down by the lake's edge are amazingly shaped crystals and rare volcanic rocks, halite being the strangest, with its egg-shaped hollowed-out rugby-ball shapes and brown crystals locking into each other. Brilliant yellow sulphur crystals grow from the water's edge. This is not a place to walk around carelessly without a guide. Here is the birthplace of a new ocean, where Africa is being ripped apart along its famous Rift Valley. Here Somalia and most of Kenya will be cut adrift by the forces from below the earth of Djibouti.

Suddenly a thunderous deafening, screeching roar breaks the silence of the desert. We jump out of our skins in fright. The French are playing soldiers across the desert, and their airforce is terrifying everyone with its low-flying supersonic fighter jets. Djibouti, it seems, is the playground of the French military. The noise is enough to awaken the demons of the dormant cones and send their boiling bellies of molten lava into crescendos of explosive rage.

The road east to Tadjoura holds more surprises: massive dried-out whirlpools of solidified lava, where hardy scrub acacias are trying to stay alive. The Land Rover can barely cope with the gradients and the gearbox sounds noisy. The views south of the narrow Bay of Ghoubbet are stupendous. The waters are almost cut off from the Red Sea. The mountains to the north are stark and rugged. Towards Tadjoura the greenery increases, and soon we can make out the Forêt du Day, a small zone of intensely forested hills. A freak of nature, born from the sea mists and very infrequent rains.

# HISTORY

It is generally agreed that human development began in Africa. Recently the oldest remains were found in Chad 300km north of N'djamena. Until the discovery in Chad, the oldest hominid had been found in Ethiopia's Danakil region. The name given to this find was Lucy. Dated at just over three million years old, these remains confirm the existence of transitional humanoids that were neither apes nor fully developed humans.

There is evidence to suggest that five main ethnic groups existed in Africa. There were the Nilotic peoples, generally taller in stature. In the north were people from whom the Berbers have descended. In the west were stocky negroid people. In central areas were the diminutive pygmies and in the east and south were the San who are now known as the Bushmen of Botswana. A date for the emergence of these groups is around 100,000 years ago. The Egyptians seem to have developed later, before or around 6000BC and separately from these groups. The Egyptian civilisation was at its zenith after 3000BC. It finally died out after being engulfed by the Nubians around 300BC. Then the Nubians too were overrun, by the Assyrians and Persians. Meanwhile from central and East Africa the Bantu people spread south between 100BC and AD200–300.

The next great civilisations to impose their will on North Africa were the Greeks and the Romans. The great cities of Carthage, El Djem, Sbeitla, Leptis Magna, Sabrata, and Apollonia arose. Further south another great kingdom, possibly with a Jewish connection, arose in the 4th century: that of Aksum in Ethiopia. Christianity spread into the empire, but in the face of the new religion, Islam, it was driven up into the highlands where it continued to flourish. Perhaps the greatest change in Africa occurred with the rise of Islam, from its beginnings in Arabia in the mid 7th century. Arab traders and slavers moved down the coast of East Africa, where the Swahili language developed. Arab zealots moved swiftly across North Africa, the Sahara and deep into West Africa.

Way to the south, the only significant civilisation to develop in the rest of the continent was centred on Zimbabwe. These famous ruins date from the 11th century. In West Africa three great civilisations or empires arose, mainly with the development of cross-Sahara trade routes using camels. The earliest was the Ghana Empire. It existed from AD700 to approximately AD1000. This was not centred on the area known as Ghana today, but located in southeastern present-day Mauritania. Later the Mali Empire arose, around AD1200, lasting until AD1500. This was the great period of wealth and trade with the cities of Djenné, Mopti and Timbuktu at their zenith. Finally the Songhai Empire gradually developed, taking over from the Mali Empire with its centre around Gao.

Slavery, which had already existed since the Arabs arrived, was further developed with the coming of the seafaring Europeans. The Portuguese began the process in 1450. Officially it was abolished in 1870, but did not completely die out. In fact tendencies towards slavery have not long been discontinued in Mauritania. The great wave of European expansion and subsequent colonisation began around the 1850s. By 1884 the great colonial powers were in such conflict over the territories that a meeting was called in Berlin to delineate the boundaries of the various countries. The British and the French took most of the continent, with Germany, Belgium and Portugal occupying most of the rest. Spain got Western 'Spanish' Sahara and Rio Muni/Fernando Po, modern Equatorial Guinea. Ethiopia remained virtually independent, but the Italians had some of its territory as well as Libya.

After World War I, Germany lost Tanganyika and parts of Togo and Cameroon, but remained influential in Namibia. Independence finally arrived, from the early 1950s onwards. Libya was one of the first to become independent, in 1951, followed by Ghana in 1952 after agitation by Nkrumah. Many countries gained independence in the 1960s, including most of East Africa, Nigeria and the French and Belgian colonies or protectorates. The last were the Portuguese colonies, finally succeeding in the years of 1974–75. Guinea Bissau, Mozambique and Angola. In southern Africa different problems existed. Zimbabwe finally gained freedom in 1980, after a protracted period under the Smith Government and various interim arrangements. Namibia was the last country to gain independence. It had been under South African administration, which had long been separated from the British yoke, but retained its unique racial separation with apartheid. South Africa finally became a multi-racial democracy in 1994.

## African explorers

Today we can pore over glossy maps and calculate travel times and distances in Africa with ease. However, the early exploration of Africa was a haphazard affair; some adventurers had official backing, others explored clandestinely, some were fanatical missionaries and others travelled with a deep faith in their hoped-for discoveries. Most set forth in the footsteps of Arab traders and slavers. An overland journey today follows these illustrious adventurers, but does not need to be so haphazardly planned!

One of the first African explorers was James Bruce, who set out for Ethiopia in 1769, ostensibly to find the source of the Nile. His journey took him into the highlands of the

## A FARM IN TANZANIA

Just south of Iringa is the Kisolanza Farm. This haven of peace sits at some 7,000ft and is much cooler. As we drove in, two young white women came across and said in perfect Sussex accents 'Do come and have a cup of tea when you're ready!' The campground was very well organised and the steaks were tremendous. For less than a pound we gorged on best fillet steak, so tender it could be cut with a butter knife. A party of four South African vehicles and their ageing occupants shared the camp.

The evening was spent exchanging stories. Where did you break down? How is your vehicle going? What sort of engine do you have? (Note that we all had Land Rovers!) Jasper and Emma, Justin and Becky had met in Nairobi after completely separate journeys from England, but lived only five miles apart in Kent and did not then know each other.

The farmhouse stands on a hill not far from the camp; the roof is thatched, the walls of local stone. Such a magnificent house could easily fit into a Dorset village. The farm had run down during the excessive socialist years of Nyerere, when landed gentry were considered undesirable in a left-leaning Utopian regime. New but admirably set bungalows have now been added to encourage eco-tourism, the new byword in development in modern-day Tanzania.

Things change.

---

country, from the port of Massawa on the Red Sea. Climbing on to the high plateau, he first visited Axum and then headed south across the Simien Mountains to the capital Gonder. Bruce was briefly appointed court physician to Ras Michael in Gonder after an epidemic of smallpox. He was also bewitched by one of his wives. After much drinking of honey wine at a wedding, he took his leave and travelled to Lake Tana and the Tissisat falls on the Blue Nile. Avoiding the various intrigues of power in Gonder he eventually made his way home via the Sudan and Nile. On his return in 1773 his exploits were doubted although his books prospered. He received no acclaim until after his death in 1794.

The Scotsman Mungo Park was another adventurer to be sent out to find answers to African geographical mysteries. Heading inland from the Gambia, he passed Ségou but got no further than Silla in his quest for the route of the Niger River. This was in 1795. He later returned to Africa in 1805 after recovering in England. This time his progress was better and he followed the river through Mali, Niger and Nigeria. He was killed at Bussa in Nigeria before completing his mission.

Three strong-minded and incompatible adventurers, Oudney, Clapperton and Denham, crossed the Sahara in 1822 via Murzuk to Bilma and Agadez. They eventually reached Lake Chad seeking routes to the Niger River. Oudney died in Nigeria and only Clapperton made any significant journeys, to Kano and Sokoto. In 1825 he again set out with Landers to find the route of the Niger. It was left to the Landers brothers to solve the mystery of the Niger and its mouth in 1830.

Stories of great wealth and gold lured others to Timbuktu. Alexander Gordon Laing was one such explorer. He travelled across the desert via Ghadames and the Fezzan. Having once been left for dead after a Tuareg raid, he reached the fabled city and lived there in a house that can still be seen today. He never returned alive though, being killed by Tuareg in 1826. The Frenchman René Caillié reached Djenné and Kabara by canoe, and arrived in Timbuktu in April 1828. He returned to France alive, crossing the Sahara to Morocco.

In 1850 Heinrich Barth and James Richardson left Tripoli southbound across the Sahara. Despite hostile Tuareg, Barth succeeded in being the first 'infidel' Christian to reach Agadez. Richardson later died, but Barth continued to explore the area of Nigeria, Cameroon and west to Timbuktu before returning alive to Germany in 1855. The Swiss explorer Johann Ludwig Burckhardt learnt Arabic and made a daring visit to Mecca, having travelled across Egypt and the Sudan. Another adventurous German, Gustav Nachtigal, explored the Sahara and in particular the unknown Tibesti Mountains. He was lucky to escape from the fiercely independent and unfriendly Tubu tribes of those mountains. The Tubu still resist outsiders today.

In 1854 Richard Burton, having studied Somali customs, made a daring visit to Harar in Ethiopia, a city of devout Muslims where no infidel was likely to survive. But survive he did, being welcomed by the Amir. On a further expedition to Somaliland, Burton travelled with John Hanning Speke. In 1856 Burton and Speke were sent by the Royal Geographical Society to discover the source of the Nile. Having caught yellow fever, both were holed up in Zanzibar until June 1857. Travelling inland, they made it to Tabora and on to Lake Tanganyika. Here they split up, with Burton continuing to look for the source of the Nile in the area, while Speke headed north to a large lake, Lake Victoria, from which he came back convinced it was the source of the Nile.

Back in England, the debate between Burton and Speke continued acrimoniously. In 1862 Speke returned to Lake Victoria with James Grant. They explored the western shore, found a river and waterfall at Jinja, headed to Lake Albert and then continued up the Nile to Khartoum. However, they did not actually follow the river from Jinja for its entire course. Burton and others, with some justification, still doubted the assumption that this was the true source of the Nile. About this time an adventurer, Baker, and his former slave girlfriend met Speke and Grant in Gondokoro. Baker and his girlfriend continued south, exploring Lake Albert and locating the waterfall later called Murchison Falls. But still the absolute facts were not settled.

After Burton returned from another journey to West Africa and Gabon in 1865, a debate was organised between Speke and Burton. This ended with the notorious self-shooting of Speke just before the meeting. The death of Speke, however, did not once and for all solve the mystery of the source of the Nile.

David Livingstone, part explorer and part missionary, arrived in southern Africa in 1835. After a series of expeditions into the Kalahari and interior, he discovered Victoria Falls in 1855. Livingstone's exploits and exploration in Africa brought him acclaim in England, but the death of his wife affected him deeply. Then, in 1865, the Royal Geographical Society asked him to seek out the source of the Nile for final clarification. Livingstone was of the opinion that the river rose well to the south of Lake Victoria, possibly in Lake Bangweulu. After a series of fruitless journeys characterised by ill health and hostile tribes, he finally arrived at Ujiji on Lake Tanganyika. This was in 1869. Joining Arab traders, he sought out the Lualaba River for the next two years. The famous meeting with Stanley occurred in Ujiji in 1871. Revived somewhat, Livingstone travelled north with Stanley up Lake Tanganyika, but the source of the Nile eluded him. He died in 1872 heading south again.

Henry Morton Stanley was an American and a different character from the stiff-upper-lipped British explorers. Yet he had as much grim determination as any of his predecessors. In 1874 he set out to explore Lake Victoria fully. He then attempted to check out Lake Albert, but warring tribes prevented this. He set out for Lake Tanganyika and then, having ascertained that it had no outlets, he headed west to the Luabala, which he followed. Continuing west, he discovered a larger river and the falls, which became known as the Stanley Falls, near modern-day Kisangani. Without knowing where his journey would take him, he finally arrived at the sea. But it was the Atlantic Ocean he found; he had followed the mighty Congo River to Boma. The mystery of the Nile had been solved, and it was Speke's original theory which proved correct.

Stanley continued to explore Africa with the celebrated Tippu Tip and a massive retinue for protection, finally mapping out the remaining geographical conundrums

## YOU'RE NEVER TOO OLD!

She sat on the deck, a large floppy hat shading her face. An English lady, without doubt, clearly much older than me. 'Where are you going?' I asked. 'We're retracing the steps of Livingstone,' Camilla replied. It transpired that she had been Profumo's secretary in the 1960s, and had married her Swiss husband Renaud just six months before the scandal broke. Just a couple of weeks ago she had celebrated her 70th birthday in the middle of the Western desert of Egypt; no champagne and caviar here, just a bottle of Coke and a few biscuits! They were travelling on public transport; across Egypt, down the Nile and across Lake Nasser on this infamous ferry, from Wadi Halfa to Khartoum on the train, cheating a bit by flying to Arusha, but then back on the road again to reach Lake Tanganyika and the dubious luxury of another African ferry.

We sought them out and miraculously found them again in Khartoum, where their son's Sudanese friend from Basel, Switzerland, took us all out for lunch in a dark low-roofed café just next to the central mosque. Wherever next would we meet, we wondered?

It was to be in Rougemont, in the Swiss Alps, where we celebrated Renaud's 80th birthday in July.

of the great central African lakes. After his death in 1905 the colonial scramble for Africa began.

## PEOPLE

Africa has a very diverse cross-section of people. In the far north are the Arabs, who migrated and brought Islam from Saudi Arabia. They mixed with the indigenous Berbers of the Maghreb. Further south are the famous nomads of the desert, the Tuareg and Tubu people of Algeria, Libya, Mali, Niger and Chad, who probably developed from the Berbers. The Moors of Morocco spread along the Atlantic coast to Mauritania. Much further to the east are the Nubia and Dinka of Sudan and the Amharic-speaking groups of Ethiopia. West Africa is well known for its diverse peoples, and it is they who add such colour and interest to trips in the region. The Fulani or Peul are the famous cattle herders. Other major West African groups are the Wolof, Bambara, Malinke, Songhai, Mossi, Bobo, Djerma, Bozo, Dogon, Hausa, Ibo and Yoruba.

In central Africa, pygmies are still found in Cameroon, the two Congos and Gabon, where the Fang are also found. Some of the Bantu-related groups in East Africa are the Buganda, Kikuyu, Masai, Rendille and Samburu. In Rwanda and Burundi the two main ethnic groups, who have been bitter enemies, are the Hutu and the Tutsi; the pygmoid Twa are only a small minority. Across southern Africa the following make up most of the people: Shona, Ndebele, Himba, Herero, Ovambo, Makua, Chewa, Basotho, Zulu and Xhosa. Finally, set apart from these Bantu peoples, are the San, who are the original Bushmen, the people who inhabited Botswana and parts of South Africa before retreating.

## RELIGION

Africa has such a rich cultural heritage that you will probably only be able to scratch the surface. As you travel through Africa, you will discover the diversity of this huge continent.

Before you leave home, get as much information as you can about Africa, its culture and people. The more you know and respect the places you plan to visit, the less likely you are to disrupt local culture when you get there, and the more you will get out of your trip. Travelling carries responsibilities as well as bringing pleasure: dress in a manner to suit the different cultures; respect people's dignity and wishes, particularly when taking photographs; respect religious sites and artefacts; keep the environment clean by burning your rubbish wherever possible; and do not encourage dependence by casually handing out gifts, unless some small service has been rendered.

Wherever you go, an understanding of local culture and history will go a long way towards enriching your experience. Making an attempt to learn about the countries you visit is one of the main differences between travellers and tourists. One of the subjects most guaranteed to cause inadvertent offence or misunderstanding is that of traditional Islam in Africa.

## Islam in Africa

Apart from the well-known countries along the North African coast that adhere to Islam, a surprising number of sub-Saharan countries also have substantial numbers, if not all of their population, observing the religion. Islam spread south across the Sahara with the caravan routes from Egypt, Libya, Tunisia, Algeria, and Morocco after its founding in the middle of the 7th century in Saudi Arabia. Places on the southern fringes of the desert became rich and powerful; places like Agadez, Gao, Djenné and Timbuktu, the most famous and mysterious of all. Vast wealth was accumulated by the empires of Ghana (not the current state), Mali and Songhai. With the coming of ships, much of the cross-Saharan trade declined and the cities were eclipsed. By now the Islamic faith had become well and truly embedded in the populations of much of West Africa. Countries like Guinea have surprisingly large numbers of devout Muslims, as do East African coastal districts. Swahili is a modified form of Arabic; the word Swahili is derived from the word for 'coast' in Arabic.

### DOWNTOWN DJIBOUTI – A MELTING-POT OF TRIBAL PEOPLE

The old colonial quarter of town has some picturesque buildings, many with arched façades that give much-needed shade to the vendors and pedestrians. There are street cafés and ancient tamarisk trees. Well-dressed businessmen mingle with entrepreneurial ladies dressed in amazingly colourful attire, laughing and gossiping over strong coffee. The African quarter and market area is totally absorbing. Shopkeepers and street vendors promote their wares, groups of men sit beside the old whitewashed mosques smoking hookah pipes and cigarettes. The women in the clothes market are deep in animated conversation. We, of course, are probably the source of most of their humorous laughter and gossip, but no-one is threatening. We drink tea; it's the milky Indian-style tea, which is a big surprise, as there aren't many Indians about. There are lots of Somalis, Ethiopian truckers, Eritrean refugees, Afar and Danakil tribals, Yemenis and Arab traders, but hardly any white faces in the markets. Djibouti city is a fascinating place and should not be missed.

Check-out time in Paradise Hotel is 13.00 but 14.00 is fine. We savour the cool luxury, watching the TV. Our world is one of make-believe; cocooned in this small place where we can travel in time and space. We are transported back to little England. The budget is being discussed – we don't know if it's over or due next week; the weather forecast is of course for rain and the cars are just as expensive as ever on *Top Gear*. Down in the car park the Land Rover is cooking, the steering wheel is too hot to touch and the guards are half-asleep in the great fog of humidity.

There are five main pillars of Islam. These are:

- Witness (*Shahadah*): submission to God (Allah) and acceptance that Mohammed is his prophet.
- Prayer (*Salat*): five times a day, at sunrise, midday, afternoon, sunset and evening. Before praying, Muslims must wash head, hands and feet. They can pray in any place that is clean and not polluted, and they must face Mecca. On Fridays at midday, it is more beneficial to pray collectively at a mosque. Otherwise they may pray alone, wherever they may be. Men and women pray separately.
- Alms giving (*Zakat*): according to the Koran, faith in God should be expressed by doing good to others. A devout Muslim should, once a year, give 2.5% of his money to others in need.
- Fasting (*Sawm*): The month of Ramadan is a holy month, when all Muslims must fast from dawn till dusk. If they are ill or travelling, or if they are pregnant women, they are permitted to postpone the fast until they are well. Elderly people and young children are excused from the fast. The purpose of the fast is to teach discipline to the soul. Eid al-Fitr is when the fast ends and all Muslims celebrate with a great feast – the sheep and goats are not so lucky, as hundreds of them are ritually slaughtered on this special day.
- Pilgrimage (*Hajj*): At least once during his lifetime, it is a sacred duty for every Muslim to go to the Ka'aba, the sacred mosque in Mecca. This should be done ideally between the seventh and tenth days of the month of Zuul-Hijja, the twelfth month of the Muslim year. This is usually between March and July, depending on the moon. The *Hajj* includes, among other things, the tawaf, seven anticlockwise circuits of the Ka'aba, prostrations at the site of Abraham, and the sacrifice of either a sheep or a camel, depending on one's wealth. This meat is given to the poor. The pilgrimage ends with another feast, the Eid al-Adha, after which the pilgrim must visit the tomb of the prophet in the holy city of Medina.

Some more basic tenets of Islam are: The **Koran** is the word of God. **Mohammed** is his prophet. The **Sunna** is the right way of life, which represents everything that the prophet Mohammed did or said. The books of **Hadith** record the Sunna, the way to live. Note that the Sunna is the guidance given by Mohammed; it is not the same as the Koran, which is the direct word of God. The Koran and the Sunna together are known as the **al-Asl**, the foundation of Islam. A **Madrasa** is an Islamic school.

Mohammed's daughter was **Fatima**. **Ali** was his cousin. Mohammed favoured Ali as his successor, and married Fatima to Ali. Those who follow Ali are known as **Shi'a** Muslims.

## Christianity in Africa

Christians probably just outnumber Muslims in Africa as a whole. The colonial expansion across Africa that began in the mid 19th century brought with it the missionaries, explorers and traders who sought to exploit Africa for its natural physical wealth as well as its people. Slavery, long endemic in the continent, had already expanded to provide cheap labour for the Arabs and later the American colonists.

Christianity found favour with the peoples of the sub-Sahara, often where slavery had its prime locations. The West African coastal people suffered the greatest impact of slavery. These areas are now some of the main heartlands of the religion. The religious divide in the countries of the Sahel, particularly Nigeria, Chad and Sudan, has been the source of communal tensions and periodic violence that continues to this day. The Coptic Christian movement found homes both in Egypt and in the highlands of Ethiopia. Further south, Christianity is the dominant faith. As with most things African, the energy and vibrancy of the people manifests in its faiths, with lively and robust forms of preaching and worship. Isolated on the highlands of Ethiopia, Christianity is the main religion. Its early roots are derived from Judaism and churches are a focal point for the very devout faithful.

## Traditional religion

Although less common, the practices of Africa's original animistic beliefs are still to be found almost anywhere except the north. Along the coast of Togo, voodoo has survived and retained its traditions. Its followers worship the cult of ancestors and fetishes. Most African animistic ideas incorporate such ideas. The Dogon people of Mali have retained their ancient beliefs. Their traditions are linked to the stars, sun and moon through their God.

## FESTIVALS

West Africa has a number of colourful and vivid festivals. In Mali there is the annual Cattle Crossing at Diafarabe. It takes place in December. This festival is when the Fulani herders reunite with their families. The famous Dogon of the Bandiagara escarpment in Mali have a number of masked dances and ceremonies, usually from March onwards after the harvest. In recent years a desert music festival has been taking place north of Gao in Mali, subject to security factors. In Niger is the famous Cure Salée around In Gall. It takes place in September and basically involves young men dressed and made up to impress and woo partners. The Bianou festival in March is another spectacle in Niger, with Tuareg riding camels into Agadez.

Across all of North Africa and amongst all the Muslim communities are the normal Islamic holidays and fastings. Tabaski, the most important festival, involves the eating of sheep and goats in large quantities and is a time when people dress in their finest clothes, particularly in places like Mali and Niger. Eid al-Fitr is the day that celebrates the end of the month-long fast of Ramadan. Eid al-Moulid is celebrated as the Prophet's birthday.

Timkat is probably Ethiopia's most colourful festival. It is the celebration of Christ's baptism. Across all of Christian Africa, Palm Sunday is a particularly colourful time for processions and gaiety. Versions of the carnival or Mardi Gras are celebrated, mainly in the ex-Portuguese colonies. There is a biannual film festival in Burkina Faso, and the Fêtes des Masques in Ivory Coast. Not so much a festival is the annual blast of technology, the dusty raid in the Sahara of the Paris–Dakar Motor Rally. Africa has it all, and always in glorious technicolour.

## ARTS AND ENTERTAINMENT
### African cultural heritage

It is a good idea to build up a knowledge and enjoyment of all things African such as its religions, music, literature and history before you leave. The visual arts are closely tied to the craft traditions of carving and weaving. These will be appreciated best as you travel.

## Art
### Sculpture

This is one of Africa's greatest art forms. Wherever you travel, you are sure to come across wonderful carvings of one kind or another, each of them distinctive to their own particular region. Of course, the main tourist areas are swamped with souvenir reproductions of little merit, but take the trouble to visit the many national museums in Africa and you will discover a treasure trove of astounding proportions.

If you would like to get a flavour for African sculpture before you go, there is much on display in European museums. A comprehensive guide to African sculpture that can be seen in England and Scotland has been published as *African Assortment* by Michael Pennie (Artworth). It discusses and illustrates works on display in 34 separate museums.

### Nigeria/Benin
The famous Benin bronzes are some of the finest art works that West Africa has produced. They date from the 10th or 11th century; the region where they were found is in today's southern Nigeria.

### Tanzania
The famous Makonde carvings are to be found along the coast in Kenya and Tanzania and are often remarkable works of art.

### Zimbabwe
It has gained a particular reputation in the world of sculpture – with some experts claiming that the country has no fewer than six of the world's top ten stone sculptors. A visit to the Chapungu Sculpture Park in Harare is an absolute must.

## Masks
These are another art form, many designs and styles having their origins in the ancient animistic beliefs. Mali and Ivory Coast are well known for their masks and Togo for its fetishes.

## Weaving and cloth
The astonishing array of colourful materials in almost any market is overwhelming. Although increasingly made locally, a lot is still imported, much of it from Holland. **Ghana** has a thriving textile industry, mostly village-based around Kumasi. Kente cloth is its most famous product. Elsewhere most of the material is produced on a small scale. Indigo cloth is produced mostly in North and West Africa, and is widely used by the **Moors** and **Tuareg** people, as well as other nomadic tribes.

## Miscellaneous
**Egypt** is famous for its **papyrus** paper and delicately painted images. **Agadez** has its silver crosses. And so on. The list is endless …

# Music
One of the easiest and most enjoyable ways to start learning about Africa is through its music. Africans will love to talk about their favourite artist. The growing interest over recent years in modern African music is a refreshing development and means a vast catalogue of material is now available.

Most good music shops stock a reasonable selection of African CDs. The variety and volume of African music means that any guide to the highlights will necessarily be a partial and personal selection. Below is a suggested list of musicians to look out for.

## Benin
One famed artist, Angélique Kidjo, who has successfully hit the European market, is worth a listen. Her albums include *Ayé* and *Fifa*, released in the late 1990s. For further information look at the website www.angeliquekidjo.com.

## Democratic Republic of the Congo (DRC)
This is the heart of African music; you will hear the sounds of *soukous* wherever you go in Africa, with its infectious jangling guitar lines and sweet vocals.

The king of *soukous*, Franco, sadly died in 1990. For a taste of him at his best listen to the 1985 release *Mario* and the compilation of his 1950s' classics *Originalité*. Franco's band, OK Jazz, was for many years effectively a training school for all of the greats of DRC music. Thankfully, they continued after their leader's death, immediately recording the impeccable *Champions Du Zaïre* (they were rejoined for this album by former member Ndombe Opetum, whose solo albums are a delight).

One former member of OK Jazz who warrants special mention is Papa Noel – if only because he rarely receives the praise he so richly deserves. Two albums, *Nono* and *Ya Nono*, are among the most prized records in our collection. Pass them by at your peril.

Franco's great rival over many years was Tabu Ley, who has a similarly large catalogue of releases. Check also on his protégés Sam Mangwana and top female vocalist Mbilia Bel.

The 1980s saw a shift in the music of the Democratic Republic of the Congo (then known as Zaïre), with the rise of a new generation of younger stars preferring to leap straight into the faster dance sections of the *soukous* style and dropping the traditional ballad sections. Top of this group of musicians is Kanda Bongo Man, possibly the most commonly played throughout Africa. Many of his albums are available, but try *Non Stop Non Stop*. Other bands at the forefront of this new wave are Pepe Kalle's Empire Bakuba, Zaiko Langa Langa and Papa Wemba.

## Gabon

An honourable mention should go to the Gabonese *soukous* band Les Diablotins. Their best-known albums are a whole series recorded in Paris in 1983 – the best is *Les Diablotins à Paris Volume 7*.

## Ghana

The greatest musical contribution from Ghana is 'highlife' – the danceband music that has developed throughout the 20th century with its synthesis of African and Western styles. The acknowledged king of highlife is E T Mensah. Look out for the excellent compilation of his 1950s' hits, released under the title *All For You*. Also look out for Daddy Lumba, Highlife 2000, entitled *Aben Woaha*.

A superb compilation of 1950s and early 1960s' highlife hits is *Akomko* – it features tracks from such greats as The Black Beats, Stargazers Dance Band and Red Spot. For a taste of more recent music from Ghana, the Guitar And The Gun compilations are also worth a listen.

## Guinea

Guinea shares the *griot* traditions of Mali and many musicians have moved between the two countries. Guinean *griot* Mory Kanté, for example, replaced Salif Keita in The Super Rail Band. He subsequently left and has released a number of excellent solo albums.

For many years, the national band of Guinea was the Beyla group Bembeya Jazz, who used modern electric instruments to interpret traditional themes. Although they have now disbanded, many of their recordings are available. Guinea's most popular performer of semi-acoustic Manding music is now former Bembeya Jazz singer Sekouba Bambina Diabaté. The all-woman equivalent band was Les Amazones (which was sponsored by the police). Two of its members, Sona Diabate and M'Mah Sylla, released an excellent album in 1988, called *Sahel*, featuring acoustic instruments.

The best-known musician from Guinea is now Mory Kanté, a wonderful singer whose breakthrough album was *Akwaba Beach*. He also appears with Kanté Manfila and Balla Kalla on the rootsy *Kankan Blues* – a much more raw sound recorded at the Rubis Nightclub in Kankan, Guinea.

## Kenya and Tanzania

East African music is dominated by three main styles – a local version of the *soukous* of the Democratic Republic of the Congo, the unique sound of Swahili Taarab music and the big-band sound of Tanzania. For *soukous* try Orchestra Virunga or Orchestra Maquis Original. For the Swahili sound, try Black Lady and Lucky Star Musical Clubs' *Nyota: Classic Taarab from Tanga*. Of the Tanzanian big bands, the all-time great was Mbaraka Mwinshehe. By the time of his death in 1979 he had recorded dozens of albums. Look out particularly for the *Ukumbusho* series.

## Mali

The traditional music of Mali is dominated by the *griots* – singers who have been charged through history with maintaining the oral literature of the area. Their pure voices typically combine with two beautiful instruments – the 21-stringed *kora* and the *balafon* (xylophone).

Since gaining independence, Mali has also produced a number of tremendous and quite distinctive large bands. Its contemporary music typically integrates traditional patterns and styles with modern instruments. Several former *griots* have made the transition.

One of the country's most successful musical exports has been Salif Keita, the singer with a voice of pure gold. If you are happy for the music to be filtered through modern Western pop, then solo albums like *Soro* and *Ko-Yan* are worth a listen. But if you want to hear Salif Keita at his best, look for the albums made between 1974 and 1984 with Les Ambassadeurs (the easiest to find is probably the 1984 release *Les Ambassadeurs Internationaux*).

One classic album from Mali that is reasonably easy to find is by Salif Keita's former group, The Super Rail Band. He left in 1973 but it was not until 1985 and the band's first UK release, *New Dimensions in Rail Culture*, that it achieved international success. This album features the voices of Sekou Kanté and Lanfia Diabate.

The Super Rail Band is based in Bamako, but the second-largest town in Mali, Ségou, is home to the excellent Super Biton Band. Their best album is simply called *Super Biton de Ségou* (we bumped into the lead singer one day in a bar in town!).

Make sure you don't bypass the work of the magnificent Ali Farka Touré. His work is some of the most accessible to Western tastes, even though his music is based on traditional forms of Malian music. He reached an even wider audience with the 1994 release of *Talking Timbuktu*, recorded with American guitarist Ry Cooder.

More recently female artists have become popular, like Nahawa Doumbia's *Didadi* and Oumou Sangare with *Bi Furu*.

## Niger

Worth looking out for is the Guez Band from Arlit. This is the new style of the Sahel.

## Nigeria

As well as having the largest population in Africa, Nigeria also has the most developed music industry. Its best-known musical style is *juju* – typically guitar-based bands, weaving melodies around a core of talking drums. Its best-known exponents are Ebenezer Obey, King Sunny Ade and Segun Adewale. A good introduction is Segun Adewale's *Ojo Je*.

No account of Nigerian music would be complete without reference to Fela Kuti, whose politically charged 'Afro-beat' music has ensured continual conflict with the authorities – he was even jailed from 1984 to 1986. A live concert is a real experience, with as many as 40 musicians on stage putting together complex patterns of cross-rhythms.

## Senegal

Another famed artist to hit the European market is Youssour N'Dour from Senegal. His albums feature a few solo hits and some with his band, the Super Etoile.

## South Africa

Paul Simon may have popularised the music of southern Africa with his *Graceland* album, but, if you enjoyed the singing featured by Ladysmith Black Mambazo, far better to check out the records from their own large output.

The music of South Africa is incredibly varied, with everything from traditional music to township jive via some of the best jazz in the world. There are a number of very good compilation albums of various artists – in particular *Zulu Jive* and *The Indestructible Beat of Soweto*. Also, listen out for Johnny Clegg who has recorded various albums. More traditional and with a Mozambique influence is Steve Newman and Tananas. The ex-exiled Miriam Makeba and Dollar Band (Abdullah Ibrahim) are also worth a listen and are traditionally South African.

## Zimbabwe

The modern music of Zimbabwe has been popularised in the West by The Bhundu Boys and The Four Brothers. Albums by both are readily available. But also try to listen to Oliver Mtukutzi and Thomas Mapfumo, Zimbabwe's number-one singers and band leaders. A classic collection of Mapfumo's earlier work is *The Chimurenga Singles*. For Mtukutzi try *Shoko*. A great introduction to the dance music of Zimbabwe is provided in the compilation of various artists on *Viva Zimbabwe*.

The live music scene in Harare used to be one of the best in the world. All the top names played most nights of the week in the various hotels, beer gardens and clubs. If the situation improves, make sure you build in enough time for the music when you reach there.

## Record stores and websites

Any of the above-mentioned music is to be found and bought locally in Africa. Always check the tapes if you can; some will be of dubious quality, but that's part of the fun of it. Better-quality recordings can be found outside Africa. If you would like to get a feel for African music beforehand, try the Africa Centre in London or www.africana.com.

# Literature

The best of modern African literature has brought together the oral traditions of the past with alien Western traditions of the novel and theatre. A good starting point for anyone interested in the whole range of contemporary African writing is the anthology *Voices From Twentieth-Century Africa – Griots And Towncriers* (Faber and Faber). It is a collection that will lead you towards the strongest writers of the continent. *The Traveller's Literary Companion to Africa* by Oona Strathem (In Print Publishing) takes readers on a country-by-country literary tour.

The following is a guide to a handful of the most important writers to look out for.

**Chinua Achebe** Nigeria's great man of letters. The two novels that are most highly recommended were written some 30 years apart and reflect themes of very different periods in the country's history. The effect on African society of the arrival of Europeans is the subject of his first novel, *Things Fall Apart* (Heinemann), published in 1958. His subject matter moves on to the problems of corruption and governing modern Africa in his 1987 novel *Anthills of the Savannah*.

**Ayi Kwei Armah** Ghanaian novelist, much influenced by black American writers. Novels include *The Beautyful Ones Are Not Yet Born*, *Why Are We So Blest?* and *Two Thousand Seasons*.

**Nelson Mandela** *The Long Road to Freedom* is the autobiography of the great man himself and should be part of any reading on South Africa.

**Sembene Ousmane** The Senegalese writer and film director is best known for his masterpiece novel *God's Bits of Wood* (Heinemann), which vividly tells the story of the great strike on the Bamako-to-Dakar railway. It is particularly recommended if you plan to take that route.

**Stanlake Samkane** Zimbabwe's best-known novelist and historian. His classic novel *On Trial for my Country* puts both Cecil Rhodes and the Matabele King Lobengula on trial to discover the truth behind the 1890 invasion of what became Rhodesia.

**Wole Soyinka** This prolific Nigerian playwright and poet was awarded the Nobel Prize for Literature in 1986. *The Man Died* (Arrow) is a vivid account of the two-and-a-half years he spent in prison at the time of the Nigerian civil war in the late 1960s. *A Dance in the Forests* is one of his most ambitious and powerful plays, steeped in the beliefs and background of a Yoruba heritage.

**Ngugi Wa Thiong'o** Kenya's greatest writer has been highly critical of his homeland and has had many conflicts with the authorities as a result, including time in jail and in exile. Earlier books concentrated on the struggle against colonialism but he then moved on to criticise post-colonial Kenya as well, most forcefully in the classic *Devil on the Cross* (Heinemann).

Not by Africans, but about Africa, is a book by **Peter and Beverly Pickford**. Their book *Forever Africa* is a visual feast of sepia and colour photographs, depicting the people, landscapes and wildlife seen on their journey from Cape Town to Tangier.

### Literary criticism

The South African critic, novelist and short-story writer **Es'kia Mphahlele** is reckoned to be the father of serious study of African literature. His book *The African Image* was the first comprehensive work of African literary criticism.

One other particularly interesting work we can recommend is *Land, Freedom and Fiction* by David Maughn-Brown (Zed). This successfully weaves together the history, literature and politics of Kenya by discussing the distortions and reworking of history by writers about the Mau Mau struggle that led to independence.

### Further information

Try the websites www.heinemann.co.uk and www.africanwriters.com.

## CULTURAL INTERACTION IN AFRICA

Africa is home to possibly the most diverse peoples on the planet, and yet it also has common themes across its vast expanse. Each area has a great mix of distinct tribal groupings, defied by the illogical borders that the modern world ascribes to the continent. It is impossible to learn the spoken word of all these differing groups, but any usage of even the most basic words will open doors and bring a greater interaction. Most guidebooks will give a few common greetings and phrases in the local language.

Despite the cultural divide, most Africans are welcoming, interested and lively. The nature of Islam in Black Africa is generally more laid back and tolerant than that in the Arab regions. This does not mean, however, that one should act in a more liberal way, particularly regarding dress. Dress, together with general appearance, is the one thing that defines your approach and can have negative as well as positive impacts. Many African societies have very elaborate greeting rituals from person to person that seem to go on and on. Some rituals amongst the nomadic peoples involve lengthy tea ceremonies and not much actual tea drinking. A simple handshake will, however, suffice for the rest of us.

## WADI HALFA

We arose early to see the famous Abu Simbel monuments. Later, as the ferry crossed into Sudanese waters, a speedboat shot up to us. Was this the police or the Customs? We could only stare in disbelief as the cables tying the barge to the ferry were disconcertingly unleashed, and our Land Rover sailed off into the distance. We'd paid too much and now they were stealing the vehicle!

We disembarked at Wadi Halfa and then the barge appeared a few moments later with the Land Rover still intact. We followed everyone to the Immigration area, at least the building was new and the hot sugary black tea in surprisingly clean glasses was more than welcome.

A largish man who could be anyone's jolly old grandfather came over. 'Where is your car? Please get it now.' Kamal Hassan Osman was the Customs man, and he wasted no time. We quickly rushed back to the ferry barge and somehow drove down two wobbly planks to get the Land Rover on to the narrow jetty. The brakes still worked. The paperwork was quickly sorted out and then we waited. Some other work had to be done. We waited and waited. We were in Sudan but we couldn't go anywhere. It was getting dark too. We sat and brewed up more and more tea.

And then without explanation we were off. Oh yes, could we give our friendly Customs man a lift to town? Did we have a choice? Off we went; we headed not into town but over some low dunes to the next bay around the lake. Here was a small settlement set in a sandy valley with some irrigation near the lake. We stopped outside a walled mud house. It wasn't much to look at from the outside, but inside it was a treasure. The elegant wooden dresser displayed exquisite bone china tea sets, cut glass and family photos. This was the house of Kamal Hassan Osman's sister. We took tea and biscuits, hardly daring to breathe in case we dropped a china cup. He spoke English well and we had a decent conversation. They showed us some photos of the old town, before the Egyptians decided to build the dam and flood the Nile valley upstream forever. Wadi Halfa has never recovered from its flooding, and there is obvious distress about the loss of their old homes and the beautiful oasis now below the waters.

After tea, we took Kamal to his own house, doing the rounds of shops, to buy fresh bread and cheese, and visit more friends en route. We were starving by now, but he invited us for dinner. His house was inside a large walled enclosure, with many rooms carpeted by sand. A big fridge took pride of place, with basic furniture and some decorations, posters and old photographs. Various nieces and nephews seemed to call by all evening and eventually we had a superb meal of beans, rice, cheese, omelette, spaghetti and goat, washed down with copious amounts of tea. His nephew invited us to a wedding party, but unfortunately it was rather late and, after our sleepless night on the ferry, we were somewhat low on energy.

# GIVING SOMETHING BACK TO AFRICA
*with Janice Booth*

No matter where you travel in Africa, you are bound to see poverty, urban squalor and occasionally genuine hunger. Life for the poor in both cities and rural areas may prove harsher than you'd imagined. Your reaction may well be a mixture of sadness, perhaps shock and often a feeling of guilt. The imbalance seems unjust, and the scale of the problem daunting. Why do some have so much when others do not? The reasons are complex, rooted partly in culture, partly in ignorance and poor education, partly no doubt in foreign exploitation – and these are only the more obvious causes.

African tradition has cast women in the role of workers, fetching water, looking after the children, cooking and washing. Men were traditionally the hunters. In rural Africa it is very common to see men sitting under trees, apparently deep in thought or conversation but otherwise inactive. As the continent becomes more urbanised, so they have needed to become more industrious, and many have enormous reservoirs of energy and initiative – but still, tradition dies hard, and 'development' often requires painful compromises. As choices increase, so do pressures. Adapting to the pace and the advanced technologies of the 21st century isn't necessarily easy.

So, where can we fit in? Isn't it enough that we've shopped in local markets, paid local mechanics, stopped at some local campsites and used local ferries? Aren't the big charities and governments dealing with 'development' as such? Have we as individuals got anything to offer (apart, obviously, from our hard-earned cash, which we don't want to throw away into such a bottomless gulf of need) that can really make a difference to this vast, teeming, vibrant, contradictory, maddening and stunningly beautiful continent? Maybe we all have different answers. Below are just a few suggestions in case you need a starting point.

## Local choices

Of course shopping locally and using the services of local people are ways to contribute. Buy souvenirs from the craftspeople who seem to have made them rather than via middlemen who will siphon off profits, and patronise small street vendors rather than big supermarkets. Don't bargain to a price below what is reasonable; the difference may be the price of a drink to you but the price of a whole family meal to the vendor. Stay in small local hotels rather than foreign chains. Use the services of a local guide, or a child who wants to help, and pay a fair rate. Bring with you only those supplies that you know you won't be able to find in Africa, and buy the rest in local stores and markets.

## Education

Education is the future of Africa. In many places you will see children dressed in smart, brightly coloured uniforms, bouncing along to school with great exuberance and energy. In others they may be ragged, crammed together on rickety wooden benches or grouped in the shade of trees, eyes fixed earnestly on the teacher and repeating by rote because they have no books. Whatever the conditions, there is an insatiable wish to learn. If you have spent time in a village and made some contact with its inhabitants, why not consider donating some pens, crayons and notebooks to the local school? (See also *Gifts* in *Chapter 2*.) School equipment is easy to buy in local markets. Ask to be introduced to the schoolteacher, so that he/she can receive and officially distribute the gift. Offer to spend some time in the school, being questioned by the children about your home country. If an adult language or literacy course is running locally, offer to drop in on that too. After all – knowledge is about stretching horizons and learning new things, which is just what you're doing by travelling; so why not make it a two-way process. Anyway, it's fun!

If you have contact with schools back in your home country, consider whether it might be possible to set up a link. If the schoolteacher wants to stay in touch and you feel able to take on a correspondence, agree to this – but do warn him/her that mail can be very slow and envelopes sometimes get lost. Maybe someone nearby has an email account. When you get home, if you feel able to undertake the sponsorship of an individual child or older student in Africa, the big international organisations offering this are easy to find via the internet. And education is a gift for life.

A warning: travellers often collect up pens/biros at home beforehand and bring them over – but, in this case, *please* check that they work and have plenty of ink before donating them. To an impoverished rural child, a new pen is a huge and thrilling gift. He/she is so proud and happy – and then so bitterly disappointed when it stops working after only a few hours. It would have been better never to have had it. (Also see *Begging*, below.)

## In the village

As you pass through – or stay in – small towns and villages, you'll come across missionaries, expatriates, aid workers and various development projects. If the work that they're doing interests you, make a note of their contact details – once back home you may be able to organise fundraising or other support. This is development 'on a human scale' – a well, a school, an orphanage, a village hall, a water pump, a plot of farmland – so that the local organisers will appreciate your individual interest as much as you enjoy being personally involved.

While you're driving, you may also spot wooden signs beside the road advertising small development projects – housing schemes, irrigation, co-operatives, agriculture – and giving a contact address or phone number. Jot them down: you never know what may be useful later.

If you felt drawn to a village or a community but didn't manage to get details of any current activity there, it's worth trying an internet search for its name when you get home – try various spellings, just in case! – as this sometimes produces unexpected contacts.

## Volunteering

If you want to return to work as a volunteer in Africa and have some relevant skills ('relevant' covers a wide range), start by checking out **Voluntary Service Overseas** (www.vso.org.uk) or **Earthwatch** (www.earthwatch.org). VSO also welcomes donations, from small amounts up to the cost of maintaining a volunteer in a developing country. An internet search for organisations using volunteers will provide many more possibilities – including ones specialising in shorter projects, which may involve anything from teaching English to manual labour. If teaching English appeals, why not take a short course in TEFL (Teaching English as a Foreign Language). An internet search will reveal various colleges; one where you can learn at a distance by post or email is **Global English** (www.global-english.com). UK-based, it has students from as far apart as Thailand and the USA. Also look at www.tefl.com.

A way to volunteer without leaving home is via the **Online Volunteering Service**; it's managed by the United Nations Volunteers Programme (UNV), which is the volunteer arm of the United Nations. See website www.onlinevolunteering.org. Volunteers need reliable access to a computer and the internet, and some relevant skill or experience. Via the OVS they undertake a variety of computer-based assignments for organisations in developing countries: for example translation, research, web design, data analysis, database construction, proposal writing, editing articles, online mentoring, publication, design...etc. Also check out **Netaid** on www.netaid.org.

## Big international charities

The big international charities are colossal, and it's sometimes hard to remember that their work does reach down to benefit the poorest at grassroots level. It's particularly hard to believe – although it's true – that they need our small donations! Most of them don't deserve their reputation for spending too much on administration, and they respond magnificently to disasters such as the 2004 tsunami in Asia. If you want to make a general donation 'for work in Africa' you could do far worse. They advertise extensively, so check their ads and their websites to see which comes closest to your interests. If it's wildlife that appeals to you, then you'll already know about the **Worldwide Fund for Nature** – WWF – which works just about everywhere and has had some remarkable conservation successes; www.panda.org.

## Smaller charities

Nowadays the smaller international charities are amazing in their range and variety – whatever you want to support, you'll find it somewhere. The handful of lesser-known ones listed below are small enough to have a personal approach but large enough to make a useful impact. This is only a tiny sample of the many available, so you'll certainly come across others in the same or different fields.

**Firelight Foundation** (www.firelightfoundation.org) This US-based organisation works through local people and groups, and currently supports projects in Cameroon, Ethiopia, Kenya, Lesotho, Malawi, Rwanda, South Africa, Tanzania, Uganda, Zambia and Zimbabwe. Its remit – which is interpreted very broadly – is 'to support and advocate for the needs and rights of children who are orphaned or affected by HIV/AIDS in sub-Saharan Africa ... and to increase the resources available to grassroots organisations that are strengthening the capacity of families and communities to care for children made vulnerable by HIV/AIDS'.

**Good Gifts Catalogue** (www.goodgifts.org) This novel idea enables you to support development schemes while remembering friends and family at anniversaries, Christmas etc. For example you can buy a 'goat for Peace' for your aunt's birthday; it'll be delivered to one of the goat schemes in Africa, and you get a card for your aunt explaining the gift. As the brochure says: 'This is no ordinary goat: this is a revolving goat. Where communities are slowly rebuilding themselves, a revolving goat (with the aid of a revolving ram) starts families. Kids go to restock families without goats. And so on. A goat is a milk and fertiliser factory and goes a long way to improving the local diet; a four-legged step towards self-sufficiency.' The goat is only one of a huge range of gifts – check the online catalogue at the website above.

**Intermediate Technology Development Group** (www.itdg.org) Founded in 1966 by the radical economist Dr E F Schumacher, the ITDG works to show that the right technologies can help people to find lasting, appropriate solutions to poverty, and that a small-scale approach can bring results that benefit whole communities long into the future. ITDG enables poor communities to discover how new technologies, adapted in the right way, can improve their lives. Current activities are in East Africa, southern Africa and Sudan, with other countries due to be added soon.

**Send a Cow** (www.sendacow.org.uk) Based in the UK, this small charity (chosen as one of its Christmas charities by the *Independent* newspaper in 2004) provides not only cows but also goats and chickens on a self-help basis to impoverished families and individuals (widows, orphans...) so that they have a means of livelihood and hope for the future. It gives training in livestock rearing and organic farming, and access to low-cost veterinary and advice services. Projects are in Ethiopia, Kenya, Lesotho, Rwanda, Tanzania, Uganda and Zambia.

**War Child** (www.warchild.org) works with children suffering the effects of conflict – current African projects are in Angola, Burundi, DRC, Ethiopia, Eritrea, Rwanda, Sierra Leone and Sudan.

**Water Aid** (www.wateraid.org.uk) is dedicated exclusively to the provision of safe domestic water, sanitation and hygiene education to the world's poorest people. In Africa, it works in Burkina Faso, Ethiopia, Ghana, Malawi, Mali, Mozambique, Nigeria, Tanzania, Uganda and Zambia.

# Begging

There's no way you can escape beggars in Africa, and how you handle the problem is a very personal matter. Remember that the 'visible' misery of those thrusting their hands out to you as you pass is not necessarily any worse than the 'invisible' misery of those suffering silently at home; a donation to a relevant charity (for the homeless, or the orphaned, or the disabled, or the abandoned ...) is likely to mean that your money is used more effectively. But sometimes it's hard to walk on by.

If you decide to give cash on the spot, then do look the person in the eyes, smile and say an appropriate 'good morning'; being given a coin is probably far less of a novelty to him or her than being treated like a human being. (And prepare for the onslaught as others nearby spot that you're a soft touch and suddenly materialise...)

Just occasionally you can turn begging into an encounter that's pleasurable for you both. Many children do it from habit and would much rather be playing; so, if you turn

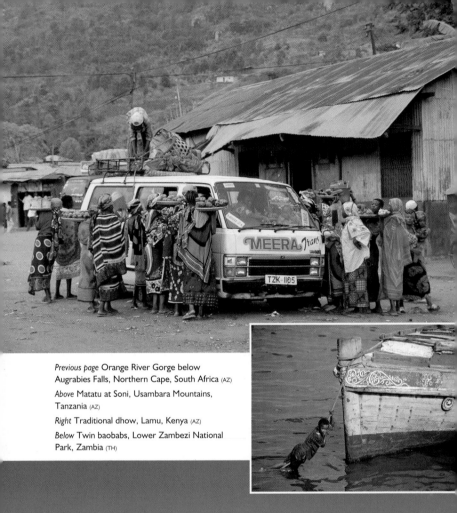

*Previous page* Orange River Gorge below Augrabies Falls, Northern Cape, South Africa (AZ)

*Above* Matatu at Soni, Usambara Mountains, Tanzania (AZ)

*Right* Traditional dhow, Lamu, Kenya (AZ)

*Below* Twin baobabs, Lower Zambezi National Park, Zambia (TH)

it into a game, they'll remember the fun of it far longer than the handing over of a coin. Also try learning 'What is your name?' in a few appropriate languages – perhaps French, Arabic and Swahili. The effect is astonishing, on someone, whether child or adult, who's used to being ignored or pushed aside. Even if you learn only their name, tell them yours and then say goodbye; you've lifted them several rungs up the scale of humanity – and again, that's what they'll remember. Or if you're refusing to give, then use their name politely as you say 'no'. In fact this is a great way to connect with children at any time; by using their name you give them dignity, and they respond.

Do bear in mind the damage you can do by giving little gifts (sweets, pens, cookies or whatever) to a child or youngster who comes up and begs, however cutely. If the begging bears fruit (and if the gift isn't immediately grabbed by a bigger child), he/she will start to pester all visitors, some of whom may react aggressively or unpleasantly. However it's fine as a 'payment' for genuine helpfulness.

## When you leave

Here's a final chance to be useful to Africa. Don't take home that T-shirt you probably won't wear again, that almost-full bottle of baby lotion, that soap, that pen, that pad of paper, that length of rope, that torch, those batteries, those duplicate tools … collect them up and give them to a local charity. Organisations looking after the homeless or running children's homes can turn pretty much anything to a good use. And then you'll have more space in your vehicle for all those bulky souvenirs that you couldn't resist.

## Tourism in general

It goes without saying that responsible tourism is vital to the future of inter-ethnic relations and cultural interaction. The actions of the visitor today are the seeds of the reaction to the visitor tomorrow. Tourism can offer Africa another source of employment, a tool for development and a direction for understanding. Eco-tourism is a new phrase in Africa, but one that will develop with greater education. It is incumbent on us to keep Africa as we found it in most aspects, and maybe somehow in other aspects to leave it a better place.

However we travel in Africa, we are always going to be seen as the rich people, but it is still a source of surprise how little this can matter sometimes. Interaction between peoples is the only way of developing greater understanding, and at least in that, if in nothing else, we may be seen to be doing some good.

182

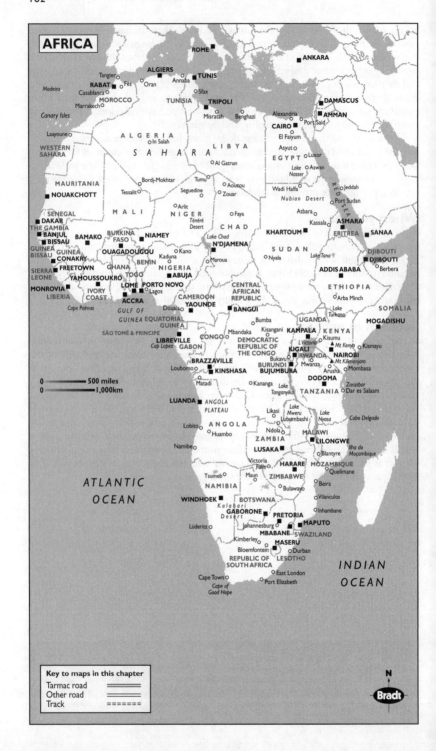

# A–Z Country Guide

> Your road is everything that a road ought to be ... and yet you will not stay in it
> half a mile, for the reason that little, seductive, mysterious roads are always
> branching out from it on either hand, and as these curve sharply also and hide
> what is beyond, [you] cannot resist the temptation to desert your own chosen
> road and explore them.
>
> Mark Twain (1835–1910)

This section, of necessity, gives just a brief introduction to each country. It includes a guide to visa requirements, some of the red tape you may encounter, an indication of fuel costs and a general overview of some of each country's highlights in Africa. Please note that fuel prices are given only as a **relative** indication, since the cost of a barrel of oil doubled in 2004 and oil prices are quoted in US dollars which have devalued significantly. We also advise you to **check the latest visa requirements**, as these change frequently. For more detail you should buy the relevant Bradt travel guide for the specific countries you intend to visit – see pages 301–2 and www.bradtguides.com.

## RED TAPE

The worst example of protracted red tape during a trip across Africa involves the obtaining of visas. Getting many of the visas in your own country can sometimes be harder than doing it in neighbouring countries en route. However, do still try to get as many as will remain valid from your home country. See advice under *Visas* in *Chapters 4* and *6*. Bear in mind that for an African to get a visa to visit almost any country outside the continent is very difficult.

You might think that driving across Africa would be a huge bureaucratic nightmare, with money disappearing from your back pocket all along the way, but it's not as bad as it might seem. In Nigeria, for example, there is an anti-corruption drive in the police force and the immigration department. We were stopped at most roadside checkposts just so they could ask after our health and wish us a safe journey. Gabon was the only country where we were really hassled by the authorities, and Equatorial Guinea, when we crossed the border for half an hour without a visa. In Cameroon we were 'fined' for travelling on the unmarked private road of the president (but only £1 sterling), and in one part of Nigeria some local bureaucrats tried to force us to pay a local road tax, which was not necessary. To stop us moving on, they threw a long plank studded with nails between our wheels. Only by standing in the middle of the road and stopping the traffic did we manage to get away, but it was an isolated incident, and we found the Nigerians perfectly civil and helpful on nearly every other occasion.

Of course we didn't visit every country in Africa on these last two trips, and no doubt things have changed and continue to change every day according to world politics. So all you can do is be flexible, keep up-to-date with websites – there are internet cafés everywhere – and keep smiling. Every country has its bureaucrats, and some of the worst are back on our own home patch! Remember that most people are kind-hearted and want to help you.

**KEY**
Capital city ■
Town ● ○
Main road
(not necessarily sealed) ▬▬▬
Other road (track) ▬ ▬ ▬
West–east routes
(identified page 22) WE1, WE2
Trans–Sahara routes
(identified pages 11–19) S1–S6
International boundary ▬ · ▬

CENTRAL & EAST AFRICA

KEY

Capital city
Town
Main road
(not necessarily sealed)
Other road (track)
West–east routes
(identified page 22)    WE1, WE2
Central African routes
(identified pages 22–25)    C1, C2
E1, E2
International boundary

SOUTHERN AFRICA

KEY
■ ○ Capital city
● Town
━━━━ Main road (not necessarily sealed)
═════ Other road (track)
─·─·─ International boundary

500 miles
1000km

# WHICH COUNTRY?

Under each country we give a brief overview of its highlights. Many African nations are currently at war, or have border disputes or tribal violence, so be prepared for some of the information to be out of date.

There are numerous guidebooks available for each individual country, giving information on public holidays, opening and closing times, specific accommodation, which bank to use, the nearest post office, shopping, markets and local attractions. We do not attempt to do that here. We have, however, listed most of the camping places/hotels that we have used, or have been told about recently. It often saves time initially to have an idea of where you can stay. Of course things change; some places shut down, grow grander or become less attractive.

Africa is so vast that at first it's daunting to decide which countries to visit and which to leave out. You cannot possibly do everything on one trip – you'll just have to go back again … and again … Each country has its own unique 'something' that you won't want to miss; landscapes, culture, people, wildlife, beaches, mountains and even rainforests with mud roads. Of course the choice is totally subjective and depends on your own personal preferences.

For wildlife we would suggest visiting southern and eastern Africa, where the majority of large national parks are located – Kruger National Park (Eastern Transvaal – South Africa), Umfolozi (Natal – South Africa), Kalahari Gemsbok Park (border of Botswana and South Africa), the Okavango Delta (Botswana), South Luangwa (Zambia), Lake Kariba (Zimbabwe), Masai Mara (Kenya) and Ngorongoro, Serengeti National Park (Tanzania). For culture and people, consider for example the Himba in Namibia, the San people in Botswana, the Masai in Kenya, the Turkana along the Jade Sea (or Lake Turkana), the Omatic tribes of southern Ethiopia or the Tuareg of the desert.

## A DOG NAMED HOPE

Having spent some time in Guinea's bustling capital city Conakry, we were keen to explore the offshore islands. We took the ferry – alone – past rusting wrecks in the harbour, and across a clear blue sea, with tropical islands dotted in the distance. Gradually our destination came closer, and soon we stepped off on to a remote beach. 'Just follow that path through the forest, and you'll reach the other side of the island in three or four minutes,' our boatman said. As we arrived, a gorgeous golden retriever appeared, with two young foreign travellers. 'He'll follow you everywhere,' they said. 'We're going back to the mainland on the boat you just came on.' So we were alone again, but for the dog.

Our room was a beautiful straw chalet overlooking a deserted beach. Later we walked along the smooth sand and lay down in the sun. The dog ran up to greet us, our own personal bodyguard. 'What's his name?' I asked the man at the restaurant, where we stopped for a drink. 'Espérance,' he replied. That means hope. In such a poor country it seemed a fitting name. 'Where are you from?' we asked, 'You speak very good English.' 'I'm a refugee from Sierra Leone,' he replied. 'I speak English, so I persuaded Madame to give me a job here for board and lodging only. She said she can't pay me anything because business is bad, but I'm happy because I have food and a roof over my head, and, above all, I am safe here. But I hope I will be able to go home soon.'

Hope again, perhaps the most important word in this vast continent, where everyone hopes for a better life.

As we left for the ferry the next day, Espérance sprang along the path to see us off. As they say, 'Hope springs eternal' in Africa.

A combination of landscapes, national parks and culture is the ideal. But it is invariably the vibrant people and colourful characters you meet who make the trip truly memorable.

The countries listed are in alphabetical order. Please note that visa prices given are approximate; they depend on your nationality and where you apply, as prices vary from country to country. Currency rates and fuel costs were correct at the time of writing, but of course are subject to significant change.

For useful websites with information on most countries in Africa, see page 304.

## ALGERIA

*Warning Having been off-limits for several years, overland travel in Algeria was again possible in the early 2000s, but is currently not recommended because of the kidnapping of 32 foreign tourists in early 2003. Groups linked to Al Qaeda are believed to be operating in the area. However, the scenery and people are outstanding and it is undoubtedly worth a visit if the situation improves. Seek sound travel advice if you do intend to visit.*

### Capital
Algiers

### Language and telephone
Arabic is the official language.
International telephone code +213

### Currency and rate
Algerian dinar (AD); US$1 = AD72.12

### Red tape
The carnet is not accepted and a *laissez passer* will be issued at the border. A currency declaration form must be completed on entry and surrendered on departure. You may or may not have to prove what you have spent when you leave. Be prepared for this.

### Visas
Visas are required for all except nationals of other Arabic countries. Israeli, South African, Malawian and Taiwanese nationality or any of these stamps in your passport will automatically mean that your visa application is rejected. Nationals of Germany, France and the United States can expect steep fees. Estimated visa costs can vary between US$55 (UK citizens) and US$100 depending on the country of application. You will also need three photographs, an invitation from the agent who is hosting you in Algeria, and an introduction from your embassy if you are not getting the visa in your home country. Double-entry visas are available. Visas are not issued at the border.

### Fuel costs
Diesel: US$0.11; petrol: US$0.22 per litre.

### Driving and roads
Drive on the right. Good surfaced roads throughout the north and most of the way down the central route to Tamanrasset and also the eastern route to Djanet. Many desert pistes of varying quality.

## African embassies

**Benin** 16 Lotissement du Stade, Birkhadem, Les Sources Birmandreis, Algiers
**Burkina Faso** 20 Rue des Cèdres, El Mouradia, Algiers
**Cameroon** PO Box 343, Algiers; tel: 02 782864
**Ghana** 62 Rue Parmentier-Hydra, Algiers
**Libya** 15 Chemin Cheikh Bachir; tel: 921502
**Morocco** 8 Rue des Cèdres, El Mouradia, Algiers
**Niger** 54 Rue de Vercors; tel: 788921
**Nigeria** 27 Bis Rue Blaise Pascal, PO Box 629, Agar Gare, Algiers; tel: 606050
**Sudan** 8 Shara Baski Brond, El Yanabia, Beir Murad Reis, Algiers
**Tunisia** 11 Rue du Bois de Boulogne, El Mouradia, Algiers; tel: 691388

## Climate

The best time to visit the desert is December to March. October, November, April and May are hotter but just about bearable. Desert temperatures are hottest in July and August.

## Highlights

The main highlight is without doubt the Sahara; Tamanrasset, the volcanic Hoggar Mountains, the hermitage of Père Foucauld, Djanet and the Tassili N'Ajjer plateau with its prehistoric art and fantastically shaped rock towers, and the remote Tassili du Hoggar in the far south. The Kasbah in Algiers is also a highlight, but it has been too dangerous to visit recently. Along the eastern coast it is said to be worth visiting Constantine, Djemila and the Kabylia Mountains. On the way south it is worth stopping in Timimoun and Ghardaia. The black Tademait plateau south of El Golea, and the Arak Gorge, are stunningly stark, and there are some beautiful sand dunes in various places along the route.

## Where to stay

Bush sleeping is a currently a dodgy option, though it is wonderful to sleep out in the open desert if you can find the right spot. If you do so, make absolutely sure you are well out of sight of the road or piste. Basic accommodation costs between US$5 and US$25 – depending on what you are after. With or without a lack of tourism in the country, the Algerians are extremely friendly and will go out of their way to help you, sometimes even offering accommodation. You can also ask to camp in the back yard of some hotels.

**Ouargla** The *Hotel Tassili* has allowed parking/camping behind the hotel. It is north of the main road.

**Ghardaia** Try either the central *Hotel El Djenoub* with secure parking nearby or the *Hotel Rym*, which has parking below. Campsite closed at the time of writing.

**El Golea** There was a nice but sandy campsite in the palmeries on the way south out of town; look for the camping sign on the gates. The central *Hotel Boustane* also has parking.

**In Salah** The *Hotel Tidikelt* allows camping outside in the garden area.

**Tamanrasset** The *Hotel Tinhinane* in the old main street has economical rooms with safe parking. There were two campsites east of town. Try the *Hotel Tahat* for a splurge with safe parking.

**Djanet** In the centre of the town is the famous and still pleasant *camping/Hotel Zeriba*.

## Other

Currency declaration forms need to be filled out on arrival and will be asked for on departure, though they may not be checked. If you are unlucky enough to be checked, it may be thorough. All other money found could be confiscated. Ensure that you get valid receipts when changing money at a bank, although the black market is thriving, particularly in euros. Remember that your declaration form needs to tally with bank receipts. But it may be that you cannot find a bank when you need to, and have to change money on the black market. Put some aside (hidden) for this eventuality. Also be aware that it is almost impossible to change travellers' cheques anywhere in the country. Take enough cash with you. Insurance must be purchased at the border or, if coming north from Niger, at Tamanrasset.

## Further information

*Sahara Overland*, Chris Scott (see *Further Information*, page 302).

# ANGOLA

**Warning** Due to the recently concluded civil war in Angola we strongly advise seeking sound travel advice if you do intend to visit. Basic information is included.

## Capital

Luanda

## Language and telephone

Portuguese is the official language.
International telephone code +244

## Currency and rate

Angolan Kwanza (AOA); US$1 = AOA85.39

## Red tape
Unknown, any news welcomed.

## Visas
Visas are required for all; applications are referred to the Direçao de Emigraçao e Fronteiras (DEFA) in Luanda and will take about two weeks. Visas cost US$50–80 and are valid for 15 or 30 days. Visas are not issued at the border.

## Fuel costs
Diesel: US$0.19; petrol: US$0.38 per litre.

## Driving and roads
Main roads were once good but we have no information about their current state.

## African embassies
**Congo Brazzaville** Rua Fernando Pessoa, Vila Alice; tel: 31 0293
**DRC** Rua Fernando Pessoa, Vila Alice; tel: 31 0293
**Gabon** Rue Eng Armindo Adrade 149; tel: 44 9289
**Ivory Coast** 41–43 Rua Karl Marx, CP 432 Luanda; tel: 39 0150 or 33 3992
**Namibia** Rua dos Coqueiro 37; tel: 39 5483
**Nigeria** CP 479, Luanda
**South Africa** Rua Kwamime Nkrumah 31; tel: 39 8726
**Zambia** Rua Rei Katyavala 1618; tel: 44 7496

## Climate
Angola has a varied climate with rains inland from October to May. The dry season is from June to August. The south coast is drier.

## Highlights
Known highlights are the Quedas do Ruacana waterfalls, when flowing, on the border with Namibia. In the southwest there is an extensive mountainous region inland from Namibe. The area close to Lubango is said to have some volcanic features, a deep fissure in the plateau.

## Where to stay
It is impossible to make many suggestions at present.

**Ruacana** It is possible to camp at *Osheja Guest House* and camp on the Namibian side.

## Further information
www.angola.org

## BENIN

### Capital
Porto Novo

### Language and telephone
French is the official language.
International telephone code +229

### Currency and rate
West African franc (CFA); US$1 = CFA502

### Red tape
Of little significance in Benin.

### Visas
Visas are required for all except nationals of the Economic Community of West African States (ECOWAS). Entry visas cost US$10–20 to US$60 for a month and are normally available at the border of Benin and Togo. You will need two passport photos. Yellow-fever vaccination certificates are also officially required, but do not often get checked.

### Fuel costs
Diesel: US$0.45; petrol: US$0.55 per litre.

### Driving and roads
Drive on the right. Most roads in Benin are paved and even those that aren't are in good condition with only a few potholes.

### African embassies
**French embassy** Av Pape Jean-Paul II/Rue 232, Cotonou; tel: 300225. British citizens with a problem should come here.
**Ghana** Rue 232/Route de l'Aéroport, Cotonou; tel: 300746. Closed in afternoon. Visa takes 24 hours; a one-month tourist visa costs CFA15,000 and needs four photos.
**Niger** Rue 651A, Cotonou; tel: 315665. A one-month tourist visa costs CFA22,500, needs two photos and takes two days. There is also a Niger consulate in Parakou, on the road to the public hospital; tel: 612827. One-month tourist visas are issued here in minutes: cost CFA20,000, two photos needed.
**Nigeria** Rue 230/Bd de France, Cotonou; tel 301142. Tourist visas issued only to residents of Benin. Transit visas available and can be extended in Lagos.

### Climate
Humid everywhere, with steady temperatures of 27°C. The dry seasons are from December to April. Northern Benin, being part of the Sahel, is less humid but very hot during March and April. Its dry season lasts from November to May.

### Highlights
The capital city of Porto Novo, which is a sleepy town, has some interesting buildings and markets. Ganvié, a village built on stilts in the middle of a lagoon and accessible only by dugout canoe, is near Cotonou. The voodoo museums of Ouidah, Grand Popo and the coastline are worth a visit. Inland are the historic palaces of Abomey. The three-storey houses of the Somba/Betamaribe people around Natitingou are worth seeing

and, in the north, the Parc National du W. The
railway, one that still works, is a fine way to travel!
And the Hotel de la Gare is a fine but crumbling
place to see in Parakou.

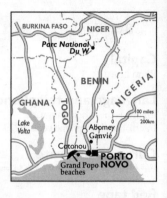

## Where to stay

**Cotonou** Finding secure parking is a problem. Try
the *Hotel de la Plage* near the beach; it had parking but
the area was not wonderful or that safe. About 14km
west of Cotonou there used to be *Camping Ma
Campagne*?

**Abomey** *Chez Monique*, a little way from the centre
of town, has a shady tropical garden and straw roof
restaurant. You can camp at the back of the hotel in
the courtyard for around US$6. The staff are extremely helpful and will go out of their
way to show you parts of Abomey, even a voodoo festival if one is in progress.

**Grand Popo** Charlie and Illya stayed at *L'Auberge de Grand Popo*, which has a hotel,
restaurant and campsite with a view of the ocean. It is an extremely beautiful setting and
they suggest that a meal at the restaurant, although a little expensive, is a must.

**Dassa** There is the *Dassa Motel* on the west side of town, past the dramatic rocks near the
ring road. Parking is available here, with good-value rooms.

**Parakou** The very rundown but atmospheric *Hotel de la Gare* has large rooms and good
parking. Nearby, just 4km away on the road to Natitigou, a new motel is due to open soon
on the barrage by the Voie de Djougou; and a new fish farm offers accommodation
overlooking a series of beautiful lakes.

## Other

Taking of photographs is permitted, but please be respectful, especially when visiting
fetish temples and shrines.

## Further information

*Benin: the Bradt Travel Guide*, Stuart Butler (due 2006).

## BOTSWANA

## Capital

Gaborone

## Language and telephone

English and Satswana are the official languages.
International telephone code +267

## Currency and rate

Pula (P); US$1 = P4.48

## Red tape

Although we had no problems, the Botswana Defence Force (BDF) sometimes take
their duties extremely seriously and can be aggressive. They are said to be best
avoided.

## Visas
Visas are not required for nationals of the USA, UK and most other Commonwealth countries, or from most of western Europe, as long as the stay does not exceed 90 days. Visas cost US$10–15. Entry permits for 30 days are issued at the border.

## Fuel costs
Diesel: US$0.45; petrol: US$0.47 per litre.

## Driving and roads
Drive on the left. There are good surfaced main roads and the rest are tracks and pistes.

## African embassies
**Angola** 2715 Phala Crescent, Gaborone; tel: 375089; CP Private Bag 111
**Namibia** BCC Building, 1278 Lobatse Rd, Gaborone; tel: 397 2685
**Nigeria** High Commission, PO Box 274, Gaborone; tel: 313561, 313563
**South Africa** Queens Rd, Gaborone; tel: 390 4800
**Zambia** PO Box 362, Gaborone; tel: 351951
**Zimbabwe** Orapa Close, Gaborone; tel: 314495

## Climate
It is hot throughout the year, with the main rainy season from December to April.

## Highlights
The Okavango Delta, Moremi Wildlife Reserve and Chobe National Park are obvious highlights. All have an array of wildlife in various environments. Maun has various campsites and organisations that arrange tours into each of these national parks. The Kalahari Desert with its vast open spaces and Central Kalahari Game Reserve is worth a visit, as are the Makgadikgadi and Nxai Pans and Tsodilo Hills with ancient San paintings.

## Where to stay
**Kanye** The *Hotel Motse* is delightful and you can camp in the orchard behind. It's rather hard to find, but is on the north side of town; ask at the fuel stations. Cost US$14 (car plus two people).

**Kang** Just about the only place on the Trans-Kalahari road between Kanye and Ghanzi with a *motel,* shop and fuel. Secure parking.

**Francistown** There are two places to camp: *Woodlands 4X4 stop* and *Marang Motel camp.*

**Maun** *Audi Camp, Crocodile Camp* and *Island Safari Lodge* all offer basic camping facilities at US$6. Each of these camps is a great stopover for planning excursions into the delta, and a safe spot for your vehicle.

**Okavango Delta** Any visit to the Okavango Delta (or any other national park in Botswana) will not be cheap, but the delta is a unique attraction. The cheapest option now is probably *Sepupa Swamp Stop,* which has camping for around US$7 per person. They can usually set up cheaper trips into the delta. Sepupa is located on the northwest side of the delta, not far from the Tsodilo Hills. The *Oddballs* camp, which lies just across the channel from Chief's Island and Moremi Reserve, is no longer the cheap option it once was.

**Moremi Reserve** There are a couple of options here: try either *Xakanaxa Campsite* or *Third Bridge Campsite*. Since these are inside the park, the costs will be higher. A rough estimate would be about US$40 per person per night.

**Chobe National Park** The main area is along the Chobe River east of Kazungula around Kasane. There is cheapish camping for US$10 each at *Kubu Camping* in Kasane. About 5km out is the *Thebe River* camping. Once inside the park, costs rise to around US$40 each at the *Ihaha Campsite*. There is also a campsite at Savuti, but this is also inside the park and will cost about US$40 per night per person. In the Chobe Forest Reserve you might look out for the new *Kavimba Community Campsite*. Previously there was the *Buffalo Ridge Campsite* costing US$6 for camping.

**Makgadikgadi and Nxai Pans** The pans can be crossed only with 4x4 and in the dry season, April to December. Only use well-marked tracks on the pans, or your vehicle will sink. It is advisable to go with another vehicle. Nata is the nearest town with places to stay. Look for *Nata Lodge* and *Sua Pan Lodge*.

**Tsodilo Hills** Getting to the Tsodilo Hills, a world heritage site, is now easier with road improvements, and is worth the effort. It is possible to camp here; try *Makoba Woods camp, Squirrel camp,* or *Malatso campsite*. It should be possible to bush camp en route.

## Other
The importing of meat is prohibited and you will get checked regularly.

## Further information
*Botswana – Okavango Delta, Chobe, Northern Kalahari: The Bradt Travel Guide*, Chris McIntyre
www.botswananet.org

## BURKINA FASO

## Capital
Ouagadougou

## Language and telephone
French is the official language.
International telephone code +226

## Currency and rate
West African franc (CFA); US$1 = CFA502

## Red tape
Police checks were once numerous, but now things are less frenetic all round. Crime in major towns is on the increase.

## Visas
Visas are required for all except nationals of ECOWAS countries. They cost US$60 to US$100 depending on country of application. Visas are not issued at the border. A *Visa Touristique Entente* covering Benin, Burkina Faso, Ivory Coast, Niger and Togo is

theoretically available; track it down via a relevant embassy or consulate. In countries where there is no representation, the French consulate usually handles Burkina visas. Vaccination certificates for yellow fever are checked.

## Fuel costs
Diesel: US$0.65; petrol: US$0.85 per litre.

## Driving and roads
Drive on the right. Main routes have mostly good surfaced roads. Secondary roads are quite reasonable, with some maintenance.

## African embassies
**French consulate** (issues visas for Central African Republic, Mauritania and Togo) Bd de la Révolution, Ouagadougou; tel: 306774
**Ghana** Av d'Oubritenga, Ouagadougou; tel: 301701
**Ivory Coast** Av Raoul Follereau/ Bd du Faso, Ouagadougou; tel: 306637
**Mali** 2569 Av Bassawarga, Ouagadougou; tel: 381922
**Nigeria** BP 132, Av d'Oubritenga, Ouagadougou; tel: 306667
**Senegal** southern end of Av Yennenga, Ouagadougou; tel: 312811

## Climate
The cool dry season is from November to mid April and the rainy season from June to September. The north has less rain and is hotter.

## Highlights
The 'Grand Marché' in Ouagadougou is a shopper's paradise. Ouagadougou is a food connoisseur's delight and known for its variety of restaurants ranging from African and European to American. Visit Banfora, which is excellent for cycling, and the surrounding area. Bobo Dioulasso, with its mud mosque, has long been a favourite. The small town of Bani, near Dori, has some amazing mosques. In the north, on the desert fringes, a melting pot of people gathers in the market of Gorom Gorom every Thursday starting at 11.00. The Parc National du W is another attraction in the southeast.

## Where to stay
**Ouagadougou** The well-established *Camping Ouaga* (follow signs to Camping Ouaga for 1km on Avenue Bassawarga) charges US$5 per person for camping and is to be used for camping only.

**Banfora** The *Hôtel le Comoé*, on the southern edge of town, may allow you to camp in their courtyard for a minimal fee, or bush camping is an option away from town. Close to Banfora are the unusually shaped hills of the Pics du Sindou. You might be able to stay at *Auberge Soutarala* in Sindou village.

**Bobo Dioulasso** As well as the main mud mosque, the biggest attractions are the Bobo (local tribe) houses, distinguished by their tall, conical roofs, in the surrounding countryside. *Casa Africa* is the said to be the best camping option, at US$6 for camping.

**Gorom Gorom** *Le Campement Hôtelier* is the only decent option and camping costs US$6 for two.

## Other
Photographic permits used to be a requirement, but this is no longer the case. Just be aware of what you are photographing and remember that photos of government institutions are completely forbidden. Video permits are required and these are issued by the Ministère de l'Environnement et du Tourisme.

## Further information
*Burkina Faso: The Bradt Travel Guide*, Katrina Manson and James Knight (due 2006)

# BURUNDI

**Warning** *Due to the ongoing political unrest in Burundi we strongly advise you to seek sound travel advice if you intend to visit. Basic information has been listed.*

## Capital
Bujumbura

## Language and telephone
French and Kirundi are the official languages.
International telephone code +257

## Currency and rate
Burundi franc (BFr); US$1 = BFr1078

## Red tape
Unknown at present.

## Visas
Visas are required for all visitors. A one-month tourist visa costs US$25–40, depending on place of issue. You will need two passport photos. Depending on place of issue, visas can be issued within 24 hours. Transit visa if issued may be US$12. Visas are not issued at the border.

## Fuel costs
Diesel: US$0.66; petrol: US$0.72 per litre.

## Driving and roads
No current information is available.

## African embassies
**DRC** Av de Zaïre
**Rwanda** 24 Av de Zaïre, Bujumbura; tel: 26865
**Tanzania** Av Patrice Lumumba, Bujumbura; tel: 24634

## Climate
The climate is varied. The general rainy season is quite long, from November to May. A dry period lasts from June until October, but seasons are not clearly defined.

## Highlights

Bujumbara has an attractive setting and some old colonial buildings. Other sights are the Parc National de la Kibira for its rainforest, the Parc National de la Rurubu, and the waterfall, Chutes de la Kagera, from Gitega.

## Where to stay

No current information.

## Further information

*Africa on a Shoestring*, Lonely Planet

## CAMEROON

## Capital

Yaoundé

## Language and telephone

French and English are the official languages.
International telephone code +237

## Currency and rate

Central African franc (CFA); US$1 = CFA502

## Red tape

You will be stopped sometimes for passport and vehicle checks. Crime is on the increase, particularly in Yaoundé and Douala. Do not carry valuables with you at any time. And beware of accidentally driving on the president's road in Yaoundé!

## Visas

Visas are required for all except nationals of Germany. Costs are US$25–70. A multiple, 90-day entry visa costs around US$65 and can be issued within 24 hours; you will need two photographs. Visas are not issued at the border. Usually, they are issued only in your country of residence and must be activated within one month of issue. We were able to get ours post-dated.

## Fuel costs

Diesel: US$0.58; petrol: US$0.76 per litre.

## Driving and roads

Drive on the right. Road surfaces range from exceptionally good tarmac to diabolically corrugated dirt, with all variations in between. North of Ngaoundéré or south and west of Yaoundé are some fairly good tarred roads. Otherwise there are some reasonable dirt roads that shut if it rains. Then there are a few awful stretches of corrugated dirt, best not dwelt on — east of the capital and on the road to Mamfe. There are also some new road projects, so the situation is improving all the time.

## African embassies

**Central African Republic** Rue 1810, Bastos, Yaoundé; tel: 220 5155
**Chad** Rue Mballa Eloumden, Bastos, Yaoundé; tel: 221 0624
**Congo** Rue 1816, Bastos, Yaoundé; tel: 221 2455
**Democratic Republic of the Congo** Bd de l'URSS, Bastos, Yaoundé; tel: 222 5103

**Equatorial Guinea** Rue 1805, Bastos, Yaoundé; tel: 221 0804

**French consulate** (issues visas for Burkina Faso and Togo) Rue Joseph Atemengué, Yaoundé; tel: 223 6399

**Gabon** Rue 1816, Bastos, Yaoundé; tel: 220 2966

**Ivory Coast** Bastos, PO Box 11357, Yaoundé; tel: 221 7459

**Niger** Tel: 221 3260

**Nigeria** off Av Monseigneur Vogt, Centre Ville, Yaoundé; tel: 222 3455

## Climate

Coastal Cameroon is very wet almost all year. The north is hot and dry, with a long rainy season from May to October. The south is hot and humid, with a short 'dryish' season from December to February and rains from March until October, with a less wet period in July and August away from the coast.

## Highlights

Climb Mount Cameroon, which is West Africa's highest mountain at 4,070m; visit the Waza and Benoué national parks. The beaches at Kribi are excellent. In the north, explore the villages and markets around Maroua, and hike in the Mandara Mountains, including Roumsiki. Southern Cameroon has some spectacular hill regions with the last of the pygmy tribes left in the area, but they are extremely difficult to reach; take an organised expedition with a volunteer organisation in Yaoundé.

## Where to stay

**Yaounde** Finding a reasonably priced hotel with parking in the capital is hard. *Hotel Meumi* is a good choice. Double rooms cost US$22.

**Buea** Buea is on the lowest slope of Mount Cameroon and is also the base camp. You must have a permit and guide; both are available in the main street in town. Climbing Mount Cameroon can take between three and four days. A good place to stay in Buea is the *Mountain Village*. In town is the *Hotel Mermoz* where a double room is US$12.

**Maroua** The best place to stay in Maroua is *Campement Bossou* at US$6. You could stay in Roumsiki at the only *Campement*, but at US$10 it is expensive.

**Garoua** Try the plush hotel, *Relais St Hubert*. It has AC rooms and secure parking. Double room costs US$30. Camping might be allowed.

**Ngaoundéré** On the south side of town try *Hotel Transcam*, which has secure parking.

**Mamfe** We stayed at the *Heritage Inn*. By chance, or perhaps because it's a good retreat, so did Charlie and Illya. We were told, 'Sorry, we have only the most expensive room left. It's $12.' This was a suite with air conditioning, sofas and a huge bathroom. We didn't mind at all! This small town is close to the border with Nigeria. Fuel comes from Nigeria and is only available from large barrels; there is no fuel station.

## Other

Photographic permits are not required but many officials will tell you that they are. If hassles continue, go to the Ministry of Information and Tourism and let them, for a small fee, write a letter stating as much. Again don't drive on the president's unmarked private road, a large roundabout area in central Yaoundé; it could be a costly error!

## Further information

*Cameroon: The Bradt Travel Guide*, Ben West.

# CENTRAL AFRICAN REPUBLIC (CAR)

**Warning** Due to the ongoing civil disturbances in the Central African Republic the information listed may be out of date. We strongly advise no overland travel into the country. Seek sound travel advice if you do intend to visit.

## Capital

Bangui

## Language and telephone

French is the official language.
International telephone code +236

## Currency

Central African franc (CFA); US$1 = CFA502

## Red tape

Avoid all military personnel and try not to stay longer than one day in one area.

## Visas

Visas are required for all and can cost as much as US$70–90. Two photos, two application forms, a yellow fever certificate, a letter from your company stating that the applicant will resume work on returning and a return ticket are all required. Nationals of Australia, New Zealand, France and the Republic of Ireland need permission from Bangui before a visa application is accepted. Visas are not issued at the border. Visas may only be given for short stays, requiring extensions in Bangui.

## Fuel costs

Diesel: US$0.65; petrol: US$0.81 per litre.

## Driving and roads

Drive on the right. There are sealed roads to the northeast and northwest of Bangui for a limited distance, but closer to the borders of Cameroon, Chad and Sudan roads are in very poor condition, particularly during the rainy season.

## African embassies

**Cameroon** Rue de Languedoc, Bangui; tel: 61 1687
**Chad** Av Valéry Giscard d'Estaing, Bangui; tel: 61 4677
**Congo** Av Boganda, Bangui; tel: 61 1877
**Democratic Republic of the Congo** Rue Gamal Abdel Nasser, Bangui; tel: 61 8240
**French consulate** (issues visas for Burkina Faso,

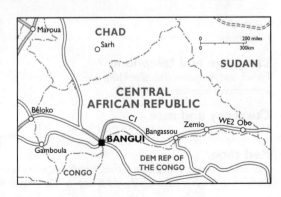

Gabon, Ivory Coast, Mauritania, Senegal and Togo) Bd Général de Gaulle, Bangui; tel: 61 3000
**Nigeria** BP 1010, Km3, Av Boganda, Bangui; tel: 61 0744 or 3910 or 3911
**Sudan** Av de la France, Av de l'Indépendénce, PO Box 1351, Bangui; tel: 61 3821

## Climate
It's hot and humid in the south, drier in the north. The rainy season is from March to October, starting later and finishing earlier the further north you go.

## Highlights
The rolling savanna forest across the border from Cameroon gives a feeling of vastness. The Chutes de Boali north of Bangui are spectacular, particularly during the rainy season. Also worthwhile are the Kembe Falls east of Sibut, and the remote forests beyond. In Bangassou you can take dugout canoe rides along the river in search of hippos. The Dzanga-Sangha Nature Reserve is opening up to tourism and has some great wildlife including lowland gorillas. The Worldwide Fund for Nature is involved: www.panda.org.

## Where to stay
**Bangui** The latest information, which is five years old, is that the *Centre d'Accueil Touristique Dalango* is still open and charges US$5 for camping. It is located in the African Quarter, on Avenue Boganda, 1.5km to the west on Km5.

**Bayanga** *Doli Lodge* is a remote and rustic eco-lodge built by the Worldwide Fund for Nature (WWF) with aid from Germany. It is used by tour operators and researchers as a base for trips into the Dzanga-Sangha Nature Reserve.

**Obo** The *Obo Mission* allowed camping and had a very well-equipped workshop some years ago! (See pages 140–1.)

## Other
We would suggest that your camera stays in its case in Bangui. Ask people in the countryside for their permission, as some in the Central African Republic are extremely sensitive about photography.

## Further information
The WWF currently have conservation, health and education projects in the CAR so their website has some relevant information: www.panda.org.

## CHAD

## Capital
N'djamena

## Language and telephone
French and Arabic are the official languages.
International telephone code +235

## Currency and rate
Central African franc (CFA); US$1 = CFA502

## Red tape
The eastern border with Sudan is currently closed, so we leave this information from the previous authors for reference should it reopen. 'On entry from Sudan at the Adré border

in Chad, we found the military and police to be extremely aggressive – and drunk. It also took up to four hours to clear all paperwork, which was not due to inefficiency, but to having to find the right person for the job who was having a game of cards with friends on the other side of town. Throughout Chad we found the military to be particularly aggressive – they are best avoided.'

When we travelled there ourselves in the desert (Ennedi plateau) in a local agent's cars, our drivers always tried to avoid police checkposts wherever possible, suggesting that the situation is not much different elsewhere in the country.

## Visas
Visas are required for all except nationals of Germany and France. Three application forms and three photos are required. Officially you also need a return air ticket. Visas are valid for three months. The estimated cost of a visa is US$30–80 depending on country of issue. Yellow-fever vaccination certificates will be checked on entry. Visas are not issued at the border. It was possible to get an invitation by fax from a local tour operator and have a visa issued at the airport on arrival by air.

## Fuel costs
Diesel: US$0.70; petrol: US$0.80 per litre.

## Driving and roads
Drive on the right. There are short sections of tarred road on either side of N'djamena; the rest are either sandy desert tracks in the north or very bad mud roads in the south.

## African embassies
**Cameroon** Rue des Poids Lourds, N'djamena; tel: 52 3473
**Central African Republic** was at Rue 1036, N'djamena; tel: 52 3206
**Democratic Republic of the Congo** Av 26 de Août, N'djamena; tel: 52 5935
**French consulate** (issues visas for Burkina Faso, Gabon, Ivory Coast, Mauritania, Senegal and Togo) Rue de Lieutenant-Franjoux, off Av Félix Eboué, N'djamena; tel: 52 2575
**Nigeria** Av Charles de Gaulle, BP 752, N'djamena; tel: 52 2498
**Sudan** off Rue de Gendarmerie, N'djamena; tel: 52 5010 or 51 3497

## Climate
The desert climate in the north is very hot and dry all year round. The heavy rains are from June to September in the south.

## Highlights
The bustling central market and Grand Marché in N'djamena are colourful. Also worth seeing are the village of Gaoui, which is just outside N'djamena, Lake Chad and Abéché, on the edge of the Sahel. The Tibesti Mountains in the north would be a highlight if they were safe and accessible. The Ennedi Plateau, including Guelta d'Archei, is accessible with a local guide and offers stunning desert scenery with natural arches, freshwater crocodiles and prehistoric rock art. Ounianga Kebir and the northern lakes are amazing.

## Where to stay
**N'djamena** There are a few hotels in N'djamena and you may be able to park in their yards. We stayed at the centrally located *Hotel Sahel*. It has a nice airy courtyard and parking. Or ask at the *Novotel* – formerly *Hotel Tchadienne* – if you can camp in their grounds. If you're lucky, you may be allowed to use the staff showers and the hotel's pool. Email facilities are available in town. *La Caravelle* is rumoured to be a new camping place near Rondpoint du Pont.

**Abéché** In Abéché Charlie and Illya were lucky enough to meet the sultan's brother (!) who put them up for the night. We would otherwise suggest bush camping. Abéché is not a very large town and the surrounding area is typical Sahel.

**Ennedi** The Ennedi Plateau is a beautiful desert area, similar to the Tassili du Hoggar in Algeria. But it is equally wild and we do not suggest going there alone. Travel with a local agent to avoid the risk of landmines remaining from the civil war. Mostly you will camp out wild, but there is a vague resemblance to a hotel in Fada, *Hotel Restaurant Emi Koussi*, where we camped in the yard. In Fada we camped at our driver's cousin's house – the toilet was just outside...

**Tibesti Mountains** There has been a long-standing border dispute between Chad and Libya, as well as fields of uncharted landmines – this tour of the Tibesti is definitely not for the faint-hearted. In fact we do not recommend you to go there at all at the moment. If and when it becomes safe, you will need enough fuel, water and food supplies for approximately 1,000km (600 miles). Bush sleeping is the only option and a travel permit for the area is required, depending on which side you come in on. Obtaining permission to travel in the area will be difficult and you will probably be rejected. If it ever becomes safe, it will still probably be best to avoid officialdom when wise and safe to do so.

## Other

A photographic permit is said to be required, but can take up to a week to issue, so most travellers don't bother. The answer is not to take any pictures, or be extremely discreet when you do. Out in the desert this is not a problem, though you should always ask if photographing people. The Tubu people are particularly averse to having their photos taken.

At the time of writing, the border between Chad and Sudan (Adré) is closed due to the situation in Darfur. How this will develop, we have no way of knowing. In any case it is a very remote and lonely area. Be careful and make sure you have sufficient supplies of fuel and food.

## Further information

www.expeditionworld.com

# PEOPLE'S REPUBLIC OF THE CONGO

*Warning Due to the on–off rebellion in the People's Republic of the Congo the information listed may be out of date. We advise against overland travel into the People's Republic of the Congo. However in 2004 a few overland trucks were trying to take the route – it may get better. Seek sound travel advice if you do intend to visit.*

## Capital
Brazzaville

## Language and telephone
French is the official language.
International telephone code +242

## Currency and rate
Central African franc (CFA); US$1 = CFA502

## Red tape
As with most war-torn countries in Africa, avoid all military personnel. It has also been advised that all travel at night be avoided here. Try to keep a low profile in Brazzaville!

## Visas
Visas are required for all except nationals of France. Two-week visas are valid from the date of entry and will cost US$70–90 depending on country of application. Visas are not issued at the border.

## Fuel costs
Diesel: US$0.50; petrol: US$0.50 per litre.

## Driving and roads
Drive on the right. Roads are extremely poor.

## African embassies
**Angola** try CP 388, Brazzaville; tel: 83 6565;
**Cameroon** Rue Général Bayardelle, Brazzaville; tel: 81 1008
**Central African Republic** Rue Fourneau, Brazzaville; tel: 81 4721
**Chad** 22 Rue des Ecoles; Brazzaville; tel: 83 2222
**Democratic Republic of the Congo** 130 Av de l'Indépendance, Brazzaville; tel: 81 3052
**France** (issues visas for Burkina Faso, Ivory Coast and Togo) Av Alfassa, Brazzaville; tel: 81 5541
**Gabon** Av Monseigneur Augouard, Brazzaville; tel: 81 5620
**Nigeria** 11 Bd du Maréchal Lyautey, Brazzaville; tel: 81 1022

## Climate
The climate is mostly hot and humid. The main drier season is from May or June to September.

## Highlights
The clean beaches along the coastline. Congolese music and food. Pointe-Noire. Parc National de Odzala for gorilla trekking. The bad roads if you like that sort of thing!

## Where to stay
**Brazzaville** It seems that in Brazzaville, as in most West and central African countries, it is expensive and difficult to find camping accommodation. You could try either of the Catholic missions in town, *Eglise Sacré Coeur* (on Avenue Maréchal Foch behind the Méridien Hotel) or the *Eglise Kimbanguiste* (on Plateau de 15 Ans, near the Hotel Majoca).

**Pointe Noire** Most accommodation is said to be along the Cité.

**Parc National de Odzala** Gorilla trekking needs to be booked through ECOFAC, Ave Marechal Foch in Brazzaville. The one-week trips including all transfer fees to and from Brazzaville, accommodation and meals, will set you back US$600. For further information try ECOFAC's website www.ecofac.org.

## Other
A photographic permit is not required, but be extremely cautious when taking photos and stay clear of all government institutions.

## Further information
*Africa on a Shoestring*, Lonely Planet

# DEMOCRATIC REPUBLIC OF THE CONGO (DRC)

**Warning** *Due to the civil war in the Democratic Republic of the Congo the information listed may be out of date. We also strongly advise no overland travel into the country. Seek sound travel advice if you do intend to visit and, depending on the state of the country, travel in convoy. The western areas may be improving.*

## Capital
Kinshasa

## Language and telephone
French is the official language.
International telephone code +243

## Currency and rate
Congolese franc (Franc Congolais: CDF); US$1= CDF430

## Red tape
Officials of the DRC are notoriously bad and known for their corruption and drunkenness (from palm wines) – avoid at all times! Never stay in one place longer than a day and never walk or drive at night.

## Visas
Visas are required for all and costs vary depending on where you get the visa. Prices range from US$50 for a one-month visa to US$100 for multiple entry. You will also need three to four photographs and an introduction letter from your embassy. Vaccination certificates are obligatory. Visas are not issued at the border.

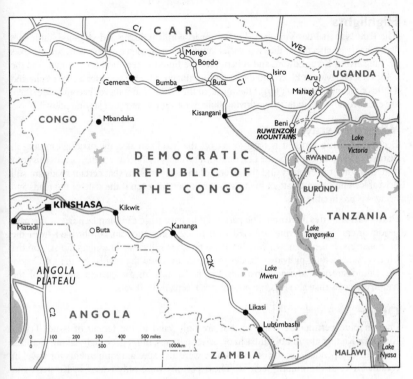

## Fuel costs
Diesel: US$0.50; petrol: US$0.50 per litre.

## Driving and roads
Drive on the right. There are not many stretches of road in the DRC that are good and they become a sea of mud during the rainy season.

## African embassies
**Benin** 3990 Av des Cliniques, Kinshasa; tel: 30 492 or 28 822
**Burundi** was at 4687 Av de la Gombe, Kinshasa; tel: 33 353
**Cameroon** Bd du 30 Juin, Kinshasa; tel: 34 787
**Central African Republic** 11 Av Pumbu, Kinshasa; tel: 33 571
**Congo** Bd du 30 Juin, Kinshasa; tel: 34 028
**Gabon** Bd du 30 Juin, Kinshasa; tel: 50 206
**Kenya** 5002 Av de l'Ouganda, Kinshasa; tel: 33 205
**Nigeria** Bd du 30 Juin, Kinshasa; tel: 33 343
**Rwanda** was at 50 Av de la Justice, Kinshasa; tel: 33 080
**Sudan** 83 Av des Treis, PO Box 7347, Kinshasa
**Tanzania** BP 1612, 142 Bd 30 Juin, Kinshasa, tel: 34 364
**Uganda** was 17 Av Tombalbaye/Av des Travailleurs, BP 1086, Kinshasa 1; tel: 22 7740
**Zambia** 54 Av de l'Ecole, Kinshasa; tel: 21 802

## Climate
It is impossible to summarise the climate for the whole of the DRC, as it is such a huge country. Along the northern route (the one taken by most travellers) the only time of year it is likely to be fairly dry is from December to February.

## Highlights

The Parc National des Virunga is known for its gorilla trekking and volcanoes (although access has been affected by the civil war). Climbing Nyiragongo is spectacular. See the lakes of Tanganyika, Kivu, Edward and Albert, plus the Epulu Reservation for pygmies, and the Okapi reserve. Mount Hoyo and the eastern mountain ridge are good for a cool respite and a taste of the villages. Don't forget the music of the DRC. And if it ever becomes safe, there are even worse roads to test your driving skills, your vehicle and your staying power!

## Where to stay

Because of dense forest it is hard to get off the 'road', so sleeping/parking/camping in disused road quarries will be the best option. Travellers used to stay at the various missions dotted around the country and this is one of the only reasons that certain roads are still driveable. The current state of the missions is uncertain, even if the state of the roads and bridges is predictable.

**Parc National des Virunga** The park used to have basic camping facilities at the park headquarters. Entry permits are paid in hard currency and can be obtained from the headquarters. It is not known whether these facilities still exist. Travellers did stay on the Uganda side, getting individual guides to take them to see the gorillas on the DRC side. We would strongly advise against this, but it depends on the current situation of the country. Access may also become possible via Goma from Rwanda.

## Other

Photographic permits are required, but are only valid in the region of issue. Try in Kinshasa, Kisangani and Lubumbashi or, easier perhaps, don't get caught taking pictures. The cost is dependent on the official! There were also special requirements for travel in central DRC in the mining regions. These permits were only issued in Kinshasa and could take up to two weeks to get. Most travellers bribed their way through these areas.

## Further information

For wildlife and nature, the website of the Institut Congolais pour la Conservation de la Nature: www.iccnrdc.cd.

## DJIBOUTI

## Capital

Djibouti City

## Language and telephone

French and Arabic are the official languages. Afars spoken elsewhere.
International telephone code +253

## Currency and rate

Djibouti franc (DFr); US$1 = 176DFr

## Red tape

None of any significance.

## Visas

Visas are required for all. They are valid for one month and cost around US$65/€50. Visas are not issued at the border. There are not many embassies; in Europe try Paris.

## Fuel costs
Diesel: US$0.55; petrol: US$0.91 per litre.

## Driving and roads
Drive on the right. The main roads to Ethiopia and
Tadjoura are generally good; desert tracks and piste
outside the main routes. Be very careful if going to
Lac Abbé, take a guide to avoid quicksands and
getting seriously lost.

## African embassies
**Egypt** Ilot du Heron, Djibouti City; tel: 351231
**Eritrea** PO Box 1944, Rue de Kampala; tel: 354951 or
350381 or 354961
**Ethiopia** PO Box 230, Rue Clochette, Djibouti City; tel: 350718
**French consulate** (issues visas for most French-speaking African countries) Av Maréchal Lyautey,
Djibouti City; tel: 352503
**Sudan** PO Box 4259, Iron House, IE12, Djibouti; tel: 356404

## Climate
The climate is generally very hot and humid on the coast, with a cooler season from
November to mid April and occasional rain during that period.

## Highlights
Djibouti City has some colourful markets, old colonial buildings, teashops and old
mosques. You could take a boat trip across the Gulf of Tadjoura, but driving there is very
spectacular with black lava flows and volcanic cones. Lac Assal lies below sea level with
amazing brilliant-white salt, sulphur and halite crystals. The Forêt du Day, a small zone of
luxuriant growth, is accessed by a shocking rocky track. Randa is a nearly defunct retreat
but a nice drive. Lac Abbé is known for its birdlife. Enjoy the flamingos and natural
chimneys formed by the escape of underground steam dotted along the foreshore.

## Where to stay
**Djibouti City** Try the *Sheraton*: it has secure parking. In town try the *Auberge Sable Blanc*
on Boulevard de la République; it may still have parking/camping. In the African quarter
there is some budget accommodation available but no obvious secure parking.

**Gulf of Tadjoura** With superb coral reefs 10m from the shore, this is a great place for a
stopover. Bush sleeping well outside the town is one option. Try *Hotel Le Golfe* or the hotel
opposite nearby, which have parking.

**Randa** Look for *Campement le Goda* just before town.

**Forêt du Day** Try *Campement de Dittilou*, but getting there is shockingly rough.

**Dikhil** Try the *Hotel le Palmerie* on the main road. Camping is not encouraged.

**Lac Assal** Bush sleeping is not recommended; stay close by at *Le Plage du Goubbet*, with
camping and small thatched huts.

**Lac Abbé** Lac Abbé can be reached only by 4x4 and requires at least two days, including
a guide. Bush camping is possible, but beware of quicksands, or better, try the new
*Campement Asbole*.

**Border: Galafi** We camped/parked here close to the Customs on our way back into
Ethiopia.

## Other
Photographic permits are not officially needed, but officials particularly may act petulantly and in any case people in Djibouti are not happy to be photographed, so beware. Djibouti is an expensive country.

## Further information
*Africa on a Shoestring*, Lonely Planet

## EGYPT

## Capital
Cairo

## Language and telephone
Arabic is the official language.
International telephone code +20

## Currency and rate
Egyptian pound (E£); US$1 = E£5.92

## Red tape
The roads south of Aswan and Ras Banas have been closed to all by the military since the tourist attacks and we suggest that you get advice on routes if you are intending to drive that way. Convoys are also compulsory between the Red Sea resorts, Luxor and Aswan.

## Visas
Visas are required for all except nationals of Malta and Arabic countries. Visas can now be obtained at airports and at some borders. For those entering by road it is better to get one in advance. One-month single-entry visas cost US$25.

## Fuel costs
Diesel: US$0.06; petrol: US$0.15 per litre.

## Driving and roads
Drive on the right. All the main routes are well surfaced. Outside the major routes you will find road signs in Arabic only. Convoys operate on the Hurghada to Luxor and Aswan routes and to Abu Simbel.

## African embassies
**Algeria** 14 Sharia Brazil, Zamalek, Cairo; tel: 341 8257
**Burkina Faso** 9 Fawakeh St, Mohamdessine, Cairo; tel: 360 8480
**Cameroon** 42 Rue Batel, Doqqi, Cairo; tel: 704622
**Chad** 12 Midan al-Rifai, Doqqi, Cairo; tel: 349 4461
**Democratic Republic of the Congo** 5 Sharia Al-Mansour, Mohammed Zamalek, Cairo; tel: 341 1069
**Djibouti** 11 Sharia al-Gezira, Agouza, Cairo; tel: 345 6546
**Eritrea** 87 Shahab St, Al Mohamdessine, Cairo; tel: 303 0517 or 334409
**Ethiopia** 6 Abdel Rahman Hussein St, Midan El-Gomhouria, Doqqi, Cairo; tel: 335 3696
**Ivory Coast** 39 Rue El Kods El Cherif, Madinet, El Mohamdessine, Cairo 11511; tel: 346 0109 or 346 4952

**Jordan** Al Shaheed Basem al Khatib, Doqqi, Cairo; 348 5566

**Kenya** 7 Sharia Mohandis Galal, Mohamdessine, Cairo; tel: 345 3907

**Libya** 7 Sharia As-Saleh Ayoub, Zamalek, Cairo; tel: 735 1864

**Morocco** A10 Rue Salah ad-Din, Zamalek, Cairo; tel: 340 9849 or 340 9677 or 341 4718

**Nigeria** 13 Gabalaya St, Zamalek, Cairo; tel: 818389

**Somalia** 27 Sharia Somal, Doqqi, Cairo; tel: 337 4038

**South Africa** 21–23 Sharia al-Giza, Giza, Cairo; tel: 571 7234

**Sudan** 3 Ibrahim St, Garden City, Cairo; tel: 794 5043 or 355 7705

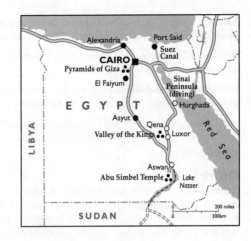

**Tanzania** 9 Sharia Abdel Hamid Lotfi, Doqqi,Cairo; tel: 704155

**Tunisia** 26 Sharia al-Gezira, Zamalek, Cairo; tel: 341 8962

**Uganda** 9 Midan al-Missaha, Doqqi, Cairo; tel: 348 6070 or 248 5975

**Zambia** 25 Abdel Monein Riad St, Mohamdessine, PO Box 253, Doqqi, Cairo 12311; tel: 361 0281–3

**Zimbabwe** 36 Wadi El Nil St, Obandessin, Cairo; tel: 351 4427

## Climate
Egypt is hot and dry for most of the year, except for the winter months of December, January and February.

## Highlights
One of the Seven Wonders of the World – the Pyramids of Giza. Also in Cairo are the Tutankhamun treasures and, close by, the Pyramid of Sakkara. The Coptic monasteries of St Paul and St Anthony are further south, close to the Red Sea coast. Along the Nile are the temples of Karnak and Luxor, plus the Valleys of the Kings and Queens in Luxor. Kom Ombo and Idfu are worth stopping at on the way to Aswan. Aswan has the Philae Temple and a pleasant riverside environment. Abu Simbel is spectacular if you have the time and money to go that far. The Sinai has its own highlights of St Catherine's Monastery, climbing Mount Sinai and the fantastic snorkelling and diving along the coast. Plus the Red Sea has the popular resorts of Hurghada and Safaga, while the western desert has the oases of Kharga and Siwa etc.

## Where to stay
**Cairo** Try the *Motel Salma*, near Wissa Wassef Art Centre just south of Giza on the Sakkara road. Camping will cost around US$5 and there's lots of space but little shade.

**St Anthony's and St Paul's monasteries** These monasteries do not encourage camping.

**Luxor** The *Rezeiky Camp* is fairly basic, but pleasant with some shade; US$10 for camping, (vehicle plus two people).

**Hurghada** Try *Hotel Snafer*, parking will be sorted out with the police for security reasons. US$10 double.

**Safaga** Camping at *Sun Beach* is the only option as far as we know. It's pleasant with a beachside tent bar. Cost US$10 (car plus two people).

**Aswan** We stayed a mile or two south of the very swish Old Cataract Hotel at the pleasant *Hotel Sara*, with safe parking and good rooms, all negotiable.

**Between Alexandria and Cairo** Try the *Fisherman's Village*, a local mini-resort in a quiet spot west of the main highway.

**Between Libya and Alexandria** We did not find anywhere, and the military do not allow desert camping. There are plenty of expensive hotels near El Alamein.

**Sinai** Try the *Pigeon House* in Na'ama Bay, Sharm el Sheikh, which had comfortable huts with fans, and serves breakfast. Accommodation costs around US$20. Nuweiba has a *camping* area.

## Other
*Baksheesh* (tipping) is widely expected, whether for somebody carrying your bags or opening a door or for a service. Haggling is an art form in Egypt and, whether it be for accommodation or curios, be aware of local prices, and never quote a price you are not prepared to pay. This includes the ferry from Aswan to Wadi Halfa.

## Further information
www.tourism.egnet.net
www.touregypt.net
www.cairo.com if you want to go web-shopping in California!

## REPUBLIC OF EQUATORIAL GUINEA

### Capital
Malabo

### Language and telephone
Spanish is the official language.
International telephone code +240

### Currency and rate
Central African franc (CFA); US$1 = CFA502

### Red tape
The police are said to be a little pushy, but if all your paperwork is in order there shouldn't be a problem. You might be allowed to cross the border for a brief visit from Cameroon, for a small fee.

### Visas
Visas are required for all and one-month visas cost US$65–80. You will also need two photographs. Visas are not issued at the border but you could ask at Ebebiyin on the northern border with Cameroon.

### Fuel costs
Diesel: US$0.56; petrol: US$0.68 per litre.

### Driving and roads
Drive on the right. Roads are mostly very poor, but new oil wealth should change this one day!

## African embassies

**Cameroon** 19 Calle de Rey Boncoro, Malabo; tel: 92263
**France** (issues visas for Burkina Faso, the Central African Republic, Chad, Ivory Coast and Togo) Carretera del Aeropuerto, Malabo; tel: 92005
**Gabon** Calle de Argelia, Malabo; tel: 93180
**Nigeria** 4 Paeso de los Cocoteros, Malabo; tel: 92487

## Climate

Equatorial Guinea has a wet tropical climate with a drier spell from June to September on the mainland. December and January are driest on Bioko Island.

## Highlights

Malabo, with its old Spanish architecture, and Luba's nightlife on Bioko Island. There's a Bioko Biodiversity Protection Program under way: see www.bioko.org. The rainforests of the mainland.

## Where to stay

**Ebebiyin** If you visit Equatorial Guinea at all by road it will be through the border here. Try at the hotels, eg: *Hotel Mbengono.*

**Bata** Finding any secure parking would be difficult in Bata. *Hotel Yessica* might have parking.

**Malabo** It's virtually certain you will only come to Malabo if you fly from Bata. The *Hostel Nely*, where the owner speaks English, is a suggestion. Cost estimated at US$12.

**Luba** Luba is southwest of Malabo and known for its nightlife with beautiful beaches. Suggested is the *Hotel Jemaro.*

## Other

Photographic permits are essential and you will be asked for your permit on a regular basis. These can be obtained from the Ministry of Culture, Tourism and Francophone Relations. You will need to type up a request, preferably in Spanish on official stationery, which will cost you US$60 and will be issued within 24 hours. Do not take pictures of any government organisations.

## Further information

www.bioko.org

## ERITREA

*Warning* The recent border disputes between Eritrea and Ethiopia have now been partially resolved. It is currently impossible to drive into Eritrea from Ethiopia. It may be possible to drive in from Kassala in Sudan, but security may be an issue. Crossing into Djibouti is said to be possible, according to one local, but check first as you might be stuck in the country. Within the country security has improved and visiting should be a pleasant experience. However, seek current advice before entering.

## Capital

Asmara

## Language and telephone

Arabic and Tigrinya are the official languages.
International telephone code +291

## Currency and rate

Nakfa; US$1 = 13.5Nakfa

## Red tape

None of any significance. Check before heading into
the Danakil areas.

## Visas

Visas are required for all and should be applied for in
your home country. Of course this is not always
possible and proof of visas from other countries, a letter of introduction from your
embassy and two photographs should suffice. A one-month visa will cost US$40–60 and
is valid from date of entry. Visas are not issued at the border. Have a valid yellow fever
vaccination certificate.

## Fuel costs

Diesel: US$0.23; petrol: US$0.37 per litre.

## Driving and roads

Drive on the right. Roads are in good condition on most major routes, deteriorating as
you get off the beaten track. On the road south from Massawa to Assab, construction
is reported to be substantially underway. It is said to be rather risky to go south of Assab
into Djibouti, but this may change. Hard information is difficult to find about this
route.

## African embassies

**Djibouti** Andinnet St, Asmara; tel: 125990
**Egypt** Marsa Fatuma St, Asmara; tel: 120056, 123603
**Ethiopia** was at Franklin D Roosevelt St, Asmara; tel: 116365; but might not be open.
**Sudan** Hazemo St, Asmara; tel: 120672

## Climate

Eritrea has a varied topography, so the climate is different in each of the three main
zones. In the highlands, the hottest month is usually May, with highs of around 30°C.
Winter is from December to February, with lows at night that can be near freezing.
Asmara's climate is pleasant all year round. Short rainy seasons are in March and April;
the main rains are from late June to early September. On the coast, travel is not
recommended between June and September, when daily temperatures range from 40°
to 50°C (and considerably hotter in the Danakil Desert). In winter months the
temperature ranges from 21° to 35°C. Rain is rare, and occurs only in winter. In the
western lowlands the rainy seasons are the same as the highlands; the temperature
pattern is the same as that of the coast.

## Highlights

Asmara is known for its pleasant ambience, Italian buildings and cool climate. The dusty
alleys of Massawa are being restored, across the first causeway on Taulud Island. Keren is a
predominantly Muslim town and has a colourful daily market, renowned for its silversmiths'
street, and the livestock market every Monday. Churches and monasteries close to the

Ethiopian border are interesting. The Danakil desert is an incredibly remote area, sparsely populated by the Afar nomads. It is said to be possible to drive through this area to Djibouti. However, with temperatures generally around 40°C, and with no facilities or main roads, it is really only for the seriously adventurous. A guide is recommended.

## Where to stay

There are said to be a few campsites, but good-value accommodation is available and rooms are usually clean and well kept. It's just a matter of finding secure parking for the vehicle.

**Asmara** There are quite a few *albergos* (inns) to be found along Liberation Avenue. For camping try the *Africa Pension*, which is an old converted villa. The *Hotel Sunshine* and *Hotel Khartoum*, which has car hire, may be possible places to park.

**Massawa** Massawa does not have any campsites, but does have accommodation on the mainland and on Taulud Island. You will need to shop around for parking if you managed to get your vehicle into the country in the first place.

**Keren**Try the *Eritrea Hotel* or the *Sicilia*, with both having shady courtyards.

## Other

There are uncharted mines throughout Eritrea, so stay on main roads rather than off the beaten track, particularly after dark, and always ask the locals for route advice. The *faranji* ('white man's') hysteria can get a bit much, but you'll become used to it and it's generally harmless.

## Further information

*Eritrea: The Bradt Travel Guide*, Edward Paice
www.eritrea.org is now for sale!

# ETHIOPIA

> Ethiopians are completely bonkers. I knew, too, that I had to visit their country.
>
> Philip Briggs, from *Ethiopia: The Bradt Travel Guide*

## Capital
Addis Ababa

## Language and telephone
Amharic is the official language.
International telephone code +251

## Currency and rate
Ethiopian birr (Birr); US$1 = 8.4Birr

## Red tape
None of any significance. Ethiopians are generally pleasant people, if more than a little inquisitive!

## Visas
Visas are required for all except nationals of Kenya. Visas are single-entry only and cost US$65. You will also need to produce an onward visa for the next country and prove you

have sufficient funds. Yellow fever vaccination certificates are mandatory. Visas are not issued at the border.

## Fuel costs
Diesel: US$0.35; petrol: US$0.45 per litre.

## Driving and roads
Drive on the right. Roads are mostly poor with some tarred sections along the major routes. The road from Addis Ababa to Moyale is nearly

all tarred, as is the new road to Djibouti, the main port now for landlocked Ethiopia. Roads in the highlands are very rough gravel and extremely slow going. The eastern highland road from Adigrat to Addis is not all tarred, as indicated by the Michelin map.

## African embassies
Just about every African country is represented in Addis Ababa and the tourist board (near Maskal Square) issues a useful booklet listing all the embassies. Here are just a few:

**Djibouti** off Bole Rd, Addis Ababa; tel: 613006
**Egypt** Entonto Av, Addis Ababa; tel: 514302
**French consulate** (issues visas for most French-speaking African countries) Omedia St, Addis Ababa; tel: 550066
**Kenya** Maryam Aba Techan St, Addis Ababa; tel: 610033
**Somaliland** tel: 635921
**Sudan** off Roosevelt St, Addis Ababa; tel: 516477
**Tanzania** Bole Rd, Addis Ababa; tel: 448155–7

## Climate
The main rainy season is from June to September, with lighter rains from February to April. In the lowlands it can get extremely hot from April to June, while the colder season in the highlands can be very cold.

## Highlights
The northern historical route includes Gonder, for its castle compound, and Bahar (Bahir) Dar beside Lake Tana, source of the Blue Nile, and close to the Blue Nile Falls. The route also includes the Simien Mountains and Axum, plus the famous rock-cut churches of both Lalibela and Tigre. South of Addis are the lakes of the Rift Valley and the Omo region, with its traditional village life and culture. Ethiopian cuisine (memorable at least), and the elaborate coffee ceremony are a must, as well as the traditional music and dance.

## Where to stay
**Addis Ababa** There are a few options apart from hotels. We stayed at the *Hotel Amba*, a small but friendly compound on Maryam Aba Techan Street, east of town. We also

camped at the *Swedish Mission*, just beyond the American embassy north towards Entoto. Cost US$6. Charlie and Illya stayed at the *Bel Air* (head east from Arat Kilo roundabout and it's on the right), camping in the shady courtyard, for US$3 per person. The manager and his wife are apparently delightful and go out of their way to help.

**Gonder** The *Terera Hotel* has a view of the Royal Enclosure – it is located just to the north. Camping costs US$3 per person. Gonder often has a shortage of water and getting a shower can be a little frenetic.

**Bahar Dar** We camped in the exotic lakeside garden of the *Ghion Hotel*. Camping cost US$6, rooms are US$12–15. It's hard to beat for a restful interlude. You could also try at the *Guna Terara Hotel* (east towards Gonder, opposite the Mobil garage) at US$3 per person. There are communal showers.

**Axum** At the time of writing, not many travellers in vehicles had visited Axum, partly because of the terrible road and the long distance. But don't let this deter you; fill up with fuel in case of shortages. Some tour groups were flying into Axum. Try the *Axum Hotel*, east of town towards Adwa and government run, for camping.

**Lalibela** We camped in the driveway of the *Seven Olives Hotel*; it's not very busy. There's a nice view and enough room to spread out. Cost US$5 per person for camping. The food is traditional Injera Wat in the restaurant. The *Roha* to the west of town also offers camping at US$6.

**Woldiya** The *Lal Hotel* allows camping in its back yard; it has a bar, comfortable lounge and good rooms. It is a super place with an amazing vegetable and fruit garden; a rare example of local personal initiative in the highlands, where fresh food other than garlic is often scarce. They will sell you some of the produce. A bread shop is also on the site. Camping US$5 for two. See box *Ethiopia in a Nutshell* in *Chapter 6*.

**Kombolcha** The *Hotel Tekle* is very good value, with pleasant rooms, restaurant and parking on a hill. Double room US$10.

**Nazret** Along the main road on the south side is the *Hotel Adama Ras* with a quiet garden and good parking. Rooms are good value, costing US$10 for a double room.

**Awasa** On the lakeside try *Hotel Woye Shebele*; it's shady and the gardens host lots of birdlife. Camping cost US$6 for two and a room will be US$12. Watch out for the monkeys.

**Yabello** The *Yabello Motel* is the only decent place, with parking and a nice garden. There is a basic garage next door if you need it! Double room costs US$12.

**The Omo region** The best bet here is to bush camp. If you decide to stay a night in Arba Minch, stay at *Rosa's Place*, where camping is allowed in the courtyard and she makes the best fish cutlets in all of Ethiopia. It makes a great break from *injera* (a large pancake-shaped substance made of *tef*, a grain that is unique to Ethiopia).

## Other

Currency declaration forms are not now needed on arrival, but keep all bank exchange receipts.

### The Julian calendar and 12-hour clock

Ethiopians use the Julian calendar, which means that their year falls seven or eight years behind the European calendar, and there are 13 months in the calendar of the Orthodox Church. Ethiopian time is also measured in 12-hour cycles starting at 06.00 and 18.00. In other words, their 19.00 is our 13.00 and vice versa. Be very aware of this when booking a bus or flight, and double-check departure times. Most banks and other such institutions have both Western and Ethiopian calendars and times.

## Further information
*Ethiopia: The Bradt Travel Guide*, Philip Briggs
www.ethiopia.org

# GABON

## Capital
Libreville

## Language and telephone
French is the official language.
International telephone code +241

## Currency and rate
Central African franc (CFA); US$1 = CFA502

## Red tape
Police are suspicious of all foreigners, so approach with care. Some officials at road check points are a little unfriendly, but not all.

## Visas
Visas are required for all and can take as long as a week to be issued, as all applications are theoretically telexed through to Libreville for approval. You may need a letter of introduction from your embassy, two photographs and US$80–100. Visas are not issued at the border. A yellow fever vaccination certificate is needed.

## Fuel costs
Diesel: US$0.52; petrol: US$0.75 per litre.

## Driving and roads
Drive on the right. Roads are a mixture of good new tarmac interspersed with generally poor corrugated dirt. Between Oyem and Ndjole there are both good and bad sections which are slowly being worked on. Libreville to Lambaréné is good but quite hilly. To Réserve de la Lopé, the road was narrow, remote and very hilly. We gave up! There is a train!

## African embassies
**Benin** Bd Léon Mba, Quartier Derrière Prison, Libreville; tel: 73 7692
**Cameroon** Bd Léon Mba, Quartier Derrière Prison, Libreville; tel: 73 2800
**Central African Republic** North of Voie Express, Libreville; tel: 73 7761
**Congo** Gué-Gué, off Bd Ouaban, Libreville; tel: 67 7078
**Democratic Republic of the Congo** Gué-Gué, off Bd Ouaban, Libreville; tel: 73 8141
**Equatorial Guinea** Route d'Ambowe, Gué-Gué, Libreville; tel: 73 2523

**Ivory Coast** Immeuble Diamant, Bd de l'Indépendance, Libreville; tel: 72 0596/73 7412
**Nigeria** Av du Président Léon Mba, Quartier de l'Université, Libreville; tel: 73 2111
**São Tomé** BP 489 Bd de la Mer, Libreville; tel: 72 0994

## Climate

The climate is hot and humid, with the dry season from May to September and another short drier spell in mid December.

## Highlights

Gabon has extensive virgin forest covering very hilly country, which can be seen by visiting the various reserves. The most famous is the Réserve de la Lopé, where one can go in search of lowland gorilla. In Libreville are extensive local markets, and a few resorts along the ocean to the beach at Cap Estérias. Lambaréné is set on the beautiful banks of the Ogooue River, with the Albert Schweizer hospital and museum.

## Where to stay

**Libreville** We stayed at the *Michele Marine*, which is one of the cheaper places but still expensive. A double room costs US$55. Camping may be possible in the parking area, but with high humidity rather unpleasant. The *Hotel Tropicana* resort, near the airport, is another pleasant and cheaper option used by expatriates. Cost: US$30 a double. It has a beachside café-restaurant, but check that the parking is secure overnight. The *Maison Libermann* on Boulevard Bessieux has been suggested and is said to be clean, quiet and offering hot showers. Camping facilities would need to be negotiated.

**Cap Estérias** Cap Estérias is just north of Libreville and very pleasant. Camping is possible at the *L'Auberge du Cap*. It also has rondavel huts and a restaurant.

**Lambaréné** We parked for free in the grounds of the *Ogooue Palace Hotel*, which is on the river to the north of town near the church and mission. The *Mission (Soeurs de la Conception)*, the red brick complex mentioned and on the nearby hill, is not that cheap and does not allow camping. They have rooms for US$18. Another suggestion was *Le Petit Auberge*, two blocks southeast of Bar Dancing Le Capitol, but camping facilities would need to be negotiated. It could be noisy!

**Réserve de la Lopé** By taking the train this is the easiest national park to get to and has abundant wildlife. In your own vehicle be prepared for a remote drive. Camping is not allowed inside the reserve. The *Hotel Lopé* is very expensive. It might be possible to stay in cheaper lodgings (*Casa de passage*) in the village, but come well prepared.

**Bitam** Try the *Hotel Escale*, which has parking and a nice restaurant.

**Oyem** South of town on the west is the *Oyem Motel* with parking and cheap rooms at US$12.

**Ndjolé** The amazing *Auberge St Hubert* on the west of town along the river looks like a hotel set on the banks of the Loire in France. The inside is not much less comfortable; a welcome retreat in a sea of jungle and pot-holed roads. Double room costs US$30. See *Est-ce que c'est la Loire* box in *Chapter 4*.

## Other

Be wary of what you photograph, as the Gabonese are quite touchy about photography and your camera could be confiscated.

## Further information

*Gabon, São Tomé & Príncipe: The Bradt Travel Guide*, Sophie Warne

## GAMBIA

### Capital
Banjul

### Language and telephone
English is the official language.
International telephone code +220

### Currency and rate
Dalasi (D); US$1 = D28.5

### Red tape
Roadblocks can be tiresome, with officials surly at the best of times.

### Visas
Visas are required for all except nationals from the Commonwealth and most EU countries, cost US$20. There are different visa requirements for nationals of the United States, Australia, New Zealand and South Africa, so it's best to check. Ensure that your passport is valid for six months or more. Yellow-fever certificates are obligatory.

### Fuel costs
Diesel: US$0.45; petrol: US$0.59 per litre.

### Driving and roads
Drive on the right. Roads along the coastal strip and the airport road are good, but inland expect some deteriorating surfaces.

### African embassies
**Guinea** 778A Daniel Goddard St, Banjul; tel: 22 6862
**Guinea Bissau** Atlantic Rd, Bakau; tel: 22 8134
**Mali consulate** VM Company Ltd, Cotton St, Banjul; tel: 22 6942
**Mauritania** off Kairaba Av, Fajara; tel: 49 6518 or 4098
**Senegal** now in Fujara; tel: 37 3752
**Sierra Leone** 67 Daniel Goddard St, Banjul; tel: 22 8206

### Climate
Cool dry season from December to April, followed by a warmer dry season and rains between June and October.

### Highlights
Visit the mysterious Wassu Stone Circles. Take a trip up the Gambia River for its birdlife, in a local boat. Relax on the beaches along the Atlantic coast and visit the market at Basse Santa Su. Banjul should be seen for its rundown ambience!

### Where to stay
**Serrekunda/Bakau** Look out for *Sukuta Camping*, which costss about US$7 for a car plus two people.

**Banjul** Banjul is not a place suitable for camping. Some years ago travellers camped at the *Black Cow Cross-Cultural Arts Centre* across the river in Bara, 300m from the ferry. It used to offer courses in traditional dance and drum.

**Fajara** You will have to shop around, but try the *The Kololi Inn*, where a double room will cost about US$8.

## Other
Crime is on the increase in Banjul, so do not walk on your own at night along the beaches of Bakau and Fajara. There have also been many complaints about beach boys, known as 'bumsters' or 'bumsan', who offer you everything and anything. Ignore them unless you would like to use one or other of their services.

## Further information
*Gambia: The Bradt Travel Guide*, Linda Barnett and Craig Emms
www.gambia.com

## GHANA

## Capital
Accra

## Language and telephone
English is the official language.
International telephone code +233

## Currency and rate
Cedi (C); US$1 = C8,910

## Red tape
There are occasional roadblocks with minimal hassle; just ensure all your paperwork is in order. Between the border of Ghana and Togo the touts can be a nightmare. Politely ignore them.

## Visas
Visas are required for all except nationals of ECOWAS countries and cost US$25–60. Vaccination certificates are obligatory. Visas are not issued at the border. On arrival you may be asked how long you intend to stay. Whatever you say could be written in your passport and you won't be able to stay for longer, despite what your visa indicates, so always state the duration of your visa.

## Fuel costs
Diesel: US$0.30; petrol: US$0.32 per litre.

## Driving and roads
Drive on the right. The coastal roads are excellent but as you move further north they get a little patchy.

## African embassies
**Benin** Switchback Lane, Accra; tel: 774860
**Burkina Faso** off 2nd Mango Tree Av, Accra; tel: 221988

Guinea Tel: 777921
Ivory Coast 18th Lane, Accra; tel: 774611
Mali 8 Agostino Neto Rd, Airport residential area; tel: 775160
Niger E 104/3 Independence Av (PO 2685); tel: 224962
Nigeria 5 Josef Tito Av; tel: 776158
Togo Cantonments Rd, Accra; tel: 777950

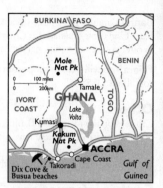

## Climate
Hot and dry in the north and humid along the coast. The rains arrive in late April and last intermittently until September.

### Highlights
The coastline from Accra to Dixcove has various former gruesome slave forts along the coast at Elmina and Cape Coast. Inland is the ancient Ashanti capital, Kumasi, known for its massive market and Kente cloth-weaving villages nearby. The Kakum and Mole national parks are worth a visit.

## Where to stay
Accra In Accra try the *Coco Beach Resort*, which used to offer camping and is 7km east of central Accra. About 25km west of Accra is Kokrobite, where a popular place is *Big Milly's*, which charges US$3 for camping. Meals are also available just outside on the beach; you can get a fine toasted egg fry with a taste of the local firewater, *apatechi*. Kokrobite is renowned for the Academy of African Music and Arts Ltd (AAMAL) with live music, drumming and dancing every weekend. A new resort has been opened here.

Elmina, Cape Coast Castle and the coast There is camping along the coast just east of Biriwa, on the beach under palm trees. Look for *Anomabu Beach Resort/Biriwa Beach Hotel*. The following detail may still be valid: the *Drum and Dance Workshop* is near Ampenyi, also known as *Ko-Sa*, which is 25km (15 miles) from Cape Coast. Turn right at the Ajensudo junction. The campsite is on the beach and costs US$3 per person.

Kumasi The *Presbyterian Guesthouse* is probably still the only place you can camp. Cost is around US$5. It's a beautiful place with huge shady trees, located close to the city centre. *Rose's Guest House* might be a possible alternative.

North to Burkina There is plenty of savanna forest where you can camp wild.

## Other
If you own a Land Rover, Accra is the place to get it fixed. Seek advice before diving into the ocean, as Ghana is plagued with dangerous currents. Photographing people is generally not a problem, but always ask beforehand and do not photograph near government institutions.

## Further information
*Ghana: The Bradt Travel Guide*, Philip Briggs
www.ghanaweb.com

# GUINEA

## Capital
Conakry

## Language and telephone
French is the official language.
International telephone code +224

## Currency and rate
Guinean franc (GFr); US$1 = GFr2,813

## Red tape
The police in Guinea like to host roadblocks at night and hold your papers until you pay a bribe. In other words, don't drive at night. If you do get caught in one of these notorious roadblocks, you shouldn't pay more than US$5 as a bribe.

## Visas
Visas are required for all and cost US$25–50. Depending on which country you are in, the Guinean embassy may ask for a letter of introduction from your own embassy. You will also need a photocopy of the identification pages of your passport. Visas issued in Africa are normally valid for two weeks only, but this depends on where you apply. They are not issued at the border.

## Fuel costs
Diesel: US$0.56; petrol: US$0.68 per litre.

## Driving and roads
Drive on the right. The roads are generally poor and those that are paved are usually pot-holed, except closer to Conakry. The road to Dalaba and Labé is not too bad. After Labé it is reported to be rough into the higher country.

## African embassies
**France** (issues visas for Burkina and Mauritania), Bd du Commerce, Conakry; tel: 41 1605
**Ghana** Pl de Martyrs, Imm Kaloum, Av de la République, Conakry; tel: 44 1510
**Guinea Bissau** Route de Donka, Conakry; tel: 42 2136
**Ivory Coast** Bd du Commerce, Conakry; tel: 45 1082
**Mali** Block de Professeurs, Conakry; tel: 46 1418
**Nigeria** Corniche Sud, Pl du 8 Novembre, Conakry; tel: 41 4375 or 46 1341
**Senegal** Corniche Sud, Conakry; tel: 46 2834
**Sierra Leone** Commune de Dixinn, Conakry; tel: 46 4084

## Climate
Guinea has a tropical climate, with a lengthy rainy season between May and October determined by altitude and location.

## Highlights
Conakry has some pleasant leafy areas and markets. There are beaches on the Iles de Los, Iles de Roume and Iles de Kassa. Most can only be reached by *pirogue*. Iles de Los has a mini-resort. You may even get a spontaneous musical performance. Some local outfits teach tourists to learn about the music and play the Kora here. Inland is the

Fouta Djalon Plateau with short treks from either
Dalaba, a pleasant hill resort, Labé or Pita.

## Where to stay

**Conakry** For a place with parking, you need to head
north of the centre. Try the *Hotel du Golfe* in
Rogbane area and, in the northern area, try *Hotel
Kaporo*. In town is the *Hotel Niger*, a seedy but cheap
place without parking. Pension Doherty was closed.

**Fouta Djalon Plateau** This plateau, with its rolling
green hills, cooler climate and some excellent hiking,
is a must for any visitor to Guinea. Stay with local
people in traditional village huts and preferably have
a local guide to translate.

**Dalaba** The *Pension Tangama* is a relaxing place with parking. Up the hill overlooking the
valley is the more upmarket *Hotel Sib*, with camping in the garden.

**Labé** Try the *Hotel Tata* with thatched huts in the garden and some parking places.

## Other

Guinea is a great country for outdoor enthusiasts, particularly cyclists and hikers, and is
also well known for its music. The Fouta Djalon is the most obvious option; remember
to carry adequate water and food with you. There is also the great biking/hiking Pita-to-
Télimélée route, which was part of the Paris-to-Dakar rally in 1995.

## Further information

*West Africa*, Rough Guides
www.boubah.com

---

## GUINEA BISSAU

## Capital

Bissau

## Language and telephone

Portuguese is the official language.
International telephone code +245

## Currency and rate

West African franc (CFA); US$1 = CFA502

## Red tape

You may find intermittent roadblocks, but locals, including government personnel, are
extremely friendly.

## Visas

Visas are required for all except nationals of Cape Verde and Nigeria. They cost around
US$10–25 and are valid for one month. Visas are not issued at the border.

## Fuel costs

US$0.44 per litre (diesel)

## Driving and roads
Drive on the right. The roads are generally poor; those that are paved are usually pot-holed.

## African embassies
**French consulate** (issues visas for Burkina, Central African Republic, Chad, Ivory Coast and Togo) Bairro de Penha, Avenida de 14 Novembro, Bissau; tel: 20 1312
**Gambia** Av de 14 Novembro, Bissau; tel: 25 1099
**Guinea** corner of Rua Ngouabi and Rua 12, Bissau; tel: 21 2681
**Senegal** off Praça dos Heróis Nacionais, Bissau; tel: 21 2944

## Climate
The hottest months are April to May, with the coolest months from December to January. Rains are from July to September.

## Highlights
Explore the Portuguese colonial areas of Bissau. In the north are the coastal mangrove swamps around Cacheu, with its tiny ruined fort. More offbeat is a visit by boat to the Bijagos Islands.

## Where to stay
**Bissau** Finding somewhere to park or camp will be difficult. Try some of the hotels and guesthouses.

**Bijagos Archipelago** These are a group of islands off Guinea Bissau. Assuming you can find secure parking for the vehicle for a night or two, your best bet is to pack an overnight bag and head over to one of the following two islands, which have some accommodation. Bolama Island is the closest to the mainland, but accommodation is basic. Bubaque Island, at the centre of the archipelago, is one of the easiest to reach. The best part is said to be Praia Bruce Beach on the southern end of the island, with some basic places to stay. Ask other travellers about any new developments.

**Cacheu** Try the *Hotel Baluarte* if it's reopened, where camping accommodation will need to be negotiated.

## Other
Guinea Bissau is one of the poorest countries in Africa. If you are invited to stay by a local person, always offer to pay for your accommodation and/or meal.

## Further information
*West Africa*, Rough Guides

# IVORY COAST (COTE D'IVOIRE)

**Warning** Due to the recent civil unrest in much of the country we strongly advise seeking sound travel advice if you do intend to visit. French troops were helping to restore some peace.

## Capital
Yamoussoukro is the official capital, though Abidjan remains the commercial and diplomatic centre.

## Language and telephone
French is the official language.
International telephone code +225

## Currency and rate
West African franc (CFA); US$1 = CFA502

## Red tape
With a sporadic civil war in the country, you can expect a lot of hassles throughout. Camping accommodation may be hard to find.

## Visas
Visas are required for all except nationals of ECOWAS countries and cost US$25–50. Citizens of the United States do not need visas for stays of up to 90 days. Vaccination certificates are obligatory. Visas are not issued at the border. A *Visa Touristique Entente* covering Benin, Burkina Faso, Ivory Coast, Niger and Togo is theoretically available; track it down via a relevant embassy or consulate.

## Fuel costs
Diesel: US$0.60; petrol: US$0.90 per litre.

## Driving and roads
Drive on the right. Good surfaced roads on main routes with mainly good dirt roads elsewhere.

## African embassies
**Benin** Rue de Jardins, Deux Plateaux, Abidjan; tel: 414413
**Burkina Faso** 2 Av Terrason de Fougères, Plateau, Abidjan; tel: 2021 1313
**France** (issues visas for Togo and Chad) Rue Lecour, Plateau, Abidjan; tel: 2020 0504/5
**Ghana** Res le Corniche, Bd Général de Gaulle, Plateau, Abidjan; tel: 2033 1124
**Guinea** Immeuble Crosson Duplessis, Av Crosson Duplessis, Abidjan; tel: 2032 9494
**Liberia** 20 Av Delafosse, Plateau, Abidjan; tel: 2032 4636
**Mali** Maison du Mali, Rue de Commerce, Plateau, Abidjan; tel: 2032 3147
**Niger** 23 Bd Angoulvant, Marcory, Abidjan; tel: 262814
**Nigeria** Bd de la République, Plateau, Abidjan; tel: 211982

*Above* Donkey cart, Riemvasmaak, South Africa (AZ)

*Above right* Likoma Island, Lake Malawi (AZ)

*Right* Dining under the stars at Xakanaxa Campsite, Botswana (CM)

*Below* River in flood, Cameroon (GR)

*Above* Mountain gorilla, Parc National des Volcans, Rwanda (AZ)

*Above right* Black-backed jackal, Hwange National Park, Zimbabwe (AZ)

*Right* The African elephant is the world's largest terrestrial mammal (AZ)

*Below* Forest buffalo, Senegal (AZ)

*Bottom right* Senegal parrot, one of almost 2,000 birds recorded in Africa (AZ)

*Bottom left* Lions are the largest African predators and common in most major game reserves (AZ)

## Climate

There are two climatic regions. In the south, the temperature remains at a steady 30°C all year round and has heavy rainfall. There are four seasons: a long dry season from December to April; a long rainy season from May to July; a short dry season from August to September; and a short rainy season from October to November. The north has a broader temperature range, with a rainy season from June to October and a dry season November to May.

## Highlights

Grand Bassam, with its old colonial-era buildings, has a stretch of bustling beachfront cafés and entertainment. Abidjan offers contrasting affluence and poverty. It has a huge market for secondhand spares, plus great supermarkets with goodies such as imported cheeses – costly but worth the taste sensation!

Yamoussoukro is fascinating, full of contrasts, with deserted streets, concrete structures and eight-lane highways lined with thousands of lights ending abruptly in the jungle. The Basilique de Notre Dame de la Paix, which resembles St Peter's in Rome, is the white elephant of Africa, built by President Houphouët-Boigney at a cost of a mere US$300 million. There is nothing else quite like it! Upcountry, Korhogo, the capital of the Senoufo, is famous for its wooden carvings and Korhogo cloth (mud-coloured designs painted on fabric). In December there are some festivals. Try to visit the pottery and blacksmith quarters, with temples for each of the crafts. Also visit Komoé National Park.

## Where to stay

**Abidjan** Abidjan has six sections – Plateau, Treichville, Marcory, Adjame, Cocody and Deux Plateau. The only camping was at *Camping Virdi* and *Camping Coppa-Cabana*. Both are on the beachfront; US$5 for camping. There is also an enormous selection of hotels from budget to top of the range.

**Grand Bassam** Grand Bassam is south of Abidjan and frequented mostly by expatriates during the weekend, so visit during the week. There isn't much camping accommodation, but a few locals have set up very rustic campsites for a minimal fee. Otherwise try one of the better hotels along the beach. Don't leave your gear lying around, as crime is rampant.

**Yamoussoukro** There is no camping in Yamoussoukro and you will have to ask one of the hotel managers if you can stay in their courtyard. Try the family-run *Motel Agip* or the *Motel Shell*.

**Korhogo** There is no camping facility in Korhogo, but budget accommodation is available. It's just a matter of finding secure parking for your vehicle.

## Other

A photographic permit is not required. But be very careful until the political problems have calmed down.

## Further information

*West Africa*, Rough Guides

## KENYA

### Capital
Nairobi

### Language and telephone
English and Swahili are the official languages.
International telephone code +254

### Currency and rate
Kenyan shilling (KSh); US$1 = KSh78.5

### Red tape
You may need to take an armed officer, or join the convoy if it's reinstated, from Isiolo to Moyale to get to Ethiopia or vice versa. See *Route Planning* in *Chapter 1* for further details.

### Visas
Visas are required by most visitors except nationals of some Commonwealth countries (passport holders of Australia, New Zealand, Sri Lanka and the UK *do* need visas). Other nationalities should check, as recent changes have been made. Visas are issued at the border for US$20–50, but fees may vary depending on nationality. Getting a visa in advance for Kenya in Tanzania, Uganda or Ethiopia is simple and hassle-free.

### Fuel costs
Diesel: US$0.75; petrol: US$0.87 per litre.

### Driving and roads
Drive on the left. Many of the roads in Kenya are excellent, but some are deteriorating fast. The roads get worse the further north you go. Around Mount Kenya some sections are quite rough, as is some of the coast road to Mombasa. Watch out for some bad driving locally.

### African embassies
**Democratic Republic of the Congo** Electricity House, Harambee Av, Nairobi; tel: 229771
**Djibouti** 2nd Floor, Comcraft House, Haile Selassie Av, Nairobi; tel: 339633
**Egypt** was at Harambee Plaza, Haile Selassie Av, Nairobi; tel: 225991
**Eritrea** New Waumuni House, Westlands, Nairobi; tel: 443164
**Ethiopia** State House Av, Nairobi; tel: 020 723035
**French consulate** (issues visas for most French-speaking African countries) Barclays Plaza, Loita St, Nairobi; tel: 339978
**Mozambique** HFCK Building, Kenyatta Av, Nairobi; tel: 222446
**Rwanda** International House, Mama Ngina St, Nairobi; tel: 212345
**South Africa** 17/18 Floor, Lonrho House, Standard St, Nairobi; tel: 215616

**Sudan** Minet-ICDC Building, Mamlaka Rd, Nairobi; tel: 720883
**Tanzania** Continental House, Harambee Av, Nairobi; tel: 331056
**Uganda** Uganda House, Baring Arcade, Kenyatta Av, Nairobi; tel: 330899
**Zambia** Nyerere Av, Nairobi; tel: 718494
**Zimbabwe** Minet-ICDC Building, Mamlaka Rd, Nairobi; tel: 721049

## Climate

Coastal areas are tropical and hot, but tempered by monsoon winds. The wettest months are April, May and November; the hottest are February and March; the coolest are June and July. The lowlands are hot and dry. Much of Kenya, however, stands at over 1,500m (4,500ft) and has a more temperate climate with four seasons. There is a warm and dry season from January to March; a rainy season from March to June; a cool, cloudy and dry season from June to October and a rainy season from November to December.

## Highlights

Visit the famous national parks: Masai Mara, Amboseli, Tsavo and Nakuru, to mention but a few. Climb Mount Kenya and visit the different lakes: Naivasha, Bogaria, Baringo, and if safe, Lake Turkana. Along the coast are many good beaches and resorts from Mombasa to Lamu. Also watch out for the various colourful tribes: Samburu, Turkana, Rendille and Masai. Eating in Kenya is a highlight too! There is great ice-cream, a cheese factory in Eldoret and superb bacon and eggs in Nairobi.

## Where to stay

**Nairobi** Most overlanders end up at either one of these camps. *Upper Hill Campsite* is on Menegari Road, just off Hospital Road, which is within walking distance of the city centre; camping costs US$3 and double rooms were US$13. Others stay at *Rangi's* in Langata, which is a little way out of town; ask around. The bar is reported to be superb. There are plenty of cheap hotels near Tom Mboya Street, but no parking. As for eating, which most overlanders do all day in Nairobi, there is Carnivore, a famous game restaurant on Langata road. For morning coffee, the Thorn Tree Café at the New Stanley has been *the* place forever.

**Eldoret** There is a good campsite just outside Eldoret called the *Naiberi River Campsite*, with the most comfortable bar imaginable. Camping costs US$6.

**Nakuru** Look for *Kembu Camping*, 20km from town going towards Njoro and Molo.

**Lake Naivasha** The lake makes a good break from the chaotic lifestyle in Nairobi. Try *Fisherman's Camp*, which has huge acacia trees, an incredible amount of birdlife, loads of water activities and a great bar. Camping costs about US$6.

**Lake Baringo** Try *Robert's Camp* on the lakeside; cost about US$5 each.

**Mount Kenya** For all information on Mount Kenya, go to the *Naro Moru River Lodge*, which also offers camping at US$5 per person. It is about 1.5km off to the left on the main Nairobi to Nanyuki road.

**Nanyuki** North of Nanyuki is *Timau River Lodge*, which has cottages and camping; cost is US$5 each.

**Maralal** Maralal, on the way to Lake Turkana, is high up in the hills and above the Lerochi Plateau. It is also famous for its Camel Derby, which takes place every October. The best place to stay is the *Yare Safari Club and Campsite*.

**Up to Lake Turkana** Bush sleeping is the best option but check the latest security warnings. The road up to Lake Turkana crosses volcanic outcrops, which means there are lots of sharp stones that make it slow going. On Lake Turkana, in Loyangalani, there were a number of campsites: *El Mol, Sunset strip, Gametrackers* and the *Oasis Lodge*.

**Moyale** You can camp outside the friendly Customs or stay on the Ethiopian side at the *Bekele Mola Motel*.

**Marsabit** The national park campsite is very expensive and rundown. The best place in town is the *Jey Jey Motel*, with cheap clean rooms and safe parking. Double room US$6. It is just off the main road. They do a superb egg and toast breakfast; yes it's sad isn't it, those little pleasures!

**Isiolo** There is a campsite on the main road about 10km south of town, the *Rangeland Camping*.

**Coastline** The options are endless, but most people rave about *Tiwi Beach*. It's south of Mombasa. *Twiga Lodge* is an old favourite. The only problem is finding safe parking facilities for your vehicle. There are various beach bungalows offering accommodation; prices range from US$3 to US$25 per person, depending on what you want. Further north up the coast is Malindi, which has the *Silversands* Campsite.

**National parks** Most of Kenya's national parks allow vehicles and have camping facilities. Be aware that the cost of taking a foreign-registered vehicle into most national parks is very high. It can cost you over US$100 per day (US$30 per person park fee and US$40 per vehicle plus US$10–20 per person camping). Another option is to organise a tour in Nairobi for the various national parks. Get some advice from the Upper Hill Campsite regarding the best and most economical tours available.

## Other

Nairobi has one of the worst reputations regarding crime and petty theft. Watch your back and find out from the locals which areas are being targeted. Don't walk around at night.

## Further information

*Kenya: The Bradt Travel Guide*, Claire Foottit
www.kenyaweb.com
www.kenyalogy.com
www.nairobi.com *news about Kenya*

## LESOTHO

## Capital

Maseru

## Language and telephone

English and Sotho are the official languages.
International telephone code +266

## Currency and rate

The maloti (LSL) is the local currency, but South African rand are universally accepted.
The current rate is US$1 = LSL6.08

## Red tape

None of any significance. Lesotho is within the South African Customs area.

## Visas
Visas are not required by citizens of the
Commonwealth and South Africa. Others visitors
should check. Visas cost US$10–15.

## Fuel costs
Diesel: US$0.54; petrol: US$0.60 per litre.

## Driving and roads
Drive on the left. Many of the roads in western
Lesotho are good and tarred, if a little narrow in
places. The roads get worse the further you go from
Maseru into the eastern mountain regions. Be
warned, crossing the Sani Pass is only possible in
summer and could be nerve-racking for some.

## African embassies
**South Africa** Bank of Lesotho Towers, Kingsway; tel: 2231

## Climate
Lesotho has a varied climate affected by a wide range of altitudes. The dry season is June
to August, with a wet season from October to April.

## Highlights
Lesotho is a mountainous enclave within South Africa. It shares the delights of the
Drakensberg range, but is much more isolated. Hiking and horseriding are the main
activities. Sani Pass is literally a high point. The culture is very strongly retained.

## Where to stay
**Maseru** The luxury *Hotel Lesotho Sun* on the hill above town may allow parking/camping.
If not try the *Lancer's Inn* off Kingsway; they have some rondavels.

**Teyateyaneng** Try the *Pitseng Guesthouse*. Camping costs US$9; car plus two people. Also
nearby is *Blue Mountain Resort*, a more upmarket establishment.

## Further information
*East and Southern Africa: The Backpacker's Manual*, Philip Briggs, Bradt Travel Guides

# LIBERIA

**Warning** Due to the ongoing political troubles in Liberia we suggest no overland
travel into Liberia. Basic information is listed but seek sound travel advice before
going.

## Capital
Monrovia

## Language and telephone
English is the official language.
International telephone code +231

## Currency and rate
Liberian dollar (L); US$1 = L$1

## Visas
Visas are required for all and cost US$30–40. Within 48 hours you also need to report to the first Bureau of Immigration that you find; they will issue you with a visitor's permit and determine the length of your stay. Vaccination certificates are obligatory. Visas are not issued at the border.

## Fuel costs
Diesel: unknown

## Driving and roads
Probably in a poor shape after so much neglect.

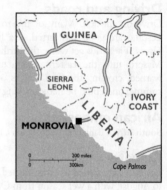

## African embassies
**Ghana** 15th St, Sinkor, Monrovia; tel: 223461
**Guinea** Tubman Bd, Monrovia
**Ivory Coast** 8th St, Sinkor, Monrovia; tel: 227436
**Sierra Leone** Hotel Africa, Monrovia; tel: 226250

## Climate
Liberia has a fairly wet climate, with the drier season from November to April.

## Highlights
Liberia has the last remaining concentration of wet tropical rainforest in West Africa. Firestone rubber plantations here were the largest in the world before the troubles.

## Where to stay
No current information is available.

## Further information
*West Africa*, Rough Guides
www.liberian-conection.com

# LIBYA

**Note** *Libya is now increasingly becoming established as a tourist destination. Apart from idiosyncrasies it is generally very safe.*

## Capital
Tripoli

## Language and telephone
Arabic is the official language.
International telephone code +218

## Currency and rate
Libyan dinar (LD); US$1 = LD1.29

## Red tape

If all your paperwork is in order, you should not experience any major hassles. Currently tourists in their own vehicles need to travel with a guide or with a guide in his own vehicle. This could change in future, so check before travelling.

## Visas

Visas are required for all. Nationals of Israel or those with an Israeli stamp in their passport will not be admitted. All visitors also need permission from the Libyan People's Bureau, ie: the embassy, which means that a tourist visa needs to be sponsored by a Libyan tour company. You will also need to have all the details of your passport translated into Arabic. Visas cost US$35 and are valid for one month. You will be required to register within 48 hours at the first police station you come across in Libya.

## Fuel costs

Diesel: US$0.05; petrol: US$0.07 per litre.
Libya has the cheapest fuel available in Africa. Sometimes travellers who only top up their tanks are not charged for the fuel!

## Driving and roads

Drive on the right. The roads on major routes are good and the rest are desert pistes and tracks. Main roads are quite busy along the northern coast near Tripoli; driving standards are rather erratic, to be kind!

## African embassies

**Egypt** Sharia al Fateh, Tripoli; tel: 660 5500
**Tunisia** Sharia al Jabah, Bin' Ashur, Tripoli; tel: 333 1051

## Climate

The best time to visit is during the northern spring and autumn months from October to early March, although you might come across the *ghibli,* which is a hot, dry and sand-laden wind that can raise the temperatures to 40+°C.

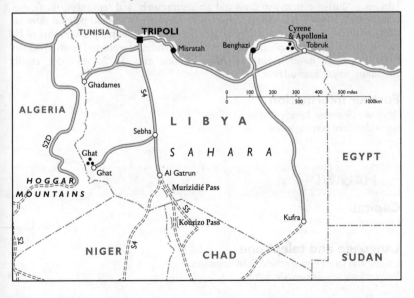

## Highlights

Tripoli has a fascinating old city medina. The magnificent Roman ruins of Leptis Magna and Sabratha should not be missed, plus the ancient Greek cities of Cyrene and Apollonia. In the west are the old granaries at Nalut and the old mud city of Ghadames. The war graves at Tobruk are sobering. In the Sahara are the 'Dune Lakes' close to Awbari and the Akakus Mountains near Ghat. Visit the prehistoric rock art and see the superb desert scenery, including some rock arches. You can't miss the billboards with the great leader's face adorned with blue sunglasses!

## Where to stay

Wild camping is the most pleasant option throughout Libya, and away from settlements this is not a problem. Always carry adequate fuel and water when visiting the Sahara. Even in the larger towns it's best to park up for the day, do what needs to be done, and leave in the early afternoon to find a camping spot. There are hotels in most major cities, but prices are high and you might be charged in foreign currency.

**Tripoli** Rather difficult and expensive, so stay at Sabratha or Zuara on the beach near the Tunisian border.

**Leptis Magna** There is a place to camp just outside the entry gate to the ruins. Across the road to the west is *a* hotel with its name in Arabic! It also allows camping.

**Awbari** In Awbari the *Africa Camp* is a pleasant place, right below the dunes.

**Siltar** It is possible to camp in the grounds of the Roman Statues, which your guide will know about.

**Ghadames** On the road into town before the old city is the *Hotel Al Waha*, which has a compound.

**Tobruk** There is a hotel with parking on the south side of town, overlooking the wide open area before the main business area. The guides know it!

## Other

Libya is a Muslim country, so dress and act appropriately, and remember, no alcohol whatsoever is allowed. It is also advisable not to mention any personal political views or criticism of the country's leadership. Libyans are sensitive towards photography, so be careful what you photograph and never ever take pictures of women. For an invitation from a Libyan travel agent try Africa Tours; fax: 21 36 13 036; email: africatours_libya@hotmail.com.

## Further information

*Africa on a Shoestring*, Lonely Planet
www.libya.com coming soon!

## MALAWI

## Capital

Lilongwe

## Language and telephone

English and Chichewa are the official languages.
International telephone code +265

## Currency and rate
Malawi kwacha (MK); US$1 = MK106.5

## Red tape
None of any significance. There are occasional roadblocks, which just check vehicle particulars and your travel itinerary.

## Visas
Visas are not required for most nationalities. A visitor's stamp is issued at the border.

## Fuel costs
Diesel: US$0.90; petrol: US$1.01 per litre.

## Driving and roads
Drive on the left. Roads throughout Malawi are generally in good condition, but there is surprisingly little traffic, especially in the north.

## African embassies
**Mozambique** Celtel Building, Rayner Av, Lilongwe; tel: 01 774100
**South Africa** Kangombe Building, Lilongwe; tel: 01 773722
**Zambia** Box 30138, Plot 40/2 Capital Hill, Lilongwe; tel: 01 731911
**Zimbabwe** Indépendance Drive, Lilongwe; tel: 01 774988

## Climate
The climate in Malawi is generally very pleasant. The rainy season is from November to March, when it can be quite grey and overcast some days.

## Highlights
The main highlight is of course the long lake, with quite a few pleasant beaches, specifically Chitimba, Nkhata Bay, Chintheche, Mangochi and Senga Bay. But there is a very high risk of contracting bilharzia if you go swimming in its attractive waters. Close to the lake is the Nyika Plateau and colonial Livingstonia. Further south are the Zomba Plateau, Liwonde National Parkwith an array of wildlife, and Mount Mulanje.

## Where to stay
### Lilongwe
The *Kiboko camp* is a good place to meet other travellers and get a feel for what to see in Malawi, with suggested campsites along the way. Cost US$3.

**Karonga** On the beachfront is the large compound, with some shade, of the *Mafwa Lakeshore Lodge and Campsite*. Camping costs US$4.

**Chitimba** There are three places: *Chitimba campsite*, *Mdokera beach* and *Namiashi Resort*.

**Livingstonia** At the time of our visit, during the rainy season, the road up from Chitimba was unusable. It is apparently better to get there from Rumphi from the south. The *Lukwe Permaculture* camp, an eco-friendly campsite, is reported to be a good place to stay.

**Nkhata Bay** Try *The Big Blue* for camping, also *Njaya Lodge* and camp. The *Mayoka village* is a picturesque place with nice rooms.

**Chintheche** We stayed at *Kande Beach*, which is lively in season. Access is down a very narrow sandy track that floods after rain, so beware. Camping costs US$6 for two.

Others with camping include *Chintheche Inn*, *Nkhwazi Lodge*, *Makuzi Beach* and *Mwaya Beach Lodge*.

**Senga Bay** Rather hard to find, but just before 'town', is *Cool Runnings*. It's signposted by a smiley face logo in places and is a shady, grassy campsite with cottages if you prefer, and lakeside restaurant. There are several other places with camping, so take your pick from *Wheelhouse Marina*, *Carolina Resort*, *Baobab* or *Steps campsite* and others.

**Cape Maclear** There is plenty of accommodation along the beachfront of Cape Maclear. The most popular are *Emmanuel's*, *Chikonde Lodge*, *Fat Monkey*, *Chirwa Lodge*, or *Steven's Place*. For a quieter alternative, and particularly if you are bringing a vehicle, try the *Golden Sands Beach Resort*. Camping costs US$3 per person and expect to party at Cape Maclear. Bilharzia and malaria are both rampant in this area, so be very, very wary of swimming and cover up fast!

**Mangochi** North of Mangochi are a number of places to stay. They include *K Lodge*, *Boadzulu Lakeshore resort*, *Nkopola Lodge* and *Palm Beach resort*.

**Blantyre** Though sometimes full, *Doogle's* on Mulomba Place is a great place with a good atmosphere, bar, food and excellent internet service. Camping costs US$3 per person. The area outside is not safe at night, but there's no need to leave the premises.

**Zomba Plateau** The Zomba Plateau is in the highlands and is a little cooler, with great hiking opportunities. You will need to find secure parking if hiking up to the plateau. The *Chitinji campsite* on the top of the plateau is run by the local community and will cost you next to nothing. Also try the *Zomba Forest Lodge* on the lower slopes and accessed by a dirt road.

**Liwonde National Park** The best place to stay is *Mvuu Camp*, which has a restaurant and open-plan bar overlooking the river. Camping will cost US$10 for two and they also arrange boat rides on the river.

## Other
In the past, under the Hastings Banda regime, if you were a man with long hair it was sheared off there and then. Fortunately, since then Malawi has calmed down considerably and is today a relaxed country in which to travel. Do not get caught with the local grass, known as 'Malawi Gold'. The police are clamping down on users and dealers. In some campsites you will find notes on signboards saying 'Hi, I am from England and am currently in jail for carrying drugs. I really just need somebody to talk to.' You have been warned.

And, we repeat, there is a high risk of bilharzia in the beautiful blue waters of the lake.

## Further information
*Malawi: The Bradt Travel Guide*, Philip Briggs
www.malawi.com

# MALI

## Capital
Bamako

## Language and telephone
French is the official language.
International telephone code +223

## Currency and rate
West African franc (CFA); US$1 = CFA502

## Red tape
Tourism has become quite important to the economy in Mali and, as a result, travel is becoming much more hassle-free.

## Visas
Visas are required for all except French nationals. A one-month visitor's visa can cost US$20–60, depending on where you apply for it. Registering with the police does not seem to be necessary any more, but check with other travellers what the current status is. Visas are not issued at the border. Vaccination certificates are obligatory.

## Fuel costs
Diesel: US$0.60; petrol: US$0.95 per litre.

## Driving and roads
Drive on the right. Roads are generally poor. The main road between Bamako and Gao through Mopti is variable. The desert piste to Timbuktu is bad and the track to Gao is very sandy. There has been some construction going on along the road into Senegal.

## African embassies
**Algeria** Bamako; tel: 220 5176
**Burkina Faso** Rue 224, off Route de Koulikoro, Bamako; tel: 221 3171
**Guinea** Immeuble Saibou Maiga, Quartier de Fleuve, Bamako; tel: 222 3007
**Ivory Coast** Lumumba Sq, Bamako; tel: 221 2289
**Mauritania** Rue 218 off Route de Koulikoro, Bamako; tel: 222 4815
**Senegal** 341 Rue 287 off Route de Koulikoro, Bamako; tel: 221 8274

## Climate

Mali spans the desert, sahel and tropical areas, creating differences across the country. The three main seasons are the rainy season June to September/October; cool dry season October/November to February; hot dry season March to June. The *harmattan*, sand-laden winds, blow from December to March.

## Highlights

Mali is one of the highlights in West Africa. It has everything that encapsulates Africa; colourful markets and people, deserts, mud architecture, river life and dramatic escarpments. Bamako has great bustling markets; Ségou, Djenné and Mopti have traditional mud-brick architecture and mosques – the mosque at Djenné is particularly spectacular. The Bandiagara Escarpment in the Dogon country is a cultural feast, with some trekking. Gao and Timbuktu, on the edge of the Sahara, are famous for their history. Getting to Timbuktu and, unlike the early explorers, getting back, is still a memorable journey even today!

## Where to stay

**Bamako** The only camping place in Bamako is the *Lebanese Mission*, near the centre of the city on Rue Poincaré. It's a rundown place but is within walking distance of everything. Camping costs US$3 per person.

**Ségou** You can try the *Office du Niger Campement* for camping, but they had no running water and were charging US$10 for camping in the car park. Also *l'Auberge* or the *Delta Hotel* out of town towards Bamako might have space.

**Djenné** The only place to stay is *Le Campement* near the Grand Mosque (which is a must-see). Your vehicle is safe in the car park and sleeping on the roof costs US$3.50 per person. It's a wonderful experience.

**Mopti** Mopti, other than being an impressive town, is the gateway to the Dogon country. For the Dogon country you'll need a guide and we would suggest hiking in the area. To really enjoy the whole area, hiking is the best bet. There are a few places to stay in Mopti – you'll have to look around. Try *Le Campement* (on the right-hand side as you come into town from the main road); camping in the car park costs US$4.

**Dogon country** For your travels in Dogon country, all fees, including accommodation, should be arranged with your guide beforehand. Meals are not included, but costs are minimal at each of the villages you stop in. Accommodation is a mattress on the roof and a wonderful experience as you hear the village sounds all around you. Take some time in choosing your guide and in negotiating the fees. You will initially be hassled, but once a guide has been chosen, the rest should disappear.

**Timbuktu** You will probably have to try the *Hôtel Bouctou*, for camping and a secure parking area. Also the *Hotel Camping Timbuktu* has been mentioned. If you are camping in the bush, be sure to keep some distance from settlements, or the police may stop you.

**Gao**
There are said to be a couple of campsites.

## Other

There have been incursions by armed rebels in northern Mali, so find out from other travellers and locals what the latest status is. Crime is on the increase in Bamako, so watch your back. It is also one of the most frenetic towns in Africa with vendors, cars, people and animals using every part of the road and pavement. It's best to walk everywhere rather than drive.

## Further information

*Mali: The Bradt Travel Guide*, Ross Velton
www.mali.com coming soon!

## MAURITANIA

### Capital
Nouakchott

### Language and telephone
Arabic is the official language.
International telephone code +222

### Currency and rate
Ouguiya (UM); US$1 = UM258

### Red tape
You will probably have to buy insurance at the border, even if you have a valid insurance for West Africa. Some of the settlements impose a 'right of passage tax' on visitors.

### Visas
Visas are required for all except nationals of Arab League countries and nationals of France and Italy. On application you will need to show your vaccination certificate and get a letter of introduction from your embassy. Three-month visas cost US$15–50. Visas are not issued at the border.

### Fuel costs
Diesel: US$0.31; petrol: US$0.59 per litre.

### Driving and roads
Drive on the right. Roads are generally in good condition on all major routes, except the road to Nema, which has deteriorated badly. Watch out for sand drifts over the roads. Around Atar some tracks are very rocky. The desert roads are typical Saharan pistes.

### African embassies
**Egypt** Rue de l'Ambassade de Sénégal, Nouakchott; tel: 529 2192
**Mali** Rue Mamadou Konate, Nouakchott; tel: 525 4081
**Morocco** Av du Général de Gaulle, Nouakchott; tel: 525 1411
**Senegal** Rue de l'Ambassade de Sénégal, Nouakchott; tel: 525 7290

## Climate

Most of the country has a true desert climate – very dry and extremely hot throughout the year. The far south has occasional rains.

## Highlights

Most travellers cross through Mauritania from Mali to Morocco or vice versa. However, the Adrar region around Atar has some rocky plateaux and the Terjit oasis. The Chinguetti and Ouadâne oases are beautiful and surreal, being partially abandoned. Further south the old oasis towns of Tidjikja and Tichit are remote and see few visitors. It is said that the Parc National du Banc d'Arguin has spectacular birdlife. Some groups do visit the country, but in general, with the lack of organised tourism, you are likely to come across some interesting experiences.

### Where to stay

For most of Mauritania, bush sleeping is the only option.

**Nouakchott** Try the central *Auberge Nomade*, just off Rue Abou Bakr, which has hot showers and a pleasant bar and eating area. You can also try the *Auberge la Dune*.

**Atar** Look out for the *Camping Bab Sahara*, otherwise there was parking in the grounds of the *Hotel Almoravides*.

**Chinguetti** The *Auberge la Rose des Sables* is a pleasant spot and has been going for years.

**Terjit** Try the *Oasis Touristique*.

**Parc National du Banc d'Arguin** The best time to visit the park is during the nesting period from April to July and October to January. The park is quite hard to get to, but information can be obtained from the park's head office in Nouadhibou.

## Other

The new road from Guergarat, the Moroccan border, to Nouakchott should be finished by the end of 2005. If not, you may still need guides for some sections. This used to cost anything up to US$150 for one vehicle crossing from Nouakchott to the Moroccan border (see *Chapter 1, Route Planning*, for further information). If you take the piste from Nouadhibou to Choum and Atar beside the railway, keep on the south side of the tracks to avoid possible old landmines.

Alcohol is not permitted except at expensive European restaurants in Nouakchott.

## Further information

*West Africa*, Rough Guides
www.mauritania.com coming soon!

# MOROCCO

## Capital

Rabat

## Language and telephone

Arabic is the official language.
International telephone code +212

## Currency and rate

Dirham (Dr); US$1 = Dr8.49

## Red tape

Officials are often extremely helpful and kind, but we can't guarantee that they are always like that. When crossing the Sahara it is advisable to have several copies of the document in *Appendix 2* plus copies of your passport and driving licence, as these are required at roadblocks in Morocco and Western Sahara.

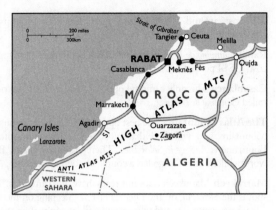

## Visas

Most visitors to Morocco do not require visas and can remain in Morocco for 90 days on entry. There are some exceptions to this rule (Israel, South Africa and others) so check before travelling. Visa fees cost around US$25–40.

## Fuel costs

Diesel: US$0.47; petrol: US$0.79 per litre.

## Driving and roads

Drive on the right. Roads are generally in good condition on all major routes, apart from the more remote desert tracks.

## African embassies

**Algeria** 46 Bd Tariq ibn Zayid, Rabat; tel: 037 76 54 74
**Mauritania** Souissi II Villa, No 226, OLM, Rabat; tel: 037 65 66 78
**Senegal** 17 Rue Qadi Amadi, Rabat; tel: 037 75 41 38
**Tunisia** 6 Av de Fès, Rabat; tel: 037 73 05 76

## Climate

Morocco has a variety of climates: Mediterranean in the north, Atlantic in the west, continental in the interior and desert in the south. The Atlas Mountains can get very cold much of the year outside the summer months. Rain is likely sometimes in winter and snow can be heavy in the mountains.

## Highlights

The Atlas Mountains are famous for their Berber villages and stunning landscape, including the Todra Gorge. Then there are the historical towns of Tangier, Fès, Meknès, Chefchaouen and Marrakech. The famous Djemaa el-Fna, a huge fair in the square of the old city of Marrakech, comes to life in the early afternoon. Between Ouarzazate and Zagora is the road of the Casbahs, with fortified mud citadels. The coastline includes the cities of Casablanca, with its superb art-deco buildings, and Rabat, famous for its magnificent architecture and lack of tourists. Essouira and Taroudant are two other places of interest.

## Where to stay

In Morocco it is generally more convenient to stay in towns rather than on the outskirts. There are hundreds of *pensions* available in all major towns at minimal cost. A double will cost around US$6. Most serve breakfast. Campsites are often reasonably convenient.

**Rabat** *Camping de la Plage* at Salé Beach is the only camping option in Rabat. Camping costs US$4 per person.

**Casablanca** The only camping option is way out of town on the road to El-Jadida. It is called *Camping de l'Oasis*.

**The Atlas Mountains** The best option is to sleep in the bush, but as you cross the Atlas Mountains you will find that most towns have campsites. In the Dadès Gorge at Boumalne is *Auberge le Soleil Bleu*. There are many nearby Berber villages and a walk is worthwhile. Todra Gorge has a couple of good campsites.

**Marrakech** Marrakech does not really have any campsites. The most popular travellers' spot is the *Hotel Ali*, on the Djemaa el-Fna. Sleeping on the roof costs US$4 per person. They have mattresses and pillows and will let you park in the basement.

**Fès** Fès is the oldest imperial city in Morocco. There are two options regarding camping – *Camping Diamant Vert* and *Camping International*. The latter can get a little noisy, as the local disco is held daily at the campsite.

**Meknès** Look for *Camping International d'Agdal* just outside Meknès (watch out for camping signs) on the way to Volubilis, the old Roman ruins.

**Agadir** The town's municipal camping site is popular with campervan retirees from Europe, but fine.

**Ouarzazate** There was a campsite just outside town, within walking distance, on the road to Tinerhir. Camping costs US$5 per vehicle.

**Zagora** It has a couple of places to camp in designated campsites with shady palm trees.

**Chefchaouen** Famous for its supply of hashish, this town in the Rif Mountains is a relaxing place. The town has a Hispanic look of whitewashed houses and tiled roofs. The only campsite was just a little out of town and signposted *Campsite (Azilan) and Youth Hostel*, just behind the Hotel Asma. Their green tea is great.

## Other

To ease the hassle factor from the hashish touts, it is best to dress conservatively and respect the culture, although you will see tourists running around with next to nothing on. Hashish is illegal and the fines for being caught with it are heavy. Beware of car-based hash sellers who block roads.

## Further information

*Morocco*, Barnaby Rogerson, Cadogan
www.marocnet.com

# MOZAMBIQUE

## Capital

Maputo

## Language and telephone

Portuguese is the official language.
International telephone code +258

## Currency and rate

Metacal (Mt); US$1 = Mt18,350. The plural of metacal is metacais.

## Red tape

There are always rumours regarding traffic officials and roadblocks in Mozambique. We had no problems but were asked if we had two warning triangles, which we did. More likely now is that officials at roadblocks want to practise their language skills and have a quick English lesson – 'Hello, how are you? Where are you going?'

## Visas

Visas are required for all and cost US$20–40. You also have to pay a border tax of US$10. It is better to pay in South African rand if you are coming in that way as it is cheaper than paying in metacal. Visas are not issued at the border.

## Fuel costs

Diesel: US$0.65; petrol: US$0.75 per litre.

## Driving and roads

Drive on the left. The main north–south highway between Malawi, Tete, Beira and Maputo is mostly OK, but some quite long sections are breaking up. Because of the floods in April 2000 the state of roads in the north is not known. There is very little traffic and there are virtually no fuel stations between the main towns. Carry enough fuel and water. (Make sure your vehicle insurance is valid; very likely you will have to buy more at the border.)

## African embassies

**France** (visas for French-speaking African countries) Av Julius Nyerere, Maputo; tel: 491774
**Malawi** 75 Av Kenneth Kaunda, Maputo; tel: 491468
**South Africa** 745 Av Eduardo Mondlane, Maputo; tel: 491614
**Swaziland** 608 Av Kwame Nkrumah, Maputo; tel: 492451
**Tanzania** 852 Av Martires de Machava, Maputo; tel: 490110
**Zambia** 1286 Av Kenneth Kaunda, Maputo; tel: 492452
**Zimbabwe** Av Martires da Machava, Maputo; tel: 490404

## Climate

The dry season is from April to September, when it is cool and pleasant. The wet season is from October/November to March when it is hot and humid. It is generally drier in the north.

## Highlights

Hectic Maputo still has some fine old colonial buildings and good nightlife. There are some beautiful beaches on the southern coast close to Inhambane at Tofo, plus Vilanculos and the lovely islands of the Bazaruto Archipelago. The northern beaches, Pemba and Ilha do Moçambique, are more remote and less inhabited. In the central bushland is the once popular Parc del Gorongosa.

## Where to stay

**Maputo** The only place to stay in town in Maputo is at *Fatima's Place* on 1317 Mao Tse Tung Road. Two vehicles can be parked in the garage and there is a security guard at night. Fatima herself is the owner and full of news about Maputo and surrounding areas. A double chalet costs US$12. Meals and drinks are available. On the main road north of Maputo (on the west side of the road) is the spacious and relaxing *Camping Casa Lila* run by a white Englishman from Kenya. It has an excellent bar and restaurant. Camping costs US$10 for car plus two people.

**Inhambane** It is probably better to camp at the *Maxixe Campismo* place across the estuary on the main road. It is signposted. Ferries sometimes run infrequently so check first.

**Tofo** There are quite a few places here, but access is tricky because of the quite deep soft sand around here. *Fatima's*, with the same owners from Maputo, have a new place with camping. Further along the beach is the sandy *Bamboozi 'Resort'* with camping. Cost US$8, car plus two people.

**Vilanculos** *Camping Vilanculos* is a well-run grassy, shaded campsite close to the beach. It is popular with South Africans but has no restaurant. Cost US$14 for two people in a car. Vilanculos is a favourite spot for travellers. Day excursions can be planned to the Bazaruto Archipelago, where the diving is said to be excellent.

**Tete** Try camping/parking at the Indian-run *Motel Tete*. Camping costs US$10 for car plus two people. There is also a simple but OK camping place on the north side of the river east of the big bridge.

**Chimoio** It's possible to camp at the windmill-style *Hotel Moinho* which is popular for its restaurant and bar. It is out of town on the road to Beira. Camping costs US$10, car plus two people.

## The north

**Chocas** One of Charlie and Illya's highlights in Africa was an area called Chocas, 21km south of Ilha do Moçambique, towards Mossaril. Camping on the beach is the only option. Water is available from wells in the village and fish is sold every morning, fresh from the ocean. You will be completely isolated except for the occasional curious villager and the expatriate community who enjoy Chocas at weekends.

**Ilha do Moçambique** It is possible to drive across to the island, as there is a 3km bridge that joins it to the mainland. There are no camping facilities on the island, so if you intend to stay the night, it is best to ask one of the restaurateurs or hoteliers to let you park in their yard. Camping is now possible on the mainland at *Camping Casuarinas*.

**Pemba** North from Ilha do Moçambique is Pemba, where you could stay for days! There was a great campsite just outside town along the coastline called *Pemba Magic*, in a beautiful setting with huge, shady baobab trees. It was run by Margot and Russell, a South African and Australian partnership. Camping costs US$3 per person.

Further up from Pemba the roads become really bad and the going is slow, but the whole northern area is wild and untamed. Villagers are surprised to see you, as not many travellers head north. It's a great adventure!

## Other

At the time of writing, the bridge between Mwambo (Mozambique) and Mtwara (Tanzania) was reportedly being rebuilt. It is predicted that this will become another transit route heading north into Tanzania. Before heading north check the status of the border crossing and the bridge for vehicles.

Do not photograph anything remotely resembling or near to a government institution.

## Further information

*Mozambique: The Bradt Travel Guide*, Philip Briggs & Ross Velton
www.mozambique.mz

## NAMIBIA

### Capital
Windhoek

### Language and telephone
English and Afrikaans are the official languages.
International telephone code +264

### Currency and rate
Namibian dollar (N); US$1 = N$6.08. The Namibian dollar has same value as the SA rand, which can be used for most transactions in Namibia. It is best to use up Namibian dollars before leaving because the reverse is not true; they cannot be used in South Africa.

### Red tape
Avoid the mining area around Lüderitz, as the police who patrol this area can be a bit overzealous. To visit a mining area, you need a special permit arranged by the mining company in Windhoek, but it could be hard to come by.

### Visas
No visas are required by nationals of Australia, Canada, Ireland, New Zealand, South Africa, the UK, the USA, and most other southern African and western European countries.

### Fuel costs
Diesel: US$0.75; petrol: US$0.78 per litre.

### Driving and roads
Drive on the left. The roads are in excellent condition except for parts of the Namib Desert, Kaokoland and Kuadom Reserve. Most secondary roads are gravel/sand/dirt but are well maintained and quite fast. Having said that, drive carefully; it would be easy to slide off if going too fast.

### African embassies
**Angola** Angola House, 3 Dr Agostinho Neto St, Windhoek; tel: 227535
**Botswana** 101 Nelson Mandela Av, Windhoek; tel: 221941
**Egypt** 10 Berg St, Windhoek; tel: 221501
**Ghana** 5 Nelson Mandela Av, Windhoek; tel: 220536
**Kenya** Kenya House, Robert Mugabe Av, Windhoek; tel: 226836
**Nigeria** (High Commission) 4 Omuramba Rd, Eros, Windhoek; tel: 232103

**South Africa** RSA House, corner Jan Jonker Strasse and Nelson Mandela Drive, Klein Windhoek, Windhoek; tel: 501 7111

**Zambia** 27 Sam Nujoma Drive, corner of Republic Rd, Windhoek; tel: 237610

**Zimbabwe** corner Independence Av and Grimm St, Windhoek; tel: 228134

## Climate

Overall the country is fairly dry. It gets quite hot in summer (October to April). Any rainfall occurs during the summer months. Winter is cool and the evenings can get quite cold. The coastal region of the Namib Desert is cool, damp and rain-free, with mist for much of the year.

## Highlights

Namibia has a long list of highlights, including Windhoek. The amazing orange/red dunes of the Namib Desert, seen as well at Sossusvlei, are spectacular. Swakopmund and Lüderitz have relics of the German colonial period. In the north is Kaokoland, with its beautiful scenery and Himba people. Then there are the national parks, including the world-famous Etosha, plus the Waterberg Plateau, the Skeleton Coast, Fish River Canyon, Kalahari Gemsbok and Namib Naukluft, all with varied wildlife.

## Where to stay

**Windhoek** A popular campsite is at *Daan Viljoen Game Park*, 18km west of town. You can pre-book at the MET in Windhoek, which handles all park bookings, or you can just turn up. Camping costs US$20 per site. Alternatively, *Arebbusch Travel Lodge* in Olympia, on the road south to Rehoboth, charges US$8 per person to camp. In town are various backpacker places, of which we stayed at the *Cardboard Box* and the *Chameleon*. Camping US$12–13; double room US$18 upwards.

**Lüderitz** Lüderitz is a surreal German colonial relic set on the edge of the Namib Desert. The only place to camp is the windy *Shark Island Campground* north of town, which costs US$8 per site. Try *Lüderitz Backpackers* for less windy conditions.

**Swakopmund** Although not as ethereal a town as Lüderitz, Swakopmund is attractive and interesting. In town try *Desert Sky Backpackers*, a well-organised place with parking. Just on the southern end of town there is *Gulls Cry Camping*. Other camping options are all out of town: try *Alte Brücke Restcamp* and, further south, *El Jada Restcamp*. Closer to Walvis Bay there is camping at *Long Beach Resort*; there are several options along the coast to the north.

**Spitzkof** It's possible to camp amongst these amazing boulders and craggy peaks. It is not far north of the main Swakopmund road.

**Solitaire** The one-horse/house town of Solitaire has a pleasant campsite and lodge. Their apple strudel is divine and the bread is superb. Camping costs US$14, car plus two people.

**Sesriem** There is a camping place and some shade. Cost around US$20 for a large pitch. Camping is not permitted at nearby Sossusvlei.

**Helmeringhausen** This is another one-horse/hotel town; the hotel is a great place to stop or stay, with more delicious apple strudel.

**Close to the Fish River Canyon** Set amongst some ancient boulders and tastefully done is the *Canyon (or Cañon) Lodge*. This is expensive and sheer luxury. They also run a place north of Hobias on the west side of the road, called *Cañon Roadhouse*, which has camping.

**Betta** Coming on the desert road south from Sesriem to Helmeringhausen there are many very expensive farm lodges. For a cheap option try the *Betta Camp*. Betta is a one-house town.

**Border with Botswana** If you are coming from Ghanzi in Botswana, where there are no camping places, wild or otherwise, close to the border with Namibia, a new campsite is open on the Namibian side of the border. It is called *Buitepos Camping*.

**Keetmanshoop** The town has a municipal caravan/camping park.

**National parks** Etosha National Park offers lodges and camps at *Namutoni, Halali* and *Okaukuejo*. The park entry fee is US$6 per person and US$6 per vehicle (entry to most Namibian parks costs around N$30–40). Camping costs US$20 for a maximum of eight people.

Fish River Canyon National Park has a very nice campsite, the *Hobas Camping*, costing US$20 for a site. Further south you can also camp at *Ai Ais Hot Springs* resort.

You are not allowed to stay overnight in the Skeleton Coast National Park, but along the coastline, south of the park, there are various very basic campsites at Mile 14, Jakkalsputz, Henties Bay, Mile 72 and Mile 108. Campsites are cheaper along this route.

**Kaokoland** Bush sleeping is the only option as you head north towards Angola. At *Epupa Falls* you can sleep under the palm trees, or in the enclosed campsite. Due to the influx of tourists, the Himba's lifestyle has been threatened. Do not give them alcohol, which you will be asked for continually.

**Rundu** Look out for the *Sarasunga River Lodge*, which offers camping for US$5 per person. Also the *N'Kwazi Lodge* near Rundu has camping and trips across the river into Angola.

**Caprivi Strip** At the Popa Falls there is camping at a few places. Look for *Ngepi Camp* for US$5 each, *Suclabo Lodge* and the *Popa Falls Restcamp*. The area is developing fast and new places are being built along the strip.

## Other

Do not photograph anything remotely close to a government institution. Crime is on the increase in larger towns, but campsites have also been targeted; lock your valuables away at night.

## Further information

*Namibia: The Bradt Travel Guide*, Chris McIntyre
www.namibiaweb.com

# NIGER

## Capital
Niamey

## Language and telephone
French is the official language.
International telephone code +227

## Currency and rate
West African franc (CFA); US$1 = CFA502

## Red tape
One of the friendliest countries we have travelled in, Niger has little red tape. However the exception is when coming from Algeria. Perhaps understandably, the border officials at Assamaka are prone to need a little something extra to do the paperwork; it is jolly hot work lifting a pen and disturbs the lethargy of the place! The old practice of getting the passport stamped in every town has all but finished, except in Arlit and places like Bilma.

## Visas
Visas are required for all except nationals of the countries of ECOWAS. One-month visas are issued within 48 hours and cost US$40–60. They are easily obtained from the countries bordering Niger (though not Mali). You'll need one to four photos for each application. Visas can be obtained in Paris for those heading south. Vaccination certificates are obligatory. Visas are not issued at the border. A *Visa Touristique Entente* covering Benin, Burkina Faso, Ivory Coast, Niger and Togo is theoretically available; track it down via a relevant embassy or consulate.

## Fuel costs
Diesel: US$0.65; petrol: US$0.95 per litre.

## Driving and roads

Drive on the right. Roads are generally in good condition, particularly along major routes: Niamey, Maradi to Zinder and via Tahoua to Agadez and Arlit. Agadez to Zinder still has about 150km of piste. Remoter routes are desert pistes and tracks.

## African embassies

**Algeria** north of Route de Tillabéri, Niamey; tel: 72 3583
**Benin** Rue des Dallois; Niamey; tel: 72 2860
**Chad** off Route de Tillabéri, Niamey; tel: 75 3464
**France** (issues visas for most French-speaking African countries) Corner of Av Mitterand and Bd de la République, Niamey; tel: 72 2722
**Mali** Bd de l'Indépendance, Niamey; tel: 75 4290
**Nigeria** Bd de la République, Niamey; tel: 73 2410

## Climate

The climate is hot and dry, except for a brief rainy season in July and August. The coolest months are December to February, when the *harmattan* blows the dust off the desert.

## Highlights

The Grand Marché in Niamey and market days in Filingué and Zinder are very colourful. Agadez is a fabulous place, with colourful Tuareg markets and traditional mud architecture; the mosque, Sultan's Palace, Hotel de l'Aïr and Vieux Quartier in particular. Taking an expedition into the remote areas of the Aïr Mountains, and/or the Ténéré Desert with Fashi, Bilma and the Djado plateau, is now possible but quite expensive.

For safety reasons, it is obligatory to have a guide with vehicle from a local tour operator and a travel permit for the area. Guides are expensive, but you can go in convoy and share the guide. It is worth every penny and is one of the most beautiful areas of Africa. It is also a wonderful introduction to the Tuareg culture. The Tuareg, the blue men of the desert, are a nomadic tribe and famous for their salt caravans to the Bilma oasis. The camel caravans continue to this day; trucks were tried but they kept breaking down, so the old faithful camels are back at work!

## Where to stay

**Niamey** The one campsite in Niamey needed repair and had no running water, toilet or shower facilities; a one-night option only. Try asking at the *Grand Hotel* if you can park/camp; it has lots of space and is the place for sundowners on the river. Also try *Hotel Sahel* further up the road. *Hotel Maourey* is a good place in town, but there is no parking.

**Dosso** The best and most entertaining place is the *Hotel Djerma*, with its good parking, pool, colourful ladies and lively atmosphere! The steaks are great. Is the pool still empty?

**Zinder** The *Hotel Damagaram*, which has an artisan shop and shady space, may allow parking/camping. There is a new campsite called *La Cafeteria* just north of town – ask locals for details. It is rumoured to double as a brothel, so take care here.

**Agadez** In Agadez the *Camping L'Escale* is a huge campsite 4km northwest of town, with lots of shade and great toilet and shower facilities, costing US$10 for two. In the city, just north of the Sultan's Palace, is *Hotel Telden*, costing US$4 for camping. It's central and has all amenities close by, including a great bar. It's also possible to park in the grounds of the classic *Hotel de l'Aïr*, with its rooftop café and view of the mosque.

**Tahoua** Try the *Hotel l'Amitié*. It may be called *Galaxie* as well.

**Arlit** There is now a small campsite in town. But you may prefer to desert camp north of town; go at least 20 kilometres away on the way to Assamaka, where you will find some low scrubby bushes you can just about hide behind. Midway between Agadez and Arlit (about 130km from Agadez) is an ancient rock art site east of the main road. It allows bush camping close by, but costs CFA500 to enter.

## Other
Dress conservatively, as dress is taken very seriously in this Muslim country. Always ask permission before taking photographs and stay clear of all government institutions. You may need to register with the local police in the odd places like Arlit, but check in case. This is referred to as '*vu au passage*'.

## Further information
*Niger: The Bradt Travel Guide*, Jolijn Geels (due 2006)

## NIGERIA

**Warning** *There have been intermittent violent clashes between Muslims and Christians. Seek sound travel advice before entering Nigeria. Most of the time things are quiet.*

## Capital
Abuja

## Language and telephone
English is the official language. Main local languages are Hausa and Yoruba.
International telephone code +234

## Currency and rate
Naira (N); US$1 = N131

## Red tape
Roadblocks are evident throughout Nigeria, sometimes within 5km (3 miles) of each other. These are police, traffic police, forestry police, fund raisers(!) and military – police! We have heard that policemen and many government employees are not always paid for long periods at a time. Some may ask for a *dash*, a little 'gift' for services rendered. It's up to you to decide each case on its merits.

## Visas
Visas are required for all except nationals of ECOWAS countries. The cost depends on your nationality, but can be from US$25–50 up to US$80 and more for double entry. You will also need two or three photographs and a letter of introduction from your embassy. Yellow fever vaccination certificates are obligatory. Visas are not issued at the border.

## Fuel costs
Diesel: US$0.20; petrol: US$0.26 per litre.
'At the time of writing there was no fuel available.' That's what Charlie and Illya wrote in the last edition and it still applied five years later. Almost the only fuel available was on the black market at US$0.40 per litre. It's totally crazy when you think that fuel is Nigeria's major income!

## Driving and roads

Drive on the right. Main roads are generally in good condition, but once on side roads watch out for pot-holes and worse.

## African embassies

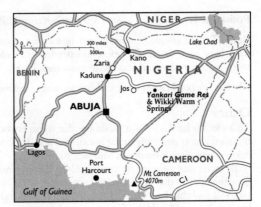

**Benin** 4 Abudu Smith St, Victoria Island, Lagos; tel: 261 4385

**Burkina Faso** 15 Norman William St, Ikoyi Island, Lagos; tel: 268 1001

**Cameroon** 5 Fermi Pearse St, Victoria Island, Lagos; tel: 261 2226

**Chad** 10 Mississipi St, Maitama, Abuja; tel: 413 0751

**French consulate** (issues visas for most French-speaking African countries) 1 Oyinkan Abayomi Drive, Ikoyi Island, Lagos; tel: 269 3427

**Ghana** 21–23 King George V Rd, Lagos Island, Lagos; tel: 260 1450

**Niger** 15 Adeola Odeku St, Victoria Island, Lagos; tel: 261 2300

**Togo** Plot 976, Oju Olobun Close, Victoria Island, Lagos; tel: 261 7449

## Climate

The south is hot and humid, with a long rainy season from March to November. The north has far greater extremes of temperature, as a result of the Saharan influence. It can be blisteringly hot. The rains last from April to September, with a shorter wet season in the far north.

## Highlights

Most travellers enjoy the north of the country. The high crime and heavy concentrations of the population in the south deter many people. Highlights of the north include Kano, Jos and the Yankari Game Reserve. Kano is famed for its old city, Sultan's Palace, mosques, dye pits and the narrow streets lined by the remains of the old city wall. The Jos Plateau is 1,200m (3,600ft) above sea level and has a relatively cool climate all year round. It is green and surrounded by rolling green hills, but check in case there has been any civil unrest recently. In the far southeast near Cameroon is the cattle ranch area of Obudu.

## Where to stay

**Abuja** We stayed at the *Hotel Luna* about 20km west of town near the main road junction. There is parking and it's friendly. A double room costs US$5.

**Lagos** The *Onikirp Hotel* on 328 Borno Avenue in Yaba has been recommended. Accommodation costs US$15 for a double. In Lagos it's essential to organise secure parking for your vehicle. Lagos lacks trustworthy campsites, and you'll have to shop around for cheaper accommodation.

**Jos** Jos has no campsite, so you'll have to ask at one of the larger hotels whether it is possible to park there for a night or two.

**Kano** The only campsite in Kano is the *Kano State Tourist Camp*, just off Bompai Road, which is friendly, secure and helpful. Camping costs US$2.50 per person. Hussein or Mohammed can fix any problems, vehicle or fuel supplies etc.

**Potiskum** Try the *FNC College*. Double room costs US$6.

**Bama** Try the government *rest house/bungalows* out of town towards the border. Rooms must have been wonderful before independence! Double room with bathroom (bath, toilet, bidet but no water) and sitting room costs US$7.

**Gboko** Try hotel *Lemba Lodge* within a secured compound.

## Other

To avoid any hassles in Nigeria, ensure that all paperwork is in order and be patient. Do not photograph any government institutions and dress conservatively, particularly in the north where there is more of a Muslim influence.

Be aware that there are frequent and long-lasting power cuts throughout the country. So, although you may have a suite of rooms (for US$5 or so) with a luxurious bathroom, you will probably have no water except in a bucket and no air conditioning except the breeze when you head outside to sleep on the roof of your vehicle!

## Further information

*Nigeria: The Bradt Travel Guide*, Lizzie Williams
www.motherlandnigeria.com

## RWANDA

**Warning** Although travel within the country is currently safe, borders with the DRC and Burundi remain sensitive. Access is normal via Uganda and Tanzania. Always heed local advice about possible trouble spots, and don't wander off the beaten track alone in unpopulated areas of the northwest or south. Conditions may change overnight so check the current situation before travelling.

## Capital

Kigali

## Language and telephone

Kinyarwanda, French and English are all official languages; English is less widespread outside Kigali.
International telephone code +250

## Currency and rate

Rwandan franc; US$1 = RFr555
Banks in Kigali can generally handle travellers' cheques (you'll get a poorer rate for them than for cash) and maybe even some VISA (card) transactions. The official and private forex bureaux just change cash – US$ or euros are best. Elsewhere in the country you're best off with cash. Moneychangers operate at border crossings. All main towns have Western Union offices if you want funds sent from home.

## Red tape

Not a great deal. There are occasional police checkpoints but they don't seem to target overlanders. Your vehicle may be checked for roadworthiness – carry two warning triangles and a fire extinguisher.

## Visas

At present visas are not required (for stays of under three months) by nationals of the UK,

Germany, Sweden, Canada, USA, Hong Kong, Burundi, DRC, Mauritius, South Africa, Tanzania and Uganda – but check in case any unfriendliness develops with these countries. For others they cost around US$35–70 and are currently obtainable at the border. You must buy separate car insurance at the border as you enter.

## Fuel costs
Diesel: US$0.72; petrol: US$0.72 per litre. Increases are probable.

## Driving and roads
Drive on the right. Roads linking main cities and border points are generally surfaced and relatively good; some smaller roads are narrow and twisty, and may be muddy (or in some areas impassable) after rain. Ask local advice, particularly in the wet season. If you don't like negotiating steep hairpin bends, stay away!

## African embassies
**Burundi** Bd de l'Umuganda, Kigali; tel: 587940/3
**Kenya** Bd de l'Umuganda, Kigali; tel: 583332/6
**Tanzania** Av de la Paix, Kigali; tel: 505400; fax: 505402
**Uganda** Av de la Paix, Kigali; tel/fax: 503537

## Climate
Rwanda is a high, hilly country and not too hot. Rainy seasons are March/May and October/November. The hottest months are August and September.

## Highlights
There are three national parks: the Volcanoes Park in the northwest (mountain gorillas, golden monkeys, Dian Fossey's grave, crater walks, trekking), Akagera Park in the east (hilly savanna, lakes, hippos, giraffe, elephant, antelope, fish eagles) and Nyungwe Forest in the southwest (chimps, colobus and l'Hoest's monkeys, orchids, birds). The National Museum of Rwanda in Butare is one of East Africa's best, with extensive displays on Rwandan history and culture. Visits to interpretive genocide memorials are possible. The tranquil lakeside towns of Kibuye and Gisenyi offer stunning views of Lake Kivu and boat trips to some islands. Permits to visit the amazing mountain gorillas (US$350) must be bought in advance from the Rwanda Tourist Board in Kigali: *Office Rwandais du Tourisme et des Parcs Nationaux* (ORTPN), BP 905; tel: 576514; email: ortpn@rwanda1.com and info@rwandatourism.com; www.rwandatourism.com. It's at the junction of Bd de la Révolution and Av de l'Armée; go there for maps, guides and other information.

## Where to stay
Rwanda is a very densely populated country and secluded spots are hard to find. All three national parks have basic (but not cheap) campsites nearby. In most towns there's a small hotel or guesthouse where you can ask to camp in the grounds.

**Kigali** The *One Love Guesthouse* (Rue de Kinamba; tel: 575412) and the *Episcopal Church Guesthouse* (Av Paul VI; tel: 573219) offer secure parking and you may be able to camp (their rooms aren't expensive anyway). Other small places keep opening – if you see somewhere that appeals, just ask.

**Lake Kivu** There's lakeside camping in Kibuye (at the *Kibuye Guest House*) and in Gisenyi (ask for details at the *Oasis Guest House* or the *Paradis Restaurant*). The steep, twisting Gisenyi-to-Kibuye road is rough going in patches but the views are amazing.

**Lake Muhazi** Beside Lake Muhazi in the east there's camping near Gahini at the *Seeds of Peace Centre* and *Jambo Beach* (on the main eastern Kigali-to-Uganda road); and on the northern shore at some idyllic small bar-restaurants (accessed via the Byumba road).

## Other
Be tactful about photos – always ask, always respect the answer, and remember that this is a country still emerging from deep trauma. Supportive tourism is a way to help.

## Further information
*Rwanda: The Bradt Travel Guide*, Philip Briggs and Janice Booth
www.rwandatourism.com
www.newtimes.co.rw *(Rwanda's English-language newspaper)*

# SENEGAL

## Capital
Dakar

## Language and telephone
French is the official language.
International telephone code +221

## Currency and rate
West African franc (CFA); US$1 = CFA502

## Red tape
Roadblocks are frequent; the police are sometimes zealous if you are in a vehicle or on a motorbike. Always adhere to all the rules and never hand over original documents.

## Visas
US and EU citizens do not need a visa, nor do citizens of most Commonwealth countries. Australians and New Zealanders are among those who do, however. A visa costs US$20–50, depending on country of application. Visitor's entry permits are issued at the border. A yellow fever certificate is obligatory.

## Fuel costs
Diesel: US$0.58; petrol: US$0.85 per litre.

## Driving and roads
Drive on the right. Roads are generally in good condition.

## African embassies
**Burkina Faso** Liberty extension, Dakar; tel: 823 9290
**Cameroon** 157 Rue Josef Gomis, Dakar; tel: 823 2195
**French consulate** (issues visas for most French-speaking African countries) 1 Rue Assane Ndoye, Dakar; tel: 839 5100
**Gambia** 11 Rue de Thiong, Ponty, Dakar; tel: 821 7230

**Guinea** Rue 7, Point E, Dakar; tel: 824 8606
**Guinea Bissau** Rue 6, Point E, Dakar; tel: 824 5922
**Ivory Coast** 2 Av Albert Sarraut, Dakar; tel: 821 3473
**Mali** Route de la Corniche Ouest, Dakar; tel: 894 6950
**Mauritania** Rue 37, Kolobane, Dakar; tel: 822 6238

## Climate

Dry from December to May; hot, humid and wet from May to June. The dry season is shorter in the south and east.

## Highlights

Dakar has some beaches not far from town for lazing and good nightlife; be careful late at night. Take a boat trip to the historic former slaving centre, Ile de Gorée. Hike in the Casamance region and enjoy the beautiful beaches of Cap Skiring. Visit the Siné-Saloum Delta and the Parc National de Niokolo-Koba. Highlights of the north include the old town of St Louis and the magnificent birdlife of the area. Senegal is also famed for its musicians, such as Youssour n'Dour and Salif Keita.

## Where to stay

**Dakar** The options for camping are all out of town – *Campement le Poulagou* near the airport, or *Yoff Village* close to the beach. Camping costs around US$3 per person. At Malika, about 20km out, is *Campement Touristique de Malika Peul* and close by is *Campement Tim Timol*.

**Ile de Gorée** Ferries leave from the wharf area in Dakar every one to two hours. The cost is US$4 per person.

**Siné-Saloum Delta** The delta is often overlooked by visitors and is a wild, beautiful area of mangrove swamps, lagoons, forests, dunes and sand islands. Camping accommodation is available at *Campement Pointe du Sangomar*, on the western edge of the delta at the tip of a narrow spit of land called Pointe de Sangomar. From here you are able to hire *pirogues* to reach the beautiful islands of Guior and Guissanor.

**St Louis** As you head south, just outside of town there is a campsite nestling off the Parc National de la Langue de Barbarie, famed for its birdlife. The *Zebrabar* is pleasant, with beautiful surroundings, and run by a Swiss family. Camping costs US$6 for a site.

**The Casamance** The best bet for accommodation is to stay at one of the local campsites called *Campements Touristiques Rurals Intégrés* (CTRI) where prices are standard at US$5 for a bed – camping costs would need to be negotiated.

**Oussoye** Has a long-standing traditional *village campement*.

The beaches at Cap Skiring are some of the nicest, but can get a little hectic. This area is worth a week's visit. Check the security situation in this area before you visit.

## Further information

*West Africa*, Rough Guides
www.homeviewsenegal.com
www.earth2000.com

# SIERRA LEONE

*Warning* Due to the recently concluded civil war in Sierra Leone it is advisable to seek further advice before travel overland. Basic information has been included. Travel in the country areas may still be ill-advised.

## Capital
Freetown

## Language and telephone
English is the official language.
International telephone code +232

## Currency and rate
Leone (Le); US$1 = Le2,355

## Red tape
Following the recent civil war, there are likely to be many road checkpoints.

## Visas
Visas are required for all, and cost around US$10–50 depending on your nationality. They are not issued at the border.

## Driving and roads
Drive on the right; the condition of the roads is unknown, but likely to be bad any distance away from Freetown.

## African embassies
**France** (issues visas for most French-speaking African countries) 13 Lamina Sankoh St, north of Siaka Stevens Rd, Freetown; tel: 222 477
**Ghana** Warpole St, Freetown; tel: 223 461
**Guinea** 6 Wilkinson Rd, Freetown; tel: 232 584
**Mali** Wilkinson Rd, Freetown; tel: 231 781

## Climate
The main rainy season is from June to September, with the rest of the year much drier.

## Highlights
Sierra Leone once had a thriving beach-holiday tourist industry, which may now be redeveloped. Freetown, although formerly rundown and crowded, is said to be experiencing a revival now that the war has finished. Its often unlit, seedy streets have a certain vibrant charm! Close by are a number of good beaches: Lumley, Lakka, River 2 and Tokey beach. Banana Island and Bunce Island, with its old fort, may be revived. In the Loma Mountains is Mount Bintumani, the highest point in West Africa at nearly 2,000m, set in a forest reserve. Also, when things improve, there is the Ooutamba Kilimi National Park.

## Where to stay
**Freetown** Out of town there is the *Hotel Cape Sierra* near Lumley beach. Currently Freetown is expensive, but as things settle down new places should open.

## Further information
*West Africa*, Rough Guides
www.sierra-leone.org

# SOMALIA

*Warning Due to ongoing civil war in Somalia it is not advisable to travel overland. Basic information has been included.*

## Capital
Mogadishu

## Language and telephone
Somali is the official language.
International telephone code: +252

## Currency and rate
Somali shilling (SSh); US$1 = SSh3,073

## Red tape
No current information

## Visas
Visas are required for all, but, with the current state of the country, anyone can probably enter without a visa – though it is not recommended! There are some reports that the breakaway northern Somaliland area around Hargeyisa may give visas, but then again it may not be safe either.

## Fuel costs
Unknown.

## Driving and roads
Drive on the right. If the Michelin map is to be believed, the roads from Mogadishu to Hargeysa were relatively new just before the troubles.

## African embassies
No African embassies are open or functioning.

## Climate
Much of Somalia is hot and dry, but there are intermittent rains in the south from March to September.

## Highlights
Formerly parts of the capital, Mogadishu, were quite picturesque, but the city has suffered from the on-going conflict. In the far north, the mountains between Berbera and Hargeysa are said to be spectacular, but it is not clear if the area is safe yet.

## Where to stay
**Hargeysa** Two hotels are said to be open and used by aid workers: *Ambassador Lion* and *Hotel Maansour*.

## Other
If you have made it to Djibouti you may hear more up-to-date news. Daallo Airlines fly to Hargeysa: www.daallo.com.

## Further information
*Africa on a Shoestring*, Lonely Planet
www.somalia.com

## SOUTH AFRICA

## Capital
Pretoria (administrative) and Cape Town (legislative)

## Language and telephone
English and Afrikaans are the official languages, with another nine local official languages – those spoken most are Zulu, Xhosa and Sotho.
International telephone code: +27

## Currency and rate
Rand (R); US$1 = R6.08

## Red tape
If you are intending to sell your vehicle in South Africa, you have to discharge your carnet by officially importing the vehicle or bike. To do this, you need a current valuation of your vehicle or bike, based on which you will pay import duty. Passports must be valid for at least six months after your date of departure from South Africa.

## Visas
Visas are not required for most holiday visitors. You'll be issued with an entry permit on arrival. If you are applying for an extended stay or work visa, which are issued free, allow a couple of weeks for the process. Visas are not issued at the border. With overland travel you may have to convince the Immigration officer that you have sufficient funds for your stay, but crossing borders is usually hassle-free.

## Fuel costs
Diesel: US$0.78; petrol: US$0.80 per litre.

## Driving and roads
Drive on the left. Roads are in excellent condition.

## African embassies

**Angola** 153 Oliver St, Brooklyn, Pretoria; tel: 012 342 0049
**Botswana** 24 Amos St, Colbyn, Pretoria; tel: 012 430 9640
**Burundi** 1090 Arcadia St, Hatfield, Pretoria; tel: 012 342 4881
**Congo** 960 Arcadia St, Hatfield, Pretoria; tel: 012 342 5508
**Democratic Republic of the Congo** 960 Arcadia St, Hatfield, Pretoria; tel: 012 342 5508
**Kenya** 302 Brooks St, Menlo Park, Pretoria; tel: 012 342 5066
**Lesotho** 1 T Edison St, Pretoria; tel: 012 460 7640
**Malawi** 209 Bauhinia Rd, Waterkloof Heights, Pretoria; tel: 012 347 6899
**Morocco** Pretoria; tel: 012 343 0230
**Mozambique** 529 Edmund St, Arcadia, Pretoria; tel: 011 336 1819
**Rwanda** 1090 Arcadia St, Hatfield, Pretoria 0083; tel: 012 342 1740; fax: 012 342 1743
**Sudan** 1203 Pretorius St, Hatfield, Pretoria; tel: 012 342 0599
**Swaziland** 715 Government Av, Arcadia, Pretoria; tel: 012 344 1917
**Tanzania** 822 George Av, Arcadia, Pretoria; tel: 012 342 4371
**Zambia** 570 Ziervogel St, Arcadia, Pretoria; tel: 012 326 1847
**Zimbabwe** 798 Merton Av, Arcadia, Pretoria; tel: 012 342 5125; fax: 012 342 5126

## Climate

The climate is extremely varied and quite localised. The summer (wet season) is from September to April in the north. Winters can be cold, particularly at night. In Cape Town the winter months (May to August) are wet and it can be very windy along the coast. June and July are the best months for game viewing. The Indian Ocean coast is driest from June to September.

## Highlights

South Africa is such a vast country that months could be spent exploring it. Highlights include the Kruger National Park and surrounding area, as well as Karoo National Park and Augrabies Falls. Of course Cape Town, Table Mountain, Cape of Good Hope and the vineyards in the surrounding area, including Stellenbosch, should be seen. East is the Garden Route along the southern coast, including Knysna, and for all surfers, Jeffrey's Bay, which is reputed to have some of the best waves in the world. Oudtshoorn has ostrich farms and the Kango caves. In the great Karoo are quirky

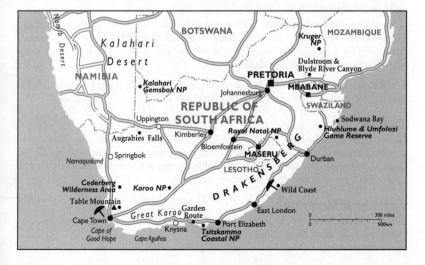

Matjiesfontein with its oddball Lord Milner hotel and railway station, plus Graff Reinet and the Mountain Zebra National Park. Natal has lush green rolling hills and incredible beaches along its coastline. The Drakensberg Mountains are spectacular, with Giant's Castle, Golden Gate park etc, as is the Cederberg Wilderness Area. Durban is known for its beaches and cosmopolitan flavour; and nearby is the wilder region of the Transkei.

## Where to stay

The options are limitless and the country is well set up for camping. Facilities are excellent. Costs are US$3 to US$10 per person, depending on the site. There are also a lot of backpacker places where parking is not usually too difficult. Here are a few pointers.

**Cape Town** There is a campsite at Muizenberg, south of town in the eastern beach area, on the way to the Cape. It's called Zandvlei Caravan Park and costs US$9 for a car plus two.

**Springbok** The *Springbok Caravan Park* with its campsite is on the ring road just south of town.

**Cederberg area** Camp at *The Baths*. It's off the main road from Citrusdal and has a natural hot pool and tranquil surroundings. Camping costs US$10. A beautiful place to stay.

**Stellenbosch** Try the *Stumble Inn Backpackers*. We parked safely outside in the street.

**Beaufort West** There is a *municipal caravan park* just on the southern edge of town. Camping for a car plus two people costs US$8.

**Gariep Dam** Beside the lake is a superb campsite costing US$9 for car plus two people, for a site with private kitchen and bathroom.

**Bloemfontein** North of the city is the *Reyneke Park* with camping areas, a peaceful spot. Cost US$12 for two.

**Pretoria** We stayed at the *North South Backpackers* in Hatfield, where the vehicle just fitted in through the archway. It's well guarded and costs US$11 to camp/park.

**Pietermaritzburg** The pleasant out-of-town *Msundzi Caravan Park* has nice camping and is about 5km out on the east side of town.

**Top of the Oliviershoek Pass** With a wonderful view across the whole range of the Drakensberg Mountains, are the relatively inexpensive *Windmill Resort* rondavel bungalows for a little luxury, and a comfortable bar too. Across the road down a steep narrow track is the *Amphitheatre Backpackers*.

**Durban** It's best to head for the beaches to the north and south, as Durban is not safe for parking overnight or even in the daytime in many areas.

## Other

Crime is on the increase in most major towns, so watch your bags and always carry minimal valuables. Most accommodation and camping places in South Africa offer to place all valuables in a safe. It is not advisable for any white person to enter a black township unless with a guide or tour company.

## Further information

*East & Southern Africa: The Backpacker's Manual*, Philip Briggs, Bradt Travel Guides
*South Africa: The Bradt Budget Guide*, Paul Ash
www.southafrica.co.za

# SUDAN

## Capital
Khartoum

## Language and telephone
Arabic is the official language.
International telephone code +249

## Currency and rate
The Sudanese dinar is the denomination of the notes, but prices are often quoted in the old Sudanese pound; US$1 = S£255 (1 dinar = S£10)

## Red tape
Sudan is wonderful to travel through, but famous for its bureaucracy. Obtaining the relevant permits is a time-consuming and frustrating task, but you have little choice. Stay within the restrictions of any permits needed, generally all in Arabic, as these may be checked on the road.

The first thing you must obtain is an Alien's Registration Stamp in your passport. This will take time and energy, as you search for the correct office in which to get the correct stamp, and then move on to the next office, and the next... And let's not forget finding the bank, where you must exchange cash in order to pay the US$20 or so for this purpose.

After this, you may need an 'Alien's Movement Permit', which states the towns and the route you intend to take. Any deviation may cause you trouble, so decide on your route before you apply. These documents were formerly required for all travel within Sudan, but we did not need one in 2004 to travel from Khartoum to Gedaref and the Ethiopian border. However, things seem to change constantly, so check at the border and in Khartoum before getting too far away.

If you cross one of the land borders, you may have to obtain your permit there; again, check if it is needed. Permits issued at borders were normally only good for travel to Khartoum, where you then needed to obtain another permit for onward travel. These permits should cost about US$20. It is worth photocopying this permit along with your passport to hand out at the police checks. It can save you some time and form-filling. At each town where you stay the night you are supposed to check in with the local police. This can become tedious, especially as the offices are often closed. It is better to camp in the bush, stopping briefly in the towns for supplies or sightseeing.

You may need to obtain a currency declaration form at the border. We did not in 2004. Also remember you cannot change any travellers' cheques in Sudan, but US dollars in cash are no problem.

## Visas
Visas are required for all and the process can be lengthy in Europe, particularly in London, as your application will first need to be approved by Khartoum. One-month entry visas cost US$75–95. Visas were said to be easy to obtain in Cairo. They are not issued at the border.

## Fuel costs
Diesel: US$0.28; petrol: US$0.36 per litre. The further north or west you go, the more expensive fuel becomes.

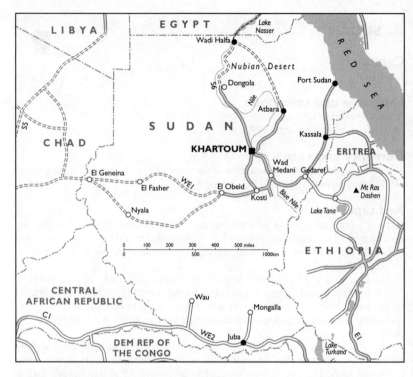

## Driving and roads

Drive on the right. All the major tarred roads are in good condition, but there are not too many of these. The road from Omdurman to Dongola is now sealed and being extended. All other roads are desert pistes and tracks.

## African embassies

**Chad** Sharia 17, New Extension, Khartoum; tel: 471084
**Egypt** Sharia al-Gamhuriyya, Khartoum; tel: 772190
**Ethiopia** Sharia 1, Khartoum 2, northwest of the cemetery, Khartoum; tel: 471156
**French consulate** (issues visas for most French-speaking African countries) Sharia 13, New Extension, Khartoum; tel: 471082
**Kenya** Sharia 3, New Extension, Khartoum 2; tel: 483834
**Libya** Block 18 Riyadh, Khartoum; tel: 222547
**Niger** Sharia 1, New Extension, Khartoum;
**Saudi Arabia** Sharia 29, New Extension, Khartoum; tel: 472583

## Climate

The summer months in Sudan are extremely hot and dry, reaching 45+°C. The best time to visit is during the winter months from December to mid March, when temperatures still reach 40°C but evenings are cool and pleasant. Should the south open up, don't go during the wet season, April to September, as roads become grim.

## Highlights

The main highlight of Sudan is its amazingly welcoming and diverse people: Arab, Nubian, Dinka, Shilluk, Nuer etc. Khartoum, the confluence of the Blue and the White

Nile, has Kitchener's old steamboat, tea shops, an impressive Central Mosque, and the Mahdi's Tomb in Omdurman. It offers fine dining at one of the restaurants along the waterfront. Further north is the Nubian Desert and the ancient pyramids of Meroe, reputed to be the oldest in the world.

Along the Red Sea, near Port Sudan and Suakin, are some reputedly excellent diving areas, with fishing excursions possible. On the way to Port Sudan, the town of Kassala is located in some spectacular rocky countryside and is on the way to Eritrea if things improve in the region. Other places that may eventually become safe are further south; the Dinder National Park and the Nile route to Juba, through the swamps of the Sudd, a naturalist's haven. To the west, but sadly off-limits due to the Darfur problems, are the volcanic mountains of Jebel Marra near El Fasher.

## Where to stay
Throughout Sudan bush sleeping is the best option, but keep a distance from settlements.

**Khartoum** There are two places that offer camping. The best and most convenient is the *Blue Nile Sailing Club*, on the southern bank of the Blue Nile near the church. It costs about US$11 for a vehicle and two people. An added bonus is the imposing presence of Kitchener's steamboat, marooned here since 1898. The other place, which we did not use, is on the road south to Wad Medani, some 10km out. It's not easy to find and has limited shade. Hotels in town to consider are the *Hotel Falcon* (US$40) and the *Akropole*, which is very expensive (US$90–150) but worth a visit. It's been run by George the Greek since time began.

**Wadi Halfa** You might get invited to stay with the Customs man, Kamal Hassan Osman, a well-known local character who has a spacious but simple house. Otherwise there is the grotty *Hotel Nile* or, much better, stay in the desert. Not always so easy, with so much paperwork to sort out here. See box on *Wadi Halfa* in *Chapter 7*.

**Atbara** The *Nile Hotel* has been recommended; there's little else.

**Meroe** Camping is permitted in the area. There is also a tastefully designed, Italian-run luxury tented camp and restaurant complex. It is not cheap.

**Gedaref** The only decent spot is the *Hotel Motwakil*, which claims to have guarded parking; it's US$26 a double. You can bush camp south of town on the grassy plains, but be careful of bush fires, which are common in the dry season.

## Other
Photography is a sensitive issue and photographic permits are sometimes needed for both a camera and a video camera. Don't take photos of anything with even the slightest military connection, including airports, government buildings, post offices, bridges, policemen and even fuel stations.

Ferries run from Port Sudan to Jeddah in Saudi Arabia.

## Further information
*Sudan: The Bradt Travel Guide*, Paul Clammer
www.sudan.com is for sale at the bargain price of only US$129,000!

## SWAZILAND

### Capital
Mbabane

### Language and telephone
English and Swati are the official languages.
International telephone code +268

### Currency and rate
Emalangeni (plural) or Lilangeni (SZL), but South African rand universally accepted.
US$1 = SZL6.08

### Red tape
None of any significance. Swaziland is within the South African Customs zone.

### Visas
Most nationalities do not need a visa. Others should check to see if they are available at the border.

### Fuel costs
Diesel: US$0.75; petrol: US$0.85 per litre.

### Driving and roads
Drive on the left. The main roads are good and secondary roads are mostly fine.

### African embassies
**Mozambique** Princes Drive, Mbabane; tel: 403 3700
**South Africa** PO Box 2507, The Mall, Mbabane; tel: 404 4651

### Climate
Swaziland has a climate generally moderated by altitude. The drier but cool season is from May to August. The main rains are from November to April.

### Highlights
On the way from Mozambique are the well-manicured sugar plantations and the Hlane Royal Park. A roadsign reads 'Motorists, beware of elephants. Cyclists and pedestrians, beware of lions!' Not far from Mbabane is the beautiful green Ezulwini valley, ancestral home of the royal family. The Mlilwane Wildlife Sanctuary near Lobamba is a delightful stop. Do go for morning or afternoon tea at Reilly's Rock, and enjoy the sumptuous colonial house, slumping in the supersoft armchairs, while the overnight guests are out. Other reserves or parks include Malolotja Nature Reserve and Mkhaya Game Reserve for black rhinos.

### Where to stay
The country is small, so almost any central location will give access to most places of interest.

**Mbabane** Try *Cathmar cottages* north of town near Pine Valley.
**Manzini** Try *Swaziland Backpackers* or *Myxo's Place,* which has village visits.

**Mlilwane Wildlife Sanctuary** There is a nice campsite in the park with well-kept gardens, bar, restaurant and inquisitive warthogs. Reilly's old house in the park is a superb colonial relic, moderately expensive but good for morning biscuits and tea. Entry costs US$4 each, and camping costs US$12, car plus two people.

## Other
With increasing crime in neighbouring South Africa, it's refreshing to visit Swaziland for its peace and tranquillity (except perhaps Mbabane and Manzini at night). Some game parks can only be paid for in rand or local currency, not other cash, even dollars.

## Further information
www.swaziland.com

# TANZANIA

## Capital
Dodoma

## Language and telephone
English and Swahili are the official languages.
International telephone code +255

## Currency and rate
Tanzanian shilling (TSh); US$1 = TSh1045

## Red tape
Watch out for radar and hefty speeding fines. Yes, even in Africa, but no cameras as yet!

## Visas
Visas are required for all except nationals of some Commonwealth countries, Scandinavia and Ireland. Things change though, so check. A visitor's pass for up to three months is issued at the border, costing US$10–50, depending on nationality: British citizens pay US$50.

## Fuel costs
Diesel: US$0.65; petrol: US$0.73 per litre.

## Driving and roads
Drive on the left. The main roads are mostly in good condition; Arusha to Dar es Salaam and on to Mbeya is fine. The road from Arusha to Ngorongoro is being tarred and should soon be completed as far as Karatu. The road south from Arusha to Dodoma is said to be atrocious.

## African embassies
**Algeria** 34 Ali Hassan Mwinyi Rd, Dar es Salaam; tel: 211 7619
**Angola** 78 Lugalo Rd, Upanga, Dar es Salaam; tel: 211 7674
**Burundi** was Plot 1007, Lugalo Rd, Dar es Salaam; tel: 23 8608
**Democratic Republic of the Congo** 438 Malik Rd, Dar es Salaam; tel: 26 6010
**French consulate** (issues visas for most French-speaking African countries) Ali Hassan Mwinyi Road, Dar es Salaam; tel: 266 6021

**Kenya** 14th Floor, NIC House, Samora Av, Dar es Salaam; tel: 211 2955
**Malawi** 1st Floor, Zambia House, Ohio St, Dar es Salaam; tel: 213 6954
**Mozambique** 25 Garden Av, Dar es Salaam; tel: 211 6502
**Rwanda** Ali Hassan Mwinyi Rd, Dar es Salaam; tel: 211 5888/9
**South Africa** Mwaya Rd, Msasani, Dar Es Salaam; tel: 260 1800
**Sudan** 64 Ali Mwinyi Rd, Dar es Salaam; tel: 246509
**Uganda** 25 Msasani Rd, Oyster Bay, Dar es Salaam; tel: 266 6730
**Zambia** 5–9 Sokoine Drive, Dar es Salaam; tel: 211 8481
**Zimbabwe** NIC House, Sokoine Drive, Dar es Salaam; tel: 211 6789

## Climate
It's hot and humid along the coast (particularly December to March). The rains are from March/April to May and in November. Inland the rains are January to April. On the central plateau it is warm and drier. The highlands are a little cooler, even cold at times.

## Highlights
In the north, Arusha is the gateway to the Serengeti National Park and Ngorongoro Crater. Climbing Mount Kilimanjaro, Africa's highest mountain, is good for those with the inclination and fitness. Zanzibar has Stone Town with its beautiful winding roads and stunning beaches. In the south are the Ruaha National Park and Selous Game Reserve. Much of the central highlands is green after the rains, and quite wild.

## Where to stay
**Dar es Salaam** Accommodation options are limited and the best bet is to go 20km (12 miles) north along the Bagamoyo road to Kanduchi Beach, where there is a choice of two campsites – the *Silversands Hotel* and the *Ndege Beach Resort*. If you are intending to stay a night in the city, try the *Hotel Kilimanjaro*, if it reopens. They used to charge hefty prices for parking the vehicle overnight.

**Bagamoyo** The only place to camp is at the *Travellers Lodge*.

**Zanzibar** Various ferries and local *pirogues* leave daily and hourly from the main wharf in Dar es Salaam. Yellow fever vaccination certificates are obligatory before a ticket is issued. Make sure you find a safe place to park your vehicle before you head over to the island. It's worth the effort as Zanzibar is really beautiful!

There is plenty of accommodation from hotels to pensions. Budget but not shoestring are the following: *Hotel Kiponda, Pyramid Hotel, Stone Town Inn*.

**Arusha** Stay at the *Masai Camp* (2.5km/1.5 miles outside on the old Moshi road). Cost US$4–5 each. If it's full of overland trucks, don't expect a quiet night in the bush. The Snake Park used to have camping west of town, but may be closed.

## *The Serengeti and Ngorongoro Crater*
As in Kenya, taking your own vehicle into the national parks is quite expensive. Of course you do retain the freedom to vary your plans with your own transport. In some circumstances it

might be easier to organise something with a tour company from Karatu or Arusha. Taking a tour might cost in the order of US$70–120 per person per day depending on the number of people. It should include all park fees, accommodation and meals.

**Lake Manyara** There are a number of camping options here outside the park around the village of Mto Wa Mbu. Look for *Panorama Campsite*, *Twiga Camp and Lodge*, *National Park Bandas Campsite* and *Holiday Fig*.

**Karatu** Further along from Lake Manyara is the small town of Karatu. The *Safari Inn* camping has a nice open garden and good facilities including restaurant/bar. Cost US$9 for two.

**Ngorongoro Crater** Ngorongoro is a magical place in fine weather. The *Simba camp* has been used for some years. Facilities are basic and costs high at US$20 per person. The views are great. Park entry was US$30 per person per 24 hours plus a vehicle fee of US$30. (Fees may have increased slightly by the time of going to press.)

**Serengeti** Covering 15,000 square miles, the Serengeti is a vast park. From Ngorongoro Crater the track passes Olduvai Gorge, famous for its early human remains, and heads to Seronera, the central area with most accommodation. The lodges are very expensive but camping in designated areas is possible for US$20 per person per day. There are also some cheapish resthouses/hostels for about US$20–30 each. Further north is Lobo with camping. The wildebeest migrations are amazing in this northern zone. Across the border in Kenya is the Masai Mara. West from Seronera is a track to Mwanza and Lake Victoria. It used to get horribly sticky and muddy in the rainy season.

## Beyond the national parks

**Kilimanjaro/Moshi** A good base for climbing Kilimanjaro is the well-known *Marangu Hotel* in Moshi. It is 10km south of the main gate to the national park and near the start of the most popular route up the mountain. The safe and attractive campsite, with hot showers and pool, costs US$3–4 per person per night. Climbs can be organised here. A more expensive option is *Coffee Tree Camping* which also organises climbs. A five-day trek will probably cost over US$500 per person all in. Beware of the altitude and **do not climb higher** if you are suffering from prolonged headaches, nausea and loss of appetite; the effects of pulmonary and cerebral oedema can be fatal.

**Same** The *Elephant Motel* south of town allows camping in its large grounds, and has showers. Camping costs US$6 for a car plus two people.

**Morogoro** Try the *New Acropole Hotel* for camping out in the yard, or take a room. The bar is lively at night, with lots of expatriates. It is Canadian-run and very friendly.

**Mikumi National Park** Try *Malela Nzuri Campsite* just off the main road on the east side of the park.

**Kisolanza Farm/Iringa** This is a wonderful stop 40km south of Iringa (email: kisolanza@cats-net.com). The farmhouse has been restored and has a spacious campsite under the trees. New bungalows have also been built if you want more luxury for a change. Local farm produce and delicious steak can be bought, to cook yourself. There is a cosy bar, but no restaurant. Camping costs US$6 for car plus two people. Closer to Iringa is the *Riverside Camp*, appropriately beside a river.

## Other

Formerly UK citizens could not get entry permits at the border but this seems to be a quirk of the past. We still advise prior checking, though. Most nationalities do need visas, but the majority can be obtained on arrival at the border. The fees vary a lot, from US$10 to US$50 for an entry permit/visa.

## Further information
*Tanzania: The Bradt Travel Guide*, Philip Briggs
*Zanzibar: The Bradt Travel Guide*, David Else
www.tanzania-web.com

## TOGO

**Warning:** At the time of going to press, the UK Foreign Office advised against all but essential travel to Togo following the presidential elections in April 2005. Visitors should keep a close eye on developments, avoid crowds and keep a low profile in case the situation deteriorates. Entry and exit points at borders are being opened and closed without warning.

## Capital
Lomé

## Language and telephone
French is the official language.
International telephone code +228

## Currency and rate
West African franc (CFA); US$1 = CFA502

## Red tape
At the border of Togo, officials may try to charge you for having your *carnet* stamped and the bureaucracy is very time consuming.

## Visas
Visas are required for all except nationals of ECOWAS countries. They are available at Togo embassies or at French consulates, where Togo has no representation. Cost US$10–20. The border may issue a 48-hour pass. A *Visa Touristique Entente* covering Benin, Burkina Faso, Ivory Coast, Niger and Togo is theoretically available; track it down via a relevant embassy or consulate. A yellow fever certificate is required.

## Fuel costs
Diesel: US$0.45; petrol: US$0.52 per litre.

## Driving and roads
Drive on the right. The roads are in generally good condition, particularly along the coast.

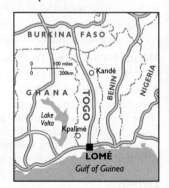

## African embassies
**French consulate** (issues visas for most French-speaking African countries) Rue de la Marina, Lomé; tel: 221 2576
**Ghana** Route de Kpalimé, Lomé; tel: 221 3194
**Nigeria** 311 Bd du 13 Janvier (Bd Greulaire), Lomé; tel: 221 3455

## Climate
The rainy season is April to July, with shorter rains in October and November. The temperature is generally pleasant in the dry season, but still hotter inland.

## Highlights

Lomé has a Fetish market. Along the coast from Lomé is Lake Togo, with its water sports, and Togoville with voodoo culture. For hiking there are the beautiful hills of Kpalimé. Visit the fortified tiered conical village compounds of the Tamberma and scenery of the Kandé area. From Kandé it's about 16km to Nadoba, the main village. Niamtougou, which has a good market, is another base for these villages.

## Where to stay

**Lomé** About 10km east of town, *Robinson Plage* hotel has camping. There is also camping at *Chez Alice*, 12km east of Lomé, on the beachfront. Camping costs US$3 per person.

**Lake Togo** This shallow lake, 30km (18 miles) east of Lomé, is popular for watersports. On the lake's northern shore lies Togoville, the centre of Togo's voodoo culture. There are no campsites in the immediate vicinity.

**Kpalimé** Try *Hotel la Détente.* There used to be a *Campement* where camping cost US$3 per person. Kpalimé is a great base for hiking enthusiasts.

**Kandé** There is the basic *Le Campement de la Nouvelle Marché* in Kandé. Bush sleeping would be another option if at all possible.

## Other

As discussed under the section on Ghana, touts at the border are frenetic and you will not be left alone. Just ignore them.

## Further information

*West Africa*, Rough Guides

## TUNISIA

## Capital

Tunis

## Language and telephone

Arabic is the official language.
International telephone code +216

## Currency and rate

Tunisian dinar (TD); US$1 = TD1.23

## Red tape

None of any significance.

## Visas

Nationals of most western European countries can stay in Tunisia for up to three months without a visa. Citizens of the USA, Canada, Germany and Japan can stay up to four months. Nationals of Australia, New Zealand and South Africa may need a visa. Visas are not issued at the border and should be applied for at any Tunisian embassy or consulate beforehand. Costs from US$5–15. Israeli nationals are not allowed into the country. Visitor's entry permits are issued at the border.

## Fuel costs
Diesel: US$0.38; petrol: US$0.70 per litre.

## Driving and roads
Drive on the right. The roads are generally in good condition. There are a limited number of tracks and pistes in the south near the borders of Algeria and Libya; some are restricted. Watch your speed if a minor road joins the major road you're on; the area around the junction may have a lower speed limit and sometimes there are police checks.

## African embassies
**Algeria** 18 Rue de Niger 100 2, Tunis
**Egypt** Av Mohammed V, Tunis; tel: 79 1181
**French consulate** (issues visas for most French-speaking African countries) Pl de l'Indépendance, Tunis; tel: 24 5700
**Libya** 35 Rue Alexander Dumas, Sfax; tel: 04 23332

## Climate
Tunisia has a Mediterranean climate in the north with cool, sometimes rainy, winters. In the south it is hotter, with a dry desert climate inland.

## Highlights
Tunisia has a number of ancient Roman sites, including that of Carthage (near Tunis), Dougga and Bulla Regia. El Djem has a gem of a Roman amphitheatre. Beaches are found south of Hammamet and on the island of Djerba. In the south are the oasis towns of Douz, for organised camel trips to 'nomadic' camps, plus Tozeur and Nefta with picturesque palmeries. In contrast, the lunar landscape of Matmata near Gabes conceals a once-busy community living underground, in caves chiselled out of the rock – you can visit their dwellings.

## Where to stay
Throughout Tunisia one option would be to bush camp, but it's quite developed, so always ask the owners of the land for permission first. There are a few campsites.

**Tunis** The *Hotel Amilcar*, north of town and close to Sidi Bou Said, is on the beach with fine views. It has safe parking and camping might be allowed. It is also possible, and currently safe, to sleep in your car at the ferry port in La Goulette.

**Nabeul** It is possible to camp at the *Hotel Les Jardins* close to the beach.

**Hammamet** There is a nice camping place with olive trees and a small hotel; take the southern motorway exit to Hammamet, and it's at the first crossroads next to a fuel station.

**Gabès** The slightly rundown *Youth Hostel* has camping in its large grounds. It's hard to find, though. When driving north to south, turn left off the main road at a roundabout with fuel station (near the new bypass ring road), and then fork left almost immediately down a narrow road through a dry riverbed on the northwest of town, passing some markets. Turn left at the end and it's on your left.

**Tozeur** There is a shady pleasant camping place south of town in the palmerie; it may be called

*Camping Beau Rivages!*

**Nefta** Try the *Hotel Marhaba*, which allows camping in the grounds. Again in the palmeries, there is also a campsite at Degache.

## Other
Tunisia is easy-going by Muslim standards, particularly in areas frequented by tourists, but outside these areas life is still conservative and revolves around the mosque, *hammam* (local baths) and cafés. Act and dress appropriately.

## Further information
*Tunisia*, Barnaby Rogerson, Cadogan
www.tunisiaonline.com

## UGANDA

**Warning:** *Uganda is generally a safe destination but with one exception. Northeast Uganda is still dominated by the LRA (Lord's Resistance Army). Always check the latest conditions before heading to this area.*

## Capital
Kampala

## Language and telephone
English is the official language.
International telephone code +256

## Currency and rate
Ugandan shilling (USh); US$1 = USh1,729
Money can be changed in Kampala. There are some ATMs but they only accept VISA credit cards. Cash US$ and cash advances can be obtained at the banks.

## Red tape
The border process is normally efficient and quick. There could be some roadblocks because of the civil war in the Democratic Republic of the Congo and an isolated mini-rebellion in the north.

## Visas
Visas are not required for nationals of Denmark, Finland, France, Germany, Israel, Japan, Sweden and most Commonwealth countries – India, New Zealand and Nigeria are exceptions. Visas cost US$25–40. They can be obtained at the border and are valid for 30 days. Students/ISS card holders can get a discount.

## Fuel costs
Diesel: US$0.68; petrol: US$0.86 per litre.

## Driving and roads
Drive on the left. The main roads are in generally good condition. Upcountry some dirt roads can be subject to wet weather.

## African embassies

**Burundi** 7 Bandali Rise, Bugolobi, Kampala; tel: 221697

**Democratic Republic of the the Congo** 20 Phillip Rd, Kololo, Kampala; tel: 233 777

**Ethiopia** Kira Rd near National Museum, Kampala; tel: 348 340

**French Consulate** (issues visas for most French-speaking African countries) 19 Lumumba Av, Kampala; tel: 342 120

**Kenya** 41 Nakasevo Rd, Kampala; tel: 258 239

**Rwanda** 2 Nakayima Rd, Kampala; tel: 258 547

**South Africa** 2b Nakasero Rd, Kampala; tel: 343 543

**Sudan** 21 Nakasero Rd, Kampala; tel: 243 518

**Tanzania** 6 Kagera Rd, Kampala; tel: 256 272

## Climate

Uganda's position on the Equator is tempered by its high altitude, giving it a very pleasant climate. The rainy seasons are March to June and October to December.

## Highlights

An undoubted highlight of Uganda is tracking gorillas in the rainforests, but it's not a cheap activity. See Murchison and Sipi Falls, Queen Elizabeth National Park, go trekking in the Ruwenzori Mountains and relax for a few days on Ssese Island. There is also whitewater rafting on the Nile, while staying in Jinja. Lake Bunyoni (near Kabale) is a very tranquil and relaxing place to spend a couple of days.

## Where to stay

**Kampala** The *Kampala Backpackers Hostel and Campsite*, Kalema road in Lungujja just off Naktete Road and west of town, has a relaxed atmosphere. Camping costs US$3 per person.

**Jinja** Apart from Speke (after he left Burton), most people stop over in Jinja for the whitewater rafting. In or close to town you can stay at either *Explorers Backpackers* or the *Timton Hotel* for camping. Not far out (9km) is Bujagali Falls. Here you can stay at *Explorers Campsite* or *Speke Camp*. Three companies were offering rafting: Adrift, Equator Rafting and Nile River Explorers. There is also a campsite at Mabira Forest.

**Fort Portal** This is the base for exploring the Ruwenzori peaks. In town the *Ruwenzori View Guesthouse* is highly recommended. Otherwise it is best to head towards the Kibale Forest National Park, south of Fort Portal, and look out for the *Safari Hotel*, on your right at the Nkingo village. Camping costs US$2.

**Ssese Islands** You'll have to leave your vehicle behind, but camping on *Buggala Island* is available. There is a 50-minute ferry from Kabassese. It was possible to ask the local fishermen to take you.

**Sipi Falls** To get to Sipi Falls you'll need to climb a steep and treacherous road up into the mountains, but it's worth the effort. Sipi Falls and the surrounding area are beautiful, with green, hilly outcrops and villages dotted around the countryside. You can stay at the *Crow's Nest Campsite*, which is eco-friendly and has a superb view of Sipi Falls. Camping costs US$3 per person. Nearby is *Moses's Campsite*.

**For gorilla trekking** The two options are Bwindi National Park and Mgahinga National Park. Most opt for Bwindi, as they have three groups of gorillas that have been habituated, while Mgahinga has only one. For either park you can get a permit in Kampala, currently costing in the order of US$300 per person. Rates may well increase in 2005. Contact Uganda Wildlife Authority on Kintu Road in Kampala for bookings. Booking is advised but it was (check this) possible to be put on standby, for a lower charge. Both parks have similar accommodation facilities and charge US$6 for a site. It can get cold up in the mountains, so come prepared. The campsite near the park headquarters costs US$3.

**Other national parks** Murchison Falls National Park and Queen Elizabeth National Park are both worth a visit. The falls are particularly spectacular, and there is abundant wildlife in the Queen Elizabeth National Park. You will need to be self-sufficient and carry all your supplies with you. During the rainy season the roads in either park can be treacherous. Camping with basic facilities costs US$6 per person; there is also self-catering, where facilities include a basic hut and a staffed kitchen. The entry charge is US$20 per person and $20 per vehicle.

**Lake Bunyoni** Bunyoni Overland Camp has excellent camping spots right on the lakeside. The camp is well maintained, and has a pleasant bar and hot showers. It is becoming a popular overlander spot, so it can be a bit crowded and noisy at times.

## Further information
*Uganda: The Bradt Travel Guide*, Philip Briggs
www.myuganda.co.ug
www.visituganda.com

# WESTERN SAHARA

*Morocco virtually annexed the northern two-thirds of Western Sahara (formerly Spanish Sahara) in 1976, and the rest of the territory in 1979, following Mauritania's withdrawal. A guerrilla war, with the Polisario Front contesting Rabat's sovereignty, ended in a 1991 ceasefire; a referendum on final status has been repeatedly postponed. In May 2003 the area was granted limited autonomy under Moroccan sovereignty. Over the next four years, some democratic reforms and institutions should be established, followed by a referendum of the Saharawi peoples. The problem is defining who is eligible to vote, and this is the daunting task that the UN has so far been unable to complete.*

## Capital
Laayoune

## Language and telephone
Arabic is the official language.
International telephone code +212

## Currency and rate
Dirham (Dr); US$1 = Dr8.49

## Red tape
Officials are often extremely helpful. When crossing the Sahara it is advisable to have several copies of the document in *Appendix 2*, plus copies of your passport and driving licence, as these are required at roadblocks in Western Sahara and in Morocco.

## Visas

Most visitors to Western Sahara/Morocco do not require visas and can remain in Morocco for 90 days on entry. Some nationalities do need visas, so it's still best to check.

## Fuel costs

Diesel: US$0.47; petrol: US$0.79 per litre.

## Driving and roads

Drive on the right. Roads are generally in good condition on all major routes, apart from more remote desert tracks. Some areas are off limits to foreigners.

## African embassies

Currently the same as those listed for Morocco.

## Climate

Western Sahara has a continental climate, with extremes in the interior and desert in the south. The south is generally hotter and inland nights can be cold in winter. Mist often hangs around along the coast, where cold currents hit hot shores.

## Highlights

The nominal capital, Laayoune, has some older mosques and buildings, but is fundamentally a fairly modern town. The beach is not far away at Laayoune Plage. The Atlantic coast is a bleak and often windswept region, but has a stark beauty of its own. Dakhla is the main point of interest in the south. Visiting Smara is now possible and some have taken the desert piste to/from Assa, east of Tan Tan. If it ever opens up, the desert inland could be a wild region to explore.

## Where to stay

There are few recognised campsites and desert camping may be preferred, but don't end up stopping by accident in any military zone that is not clearly defined.

**Laayoune** Try the nearby *Laayoune Plage* where there was, some years ago, a fenced area with a few facilities.

**Dakhla** There was said to be a proper place to camp.

## Other

In 1975 the area was evacuated by the Spanish, and both Morocco and Mauritania raised claims to the territory, because of phosphate in the area. The two countries fought over the occupied territory of Western Sahara until 1996, when a ceasefire was reached. Since then, the Moroccans have occupied the region and have been allowing convoys through. The Saharawi people have been in conflict through their active movement, the Polisario. No permanent solution has been concluded as yet.

## Further information

*Morocco*, Barnaby Rogerson, Cadogan
www.marocnet.com

# ZAMBIA

## Capital
Lusaka

## Language and telephone
English is the official language.
International telephone code +260

## Currency and rate
Zambian kwacha (ZK); US$1 = ZK4610
Most tourist places and hostels quote their rates in US$ and can be paid in cash US$.
Money can be changed in Lusaka at one of the many exchange bureaux. In other parts of
the country it is far more difficult, so stock up on your kwachas in Lusaka.

## Red tape
None of any significance.

## Visas
All visitors except citizens of some Commonwealth countries need a visa. British and Irish
citizens do need visas and may need to get them in advance. A single-entry visa costs
US$25–50. Visas can be obtained at the border and are valid for 30 days. You may be able
to get a free visa by invitation. To arrange this, contact one of the popular guesthouses (eg:
Chachacha in Lusaka, Jolly Boys or Fawlty Towers in Livingstone) and they will send a
fax to the border.

## Fuel costs
Diesel: US$0.49; petrol: US$0.53 per litre.

## Driving and roads
Drive on the left. Roads have deteriorated, with the worst bitumen in the east and the south.

## African embassies
**Botswana** Pandit Nehru Rd, Lusaka; tel: 252058 or 250019
**Democratic Republic of the Congo** 1124 Parirenyetwa Rd, Lusaka; tel: 235679
**Malawi** 31 Bishops Rd, Kabulonga, Lusaka; tel: 265764
**Mozambique** Kacha Rd, Lusaka; tel: 239135
**Namibia** 30b Mutende Rd, Woodlands, Lusaka; tel: 260407
**South Africa** 26 Cheetah Rd, Kabulonga, Lusaka; tel: 260999
**Tanzania** Ujaama House, 5200 United National Av, Lusaka; tel: 253222
**Zimbabwe** 11058 Haile Selassie Av, Lusaka; tel: 254006

## Climate
It is sunny but cool from May to September and hot from October to November. The
rains are from November to April (most parks and other resorts shut down during this
time, as the majority of roads are impassable).

## Highlights
Victoria Falls is the most imposing sight. You can try whitewater rafting and bungee jumping
if you need more adrenalin highs than just driving on Zambian roads. Try taking an easy
canoe ride down the Zambezi if you actually want to enjoy the surroundings. A trip to the

South Luangwa National Park, which has a varied array of wildlife, is highly recommended, and in the north are the Kalambo Falls.

## Where to stay

**Lusaka** Camping is possible at the *Chachacha Guesthouse* (email: cha@zamtel.zm). There are two camping options a little out of town – *Pioneer Campsite* (signposted 5km south of the Great East Road, 18km east of the city centre, 3km east of the airport turn-off) or *Eureka Camping Park* (10km south of the city on Kafue Road). Both charge US$6 for the site and facilities are excellent. Both have nearby transport into Lusaka.

**Victoria Falls (Zambia side)** There are plenty of backpacker places in Livingstone that also offer camping. Their names are liable to change periodically, even if the premises don't. Suggested places are *Fawlty Towers* (ahorizon@zamnet.zm), *Grotto*, *Geckos* and *Jolly Boys* (jboys@zamnet.zm). Upstream from Victoria Falls is Bovu Island. It is popular, so it may be worth checking beforehand (tel: 323 708; email: jungle@zamnet.zm). Camping costs US$3–4 per person. There is now an entrance charge of US$10 to visit the Victoria Falls Park.

**South Luangwa National Park** Park entry is US$20 per person. In general the wildlife is prolific, but the season may dictate the actual abundance of animals you find. There are also reasonable camping opportunities just outside the park and facilities are good at each of the camps. Camping costs US$5 per person.

## Other

Crime is on the increase in Lusaka. Do not walk anywhere at night; take a taxi. Be careful around Victoria Falls after dark and watch out for petty theft.

## Further information

*Zambia: The Bradt Travel Guide*, Chris McIntyre
www.zambia.co.zm

# ZIMBABWE

**Warning** At the time of writing there are sporadic violent disputes in Zimbabwe sometimes between President Mugabe's 'war veterans' and white farmers. Check locally if possible before contemplating a trip to the country. Most travellers have stated that tensions are running high. There is no fuel in most of Zimbabwe.

## Capital

Harare

## Language and telephone

English, Shona and Sindebele are the official languages.
International telephone code +263

## Currency and rate

Zimbabwe dollar (ZD); US$1 = Z$5,580. Rampant inflation is now the norm, so rates will fluctuate dramatically.

## Red tape

With the current problems in Zimbabwe, there are now major roadblocks and frequent police checks.

## Visas

Visas are required for most nationalities now. They vary in cost; some are free, others are US$30–50. British visitors now need a visa; fee US$55. Yellow-fever vaccination certificates are obligatory. A visitor's entry pass may be issued at the border.

## Fuel costs

Diesel: US$0.50; petrol: US$0.70 per litre. Due to severe shortages, these could change drastically.

## Driving and roads

Drive on the left. Roads are in relatively good condition.

## African embassies

**Angola** Doncaster House, 26 Speke Av, Harare; tel: 790075
**Botswana** 22 Phillips Av, Belgravia, Harare; tel: 729551
**Kenya** 95 Park Lane, Harare; tel: 792901
**Malawi** Malawi House, 11 Duthie Rd, Alexandra Park, Harare; tel: 798584
**Mozambique** 152 Herbert Chitepo Av, Harare; tel: 253871
**Namibia** 69 Borroedale Rd, Harare; tel: 8855845
**South Africa** Temple Bar House, 7 Elcombe Av/2nd St, Belgravia, Harare; tel: 753147
**Tanzania** 23 Baines Av, Harare; tel: 721870
**Zambia** 6th Floor, Zambia House, 48 Union Av, Harare; tel: 773777

## Climate

Because of its generally higher altitude the country has a temperate climate. The rainy season is December to March and cool season May to September.

## Highlights

In the east are the highlands and Chimanimani National Park. Perhaps the best-known site is the Great Zimbabwe ruin near Masivingo. In the northwest is the Lake Kariba district, with its lake of dead trees. Victoria Falls offers a variety of activities, from whitewater rafting to helicopter rides over the falls. Other national parks are Hwange, Mana Pools, Matobo and Matusadona.

## Where to stay

**Harare** Most overlanders used to head for *Backpackers and Overland Lodge*, Twentydales Road. Camping costs US$3. You might also try the *Hillside Lodge*. Don't walk around at night.

**Bulawayo** The *Municipal Caravan Park and Camp Site* or *Packers Rest* were said to be good for camping. Don't walk around at night.

**Mutare** Look for the *Municipal Caravan and Camping Park* on Harare road. Don't walk around at night.

**Chimanimani National Park** *Heaven Mountain Lodge* is a great place to stay before trekking up the mountain. You can leave your vehicle at the park entrance and take all necessary goods with you while trekking the area for a few days. You'll need to be self-sufficient; camping is possible in the various caves and lodges dotted around the area. Park entry fees are US$5 per day.

**Victoria Falls** Many travellers go to the *Victoria Falls Restcamp and Lodges* or *Victoria Falls Backpackers*. Other places were *Club Shoestring* and *Tokkie Lodge*. Facilities are reasonable and all are within walking distance of the action; be very careful after dark though. Camping costs US$4–5 per person. There is now an entrance charge of US$20 to visit the Victoria Falls Park.

**Great Zimbabwe National Park** Park entry fees are US$5 and the campsite in the actual ruins is shady and comfortable, with excellent facilities. Camping at *National Park* costs US$5–6 for the site. Watch out for the vervet monkeys; they'll steal anything.

## Other

The economic situation in the country is very bad, so expect shortages of fuel and supplies. So far tourists have not been affected directly, but seek the latest advice. Zimbabwe has a significant tsetse-fly problem, particularly along Lake Kariba. You will see blue-and-silver screens dotted along the side of roads, which attract the flies. Tsetse flies can give a very vicious bite, so beware. You may also come across tsetse-fly control stations, where two people with a butterfly net in either hand search every part of your vehicle for the elusive fly. This is a genuine search; you are very unlikely to be asked for any 'donation', but the experience may keep you amused for days. And don't wear blue; it's the flies' favourite colour.

## Further information

*East and Southern Africa: The Backpacker's Manual*, Philip Briggs, Bradt Travel Guides
www.zimbabwe.net

---

### THE END

A hazy sunshine greeted us as we parked by the seaside. A couple of tour buses pulled up for the view. At this point we were more troubled by our lack of communication with the shipping agents. The Internet had crashed at the café. How and when were we going to get the Land Rover home? It's a pity that we took in the significance of the view from the car park too hurriedly. It should have been a moment to savour.

Table Mountain was clearly in the picture; the symbolic end of our trip, which had taken us from the Sudan Embassy in London to Cape Town.

Well we had made it, but nobody else knew that. American tourists poured from the coach; if it was Wednesday, it must be Cape Town.

# Appendix 1

## LANGUAGE
### French and Arabic translation list

You may well speak normal conversational French, but possibly the technical terms for vehicle parts will not spring easily to mind. And as for Arabic, it's probably safe to assume you know nothing, as we did! *Salaam Aleikum* with a smile can get you a long way, but you can still find yourself stuck in smaller towns, sometimes even in major cities, if you do not know the translation of a specific vehicle part, spare or tool. For the Arabic translation we have used more of a general dictionary, including some vehicle parts, spares and tools.

We have tried to list (in alphabetical order) all relevant vehicle parts in French and some of the parts in Arabic. The Arabic translation is phonetic, ie: the way one would say it rather than spell it.

### French

| | | | |
|---|---|---|---|
| accelerator jet | *gicleur de pompe* | crankshaft | *vilebrequin* |
| alternator | *alternateur* | crescent spanner | *clé plate* |
| anti-roll bar | *barre de stabilisateur* | crown wheel and pinion | *couple conique* |
| armature | *induit de démarreur* | CV joint | *joint homocinétique* |
| axle casing | *corps de pont* | cylinder block | *bloc-cylindres* |
| ball bearings | *roulement à billes* | cylinder head | *culasse* |
| ball joint | *rotule* | differential | *différentiel* |
| battery | *batterie* | dipstick | *jauge d'huile* |
| bearing | *coussinet* | disc brakes | *freins à disque* |
| body | *carrosserie* | distance recorder | *compteur kilométrique* |
| bolt | *boulon* | distributor | *allumeur* |
| brake hose | *flexible de frein* | engine mounting | *tampon* |
| brake lining | *garniture de frein* | exhaust valve | *soupape d'échappement* |
| brake master cylinder | *maitre-cylindre* | fan | *ventilateur* |
| brake shoe | *mâchoires de frein* | fan belt | *corroie de ventilateur* |
| bumper | *pare chocs* | float | *flotteur* |
| camshaft | *arbre à cames* | float chamber | *cuve à niveau constant* |
| carbon brush | *balai* | flywheel | *volant* |
| carburettor | *carburateur* | fracture in tyre | *déchirure* |
| chassis | *chassis* | fuel gauge | *indicateur de niveau, jauge* |
| clutch | *embrayage* | | |
| clutch master cylinder | *pompe d'embrayage* | fuel line | *canalisation* |
| clutch plate | *disque d'embrayage* | fuel pump | *pompe à essence* |
| clutch slave cylinder | *recepteur d'embrayage* | fuel tank | *réservoir* |
| coil | *bobine d'allumage* | fuse | *fusible* |
| condenser | *condensateur* | gasket | *joint* |
| conrod | *bielle* | gear box | *boite de vitesses* |
| contact points | *jeu de contacts, rupteur* | generator | *dynamo* |
| cotter pins | *bagues d'appui* | gudgeon pin | *axe de piston* |

| | | | |
|---|---|---|---|
| hammer | *marteau* | rocker | *culbuteur* |
| handbrake cable | *cable de frein à main* | rockershaft | *axe de culbuteur* |
| handbrake lever | *levier de frein à main* | rotor arm | *rotor de distributeur* |
| heater plug | *bougie de préchauffage* | rubber bush | *coussinet en caoutchouc* |
| hose | *durite* | screwdriver | *tournevis* |
| ignition switch | *contacteur d'allumage* | set of pads | *jeu de mâchoires* |
| inlet valve | *soupape d'admission* | shock absorber | *amortisseur* |
| jack | *cric* | slow idle jet | *gicleur de ralenti* |
| leaf spring | *lame de ressort* | socket | *douille* |
| leakage | *fuite* | socket spanner | *clé à tube* |
| limited slip differentials | *différentiel autobloquant* | solenoid | *solenoid, bendix* |
| lock nut | *contre écrou* | spanner | *clé* |
| locking washer | *arrêtoir* | spare wheel | *roue de secours* |
| main jet | *gicleur d'alimentation* | spark plug | *bougie* |
| manifold | *collecteur* | speedo cable | *flexible de tachymètre* |
| needle valve | *pointeau* | speedometer | *compteur, tachymètre* |
| nut | *écrou* | spring | *ressort de suspension* |
| oil cooler | *radiateur d'huile* | starter motor | *démarreur* |
| oil filter | *filtre à huile* | steering column | *colonne de direction* |
| oil seal | *bague d'étanchéité* | steering wheel | *volant de direction* |
| patch | *rustine* | thermostat | *thermostat* |
| petrol cap | *bouchon de réservoir* | third gear | *pignon de la troisième* |
| piston | *piston* | | *vitesse* |
| piston ring | *segment* | | *(1 première, 2 deuxième,* |
| pitman arm | *levier de direction* | | *4 quatrième)* |
| pliers | *pince* | throttle valve | *papillon* |
| pressure plates | *plateau de pression* | tie road | *barre de connexion* |
| propeller shaft | *arbre de transmission* | torque spanner | *clé dynamométrique* |
| pulley | *poulie* | tube | *chambre à air* |
| puncture | *crevaison* | tyre | *pneu* |
| push rod | *tige de culbuteur* | tyre lever | *démonte pneu* |
| (motor/engine) | | universal joint | *cardan de roue* |
| push rod | *tige de poussoir* | valve cover | *couvercle de culasse* |
| (transmission) | | valve guide | *guide de soupape* |
| push rod tube | *couvercle de tige* | valve spring | *ressort de soupape* |
| radiator | *radiateur* | water pump | *pompe à eau* |
| rear axle | *pont arrière* | wheel | *roue* |
| regulator | *régulateur* | wheel hub | *moyeu de roue* |
| release bearing | *butée d'embrayage* | wheel rim | *jante* |
| ring spanner | *clé à oeillet* | windscreen | *pare-brise* |

## Arabic

When reading the imitated pronunciation, stress that part of the word which is underlined. Pronounce each word as if it were an English word and you should be understood sufficiently well.

## General

| | | | |
|---|---|---|---|
| accident | *haad̲e̲thah* | coffee | *qah̲wah* |
| accommodation | *m̲askan* | doctor | *tab̲ee̲bh* |
| border | *hod̲oo̲d* | drinking water | *maa' lesh-sh̲or̲b* |
| bread | *khobz* | east | *sharq* |
| camel | *j̲amal* | encampment made | *douar* |
| campsite | *moA̲skar* | up of tents | |

| | | | |
|---|---|---|---|
| exchange rate | *seAr at-taHweel* | road | *shaareA* |
| flat stony plain | *hammada* | road or piste | *tric* |
| go away! | *emshee!* | sick | *mareeD* |
| greeting | *Salaam al Laikoum* | Sir | *Sidi* (only used for a |
| How long will it take? | *Qad aysh waqt* | | person of higher |
| | *tastaghreq be-taakhoz?* | | standing than |
| How much? | *Kem?* | | oneself) |
| journey | *reHlah* | small shops | *souks* |
| map | *khareeTah* | small rock standing in | |
| married | *motazawaj* | the plain | *gara* |
| morning | *sabaah* | south | *janoob* |
| mountain | *jebel* | stop! | *geff!* |
| night | *layl* | tea | *atai* |
| no (response) | *laa* | thank you | *shokrahn* |
| north | *shemaal* | tip | *baqsheesh* |
| office | *maktab* | valley between dunes | *gassi* |
| passport | *jawaaz safar* | water | *mey* |
| policeman | *shorTee* | west | *gharb* |
| police station | *noqTat ash- shorTah* | Where can I park? | *Wayn awqef as-* |
| post office | *maktab bareed* | | *sayaarah?* |
| reply to greeting | *al Laikoum salaam* | yes | *noAm* |
| riverbed | *oued* | | |

## Vehicle

| | | | |
|---|---|---|---|
| accelerator | *dawaasat al-banzeen* | inner tube | *anboob daakhelee* |
| anti-freeze | *moDaad let-tajmeed* | long (as in How long?) | *taweel* |
| battery | *baTaareeyah* | mechanic | *meekaaneekee* |
| brake | *faraamel* | motorbike | *daraajah bokhaareeyah* |
| breakdown | *Ta Atal* | oil | *zayt* |
| camshaft | *amood al-kaamah* | park (as in park the | |
| car | *sayaarah* | vehicle) | *hadeeqah* |
| carburettor | *karboraateere* | piston | *makbas* |
| clutch | *debreiyaaj* | puncture | *thaqb* |
| diesel | *deezel* | radiator | *raadiyateer* |
| distributor | *destrebyooter* | screwdriver | *mafakk* |
| drive | *yasooq* | seatbelt | *hezaam al-maqAd* |
| to drive | *yasooq* | spanner | *meftaaH sawaameel* |
| engine | *moHarrek* | spares | *qeTaA ghiyaar* |
| exhaust | *shakmaan* | spark plug | *belajaat* |
| fan belt | *sayr al-marwaHah* | speedometer | *adaad as-sorAh* |
| funnel | *qomA* | spring | *soostah* |
| garage (for fuel) | *maHaTTat banzeen* | steering wheel | *ajalat al-qiyaadah* |
| garage (for repairs) | *garaaj meekaaneekee* | to tow | *yasHab* |
| gears | *geer* | transmission | *naql al-Harakah* |
| handbrake | *faraamel* | tyre | *'eTaar or Taayer* |
| ignition | *jehaaz al-eshAal* | wheel | *ajalah* |
| indicator | *mo'asher* | | |

# **Appendix**

## PERSONAL DETAILS

Wherever you plan to go in Africa, it's worthwhile having some copies of the following information sheet in order to speed up some of the bureaucracy .Use A4 paper, then use this and copies of your passport and driving licence for presentation as required. Of course, the information can be written out at each police post, but the officials don't mind the copied material, so why waste time?

Surname . . . . . . . . . . . . . . . . . . . . . . . . . . . . . . . . . . . . . . . . . . . . . . . . . . . . . . . . . . . . . . . . . . . . . . . . . . . .

Name . . . . . . . . . . . . . . . . . . . . . . . . . . . . . . . . . . . . . . . . . . . . . . . . . . . . . . . . . . . . . . . . . . . . . . . . . . . . . . . . .

Date of birth . . . . . . . . . . . . . . . . . . . . . . . . . . . . . . . . . . . . . . . . . . . . . . . . . . . . . . . . . . . . . . . . . . . . . . . . . . .

Place of birth . . . . . . . . . . . . . . . . . . . . . . . . . . . . . . . . . . . . . . . . . . . . . . . . . . . . . . . . . . . . . . . . . . . . . . . . . .

Nationality . . . . . . . . . . . . . . . . . . . . . . . . . . . . . . . . . . . . . . . . . . . . . . . . . . . . . . . . . . . . . . . . . . . . . . . . . . . . .

Passport number . . . . . . . . . . . . . . . . . . . . . . . . . . . . . . . . . . . . . . . . . . . . . . . . . . . . . . . . . . . . . . . . . . . . . . . .

Date of issue . . . . . . . . . . . . . . . . . . . . . . . . . . . . . . . . . . . . . . . . . . . . . . . . . . . . . . . . . . . . . . . . . . . . . . . . . . . .

Date of expiry . . . . . . . . . . . . . . . . . . . . . . . . . . . . . . . . . . . . . . . . . . . . . . . . . . . . . . . . . . . . . . . . . . . . . . . . . . .

Place of issue . . . . . . . . . . . . . . . . . . . . . . . . . . . . . . . . . . . . . . . . . . . . . . . . . . . . . . . . . . . . . . . . . . . . . . . . . . .

Profession . . . . . . . . . . . . . . . . . . . . . . . . . . . . . . . . . . . . . . . . . . . . . . . . . . . . . . . . . . . . . . . . . . . . . . . . . . . . . .

Marital status . . . . . . . . . . . . . . . . . . . . . . . . . . . . . . . . . . . . . . . . . . . . . . . . . . . . . . . . . . . . . . . . . . . . . . . . . . .

Permanent address . . . . . . . . . . . . . . . . . . . . . . . . . . . . . . . . . . . . . . . . . . . . . . . . . . . . . . . . . . . . . . . . . . . . . . .

Father's name . . . . . . . . . . . . . . . . . . . . . . . . . . . . . . . . . . . . . . . . . . . . . . . . . . . . . . . . . . . . . . . . . . . . . . . . . . .

Mother's name . . . . . . . . . . . . . . . . . . . . . . . . . . . . . . . . . . . . . . . . . . . . . . . . . . . . . . . . . . . . . . . . . . . . . . . . . .

Purpose of visit . . . . . . . . . . . . . . . . . . . . . . . . . . . . . . . . . . . . . . . . . . . . . . . . . . . . . . . . . . . . . . . . . . . . . . . . . .

Coming from . . . . . . . . . . . . . . . . . . . . . . . . . . . . . . . . . . . . . . . . . . . . . . . . . . . . . . . . . . . . . . . . . . . . . . . . . . . .

Going to . . . . . . . . . . . . . . . . . . . . . . . . . . . . . . . . . . . . . . . . . . . . . . . . . . . . . . . . . . . . . . . . . . . . . . . . . . . . . . . .

Driving licence number . . . . . . . . . . . . . . . . . . . . . . . . . . . . . . . . . . . . . . . . . . . . . . . . . . . . . . . . . . . . . . . . . . .

# **Appendix**

## CHECKLIST

Below is an example of a useful checklist so that you can see at a glance whether you have everything you will need.

| ITEM | HAVE OR NOT | DETAILS | COST |
|---|---|---|---|
| **Finances** | | | |
| Travellers' cheques | | | |
| US dollars | | | |
| British pounds | | | |
| Euros | | | |
| Other denominations | | | |
| Credit cards | | | |
| | | | |
| **Route planning** | | | |
| Where, ie: planned route | | | |
| For how long | | | |
| Suggested itinerary | | | |
| *Guidebooks and maps* | | | |
| *Africa guidebooks* | | | |
| North Africa | | | |
| West Africa | | | |
| Central Africa | | | |
| East Africa | | | |
| South Africa | | | |
| *Africa maps* | | | |
| Bartholomew (Continental Travel Map) Africa | | | |
| Michelin 741 – North and West | | | |
| Michelin 745 – North East | | | |
| Michelin 746 – Central and South Africa | | | |
| Michelin 743 – Algeria & Tunisia | | | |
| Michelin 742 – Morocco | | | |
| Michelin 747 – Ivory Coast | | | |
| | | | |
| **Bureaucracy** | | | |
| *Visas* | | | |
| For which countries | | | |
| Cost estimate | | | |
| Can get beforehand | | | |
| Other | | | |

| ITEM | HAVE OR NOT | DETAILS | COST |
|---|---|---|---|
| **Paperwork** | | | |
| *Passport* | | | |
| Validity | | | |
| Number of unused pages | | | |
| *Vaccination certificates* | | | |
| Cholera | | | |
| Diphtheria | | | |
| Hepatitis A and B | | | |
| Meningitis | | | |
| Polio | | | |
| Rabies (optional) | | | |
| Tetanus | | | |
| Tuberculosis | | | |
| Typhoid | | | |
| Yellow fever | | | |
| NB: Certificate signed by GP/clinic | | | |
| *Other* | | | |
| Bond or insurance | | | |
| *Carnet de passage (carnet)* organised for every country mentioned that you will visit | | | |
| International certificate for motor vehicles, ie: *carte grise* (grey card) | | | |
| *Insurance* | | | |
| Medical insurance | | | |
| Vehicle insurance (optional) | | | |
| International driving licence | | | |
| References | | | |
| in English | | | |
| in French | | | |
| Passport photos | | | |

## Vehicle selection

| ITEM | HAVE OR NOT | DETAILS | COST |
|---|---|---|---|
| **4x4/2WD** | | | |
| Type | | | |
| Registration number | | | |
| Chassis number | | | |
| Engine number | | | |
| Other | | | |
| **Motorbike** | | | |
| Type | | | |
| Registration number | | | |
| Chassis number | | | |
| Engine number | | | |
| Other | | | |
| **Bicycle** | | | |
| Type | | | |
| Other | | | |

| ITEM | HAVE OR NOT | DETAILS | COST |
|---|---|---|---|
| **4x4/2WD** | | | |
| *Preparation* | | | |
| Sleeping requirements | | | |
|   Tent | | | |
|   Rooftop tent | | | |
|   Inside the vehicle | | | |
|   Mattresses | | | |
|   Pillows | | | |
|   Sleeping bags | | | |
|   Covers for pillows, etc | | | |
| Roof rack | | | |
| Security | | | |
|   Padlocks and hasps | | | |
|   Windows | | | |
|   Curtains | | | |
|   Safety box | | | |
|   Alarm system (optional) | | | |
| Bull bar | | | |
| Baffle/bash plate | | | |
| Suspension | | | |
| Heavy-duty suspension fitted | | | |
| Spare battery and split charge system | | | |
| Oil cooler | | | |
| Raised air intake | | | |
| Tyres | | | |
| Spare tyres | | | |
| Inner tubes | | | |
| Valves | | | |
| Foot or electrical tyre pump | | | |
| Tyre repair kit | | | |
| Pressure gauge | | | |
| Fuel and water tanks | | | |
|   Capacity | | | |
|     Fuel | | | |
|     Water | | | |
| Storage boxes | | | |
| Seat covers | | | |
| Steering-wheel cover | | | |
| Stereo | | | |
|   Type and make | | | |
|   Serial number | | | |
| Canopy | | | |

## Equipment

| ITEM | HAVE OR NOT | DETAILS | COST |
|---|---|---|---|
| Recovery gear | | | |
| Electronic or manual winches | | | |
|   Type and make | | | |
|   Guarantees | | | |
| High-lift jack | | | |

| ITEM | HAVE OR NOT | DETAILS | COST |
|---|---|---|---|
| Hydraulic jack | | | |
| Blocks of wood to jack on | | | |
| Sand ladders | | | |
| Towing points | | | |
| Towing straps | | | |
| Shackles | | | |
| Compass and/or Global Positioning System (GPS) | | | |
| Type and make | | | |
| Mounting and storage system | | | |
| Serial number | | | |
| Guarantee | | | |
| Shovel or sand spades | | | |
| Axe or machete | | | |
| Warning triangles (2) | | | |
| Jerrycans | | | |
| Carrying capacity for: | | | |
| Fuel | | | |
| Water | | | |
| Oil | | | |
| Fire extinguisher | | | |
| Water | | | |
| Water purification (eg: Chloromyn T, Puritabs) | | | |
| Water filter | | | |
| Type | | | |
| Capacity of filter before replacement | | | |
| Guarantee | | | |
| Table and chairs | | | |
| Mosquito net/s | | | |
| Refrigerator | | | |
| Type and make | | | |
| Runs on 12V DC or 240V AC or gas or all three | | | |
| Serial number | | | |
| Guarantee | | | |
| **Lighting** | | | |
| Car lights | | | |
| Fluorescent strip light | | | |
| Map light | | | |
| Torch and batteries | | | |
| **Cooking equipment** | | | |
| Petrol stoves | | | |
| Kerosene stoves | | | |
| Container for kerosene | | | |
| Meths burners | | | |
| Container for methylated spirits | | | |
| Gas stoves | | | |

| ITEM | HAVE OR NOT | DETAILS | COST |
|---|---|---|---|
| Gas bottle fitted | | | |
| Cooking utensils | | | |
| Saucepan | | | |
| Deep straight-edged frying pan | | | |
| Cooking pot or cast-iron pot | | | |
| Kettle | | | |
| Pressure cooker or wok (optional) | | | |
| Decent sharp knife | | | |
| Wooden spoon | | | |
| Strainer (optional) | | | |
| Tin-opener | | | |
| Bottle-opener | | | |
| Chopping board | | | |
| Plates and bowls (plastic or enamel) | | | |
| Mugs (plastic) | | | |
| Assortment of cutlery | | | |
| Matches and/or firelighters | | | |
| Fire grill (optional) | | | |
| **Cleaning up** | | | |
| Plastic bowl | | | |
| Washing-up liquid | | | |
| Washing-up cloth | | | |
| Scourer (optional) | | | |
| Drying-up cloth | | | |
| **Spares and tools** | | | |
| Workshop manual | | | |
| 3 x oil filters | | | |
| 4 x fuel filters | | | |
| 2–3 x air filters | | | |
| Engine oil (enough for two changes) | | | |
| 5 litres of gearbox and differential oil | | | |
| Grease | | | |
| 1–2 litres brake and clutch fluid oil | | | |
| 1–2 litres coolant (you can use water) | | | |
| Heater plugs/spark plugs | | | |
| One spare diesel injector | | | |
| Set of engine gaskets | | | |
| Set of all oil seals | | | |
| Set of wheel bearings | | | |
| Set of engine mounts | | | |
| Set of radiator hoses | | | |
| Accelerator cable | | | |
| 2 x fanbelts | | | |
| Set of brake pads | | | |
| Brake master cylinder rubbers | | | |

| Item | Have or not | Details | Cost |
|---|---|---|---|
| Clutch master and slave cylinder rubbers (as above) | | | |
| Wheel cylinder kit – rubbers (or kit for disc brakes) | | | |
| Water pump | | | |
| Lift pump | | | |
| Suspension rubbers and bushes | | | |
| Condenser | | | |
| Distributor cap | | | |
| Contact breaker points | | | |
| Spare fuel cap | | | |
| Spare radiator cap | | | |
| U-bolts centre bolts for leaf springs | | | |
| Main leaf springs (coil springs rarely break with careful driving) | | | |
| Track rod ends | | | |
| Clutch plate | | | |
| Wheel nuts | | | |
| Water temperature sensor unit | | | |
| Sump/gearbox drain plugs | | | |
| Propshaft UJ | | | |
| Brake hose | | | |
| Alternator (complete or at least the brushes) | | | |
| Fuses | | | |
| Light bulbs | | | |
| **Other optional parts** | | | |
| Starter (for remoter areas) | | | |
| Fan (for remote areas) | | | |
| Injector pipes | | | |
| Injector pump (for remote areas) | | | |
| Injector pump solenoid if applicable | | | |
| **Useful items** | | | |
| Funnel (make sure it fits the filler of your fuel tank) | | | |
| Jubilee clips | | | |
| Cable ties | | | |
| Electrical tapes | | | |
| Electrical wires | | | |
| Masking tape/duct tape | | | |
| Assortment of wire | | | |
| Assortment of nuts, bolts and washers | | | |
| Plastic fuel line and connectors | | | |
| Contact adhesive | | | |
| Prately putty/flexible 'bathroom' sealant | | | |
| 2m fuel hoses (long enough to be used as a siphon) | | | |
| Rapid araldite/plastic metal glue | | | |

| ITEM | HAVE OR NOT | DETAILS | COST |
|---|---|---|---|
| Plastic padding/instant fibreglass | | | |
| Instant gasket paste | | | |
| Exhaust repair putty | | | |
| Gasket paper | | | |
| Can of WD40 or Q20 | | | |
| Radiator sealant | | | |
| Towing eye/cable | | | |
| Assorted small sheet metal, short drain piping, square tubing etc | | | |
| Assorted bits of rubber, inner tube, old stockings | | | |
| Old rags – lots and lots | | | |
| **Tools** | | | |
| Good set of spanners (imperial or metric as required) | | | |
| Good set of sockets with power bar and ratchet | | | |
| Extra large sockets (check sizes needed) | | | |
| Assortment of screwdrivers | | | |
| Adjustable spanner | | | |
| Mole wrench (large and small) | | | |
| Pipe wrench | | | |
| Grease gun | | | |
| Metal and rubber hammers | | | |
| Torque wrench | | | |
| Pliers (various) | | | |
| Circclip removers | | | |
| Multi-size puller | | | |
| Jump leads | | | |
| Set of feeler gauges | | | |
| Hacksaw and spare blades | | | |
| Multi-meter electrical tester | | | |
| Flat metal file | | | |
| Small round file | | | |
| Coarse flat file | | | |
| Hand drill and kit (9V cordless drills can be connected directly to your battery) | | | |
| Tyre levers | | | |
| Tyre valve tool | | | |
| Set of Allen keys | | | |
| Centre punch/assorted punches and metal drifts | | | |
| Wet and dry sandpaper | | | |
| Length of pipe (to extend your power bar for those stubborn nuts) | | | |
| Arc welding rods – a few | | | |
| G clamp/small vice to attach to bumper | | | |
| Magnetic retrieving tool | | | |

| ITEM | HAVE OR NOT | DETAILS | COST |
|---|---|---|---|
| **Motorbike** | | | |
| ***Spares and tools*** | | | |
| Repair manual | | | |
| 1 x spare rear tyre | | | |
| 1 x front and rear heavy duty inner tubes | | | |
| 1 x good-quality puncture repair kit with lots of patches | | | |
| 1 x small mountain bike pump | | | |
| A few spare spokes | | | |
| Connecting links for chain | | | |
| 1 x clutch lever | | | |
| 1 x brake lever | | | |
| 1 x clutch cable | | | |
| 1 x throttle cable(s) | | | |
| 1 x air filter | | | |
| 3 x oil filters | | | |
| 1 x fuel filter | | | |
| 2 x spark plugs | | | |
| Fuel hose and jubilee clips | | | |
| Bulbs and fuses | | | |
| Electrical wire and connectors | | | |
| Assorted nuts, bolts and washers | | | |
| Main gaskets | | | |
| Duct tape | | | |
| Assorted cable ties (lots) | | | |
| Spare bungee rope/straps | | | |
| Instant gasket | | | |
| Silicon sealant | | | |
| Epoxy glue | | | |
| Liquid steel | | | |
| Loctite (for nut threads) | | | |
| Small tub of grease | | | |
| About 1 litre engine oil (for top-up and oiling air filter) | | | |
| Standard small toolkit (combination spanners, $3/8''$ drive ratchet + relevant sockets, screwdrivers) | | | |
| Leatherman's or Swiss Army knife | | | |
| Feeler gauges | | | |
| File | | | |
| Spark plug spanner | | | |
| Tyre levers | | | |
| ***Personal equipment*** | | | |
| Jacket with built-in shoulder and elbow pads | | | |
| Spine protector with a waist band | | | |
| Full-length motorcross-style boots (optional) | | | |

| ITEM | HAVE OR NOT | DETAILS | COST |
|------|-------------|---------|------|
| Helmet and goggles | | | |
| Gloves | | | |

## Bicycle
### *Spares and tools*

| ITEM | HAVE OR NOT | DETAILS | COST |
|------|-------------|---------|------|
| Panniers – Overlander by Carradice | | | |
| 2 x spare tyres | | | |
| 10 x inner tubes | | | |
| Puncture repair kit | | | |
| Cables | | | |
| Brakepads | | | |
| Grease and oil | | | |
| Bearings | | | |
| Wires and straps | | | |
| Pliers | | | |
| Set of Allen keys | | | |
| Cable cutter | | | |
| Spoke tensioner | | | |
| Set of spanners | | | |
| Screwdriver | | | |
| Bottom bracket tensioner | | | |
| Front bearing spanner | | | |
| Spokes | | | |
| Box of nuts and bolts, etc | | | |
| Chain link extractor | | | |
| Toothbrush | | | |

### *Personal equipment*

| ITEM | HAVE OR NOT | DETAILS | COST |
|------|-------------|---------|------|
| Helmet | | | |
| Gloves | | | |
| Sunglasses | | | |
| 2 x whistles (as a warning and signal) | | | |
| Compass | | | |

## Camping: Motorbike/bicycle

| ITEM | HAVE OR NOT | DETAILS | COST |
|------|-------------|---------|------|
| Tent | | | |
| Sleeping mat | | | |
| Sleeping bag | | | |
| Nylon string | | | |
| Towel | | | |
| Torch | | | |
| Thermarest mattress | | | |

### *Cooking*

| ITEM | HAVE OR NOT | DETAILS | COST |
|------|-------------|---------|------|
| Stove, eg: MSR high-quality petrol stove or Coleman's multi-fuel cooker | | | |
| 2 x spoons | | | |
| 2 x plastic bowls | | | |
| 2 x plastic cups | | | |
| Saucepan | | | |

| ITEM | HAVE OR NOT | DETAILS | COST |
|------|-------------|---------|------|
| Penknife | | | |
| **Water** | | | |
| 2 x Travelwell military water purifiers | | | |
| 2 x 10-litre water bags | | | |
| Water bottle | | | |
| Filter | | | |
| **Food** | | | |
| Salt and pepper | | | |
| Herbs and spices | | | |
| Tea and coffee | | | |
| Sugar | | | |
| Powdered milk | | | |
| Muesli/cereals/oats | | | |
| Jam/marmalade | | | |
| Rice and pasta | | | |
| Tubes of tomato puree | | | |
| Stock cubes | | | |
| Marmite/Vegemite | | | |
| Tinned meat | | | |
| Tinned vegetables and fruit | | | |
| Packets of instant foods, ie: ready-made pasta, etc. | | | |
| Oil | | | |
| Vinegar | | | |
| Flour or cornflour | | | |
| Dried beans | | | |
| Mustard | | | |
| Kendal mint cake | | | |
| Dried mushrooms or other | | | |
| Dried fruit and nuts | | | |
| Biscuits and crackers | | | |
| Boiled sweets | | | |
| Packets of dried food (specific for cyclists and bikers) | | | |
| Instant mashed potato | | | |
| Small packets parmesan cheese | | | |

# Medical kit

Seek medical advice before use of any medicaments and read the instructions.

## Analgesics (painkiller)

| | | | |
|------|------|------|------|
| Aspirin for sore throat and mild pain | | | |
| Paracetamol for mild pain and temperature | | | |
| Ibuprofen for joint inflammation and pain | | | |
| Paracetamol/codeine for moderate pain | | | |

| ITEM | HAVE OR NOT | DETAILS | COST |
|---|---|---|---|
| **General** | | | |
| Buccastem for severe nausea, vomiting and vertigo | | | |
| Loperamide for acute diarrhoea | | | |
| Oral-rehydration sachets for dehydration | | | |
| Senokot tabs for constipation | | | |
| Merocaine lozenges for sore throats | | | |
| Indigestion tabs for excessive acid and indigestion | | | |
| Loratidine for allergies | | | |
| Pseudoephedrine (Sudafed) for nasal and sinus congestion | | | |
| Clove oil for toothache | | | |
| **Antibiotics** | | | |
| Amoxycillin for chest, ear, cellulitis and urinary tract infection (general antibiotic) | | | |
| Ciprofloxacin for gut and urinary tract infections | | | |
| Tinidazole for amoebic dysentery and giardia | | | |
| Flucloxacillin for skin infections | | | |
| Erythromycin for skin and chest infections (if allergic to penicillin) | | | |
| Mebendazole for thread-, round- and hookworm infections | | | |
| **Malaria (prevention and treatment)** | | | |
| Anti-malarial tablets | | | |
| Quinine sulphate and Fansidar | | | |
| Quinine sulphate and doxycycline | | | |
| Fansidar | | | |
| **Bilharzia** | | | |
| Biltracide | | | |
| **Eye, ear and nose** | | | |
| Chloramphenicol for eye infections | | | |
| Normal saline sachets for eye wash | | | |
| Eye bath as an eye-wash unit | | | |
| Ear drops | | | |
| Nose drops | | | |
| **Powder and creams for the skin** | | | |
| Hydrocortisone for skin allergies and insect bites | | | |
| Lactocalamine for sunburn, itching and rashes | | | |
| Daktarin cream for fungal infections | | | |

| Item | Have or not | Details | Cost |
|---|---|---|---|
| Cicatrin powder for wound infections (antibiotic) | | | |
| Magnesium sulphate for treatment of boils | | | |
| **Comprehensive first-aid kit** | | | |
| Granuflex dressing for tropical ulcers | | | |
| Gauze swabs for cleaning wounds | | | |
| Melolin of varying sizes for non-sticky wound dressing | | | |
| Micropore or zinc-oxide tape used as surgical tape | | | |
| Assortment of plasters | | | |
| Crepe bandage for muscular injuries | | | |
| Steristrips for wound closures | | | |
| Wound dressing for heavily bleeding wounds | | | |
| Triangular bandage for securing broken limbs | | | |
| Safety pins | | | |
| Steripods (disposable antiseptic sachets) | | | |
| Water gel or Jelonet dressing for burns | | | |
| Scissors | | | |
| Tweezers | | | |
| Disposable gloves | | | |
| Lancets (sterile needles which can be used for popping blisters) | | | |
| Betadine as antiseptic solution | | | |
| **Sterile surgical equipment (optional)** | | | |
| Sterile surgical gloves | | | |
| Scalpel (disposable) | | | |
| Mersilk suture of varying sizes | | | |
| Suturing forceps | | | |
| Stitch cutter | | | |
| Dental needles | | | |
| Syringes of varying sizes | | | |
| Variety of needles | | | |
| Pink and green Venflon for intravenous administration | | | |
| Sterile gauze to cleanse area of sterilisation | | | |
| Medical set for intravenous administration | | | |
| **Other items for the medical kit** | | | |
| Thermometer | | | |
| Permethrin mosi-net treatment | | | |
| Repellent coils to burn at night | | | |
| Insect repellent | | | |

| ITEM | HAVE OR NOT | DETAILS | COST |
|---|---|---|---|
| Anti-itch cream | | | |
| Flu medication | | | |
| Medication for personal ailments | | | |
| Condoms, pill or other | | | |
| Tampons | | | |

## Personal kit
### Clothes

| ITEM | HAVE OR NOT | DETAILS | COST |
|---|---|---|---|
| Jeans | | | |
| T-shirts | | | |
| Light cotton trousers | | | |
| Skirt | | | |
| Tunic dress | | | |
| Trousers and shirt | | | |
| Swimming costumes | | | |
| Wraparound skirts (also used as towels) | | | |
| Light scarf or shawl | | | |
| Sweatshirts | | | |
| Thick jerseys | | | |
| Woolly hats | | | |
| Hiking boots | | | |
| Sandals | | | |
| Raincoats | | | |
| Socks and underwear | | | |

### Toiletries

| ITEM | HAVE OR NOT | DETAILS | COST |
|---|---|---|---|
| Soap | | | |
| Shampoo | | | |
| Flannel | | | |
| Toothbrush & toothpaste | | | |
| Towels (or sarongs) | | | |
| Portable washing machine | | | |
|   Bucket with lid | | | |
|   Washing liquid/powder | | | |
|   Nylon or other string | | | |
|   Clothes pegs | | | |

### Miscellaneous

| ITEM | HAVE OR NOT | DETAILS | COST |
|---|---|---|---|
| Pens and pencils | | | |
| Writing paper | | | |
| Diary or other writing material | | | |
| Address book | | | |
| Games/playing cards | | | |
| Books and magazines | | | |
| Music on either tapes or CD | | | |
| Short-wave radio | | | |
| Pocket calculator | | | |
| Swiss Army knife or Leatherman's | | | |
| Hammock | | | |

| ITEM | HAVE OR NOT | DETAILS | COST |
|---|---|---|---|
| Binoculars and various books on fauna, flora and wildlife | | | |
| Driver's logbook | | | |
| Gifts | | | |
| **Photographic equipment** | | | |
| Dust-proof storage system | | | |
| Camera | | | |
| Polaroid camera | | | |
| Lens/es | | | |
| Cleaning gear | | | |
| Film | | | |
| Other | | | |
| Serial number(s) | | | |

# Appendix 4

## VISA REQUIREMENTS AT A GLANCE
*For details see country entries*

| Country | Visa requirements | Approx cost |
|---------|-------------------|-------------|
| Algeria | Required for all except nationals of other Arabic countries; if you have a stamp from Israel, South Africa, Malawi or Taiwan in your passport the visa application will be rejected; 30-day tourist visas are available | US$55–100 |
| Angola | Required for all; visa applications are referred to Direçao de Emigraçao e Fronteiras (DEFA) in Luanda and take about two weeks to issue. | US$50–80 |
| Benin | Required for all except nationals of the Economic Community of West African States (ECOWAS); 48-hour entry visas are available and can be extended in Cotonou | US$10–20 |
| Botswana | Not required for nationals of USA, UK, Germany, Netherlands and most Commonwealth countries | US$10–15 |
| Burkina Faso | Required for all except for nationals of ECOWAS | US$60–100 |
| Burundi | Required for all nationals *Transit visa* | US$12 |
| | *1-month tourist visa* | US$25–40 |
| Cameroon | Required for all except nationals of Germany *9-day multiple-entry visa (cost depends on nationality)* | US$25–70 |
| Central African Republic (CAR) | Required for all; nationals of France, Australia, New Zealand and the Republic of Ireland need to get permission from Bangui before entry | US$70–90 |
| Chad | Required for all except French and German citizens. Valid up to three months. | US$30–80 |
| Congo (People's Republic) | Required for all except nationals of France *2-week visa* | US$70–90 |
| Democratic Republic of Congo (DRC) | Required for all | US$50–100 |
| Djibouti | Required for all | US$65 (€50) |
| Egypt | Required for all except nationals of Arab countries and Malta | US$25 |
| Equatorial Guinea | Required for all | US$65–80 |
| Eritrea | Required for all | US$40–60 |
| Ethiopia | Required for all except Kenyan nationals | US$65 |
| Gabon | Required for all; all applications need to be referred to Libreville and can take up to a week to issue | US$80–100 |

| Country | Visa requirements | Approx cost |
|---|---|---|
| Gambia | Required for all except for nationals of Commonwealth countries | US$20 |
| Ghana | Required for all except nationals of ECOWAS | US$25–60 |
| Guinea | Required for all | US$25–50 |
| Guinea Bissau | Required for all except nationals of Cape Verde and Nigeria | US$10–25 |
| Ivory Coast (Côte d'Ivoire) | Required for all except nationals of ECOWAS; US passport holders don't need visas for stays up to 90 days | US$25–50 |
| Kenya | Required for all except nationals of most Commonwealth countries (nationals of Australia, New Zealand and UK do need visas). | US$20–40 |
| Lesotho | Required for all except nationals of Commonwealth countries and South Africa | US$10–15 |
| Liberia | Required for all; entry and exit permits are also required | US$30–40 |
| Libya | Required for all; independent tourist visas not issued to nationals of Australia, New Zealand, Great Britain, USA or Canada without approval of Libyan People's Bureau; all details of your passport must be translated into Arabic; nationals of Israel are not permitted entry; an Israeli stamp in your passport will deny you entry | US$35 average |
| Malawi | Not required for most nationals | n/a |
| Mali | Required for all except nationals of France | US$20–60 |
| Mauritania | Required for all except nationals of France and Italy and Arab League countries | US$15–50 |
| Morocco | Not required for most nationals except Israel and South Africa | |
| | 1-month visa | US$25–30 |
| | 3-month visa | US$35–40 |
| Mozambique | Required for all | US$20–40 |
| Namibia | Not required for most nationals | |
| Niger | Required for all except nationals of ECOWAS | US$40–60 |
| Nigeria | Required for all except nationals of ECOWAS | US$25–50 |
| Rwanda | Not required for nationals of several countries | US$50–70 |
| Senegal | Required for all except nationals of the EU, Commonwealth countries and USA | US$20–50 |
| Sierra Leone | Required for all | US$10–50 |
| Somalia | Required for all | Not known |
| South Africa | Not required for most nationals | n/a |
| Sudan | Required for all | US$75–95 |
| Swaziland | Not required except for nationals of Germany and France | Free (issued at border) |
| Tanzania | Required for all except nationals of some Commonwealth countries, Scandinavia and Iceland | US$10–50 |
| Togo | Required for all except for nationals of ECOWAS; 48-hour transit visas available at the border | US$10–20 |
| Tunisia | Not required for most nationals | US$5–15 |
| Uganda | Required for all except nationals of Denmark, Finland, France, Germany, Israel, Japan, Sweden and most Commonwealth countries (nationals of New Zealand, Nigeria and India require visas | US$25–40 |
| Zambia | Required for all except nationals of Commonwealth countries (British and Irish nationals require visas) | US$25–50 |
| Zimbabwe | Now required for most nationals | US$30–55 |

# Appendix 5

## FURTHER INFORMATION
### Books
#### History and politics

Goldsworthy, David *Tom Mboya: The Man Kenya Wanted To Forget* Heinemann. Fascinating book
on the former Kenyan trade union leader and politician who was murdered in 1969. Provides
an insight to Kenya's history in the 1950s and 1960s.

Mandela, Nelson *A Long Walk to Freedom* Little Brown, 1995. The autobiography of Nelson
Mandela and the ANC. Great insight into the apartheid era of southern Africa.

Marable, Manning *African and Caribbean Politics* Verso. A good overview to African history and
politics, with particular reference to Ghana.

Matar, N I *Islam for Beginners* Writers and Readers, 1992. A brief introduction to the basic precepts
of Islam.

Moorehead, Alan *The Blue Nile* Hamish Hamilton, 1972. The story of the exploration and history
of the Blue Nile River.

Moorehead, Alan *The White Nile* Penguin, 1972. The story of the exploration and history of the
White Nile River.

Odinga, Oginga *Not Yet Uhuru* Heinemann. Autobiography of the man who went from being
Kenya's vice-president under Jomo Kenyatta to a leading opposition force in exile.

Panaf Books *Kwame Nkrumah*. An introduction to the man who led Ghana to freedom in 1956 and
also led the Pan-African liberation movement.

Panaf Books *Sékou Touré*. The story of Guinea's unique road to independence and of its
charismatic first leader.

Pakenham, Thomas *The Scramble for Africa* Abacus, 1992. A briskly readable and well-indexed
account of Africa's development – and its colourful cast of characters – from 1876 to 1912.

Pathfinder *Thomas Sankara Speaks*. Key speeches by the inspiring and popular former president of
Burkina Faso.

Reader, John *Africa: A Biography of the Continent* Penguin, 1998. The complete reference book:
Africa from its origins until the end of the 20th century, presented vividly and accessibly.

### Travel guides
#### Bradt guides (www.bradtguides.com)

*Botswana: Okavango, Chobe, Northern Kalahari* Chris McIntyre
*Cameroon* Ben West
*East & Southern Africa: The Backpacker's Manual* Philip Briggs
*Eritrea* Edward Denison/Edward Paice
*Ethiopia* Philip Briggs
*Gabon, São Tome & Príncipe* Sophie Warne
*Gambia, The* Craig Emms/Linda Barnett
*Ghana* Philip Briggs
*Kenya* Claire Foottit
*Malawi* Philip Briggs

*Mali* Ross Velton
*Mozambique* Philip Briggs/Ross Velton
*Namibia* Chris McIntyre
*Nigeria* Lizzie Williams
*Rwanda* Janice Booth/Philip Briggs
*South Africa: Budget Travel Guide* Paul Ash
*Southern African Wildlife* Mike Unwin
*Sudan* Paul Clammer
*Tanzania* Philip Briggs
*Uganda* Philip Briggs
*Zambia* Chris McIntyre
*Zanzibar* David Else

## Others

*Africa On A Shoestring* Lonely Planet. The classic budget travellers' guide to Africa. A mine of information, although you do have to remember that with a vast number of contributors its accuracy does vary considerably. Not very helpful on places to stay if you have your own vehicle to worry about.

de Villiers, Marq and Hirtle, Sheila *Into Africa* Weidenfeld & Nicolson in Great Britain, Jonathan Ball Publishers in South Africa, 1997

Glen, Simon *Sahara Handbook* Roger Lascelles. Now out of print. Although dated, a very comprehensive reference book.

Oliver, Roland *The African Experience*, Pimlico, 1991

Philips *Essential World Atlas,* in association with the Royal Geographical Society with the Institute of British Geographers, 1998

Running Press *The Quotable Travellers*, 1994

Scott, Chris *Desert Biking: A Guide to Independent Motorcycling in the Sahara* The Travellers' Press. A mine of information for those planning a trip by motorbike – although specifically covering the requirements of desert biking rather than for a comprehensive African trip. Lots of advice on bikes and equipment as well as details of a number of North African routes. Available from the Travellers' Bookshop in London or from www.amazon.co.uk

Scott, Chris *Sahara Overland* Trailblazer, 2004

St Pierre White, Andrew *The complete guide to a Four Wheel Drive in Southern Africa* National Book Printers, 1998/1999

*The Rough Guide to West Africa* A substantial and excellent country-by-country guide to this extraordinary region.

For maps, see page 6.

## Language

Berlitz *Arabic for Travellers*
Berlitz *Swahili Phrase Book and Dictionary*
Eyewitness Travel Guides *Arabic Phrasebook*
Lonely Planet *Swahili Phrasebook*

## Wildlife

Enthusiasts may need information tailored to a specific country or area; in this case see recommendations in the appropriate travel guides.

Kingdon, Jonathan *The Kingdon Field Guide to African Mammals* Academic Press, 1997.
   Recommended by Philip Briggs, author of many Bradt Africa guides, as 'the most detailed, thorough and up-to-date of several field guides covering the mammals of the region'.

Ber Van Perlo *Illustrated Checklist to the Birds of Eastern Africa* (Collins, 1995) and *Illustrated Checklist to the Birds of Southern Africa* (Collins, 1999) between them cover bird species recorded in countries including Eritrea, Ethiopia, Kenya, Uganda, Rwanda, Tanzania, Zambia, Malawi and South Africa.

## Other useful reading

Barker, Hazel *Senile Safari: A Journey from Durban to Alexandria*. A retired couple's drive through Africa. Available from the author: 18 Louisa Rd, Birchgrove, Sydney, Australia; tel/fax: +61 2 810 5040.

Hibbert, Christopher *Africa Explored* Penguin books, 1982

Melville, K E M *Stay Alive In The Desert* Roger Lascelles. All you need to know about desert survival – but in far more detail than most travellers will ever need.

Pandora *Half The Earth*. Excellent collection of guidance and personal encounters by women travellers, based on their experiences around the world.

Simon, Ted *Jupiter's Travels* Penguin. The classic story of a round-the-world journey by motorbike – includes the trip from Tunis to Cape Town. As this was undertaken in 1974 to 1978, hard information is rather out of date (he rides through Libya). But it is the spirit of the book that makes it unmissable.

## Easy reads

Blixen, Karen *Out of Africa* Putnam & Co Ltd, 1937 (1st edition)

Foden, Giles *The Last King of Scotland* and *Ladysmith*. *The Last King of Scotland* revolves around Idi Amin through the eyes of his personal physician. *Ladysmith* is about the British occupation of this small town in southern Africa. Both are superb reads.

Galman, Kuki *I Dreamed of Africa*. This author has written several novels regarding her time with her family in Kenya.

Godwin, Peter *Mukiwa*. Rhodesia 1964 as seen through a young boy's eyes and his steady growth to the freedom of Rhodesia, now known as Zimbabwe.

*Mail and Guardian Bedside Book* (1999) is a selection of superb journalism from Africa's best.

## Sourcing African literature and maps

All of the above-mentioned books can be ordered through Amazon on www.amazon.co.uk or www.amazon.com. All Bradt guides are available via www.bradtguides.com. Old, out-of-print books (in bookshops worldwide) can sometimes be tracked down via www.usedbooksearch.co.uk.

## UK

**Africa Book Centre Ltd** 38 King St, London WC2E 8JT; tel: 020 7240 6649 or 0845 458 1581; fax: 020 7836 1975; www.africabookcentre.com

**Blackwells** 100 Charing Cross Rd, London WC2H 0JG; tel: 020 7292 5100; fax: 020 7240 9665; email: london@blackwell.co.uk; www.blackwells.co.uk. For all literature and maps. Many shops countrywide.

**Stanfords** 12–14 Long Acre, London WC2E 9LP; tel: 020 7836 1321; fax: 020 7632 8928; www.stanfords.co.uk

**Map World Direct Ltd** 25 Saltersford Lane, Alton, Staffs ST10 4AU; tel: 01538 703842; email: service@map-guides.com; www.map-guides.com

## USA

**Book Passage** 15 Tamal Vista Bd, Court Madera, California; tel: 415 927 0960; fax: 415 924 7909; email: messages@bookpassage.com; www.bookpassage.com; also in San Francisco.

**California Map and Travel Center** 3312 Pico Bd, Santa Monica, California; tel: 310 396 6277; fax: 310 392 8785; email: topo@mapper.com; www.mapper.com

**The Savvy Traveller** 310 South Michigan Av, Chicago, IL 60604; tel: 888 666 6200 (toll free); fax: 312 913 9866; email: mailbox@thesavvytraveller.com; www.thesavvytraveller.com

**Wide World Books and Maps** 4411A Wallingford Av North, Seattle, WA 98103; tel: 888 534 3453 (toll free) or 206 634 3453; fax: 206 634 0558; email: travel@speakeasy.net; www.wildworldtravels.com

## South Africa
**Exclusive Books** has 30 stores, including: Shop U30, Hyde Park Corner, Jan Smuts Av, Craighall, Johannesburg/Gauteng; tel: 011 325 4298; fax: 011 325 5001; email: hydepark@exclusivebooks.co.za; www.exclusivebooks.co.za
**Facts & Fiction** Shop 346–350, Rosebank Mall, Bath Av, Rosebank, Johannesburg/Gauteng; tel: 011 447 3039/3028; fax: 011 447 3062; email: rosebankmall@exclusivebooks.co.za; www.exclusivebooks.co.za. There is also a branch in Gaborone, Botswana; email: nikid@ exclusivebooks.co.za

# Useful websites
## Expedition planning
www.expeditionworld.com Some photos taken by the authors on their Africa trips
www.africanet.com Africanet (general info on Africa including history and politics):
www.bradtguides.com Bradt Travel Guides
www.wtgonline.com Columbus World Travel Guide
www.africa-overland, www.overlandclub.com.com Independent Africa Overland Club (a general overview on travelling overland in Africa)
www.sites.netscape.net/kingmill/africa Kingsmill (a personal journey into Africa, including crossing Sudan)
www.klaus.daerr.de/sahara Klaus Daerr Expedition (in German only but excellent information on the Sahara)
www.sahara-overland.com Sahara Travel Information (specific to Saharan countries with travellers' tales and much more)
www.geocities.com/MotorCity/1197/driving.html Tips for driving in Africa

## Other useful sites
www.africa.com
www.africaguide.com An excellent source of general information on individual African countries.
www.africanconnections.com
www.africanet.com
www.africaonline.com
www.arab.net
www.ase.net A useful source of information on accommodation.
www.backpackafrica.com
www.escapeartist.com
www.finance.yahoo.com/currency
www.geography.about.com
www.i-cias.com
www.infoplease.com
www.interknowledge.com
www.odci.gov CIA website including details of every African country
www.places.co.za For countries in southern Africa and strangely, the Maldives
www.safarinow.com
www.sas.upenn.edu/African_Studies An excellent site from the University of Pennsylvania
www.travelinafrica.co.za Includes visa information in some detail
www.wncountries.com World news for every country
www.worldtravelguide.net
www.yellowpages.co.za

# Index

**In this index page references in bold type indicate main entries**